West's Law School
Advisory Board

EFFECTIVE APPELLATE ADVOCACY

BRIEF WRITING AND ORAL ARGUMENT

Third Edition

By

Carole C. Berry

Professor of Law
Capital University Law School
Columbus, Ohio

AMERICAN CASEBOOK SERIES®

THOMSON

WEST

Mat #40134030

American Casebook Series and West Group are trademarks registered in the U.S. Patent and Trademark Office.

COPYRIGHT © 1998, 1999 WEST GROUP
COPYRIGHT © 2003 By WEST GROUP
         610 Opperman Drive
         P.O. Box 64526
         St. Paul, MN 55164–0526
         1–800–328–9352

All rights reserved
Printed in the United States of America

ISBN 0–314–14585–0

TEXT IS PRINTED ON 10% POST CONSUMER RECYCLED PAPER

Dedication

———

To Beth Ann,
Daughter Extraordinaire

*

Preface

The third edition of this book reflects some minor changes in or interpretation of the Federal Rules of Appellate Procedure, the Rules of the Supreme Court, the various Circuit Rules and the Internal Operating Procedures of the Circuits. However, of paramount importance, it expands the ethics of appellate practice into its own chapter. The persuasion chapter has been revamped to reflect a new model and to include some ancient notions of argument that are useful today when writing or speaking persuasively. The standards of review sections have been enhanced and reference is made to helpful web sites of the various courts as well as information contained within those sites. New exercises have been added to reflect the changes in the chapters and to expand the new material.

The goal of the book has not changed. It is to produce a book that can be used in law schools in the semester in which brief writing and oral argument are the main topics. I also believe it will be helpful to lawyers embarking on a career as appellate advocates.[1]

The basic layout of the book has not radically changed. My analysis begins with an overview of appellate procedure. It then explores the ethics of appellate practice. The heart of the book explores the constructs of solid brief writing and oral argument. Together with the example briefs, the reader is invited to analyze, in detail, what it means to thoroughly prepare a persuasive document and an effective and convincing oral argument.

Once again, it is my hope that the advocate will face an appellate court and state confidently "[m]ay it please the court * * *" and it will.

CAROLE C. BERRY
Professor of Law

Capital University Law School
Columbus, Ohio
June 2003

*

---

[1] There are sections in the book that would be helpful to experienced advocates if only to make them consider, or reconsider, some of the constructs of truly excellent advocacy.

Acknowledgments

The third edition was helped along by student research assistant Jacqueline Ferris. I would also like to acknowledge the library staff at Capital University Law School.

My spouse, Robert C. Berry, has again acted as my chief editor. I'm piling up indebtedness to him.

I again reiterate my thanks to the law offices of Robert S. Bennett for supplying the briefs for the Petitioner in *Clinton v. Jones* and Gil Davis for the Respondent's brief and other materials from the Eighth Circuit.

Thanks also to Capital University Law School and particularly Dean Steven C. Bahls for the continuous support of resources.

*

Summary of Contents

*

Table of Contents

EFFECTIVE APPELLATE ADVOCACY

BRIEF WRITING AND
ORAL ARGUMENT

Third Edition

*

Chapter One

THE DECISION TO APPEAL

Analysis

1.00   INITIAL CONSIDERATIONS

Preparation for the appeal of a case begins long before the case even goes to trial. The merits of the case are raised in the complaint and the answer, and other pretrial devices such as motions to strike, for summary judgment and other proceedings. These assist to formulate the issues, not just for the trial, but for a possible appeal as well. The deliberate attorney must always be cognizant of what will happen after the trial—win or lose.

In the normal course of events, if settlement is not attained, the trial will proceed, and usually there is a winner and there is a loser.[1] Then the question is whether one party or the other (or both in the event that each is disgruntled) should apply for review to a higher court.

1.01   Jurisdiction of appellate body

There are multiple factors to consider before an appeal is filed. First, counsel must ascertain whether the court or agency has jurisdiction to review the order or judgment. For example, in a worker's compensation case in Ohio, the issue of extent of disability suffered by an injured worker is not an appealable order beyond the Industrial Commission.

---

1. Remember: both parties technically can win and both can lose. See the discussion at § 3.12.

1

Therefore, a court does not have jurisdiction to hear an appeal as it relates to that issue.

1.02   Grounds for appeal

If the court has jurisdiction, the next question is whether there are grounds for appeal. In most instances, this consideration has nothing to do with the strength of the case but depends on whether the issue or issues were preserved at trial. Even the most powerful and meritorious claim will fail on appeal if the issues sought to be raised on appeal were not preserved by timely objection at the trial or presented in the record before the higher court.[2]

A timely objection should always be raised at the time evidence is either admitted or excluded by the trial judge. An explanation should follow and proof should be offered as to the admissibility or inadmissibility of the evidence. This also applies to the conduct of opposing counsel, if potentially prejudicial. The conduct need not be mischievous, such as attempting to slide information to the jury that clearly is inadmissible. The objection must be made; thus the issue is preserved for appeal. Finally, a timely objection must be made to a perceived improper jury instruction or to an instruction that is requested but not granted.

1.03   Probability of success

Even if issues are preserved at trial, a myriad of other concerns face the prospective appellant. Chief among them is a candid evaluation of the probability of success. Reversal rates are notoriously low. Figures available for the Federal Circuits for the 12–month period ending in September 30, 2001 and shown below, indicate just how dismal the chances are for a successful appeal.

Table 1–A: Appeal Reversal Rates of the Federal Circuits	
D.C. Circuit	7.5%
First Circuit	7.3%
Second Circuit	1.7%
Third Circuit	10.5%
Fourth Circuit	7.0%
Fifth Circuit	8.8%
Sixth Circuit	10.9%
Seventh Circuit	14.5%
Eighth Circuit	8.8%
Ninth Circuit	9.4%
Tenth Circuit	12.2%
Eleventh Circuit	10.1%
All Circuits	9.1%

2.   But see § 3.02 which discusses the possibility of jurisdictional questions first raised and the "plain error" rule.

The table may be somewhat misleading in that it presents only those cases listed as complete reversals. Cases reversed in part are not included. An appellant may obtain the desired result if a case is affirmed in part and reversed in part.

The following chart indicates the reversal rate for the years 1987–2001, which is even more discouraging to the appellant.

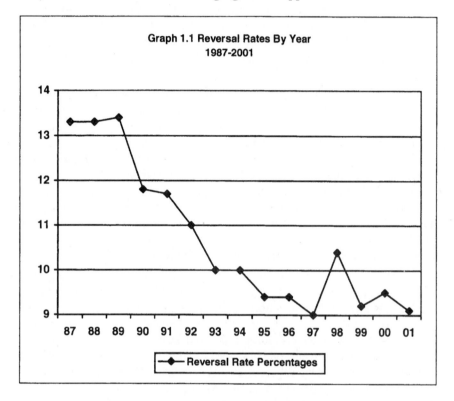

One avenue an attorney might investigate is whether it is possible to obtain information about the reversal pattern or rate of the judge, panel or agency to which the argument will be made. In the end, all available figures should be analyzed before making the final decision to appeal.

1.04 Economic and other costs of an appeal

The potential costs of an appeal are daunting. One must consider these costs will be in addition to the monies spent at trial and might well surpass those amounts. Factors to be considered are the client's ability to bear the costs, the effect of the judgment on the client, the government, the industry or the community, the likelihood of success of the appeal, and other intangible values as discussed below. The attorney must advise the client that an appeal involves a substantial commitment of resources which include both attorney fees and court costs.

If the appeal has any chance of success, the attorney handling the case must commit great amounts of time to prepare for the appeal. He or she must review the record carefully, plan the strategy to be used, research the law in preparation for writing the brief, write the brief, prepare and present the oral argument and generally handle miscellaneous matters attendant to an appeal.

While it is impossible to estimate exactly what ultimately will be charged, an honest assessment of the attorney's fees must be made to advise the client of those costs.[3] Court costs must also be appraised.

Along with court fees, security bonds may also be an expense.[4] In addition, most appeals require a transcript of the record from the court below. The cost of transcribing a trial record can easily run into the hundreds of dollars; in the case of a lengthy trial, this becomes thousands of dollars. Many courts require that the parties prepare and print an appendix which contains the important parts of the record. While printed briefs are still required by the Supreme Court of the United States,[5] most courts allow briefs to be reproduced by "any process that yields a clear black image on light paper."[6] Often, reproduction of multiple copies of both the appendix and the brief are necessary, forcing the cost of printing into the hundreds of dollars. If the appeal is not successful, the losing party may be assessed the costs of the winning party which, in effect, doubles the cost to the appealing party.

How the adverse judgment, if not appealed, will affect other parties should be considered. For example, a judgment in a criminal tax fraud case may trigger a suit for money damages in a civil suit involving tax liability. Also, at the present time, the tobacco industry is acutely aware of the horrific effect that a successful civil suit may have on bolstering the demands of hundreds of thousands of people who claim death and damage from the use of tobacco. In other words, there is often more at stake than just an adverse decision as it relates to the parties to the action.

Time constraints must also be considered. One must remember that the time necessary to perfect and process an appeal may take years. Usually this is not the case; but, depending on the appellate court backlog, the complexity of the case, and a myriad of other potential problems, delays may be substantial. Assuming that the issues on appeal are meritorious,[7] the inquiry must be whether the delay will benefit or adversely affect the client. At times, a delay will benefit the client in allowing time for assets to be marshaled to pay the judgment. Settlement may be more attractive to the winning party in view of a lengthy delay. On the other hand, a lengthy appeal may prolong the personal trauma.

---

3. Indeed, the Model Rules of Professional Conduct Rule 1.5 cmt. (1983) requires an attorney to indicate to the client factors that will be taken into account when fixing the fee to be charged. In other words, the attorney must give the client some idea about the cost of the appeal.

4. *See* § 3.31.

5. *See* Sup. Ct. R. 33(1)(a).

6. *See* Fed. R. App. P. 32(a)(1)(A).

7. *See* the discussion at 2.60 on the rules and risks of sanctions.

For the most part, people want closure when it comes to lawsuits. The prospect of further action may be far more damaging than simply paying the judgment and getting on with life.

Unquantifiable aspects of an appeal should be considered. There may be personal privileges or rights that deserve protection. For example, a questionable judgment against a doctor for medical malpractice may very well damage a successful practice. Along similar lines, criminal sanctions resulting in probation follow a person throughout life (unless expunged) and may harm future employment and personal advancement. While not specifically quantifiable, the results are potentially devastating. In these situations, an appeal may be the only recourse to avoid such unfortunate results.

1.05 Other considerations

The above are the major factors to consider when deciding whether to appeal, but other matters should also be examined. First, do trends in the court appear to favor the type of appeal contemplated? With changes in court personnel, the focus on certain issues may change. For example, the matter of the death penalty has taken several twists and turns over the years. Further, some courts are simply more interested in certain types of cases; thus a trend may emerge. Philosophies may change with a shifting membership of the court. Recall the liberal nature of the Warren Court, and compare it to the more conservative nature of the Rehnquist Court. Other appellate courts witness the same change in dynamics and direction.

Second, will the adverse decision set a precedent that should be challenged? Attorneys who deal with similar cases on an ongoing basis must be concerned about a decision that, if left uncontested, is potentially devastating, not only in the instant case but also for future cases. Conversely, if the appeal is likely to be adverse to the appellant, perhaps it is better to have the lesser precedent of a trial court decision.

1.10 STANDARD OF REVIEW

In evaluating the chances of a successful appeal, the attorney must carefully consider the standard of appellate review. The standard used will determine both the nature and the degree of error the appellant must prove to obtain a reversal of the trial court decision. The standard informs the attorney how much deference the appeals court normally gives to the actions of the trial court. It also provides significant insight into the chance of a successful appeal. If the standard is restrictive, the chance of a successful appeal is diminished. If, however, the appeals court is free to consider the matter *de novo*, the appellant has a better chance to prevail on appeal.

Consideration of the standard must be undertaken early in the decision to appeal. The appellant must be able to demonstrate to the court that the issues presented comply with the standard, while the appellee must show that the standard has not been met. For both sides, what is argued and how it is argued, i.e., the issues and their focus, must center on the question of the standard of review to be applied.

In some jurisdictions, rules which describe the contents of the brief specifically require that the advocate indicate the standard of review. More particularly, some appellate court rules require the standard of review to be set out in a separate section of the brief. Other sets of rules do not speak to the issue but rather leave the brief writer to decide where to include the discussion. However, to maximize the chances of success, a skillful advocate will carefully weave the standard concept throughout the development of the brief, and ultimately into the oral argument. This is especially true if the standard of review is favorable to the client's position.

One cautionary note is offered the brief writer. Standards of review are applied by appellate courts on an issue by issue basis. Therefore, if the appeal presents multiple issues for which different standards may apply, each issue must be addressed as to the appropriate standard that the appellate court should employ. For example, assume an appeal in which there is a questions of statutory construction and an evidentiary question. The former would be reviewed *de novo* and the latter likely would be reviewed based on the clear error standard or the abuse of discretion standard.[8]

A detailed analysis of various standards of review in different jurisdictions is beyond the scope of this book.[9] The text, Federal Standards of Review,[10] is comprehensive and helps provide a full understanding of the various federal standards. The following discussion is meant only to introduce some of the basic concepts of the federal standards of review in civil matters. There are also federal standards that deal with a criminal appeal. As always, there is no substitute for research of the matter, as jurisdictions vary substantially.

1.11   Questions of law

The appellate court reviews questions of law *de novo*. A question of law on appeal is accorded no deference by the appellate court, and it is free to decide the issue presented to it as if it had not come before the

---

8.   Both concepts are developed below.

9.   But as an example, the Fifth Circuit has an extensive section that covers the standard of review that must be articulated. Rule 28.2.6 states in relevant part: "In implementing FRAP 28(a)(9)(B), appellant must include a statement of the Standard of Review for each contention, which statement may appear in the discussion of each issue or under a separate heading placed before the discussion of the issues. For example, where the appeal is from an exercise of district court discretion, there shall be a statement that the Standard of Review is whether the district court abused its discretion. The appropriate standard or scope of review for other contentions should be simi-larly indicated, e.g., that the district court erred in formulating or applying a rule of law; or that there is insufficient evidence to support a verdict; or that fact findings of the trial judge are clearly erroneous under Fed. R. Civ. P. 52(a); or that there is a lack of substantial evidence in the record as a whole to support the factual findings of an administrative agency; or that the agency's action, findings, and conclusions should be held unlawful and set aside for the reasons set forth in 5 U.S.C. § 706(2)."

10.   Steven A. Childress & Martha S. Davis, Federal Standards of Review (3d ed. 1999).

trial court in the first place. This is as it should be because the purpose of an appellate court is to maintain consistency and uniformity in the law throughout the jurisdiction. Interpretation of legal issues is, therefore, squarely within the province of the appellate court as it strives to honor the notion of *stare decisis* as it builds on the common law.

1.12 Questions of fact

The standard of review for questions of fact depends on whether a judge sitting in a nonjury trial made the decision or whether the jury made the finding. Subtle differences may be found in the two standards. Appellate review of the facts determined by the trial judge's factual findings is controlled by Federal Rule of Civil Procedure 52(a). It states in relevant part:

> Findings of fact, whether based on oral or documentary evidence, shall not be set aside unless clearly erroneous, and due regard shall be given to the opportunity of the trial court to judge of the credibility of the witnesses.

The "clearly erroneous" standard was discussed in the case of *Anderson v. City of Bessemer City*,[11] in which the Supreme Court made clear the parameters of the appeals court to reverse the district court decision based on the facts. In that case the Court said:

> The clearly erroneous standard of Fed. R. Civ. P. 52(a) plainly does not entitle a reviewing court to reverse the finding of the trier of fact simply because it is convinced that it would have decided the case differently * * *. In applying the clearly erroneous standard to the findings of a district court sitting without a jury, appellate courts must constantly have in mind that their function is not to decide factual issues *de novo*. If the district court's account of the evidence is plausible in light of the record viewed in its entirety, the court of appeals may not reverse it even though convinced that had it been sitting as the trier of fact, it would have weighed the evidence differently. Where there are two permissible views of the evidence, the factfinder's choice between them cannot be clearly erroneous.[12]

On the other hand, the deference given to jury findings springs from a notion found in the Seventh Amendment to the Constitution which provides that no fact found by a jury "shall be otherwise re-examined in any Court of the United States, than according to the rules of the common law." As noted:

> [u]nder the 'rules of common law,' judicial examination of jury verdicts is generally limited to determining whether the evidence in the record is sufficient to support the finding, i.e., whether there is evidence from which reasonable minds could have reached the conclusions reached by the jury.[13]

11. 470 U.S. 564 (1985).

12. *Id.* at 573–74 (citation omitted).

13. Daniel John Meador & Jordana Simone Bernstein, Appellate Courts in the United States 63 (1994).

It would appear that appellate courts may overturn judge findings if supported by some evidence but may not overturn jury findings with the same evidence.[14]

The underlying burden of persuasion complicates the matter as it relates to the factfinder at the trial court level. For example, if a party must establish a particular fact by clear and convincing evidence and does not do so, the jury verdict may not stand. This is true if it is determined that a rational juror could not have found that the standard of clear and convincing evidence was met. Simply put: is there evidence that a rational jury could find for the prevailing party on the clear and convincing standard? The appellate court is more likely to defer to the trial court decision if the record reflects that the proper standard was applied by the trier of fact.

1.13   Mixed questions of law and fact

The civil rules and custom have basically drawn two lines as they relate to standards of review. Either the matter is one of factual determination or one of legal determination. Factual determinations are dictated by Rule 52(a) if judge-made and by common law if the jury is the decision maker. Legal issues have always been reviewed *de novo*. It would appear, then, that the lines are fairly distinct.

Nothing could be further from the truth. Often, the appellate court is faced with an issue which presents both law and fact. Then what standard is applied? As noted by authors Meador and Bernstein, "[o]f all of the unclear lines in our jurisprudence, the law-fact line can be among the unclearest."[15]

Questions about who did what, how, when and why are fairly conclusively questions of fact. Inferences of ultimate fact which results from a conclusion based on facts are usually treated as a factual issue. The pivotal question is which decision maker is in the best position to decide the issue. If the answer is those people who observed the witnesses and assessed their credibility, the matter likely will be deemed to be fact. If the question is which legal doctrine to apply to a given set of facts, the matter is one of law.

The problem comes when the appellate court is asked to review the application of a legal principle as it relates to a set of facts. For example, in a defamation case the defendant's conduct is a matter of fact as it relates to malice. The standard for determining malice is a legal issue. Likewise dispositive motions such as a motion for summary judgment or for judgment on the pleadings may rest upon factual as well as legal argument. These distinctions, especially where constitutional issues are concerned, are many times even more blurred.

Mixed questions are best assessed based on who is in the superior position to determine the issue AND how important the notion of

---

14. *Id.* at 64.

15. Meador & Bernstein, *supra* at note 13.

jurisdiction wide uniformity rates in the mix. If the matter is one of evaluating testimony, it is likely one of fact. If uniformity is needed and the issue is one of policy, the appellate court will likely come down on the side of law. In the end, when issues of fact and law appear to collide, the wise advocate argues the position most advantageous to the case.

1.14 Questions within the trial court's discretion

As the title indicates, there are issues that are deemed to be within the trial court's discretion. In these matters, the judge has wide latitude within which to make decisions. Appellate deference is at its maximum, and the standard applied is abuse of discretion or arbitrariness.

For example, during a trial a judge makes numerous decisions that are procedural in nature, such as matters relating to the pleadings, joinder issues and various motions. Errors made with respect to these rulings are usually left untouched unless abuse or arbitrariness can be shown.

This standard is a difficult one to establish, and most attempts at reversal under it are unsuccessful. An appellate court would have to find that "no reasonable [person] would take the view adopted by the trial court"[16] to justify overturning a trial court judge's decision. While a reversal in discretionary matters is uncommon, nevertheless the appellate court remains the final arbiter on these and other more substantive decisions.

The abuse of discretion standard is also applied to administrative officials who have been given specific authority to make decisions within an agency. In order to prevail, an appellant must show that the administrator acted arbitrarily, capriciously, or not in accordance with the law.[17]

Counsel is again cautioned that the foregoing is merely an overview of the notion of standard of review. These issues are far more complicated than presented. It is strongly suggested that, prior to advising a client about the wisdom of taking an appeal, counsel review the burden of persuasion required by the factfinder, together with the standard of review the appellate court will use. Only then can other considerations, such as time constraints, money constraints and other obstacles, be evaluated.

1.20 INSTITUTIONAL CONSIDERATIONS

Serious institutional concerns as to appellate practice center on the inundation and subsequent crisis of volume of cases filed in the U.S. courts. The following chart shows the growth in appellate filings for the period from 1987 through September 30, 2001.

16. *Delno v. Market Street Ry.*, 124 F.2d 965, 967 (9th Cir.1942).

17. Admin. Procedure Act. § 10(e), 5 U.S.C. § 706 (1994).

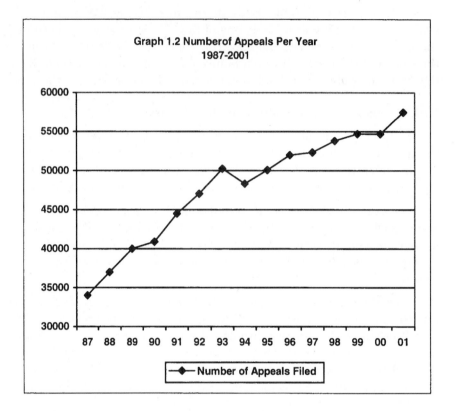

As one writer stated:

The appellate structure of our judicial system resembles a great full-rigged ship, some of whose seams have been opened below the water line by the incessant pounding of the seas. The crew has vigorously manned the pumps in order to prevent the vessel from foundering. However, try as they may, with might and main, the crews of appellate judges are able to do no more than maintain a precarious balance between sinking and sailing.[18]

Studies have been conducted and volumes written on this topic. Most commentators conclude that the number of appeals filed far outweigh the number of new judges appointed to decide those cases.

Remarkably, even with the off-the-charts level of growth in appeals filed, the courts of appeals collectively remain somewhat current. This is explained, in part, by innovations and "reforms" instituted at the appellate level. Some innovations do not benefit litigants. For example, in some circuits, the issue is deemed unworthy of oral argument unless the matter is complex or profound.[19]

18. Joseph R. Weisberger, *Appellate Courts: The Challenge of Inundation*, 31 Am. U. L. Rev. 237 (1982).

19. Many appellate lawyers, as well as judges, deem oral argument to be not only desirable but also necessary regardless of the profoundness or complexity.

On the other hand, reform techniques have moved the cases through the system to at least maintain a stabilized backlog. Some noteworthy reforms include case flow management, multiple tracking systems for different types of appeals, pre-argument settlement conferences and the summary disposition of certain types of cases.

These reforms have been met with both praise and skepticism. Those who believe the reforms are beneficial point to the increased number of cases disposed of per sitting judge. The skeptics claim the quality of the appellate process has deteriorated. They assert that the appeals process is far different than before the reforms and that the reforms have so misshaped the quality of the appellate procedure to make it unrecognizable.

1.30　APPEALABLE ORDERS AND JUDGMENTS

1.31　The finality doctrine

One of the best known rules of appellate procedure is that the judgment or order from the lower court must be "final" before it will be reviewed by a higher court. This principle is found throughout appellate practice in statutes, rules and judicial decisions. At the federal level, 28 U.S.C. § 1291 controls appeals from final judgments in the district courts. It provides:

> The courts of appeals (other than the United States Court of Appeals for the Federal Circuit) shall have jurisdiction of appeals from all final decisions of the district courts of the United States * * * except where direct review may be had in the Supreme Court * * *.

A final judgment is one that resolves all issues between all parties to the suit, leaving only the judgment to be executed. This seems more simple than it is. The problem lies in determining what is a final judgment. Over the years, this issue has spawned massive litigation, leaving its resolution in flux at best and totally perplexing at worst. This is true at both the state and federal level.

Several justifications argue for limiting appeals to final judgments. Economical considerations rank high on the list—namely, economy of time and economy of money. Obviously, if every adverse ruling was appealable, the costs in attorney fees would be staggering. Likewise, so would the backlog of appellate cases. To decide each individual issue "piecemeal" would represent a horrendous waste of court time. Further, with litigation tied up in the appeals court, the trial court case, from which it was appealed, may well come to a halt. The results of the appeal could potentially lead to relitigating aspects of the case, with further delays. The whole process would founder. Simply put, efficient judicial administration would disappear. Justice Frankfurter recognized the importance of the finality doctrine when he said:

> Congress from the very beginning has, by forbidding piecemeal disposition on appeal of what for practical purposes is a single

controversy, set itself against enfeebling judicial administration. Thereby is avoided the obstruction to just claims that would come from permitting the harassment and cost of a succession of separate appeals from the various rulings to which a litigation may give rise, from its initiation to entry of judgment. To be effective, judicial administration must not be leaden-footed. Its momentum would be arrested by permitting separate reviews of the component elements in a unified cause.[20]

For the most part, the finality doctrine works. However, in some situations, the rule is a hardship on litigants. Consider a case in which a preliminary injunction is denied. The harm to the moving litigant may never be redressed in an appeal from the final judgment. Also, preliminary orders involving matters of change of venue, class action, bail or the use of alleged privileged testimony may never be remedied if the litigant is required to wait for the final judgment.

As a result, exceptions to the finality doctrine have all but swallowed the rule in some jurisdictions. In his seminal article entitled *The Final Judgment as a Basis for Appeal,* Crick noted that the final judgment rule and its exceptions have caused more litigation than they have prevented.[21]

1.32   Exceptions to the finality doctrine

It has been observed by one scholar that "[e]ach refinement or exception has reduced the effectiveness of the final judgment rule, with the result of making the final judgment rule honored as much in the breach as in the observance."[22] The following sections detail the extent of the exceptions to the rule.

1.32–1   Review of interlocutory orders as a matter of right

As previously noted, 28 U.S.C. § 1291 mandates that only final decisions of the district courts are appealable. Section 1292(a)(1–3) sets out the exceptions to this rule. At the federal level, the appeals courts have jurisdiction to review orders that grant, modify, continue or deny injunctions. The same is true for orders to appoint receivers, or to refuse orders to conclude a receivership or take steps to accomplish the purposes of the receivership, such as directing the sale or other disposal of property. Interlocutory decrees of district courts that determine the rights and liabilities of the parties to an admiralty case, in which appeals from a final decree would be allowed, also fall within the category of review as of right.

As one would expect, state statutes which allow a review as of right vary greatly. Injunctions and receiverships are reviewable in most states,

---

20. *Cobbledick v. United States,* 309 U.S. 323, 325 (1940).

21. Carleton M. Crick, *The Final Judgment as a Basis for Appeal*, 41 Yale L.J. 539, 553 (1932).

22. Robert J. Martineau, Modern Appellate Practice—Federal and State Civil Appeals § 4.1 (1983).

but consistency ends there. Some states allow exceptions for certain orders in probate and tax, orders to terminate parental rights, orders to change or refuse to change venue, and orders to grant or deny a new trial. New York virtually allows the right of appeal from any interlocutory order which "involves some part of the merits" or "affects a substantial right." Commentators conclude that in New York just about any order can be appealed, as a matter of right, to the intermediate appellate court. Most states are not this permissive. As usual, the advocate must become familiar with the exceptions, as of right, to the finality doctrine in the state in which the trial is conducted.

1.32–2   Discretionary review of interlocutory orders

At the federal level, 28 U.S.C. § 1292(b) controls discretionary review of an interlocutory order. It reads:

> When a district judge, in making in a civil action an order not otherwise appealable under this section, shall be of the opinion that such order involves a controlling question of law as to which there is substantial ground for difference of opinion and that an immediate appeal from the order may materially advance the ultimate termination of the litigation, he shall so state in writing in such order. The Court of Appeals which would have jurisdiction of an appeal of such action may thereupon, in its discretion, permit an appeal to be taken from such order * * *.

Known as the Interlocutory Appeals Act, this section handles situations that, while not specifically named in the "review as of right" section of the statute, nonetheless need immediate attention.

District court certification brings the matter to the appeals court, but this does not guarantee that the appeals court will hear the matter. As noted in *Coopers & Lybrand v. Livesay*:

> [E]ven if the district judge certifies the order under § 1292(b), the appellant still "has the burden of persuading the court of appeals that exceptional circumstances justify a departure from the basic policy of postponing appellate review until after the entry of a final judgment."[23]

Some states do not permit discretionary review. If the right is not specified in the statute, no right exists. However, many states do follow the federal standard; they examine whether the issue raises a controlling question of law, whether substantial grounds exist for differences of opinion, and whether the appeal will advance the termination of litigation. Other states provide that an order may be reviewed if the appellant will suffer substantial harm if the appeal is delayed until after the trial. Others speak of the inadequacy of the appeal after judgment, while still others require that the question be important and doubtful. Simply put, to determine appealable orders, individual states run the gamut from the

---

23. 437 U.S. 463 (1978) (quoting *Fisons*   (7th Cir.1972)).
Ltd. v. United States, 458 F.2d 1241, 1248

very restrictive, to the federal model which is mildly restrictive, to nearly an "anything goes" model.

It is important to research a particular jurisdiction's interpretation of the language of the various statutes. Very narrow statutes may be construed broadly, and, conversely, very broad statutes may be construed narrowly. The words are important, but the interpretation given the words is what must be ascertained to determine the possibility of interlocutory review.

If counsel believes that review is needed, and the issue falls within either a right to appeal or potential discretionary review, the appeal must be brought to the attention of the reviewing court. Jurisdictions handle such appeals in one of two ways. Many jurisdictions require that the trial court certify that the issue satisfies the standards for such review. This is the method used by the federal courts. Independently, the appeals court then determines if it will take the appeal. In other jurisdictions, the matter need only be appealed to the reviewing court, with no certification by the lower court.

Quite obviously, the latter approach is both quicker and easier. Only one application must be filed in only one court. This method eliminates the potential difficulty for the trial judge who issued the order to evaluate objectively whether that order should be reviewed. The downside is that none of the appeals are filtered through the trial court. They go directly to the court of appeals, a practice that may result in a burdensome number of requests for certification to review.

If a jurisdiction requires trial court certification, and that court refuses to certify, the trial court's action is conclusive. This creates an anomalous situation for the trial judge, who is put in the position of determining whether his or her own ruling is subject to immediate appeal. For some judges, this action is welcome. For others, it may be threatening. A few states have alleviated the problem by allowing the party against whom the certification was denied to appeal to the supreme court for discretionary interlocutory relief. Perhaps the best approach would be to allow the trial court to present its views on the matter, with the ultimate decision to be made by the court of appeals.

Review may extend beyond the intermediate appellate court. This is true in the federal system and most jurisdictions that have two tiers of appellate review. The fact that the request for review is interlocutory in nature and not a final order presents no jurisdictional problems, but could militate against review. By nature, appellate courts review final orders, and if discretionary, prefer to allow the matter to come to its logical conclusion. Some states have solved the problem by restricting supreme court review to circumstances in which the decision of that body would be dispositive of the issue.

1.32–3   Judge-made exceptions

Section 1291 of 28 U.S.C. gives courts of appeals jurisdiction over final decisions of the district courts. Similarly, § 1257 allows review by the Supreme Court over "final judgments or decrees rendered by the highest court of a State in which the decision could be had." These two sections both require a "final order." What constitutes a final order has been the subject of numerous cases which have interpreted that language. A final order has come to mean something far less than an end or termination of the litigation. The courts' "interpretations" provide further exceptions to the finality doctrine.[24] Discussion of § 1291 is illustrative of the notion of judge-made law and the finality doctrine.

Cohen v. Beneficial Industrial Loan Corp.,[25] announced the collateral order doctrine, which allows review of a matter prior to the termination of litigation. In reference to the lower court decision, the Supreme Court in *Cohen* set the standard for review. It said:

> This decision appears to fall in that small class which finally determine claims of right separable from, and collateral to, rights asserted in the action, too important to be denied review and too independent of the case itself to require that appellate consideration be deferred until the whole case is adjudicated. The Court has long given this provision of the statute this practical rather than a technical construction.[26]

In the years that followed the *Cohen* decision, courts defined and redefined the exception. In the case of *Coopers & Lybrand v. Livesay,*[27] the Court stated:

> To come within the "small class" of decisions excepted from the final-judgment rule by *Cohen*, the order must conclusively determine the disputed question, resolve an important issue completely separate from the merits of the action, and be effectively unreviewable on appeal from a final judgment.[28]

While refining the meaning, nevertheless, the Supreme Court has always maintained that, indeed, a small class is just that—a small class. In *Richardson–Merrel Inc. v. Koller,*[29] the Court stated "we decline to 'transform the limited exception carved out in *Cohen* into a license for broad disregard of the finality rule imposed by Congress in § 1291.' "[30]

Review of § 1291 jurisprudence indicates that, while the Court espouses a limitation on exceptions to the finality doctrine, new exceptions continue to be articulated. In the 1996 case *Behrens v. Pelletier,*[31] the Court held that two interlocutory appeals were proper in the matter of deciding qualified immunity. In a strongly worded dissent, Justice Breyer accepted that one interlocutory appeal was permissible but drew the line at allowing two reviews of a pretrial motion to dismiss the case

---

24. *See United States v. MacDonald,* 435 U.S. 850 (1978).

25. 337 U.S. 541 (1949).

26. *Id.* at 546 (citations omitted).

27. 437 U.S. 463 (1978).

28. *Id.* at 468 (footnote and citations omitted).

29. 472 U.S. 424, 440 (1985).

30. *Id.* at 440 (quoting *Firestone Tire & Rubber Co. v. Risjord,* 449 U.S. 368, 378 (1981)).

31. 516 U.S. 299, 304 (1996).

based on immunity. He quoted and cited both the *Richardson–Merrell* and the *Firestone* cases, which demand caution in expanding judicial exceptions to the finality doctrine.

While judge-made law has not swallowed the rule, there definitely have been inroads into the finality provisions of § 1291. Similar jurisprudence has followed § 1257, previously mentioned, which allows Supreme Court review of state supreme court cases.

1.32–4 Judgment final as to some but not all claims or parties

Rule 54(b) of the Federal Rules of Civil Procedure provides another way for a court of appeals to review a partial judgment of the lower court. The rule provides:

> When more than one claim for relief is presented in an action, whether as a claim, counterclaim, cross-claim, or third-party claim, or when multiple parties are involved, the court may direct the entry of a [1] final judgment as to one or more but fewer than all of the claims or parties [2] only upon an express determination that there is no just reason for delay and upon an express direction for the entry of judgment.

Similarly, many states, by statute or court rule, allow a similar action. It makes sense. The federal rules, as well as those of most states, encourage liberal joinder of claims and parties. The idea is to get the entire matter before the court, rather than to litigate the same issues involving multiple parties over and over again. This rule allows the appeal of orders that cannot meet 1292(b) standards but nevertheless disposes of some aspect of the lawsuit.

Under Rule 54(b) and similar state statutes and rules, in order to request review in the appellate court, the lower court must direct an entry of judgment on one or more claims or parties *and* certify that there is no just reason to delay appeal from that judgment. Even with the certification, there are no guarantees that the court of appeals will accept the appeal. First, the higher court will examine whether the finality requirements meet the standards of § 1291. Second, the judge's certification that there is "no just reason for delay" will be scrutinized. The reasons given must be specific and relevant and not simply the bald statement that, in fact, there is "no just reason for delay." In most appellate courts, that assertion will invoke a finding of "abuse of discretion" by the lower court judge, thus defeating the appeal.

The difficulty comes when claims in the trial court are intertwined. In that instance, the court of appeals may dismiss the appeal, even if there is certification by the lower court judge. This ruling reduces the possibility there will be parallel proceedings in either one or both courts that will lead to an inconsistent result. However, the Supreme Court has emphasized that the lower court's opinion should be given deference, because "the task of weighing and balancing the contending factors is peculiarly for the trial judge who can explore all facts of the case."[32]

The question of whether to seek certification for an appeal, when less than all claims have been determined, is a decision that must be carefully considered. It may be strategically attractive to settle some of the claims as to some of the parties. On the other hand, it may well be strategically sound to see what happens during the remainder of the case. Whatever the decision, the appellant should note carefully that: (1) the trial court's certification gives that part of the case the status of a final judgement; (2) this starts the statute of limitations running as it relates to any appeal; and, (3) it makes the order res judicata if the matter is not reversed.

1.32–5 Extraordinary writs

Extraordinary writs have a long and rich history in the United States. A discussion of all the various writs and their functions is beyond the scope of this book. However, it is instructive to explore, as an example, the workings of the writ most widely used by an appellate court. First, there must be a short background explanation of the writ system.

Some interlocutory orders may be reviewed via extraordinary writs. Technically, use of the writs is a separate and distinct proceeding which is begun in the appellate court. The All Writs Act found in 28 U.S.C. § 1651 provides the authority for their use. It authorizes the various federal courts of appeals to review and control the power of the district courts prior to a final judgment. In effect, it takes the place of an appeal and is, therefore, an exception to the final judgment rule.

While there are many extraordinary writs, the one most often employed is mandamus. Mandamus is to be used, however, only in limited circumstances. As defined in *Heckler v. Ringer*,[33] "[t]he common law writ of mandamus * * * is intended to provide a remedy for a plaintiff only if he has exhausted all other avenues of relief and only if the defendant owes him a clear non-discretionary duty."[34]

Usually the action requests that the court of appeals order the lower court judge to act or to refrain from acting in a particular manner. The litigants in the action are normally the real parties in interest, though occasionally the judge is the subject of the challenge.

Hahnemann University Hospital v. Edgar,[35] presents an excellent example of this route to appeal. In that case, the parents of a female patient at a mental hospital brought an action against the hospital and

32. *Curtiss–Wright Corp. v. General Electric Co.*, 446 U.S. 1, 12 (1980), *vacating and remanding* 597 F.2d 35 (3d Cir.1979).

33. 466 U.S. 602 (1984).

34. *Id*. at 616. It is interesting to note that older Supreme Court cases were very restrictive in allowing mandamus. However, in the 1940's, the Court loosened the stan-

dards for granting mandamus, only later to return to a stricter view of its use. More recent cases put renewed stress on the final judgment rule and the extraordinary nature of a mandamus action.

35. 74 F.3d 456 (3d Cir.1996).

sought disclosure of records relating to two male patients. The patients had allegedly raped their daughter while she was hospitalized. The hospital, claiming confidentiality of psychiatric records, refused a district court order to produce the records. In addition to the order to produce the documents, the court ordered the hospital to pay $1,000 per day until it complied with the order. The hospital filed a Writ of Mandamus claiming that an appeal after a final decision was inadequate since compliance with the production orders would destroy the right sought to be protected. The court of appeals held that the hospital's right to the writ was clear and indisputable and that the district court exceeded its authority in compelling the hospital to produce the records.

To summarize, writs are at times available to a party in the federal system, but only in limited circumstances. The matter must be of substantial importance, the judge in the lower court must have exceeded his or her power, and there can be no other adequate remedy available.

State systems have handled the matter in several different ways. Some states have extremely relaxed rules for granting writs, while others are fairly strict. In contrast, some states have abolished the use of the writs altogether and simply have created new remedies for reviewing orders that are unappealable.[36] Counsel must examine the case law of the jurisdiction to determine when the writs or substitute actions are allowed, as well as the procedure for invoking them.

1.32–6 Contempt of court

Robert Stern notes that contempt of court is a "hazardous route for obtaining interlocutory review * * * of a nonappealable order."[37] Contempt proceedings may arise if a lawyer deliberately disobeys the direct order of the trial judge. For example, if the judge specifically asks for information that the lawyer possesses and the lawyer refuses to divulge that information, the judge could impose the sanction of contempt of court. While the order to divulge the information is not appealable, the contempt citation is a separate appealable order. Obviously, this tactic should be used only in those cases in which the party or the lawyer to be disciplined figures the appellate court will be sympathetic, the injuries, if the order is followed, will be irreparable, and the cause serious enough to warrant the risk of punishment. No lawyer wants to be in the unenviable position of disobeying a court order, especially when the outcome of the sanctions are unknown and potentially costly.

1.40 SETTLEMENT AS AN ALTERNATIVE TO AN APPEAL

Often, there is a great attraction to settle a dispute after the trial court judgment. At that time, everyone knows the players and both the strengths and weaknesses of the case. Prior to the trial, parties have far

---

36. These remedies are called by a variety of names such as "special action", "discretionary review" and "application for extraordinary appeal". In effect, they all reach the same end although some apply stricter standards when allowing such review.

37. Robert L. Stern, Appellate Practice in the United States 99 (2d ed. 1989).

less information upon which to base a settlement. Some have inflated ideas about the worth of the case, while others simply are not sure of the value. In some instances, those considerations may encourage settlement, while in others it promotes a "let's wait and see" attitude.

Once the judgment is rendered, there are a number of reasons why settlement may be negotiated. For the winning party with a money judgment, the time value of money must be considered. It may be better to settle for less and have the money in hand than to wait for the appeals process to run its course. In addition, there is always the possibility that the case will be lost on appeal, and suddenly the winner becomes the loser. Also, the money taken in settlement may be more than winning on appeal, when one considers the costs of defending the appeal. Finally, there is a great deal to be said for simple closure. Lawsuits are stressful and worrisome. Finality may be very attractive.

The loser faces much the same situation. The additional costs for the appeal are added to the knowledge that most cases are not reversed on appeal.[38] Negotiations, especially with a willing winner, may well garner the losing party a settlement considerably lower than the original judgment. And, again, there is the matter of closure.

1.50   THE CLIENT AS THE FINAL DECISION–MAKER

The decision to appeal rests with the client, and the attorney is ethically bound to respect the client's wishes.[39] This rule makes ultimate sense, because the client is the litigant and the person who will eventually suffer the results of the judgment. It is also the client who will pay the costs of the appeal. The attorney's role in the decision must be one of an advisor. The attorney presents the strengths and weaknesses of the case, along with a suggested course of action. In the end, however, the client must be the decision-maker.

At times, the matter becomes complicated because the client wishes to delay the ultimate outcome. In a civil case, this may mean a delay in payment of the judgment, though there are costs associated with delay. In a criminal case, assuming that the defendant can make bail, it means postponing a prison sentence. As a result, appeals of questionable merit are filed, thus further clogging the appellate system. Nevertheless, an attorney is bound by his client's wishes, unless the appeal is completely frivolous.[40]

EXERCISE

Jones, a resident of the State of Oregon, sued Smith, a resident of California, claiming that Smith was in breach of contract to sell Jones a painting. The painting was housed in Smith's summer residence. The contract specified that Jones agreed to pay Smith $50,000 for the

38. *See* § 1.03 on the reversal rates of courts.

39. *See* Model Rules of Professional Conduct Rule 1.2(a) (1983).

40. *But see* § 2.60 regarding sanctions. An attorney is not bound to put himself or the client in jeopardy. This matter should be carefully explained to the client.

painting, which Jones now claims is worth $80,000. Thus the basis of the lawsuit. Because there is diversity of citizenship and the amount of the claim is above the federal threshold, the suit was properly commenced in a federal district court in California.

The defendant Smith answered the complaint, claiming impossibility of performance, because the painting was no longer at the summer home and its whereabouts is unknown. The usual interrogatories were filed by the plaintiff requesting information about events leading to the disappearance of the painting. Defendant Smith filed a motion to extend the time to answer the discovery. The plaintiff opposed the motion, claiming that time was of the essence in order to protect his interest in the painting. The judge granted the motion to extend the time to answer the interrogatories.

Subsequent discovery uncovered the fact that the painting had been stolen. A police report was produced as evidence of this fact. Upon completion of the discovery process, defendant Smith filed a Motion for Summary Judgment claiming that, because the painting was no longer in his possession (he produced a police report to verify that the painting indeed had been reported stolen), he could no longer perform the contract through no fault of his own. The judge granted the Motion for Summary Judgment, holding that the defendant was entitled to judgment as a matter of law. In his decision, the judge wrote that there was no genuine issue of material fact—the painting was gone, *ergo* the defendant could not perform.

The plaintiff Jones appealed to the Ninth Circuit Court of Appeals. As it relates to the two motions, what standard of review would you articulate in your brief in support of the plaintiff Jones.

Chapter Two

ETHICS AND THE APPELLATE PROCESS

Analysis

2.00   INTRODUCTION

Lawyers who handle appeals face ethical problems that are "practice specific." Just as a trial lawyer encounters ethical questions that a consultant does not, the appellate lawyer has special concerns not associated with other areas of practice. This chapter deals with the issues encountered by the appeals lawyer and the possible sanctions imposed for violation of established ethical standards.

Legal ethics are generally understood to be standards of conduct among members of the legal profession as relates to their moral and professional duty toward each other, their clients and the court. More specifically, a lawyer's ethics describe behavior that is expected of the lawyer as he or she interacts with clients, other lawyers, and the judiciary. Fortunately, over the years, courts have clarified ethical violations and the appeals process. Primarily, the concerns center on (1) the initiation of the appeal, (2) the duty of competence, (3) diligence, (4) positional conflicts, and (5) candor and professionalism.

2.10   INITIATION OF THE APPEAL

The threshold issue an appellate lawyer must consider is whether to initiate an appeal. First, an appeal should never be a reaction to an adverse judgment—simply a way to preserve the client's rights. Rather, careful consideration must be given to determine if there are sufficient grounds for appeal. If there are not, no appeal should be taken. Second, an appeal should not be taken merely to harass the winning party or delay the outcome of the litigation. Third, the appeal must have legal merit. The key to all three is good faith—in purpose and in argument. An appeal initiated to delay the outcome and without careful consideration of the merits is often deemed to be frivolous.

The rules of conduct specifically require that "[a] lawyer has a professional obligation to the client, the court and the adversaries to ensure that actions commenced and positions advanced are not frivolous or meritless."[1] What constitutes frivolous has been addressed by many courts. There is no consensus as to its definition.

Over the years, courts have been cautious about declaring an appeal as frivolous. To do so could have a chilling effect on novel ideas and theories of law yet undeveloped. There is a fine line between zealously representing a client and promoting a claim that has no merit. Yet the line must be drawn, and the deliberate lawyer must determine whether the claim is novel and supportable in law or frivolous with no colorable arguments or merit. Remember: the lawyer does not have to believe that the appeal will ultimately succeed. He only needs to have "a good faith argument for an extension, modification or reversal of existing law."[2]

In summary, there is no bright line test to determine whether an appeal has merit or is frivolous. Courts that confront this issue must struggle with the elimination of frivolous appeals without discouraging the advancement of potentially worthwhile claims. Accordingly, prior to the initiation of an appeal, counsel must be certain the motives are proper and the arguments have merit. In the end, if the client insists on filing a frivolous appeal, it is the lawyer's obligation either to decline to file, or withdraw from representation.

2.20 DUTY OF COMPETENCE

The Model Rules of Professional Conduct, Rule 1.1 requires that "[a] lawyer shall provide competent representation to a client. Competent representation requires the legal knowledge, skill, thoroughness, and preparation reasonably necessary for the representation." The duty of competence is an ethical essential for all lawyers. The appellate lawyer is especially challenged for two reasons. First, the appellate process is highly technical in nature. Second, the technology of legal research is evolving at an exponential rate.

The decision to appeal leads the lawyer down a new path. It can be hazardous unless the journey is undertaken with care. A reading of the rules that govern the procedures for appeal seem reasonably straightforward. But for one who does not routinely practice in the area, they can be a trap for the unwary. As an example, the rules call for the appellant

1. Center for Professional Responsibility, A.B.A. Annotated Model Rules of Professional Conduct 298 (4th ed. 1999).

2. Model Rules of Professional Conduct Rule 3.1 (1983).

to state the standard of review the appellate court should use. This simple directive requires a vast amount of knowledge as it relates to the specific standards. A further complication is the wide divergence of standards through the various courts of appeals at both the federal and state level.

As a second example, trial court rules allow for liberal amendments. This is not the case in appellate practice. A notice of appeal that fails to list all individuals separately and includes them under "et al." has effectively named only the first party. Et and al. are not a part of the appeal.

Appellate courts have little patience with lawyers who do not understand or follow the rules. Failure to follow the rules may lead to sanctions, or in the worst scenario, dismissal of the appeal. For example, one court simply refused to consider the last twenty-one pages of a brief, which exceeded the page limit as specified by the rules. Another court leveled sanctions and dismissed an appeal because counsel failed to follow the rules when preparing the brief. A trial lawyer cannot assume competence at the appellate level based on past performance in the trial court. A novice appellate lawyer must carefully study case law and secondary authority to learn the innuendoes of the appeals process.

The second challenge mentioned above is that the world of legal research has changed dramatically over the last several years. Keeping current is a full time job. Lawyers who do not routinely handle cases of similar substance often find themselves scrambling to discover the most recent authorities. Without doubt, computer assisted legal research (C.A.L.R.) has becoming more and more indispensable in order to stay proficient. It has quickly become a standard research technique, the information of which can be deemed to fall within the public domain. Once in the public domain, lawyers who fail to discover computer sources may be deemed guilty of malpractice or worse. And, the use of computers for research continues to grow as more and more sources are available at no cost to the practitioner. Much of the high technology research is now accessible through the Internet on various sites catering to case research, legislative research and research of a general nature. One can hardly argue that availability is lacking when the sources may be accessed for free.

In keeping with the Internet explosion, federal circuits routinely post important information on their web sites. Each circuit has a web site that can be accessed through www.ca6.uscourts.gov. (Of course, the correct circuit must be inserted) Both the local court rules and the internal operating procedures can be found on many of the circuit court web sites. In addition, attorneys should be aware of the PACER system. PACER (Public Access to Court Electronic Records) allows access to docket sheets and other case information that were previously available only by visiting the courthouse.[3] Also, many circuits allow electronic

---

3. Information regarding PACER is available at http://pacer.psc.uscourts.gov or PACER@psc.uscourts.gov.

filing of documents. Each circuit's web site provides useful information about available services.

Lawyers are expected to show competence both procedurally and substantively. Lack of either can lead to ethical charges as they relate to the canon of competence.

2.30 DILIGENCE

The matter of diligence would seem to fit within the category of competence, at least as it relates to timely filings. However, when it comes to timely filings, the matter may not be one of competence in the sense of failure to understand the rules. Rather, timely filings can go to the matter of whether the attorney has acted in a diligent manner in pursuing the case. For example, a federal appeals court imposed, as a sanction, a three-month suspension from appearing before it when an attorney continually petitioned the court for extensions to file briefs and filed late briefs. In another case, the attorney was found in contempt of court after he failed to comply with an order setting a deadline for filing an initial brief and requesting a twentieth extension. This case was especially egregious because the appeal was from a death penalty.

However, the notion of diligence goes to issues other than timely filings. Delaying tactics may also lead to trouble for an attorney. For example, some lawyers have been known to file an appeal simply to prevent the judgment from being enforced. There may be no appealable issue, but rather the appeal is filed merely to delay the inevitable. Clearly this type of appeal could be deemed frivolous. Whatever the label, it is unethical to proceed in this manner.

Diligence also requires the attorney to keep the client informed of the progress and outcome of the appeal. Some state court rules specifically address the duty.

2.40 POSITIONAL CONFLICTS

The literature is replete with the relationship between the ethical rules and conflicts of interest. As with the trial lawyer, the appellate lawyer must examine the usual issues that potentially generate a conflict of interest. These may include conflict between current clients, conflict between a current client's interest and a former client's interest, and conflicts that affect the quality of representation for the client.[4] However, as noted by one scholar, "[t]he rules do not provide guidance on positional conflicts occurring when two clients have differing political or ideological views, or economic or legal interests that affect each other adversely. In the rarefied atmosphere of appellate practice, such conflicts can and do occur."[5]

---

4. For a detailed discussion of Model Rules of Professional Conduct Rule 1.7, which addresses the conflicts of interest question *see* Center for Professional Responsibility, A.B.A., annotated Model Rules of Professional Conduct 93 (3d ed. 1996).

5. J. Michael Medina, *Ethical Concerns in Civil Appellate Advocacy,* 43 Sw. L.J. 677, 690 (1989).

Positional conflicts arise because: (1) the appellate bar, or those firms that do the bulk of the appellate work, is a smaller body than the trial bar; and, (2) firms tend to polarize their appellate work. It is not unusual for a law firm to be aligned with management as opposed to labor, or represent plaintiff rather than defense clients. For example, in a state that has enacted legislation prohibiting affirmative action, a conflict may arise if an associate represents students for affirmative action, while a firm member sits on the Board that represents the state universities. The victor for either side would have a difficult time explaining to the opposing party how the same law firm represents such opposite ideologies.

When an appellate lawyer is confronted with a significant positional conflict, careful thought must be given to, (1) whether the same issues will be raised in each litigation, (2) the impact of one client's interests prevailing over those of another client, and (3) the overall importance of the issue. If the lawyer can utilize Rule 1.2(c) and limit the objectives of the representation of the client, the positional conflict may be eliminated. If a limited representation is sought, the lawyer must consult with the party represented. However, when limited representation is not an option, full disclosure must be made to both parties. Should both clients understand the potential positional conflict and agree to the lawyer's representation, the ethical concerns are met. When one client objects to the lawyer representing both interests, then the lawyer should withdraw from one side or the other.

2.50 CANDOR AND PROFESSIONALISM

The notions of candor and professionalism are inextricably connected because lack of one necessarily implies lack of the other. For purposes of this chapter, they will be separately discussed, but they are assumed to be overlapping concepts having to do with truthfulness and honesty coupled with the appropriate outward manifestations of a lawyer's behavior.

2.51 Candor

In appellate advocacy, attorneys may find themselves on the proverbial "horns of a dilemma." On the one hand, the attorney owes a duty to clients to represent their claims in the best possible light. On the other hand, the attorney owes a duty to the court to represent the case truthfully in all respects. These divergent loyalties may create serious tension. If the two collide, the duty to the court is paramount and must prevail. In other words, if the issue is choosing between a course of conduct that will benefit the client but is not true to the court, the attorney is ethically bound to the court.

The dilemma presents itself in a case in which an appeal has been perfected, briefs have been filed, and there is nothing to do but wait for a court decision. During the interim, the parties settle the matter. Nevertheless, the client insists on, and opposing counsel is not adverse to, obtaining the court's ruling. The scenario may occur if a client wants a definitive answer to the legal issues raised, particularly when it may affect, for example, other future actions of the client. However, since courts refuse to decide moot or fictitious appeals, lawyers have a duty to inform the appellate court of the settlement. As noted in *Douglas v. Donovan,* "[i]t is one thing to argue that settlement does not moot a particular case; it is quite another to promote an advisory opinion by disguising a settlement in order to hide it from the court's consideration."[6]

The rules require disclosure of the settlement, and court cases have held in that manner. Attorneys are obligated to keep the court apprised of all developments and it is unethical to maintain a moot appeal. If there is no controversy, there is no case.

Similarly, if, during the interim between the appeal and the decision, something happens to moot the issue other than settlement, that fact must also be disclosed. For example, in a United States Supreme Court case involving a license revocation, when the issue became moot because the business ceased to exist, in dismissing *certiorari,* the court held that counsel is required to inform the Court, without delay, of any development that could effectively deprive the Court of jurisdiction. Simply put, if the basis of the appeal no longer exists, the issue is moot, and the attorney must advise the court of that fact.

The record provides fertile ground for attorneys to act unethically. The canons require a fair portrayal of the record. Violations include misrepresentation or distortion of the facts as well as making false statements not supported by the record. For example, in *Loza v. State,*[7] the appellant asserted that he had challenged certain instructions given in the trial court, but a review of the record showed no such challenges. While clearly an attorney should cast the facts in a light most favorable to the client, it is inappropriate deliberately to misstate them. Editing or cropping the facts to eliminate material critical to an accurate portrayal of the lawsuit is likewise unethical, as well as taking quotations out of context to bolster unfavorable facts. In the end, the facts may be "swayed" to the client's position, but they must be complete and accurate.

Lawyers also get into trouble editing the case law. Quoting material from cases can be extremely beneficial to show parallels to the client's case and thus helps the court understand the client's position. The rub comes when attorneys lift words out of context or simply leave out portions of a quote so as to distort the meaning of the case. As well, attorneys must take care that proper attribution is given to sources that are not original. Courts are not amused by the discovery that materials seemingly written by the attorney actually originated from another source.

6. 704 F.2d 1276, 1280 (D.C.Cir.1983).   **7.** 325 N.E.2d 173 (Ind.1975).

Perhaps the most galling of the duties owed to the court is the duty to disclose adverse precedent if it exists. Model Rule 3.3(a)(3) requires the attorney to disclose "legal authority in the controlling jurisdiction known to the lawyer to be directly adverse to the position of the client and not disclosed by the opposing counsel." This situation does not arise often, but the concept is longstanding in the ethics literature. Its interpretation has been rich in controversy. The issues that have surrounded this duty include, but are not limited to: whether the overlooked decision is one the court clearly needs to decide the appeal; what decisions need be disclosed dependent on the level of the court; whether failure to disclose would, in the eyes of the judge, constitute lack of candor; and, how adverse the case must be before disclosure is necessary.

The duty of candor continues throughout the appellate process, including oral argument and post-argument appeals. Dedication to the accuracy of the facts and the law remain sacrosanct until the appeals have concluded and the case is over.

2.52 Professionalism

The notion of professionalism encompasses all manner of lawyer conduct and demeanor during the appellate process. Lawyers have been censored and sanctioned for disparaging remarks directed at opposing counsel, the court and other parties to the action. As one judge noted "[y]ou can think it, but you better not say it."[8]

Simply put, ethics demand that lawyers be civil. This is not a new concept but one that continues to garner more and more attention in the law and generally in society. Somehow courteous, polite, respectful behavior seems to have eluded some members of the bar. Appellate advocacy has not escaped the fray.[9] The results can be disastrous. An uncivil tone or comment in a brief can result in it being stricken. An uncivil tone or comment in oral argument can lead to sanctions. The final result generally will not be in the best interest of the client or the cause.

2.60 SANCTIONS

Courts have great power to discipline. Rule 11 of the Federal Rules of Civil Procedure, along with statutes, other Federal rules and "the inherent power of courts",[10] define those powers in the form of sanctions. Sanctions extend to attorneys, their firms and their clients. Parties may be sanctioned for violating appellate rules and procedures, utilizing unfair or dilatory practices and fraud. In particularly grievous cases, the

---

8. *Vandenberghe v. Poole,* 163 So.2d 51, 52 (Fl.Dist.Ct.App.1964).

9. In a state court case, an attorney was disbarred for, among other acts, alluding to the court as a "kangaroo court" and the judge as a "horse's ass." While the attorney's actions may seem extreme, this illus-trates the depth to which the bar has sunk insofar as civility is concerned. The case also demonstrates courts' unwillingness to put up with such behavior.

10. *See Chambers v. NASCO, Inc.,* 501 U.S. 32 (1991).

court may report the attorney to the appropriate authorities for disbarment procedures.

Sanctions that can be imposed include, but are not limited to, suspension from practice before the court, assessment of costs and fees of opposing counsel, order of contempt, reprimand and dismissal of the appeal. Generally, the attorney or party to the appeal is given notice and a hearing before sanctions are imposed, but there are instances in which a hearing is not required.

While sanctions protect both the system and the parties in the appellate process, there are at least two problems with their use. First, for a variety of reasons, sanctions may be applied in an uneven manner. What is offensive conduct to one judge may very well be overlooked by another. Second, because of the threat of sanctions, some novel causes may not be pursued, thus chilling the notion of zealous advocacy. For these reasons, sanctions should be cautiously imposed but are appropriate for egregious misrepresentations and unbecoming behavior.

EXERCISES

I.   Lawyers are cautioned always to be cognizant of the rules of appellate procedure. The Fifth Circuit, for example, issues a checklist to lawyers to make certain that the briefs filed before the court comport with the rules. Assume an appeal to a superior court in which the notice of appeal, which was timely filed, erroneously recites that the appeal is from an "order for judgment," rather than "judgment." The appeal is dismissed and cannot be resubmitted.

A.   The client files an ethical grievance against the attorney claiming he was incompetent, a violation of the canons. Argue the case for the attorney.

B.   Argue for the client. Are there alternative routes the client could take to obtain satisfaction?

C.   Having considered both sides, is this act an ethical violation under the "duty of competence" canon?

II.   A contentious area in appellate practice involves frivolous appeals. Many judges claim they "know a frivolous appeal when [they] see it," but have a difficult time articulating a standard for judging frivolous appeals. Admittedly, there is a fine line between a novel theory of appeal and a frivolous claim. Thus assume the following:

A.   The client wants to appeal a case but the basis for filing the appeal is thin, verging on non-existent. Explore the various competing interests the attorney has as well as her obligation to all parties.

B.   In the same scenario, would the lawyer's duties change if the firm also represents clients with opposing interests to those that were litigated and are now considered for appeal?

III.   A chief issue in appellate practice centers on the matter of candor to the court. Assume in oral argument that on three different occasions, the lawyer for the appellant makes the claim, "[i]t is without contradiction that * * *." In fact, the matter is in controversy, though not dispositive of the case on appeal.

Explore the ethical implications of making these kinds of statements in oral argument.

IV. Fifteen years ago, your firm defended a lawsuit against a small factory that manufactured a plastic material used to make children's toys. The lawsuit centered on the residue of the process for manufacturing the plastic, which was stored in barrels. The claim was the barrels had leaked poisons (specifically named) into the ground. Because the factory was situated on the extension of a river (which was, at the point of the factory, a large stream) the contentions of the plaintiffs (who owned property down stream) were that the leakage was polluting the waters both beneath the earth and in the stream.

The trial was a mixed bag. Your client was ordered to clean up the site but not the ground water stream. The factory appealed and lost again in the intermediate court of appeals. Thus you client was forced to spend large sums of money to comply with the court's order. Nevertheless, the factory has continued on as clients and, in fact, the firm has represented it on other matters, ranging from land acquisition for expansion to permits for the development of new products.

As for the lawsuit, the clean up was completed, the factory sued the barrel manufacturers and life went on.

Recently, a prospective client came to see you. This is a well-funded group that is interested in conservation and the environment. Because this is also an interest for you, you were more than happy to consider their representation. Among their several projects is to clean up a certain stream that, as you can guess, was the subject of the lawsuit fifteen years ago.

What is your answer to them as they offer you a healthy retainer insofar as the firm representation? Are there ethical issues? If so, what are they and how can you resolve them?

Chapter Three

TECHNICALITIES OF THE APPEAL

Analysis

3.00 INTRODUCTION

In the United States, the appellate process is so ingrained in our notion of justice that most people believe it is a right with Constitutional guarantees. This is not so.[1] However, in the interest of fairness and justice, the appellate process is favored by both legislatures and courts.[2] States generally provide that an aggrieved party has one appeal as a matter of right regarding the merits of the case.

An appeal is generally defined as the removal of a cause from an inferior tribunal to a superior tribunal. Generally, when one thinks of the appellate process, one thinks in terms of the state or federal court system, but there are other appellate forums. Many administrative agencies provide for an appeal within the agency structure, and in some instances, direct appeals to the court system. It is important that counsel have a clear understanding of why the process functions as it does and, more importantly, how it functions.

---

1. In the 1930 case of *Dohany v. Rogers,* 281 U.S. 362 (1930), the court noted that the due process clause of the Constitution does not guarantee any particular form under which states must operate with respect to procedure, including appellate procedure. Speaking to the right of appeal, the Court said under the Constitution, "no man may claim * * * a right of appeal." *Id*. at 369.

2. For an interesting counter argument on whether the appeals process is useful, see Irving Wilner, *Civil Appeals: Are They Useful in the Administration of Justice?*, 56 Geo. L.J. 417 (1968).

3.01 The purpose of the appeal

The loftiest goals of the appeal are to achieve justice and maintain uniformity within a particular jurisdiction. Most people will agree that two individuals on any given day can view a set of facts, and the application of law to those facts, from different perspectives. That being the case, a different result may be reached in cases with virtually identical facts. With the enormous number of judges administering the judicial system, there must be a process to settle what the law is or what it should be. The appellate procedure supplies the process. Simply put, the appeal allows a fresh look at the outcome of a trial. Corrections may be made in errors of judgment as they relate to interpreting the application of law to facts, policy and the like. Uniformity in judicial decisions and, thus, in justice is the goal.

Equally as important, the availability of appeal may actually prevent acts of unfairness and provide a stimulus to avoid mistakes at earlier stages of the judicial process. Few judges enjoy the prospect of having their actions and opinions overruled by a superior tribunal. The appeal acts as a type of check on impulsive or ill-conceived consequences. As Judge Coffin observed, "a human being vested with the responsibility of passing judgment is never so wise, so pure, so alert as to make a 'second opinion' redundant."[3]

3.02 The appellate courts and how they function

The primary function of appellate courts is to correct errors made by the trial court, intermediate appellate courts (if speaking of the court of last resort) and administrative agencies. When an appeal is taken, the appellate court must determine whether the decision of the lower court or agency was correct, or within a reasonable range of allowable error for the administrator or trial court decision-maker. It is not the goal of the appellate court to ensure that each party to the suit has a perfect trial. Rather, the question is whether harm results to a party because of the lower tribunal's mistake or omission.

Generally those errors focus on something the lower court does or refuses to do. For example, if the plaintiff requests a particular jury instruction, reversible error may occur in one of two ways: if the court refuses to give the instruction and harm results *or* if the judge gives a different instruction with resultant harm. In either case, trial counsel must object to the inclusion or omission in order to raise the matter on appeal. However, a trial court's failure to give the proper instruction to the jury does not present an appealable issue if trial counsel does not object to the errant instruction. The time to correct an error or omission is during trial. The objection allows the judge to make a correction and resolve the issue without an appeal.

---

3. Frank M. Coffin, The Ways of a Judge: Reflections from the Federal Appel- late Bench 16 (1980).

There are notable exceptions to trial counsel's objection to preserve an issue for appeal. First, an appeal will be allowed in the event that an issue is raised for the first time at the appellate court level. An example might be a criminal defendant's claim that he has been represented by ineffective counsel. Second, appellate courts also allow an appeal for "plain error." Plain error is defined as a matter that the judge should have recognized as error and resolved on his own motion. It must also affect a substantial right of the party against whom the error is committed. Failure to declare a mistrial upon learning that a defense lawyer had contacted members of the jury in a criminal case likely would be deemed plain error. Third, at times an issue may be preserved even though a specific objection is not raised during the trial. For example, in the case of *Judd v. Rodman,*[4] counsel for Judd made a motion *in limine* during a pretrial conference. The motion was denied. The appeals court stated, as a general proposition, a motion *in limine* that is denied does not preserve a party's objection for purposes of appeal, but under certain circumstances, it may be adequate to preserve the error. In that case, because there was good cause shown, the motion *in limine* did preserve the issue for appeal, and Judd did not waive her objection.

In conclusion, the error charged either must be noted during the trial and result in harm to the complaining party, or it must fall within one of the exceptions noted above. Remember: the appellate court's task is not to perfect the record but rather to ensure that the lower court's actions were fair and just.

A second function of the appellate process is known as institutional review. Trial courts, by their nature, operate independently from each other. Absent appellate review, great divergences in findings and results might potentially develop, thus weakening the judicial system. Appellate review provides for the continued development and unification within a jurisdiction. Institutional review then is concerned with the judicial impact a decision may have on the populous in general.

Perhaps Professors Carrington, Meador and Rosenberg in their work *Justice on Appeal* stated it best when they noted that:

> On the one hand, appellate justice is preoccupied with the impact of decisions on particular litigants, but on the other it is concerned with the general principles which govern the affairs of persons other than those who are party to the cases decided.[5]

All appellate courts engage in error correction and deal with institutional concerns. However, as a case rises in the judicial system, the error correction function diminishes and the institutional function increases. Thus, intermediate appellate courts generally concentrate on correcting errors of the trial court in individual cases, while courts of last resort typically focus on issues for the public good and its institutions.

4.   105 F.3d 1339 (11th Cir.1997).

5.   Paul D. Carrington, et. al., Justice on Appeal 3 (1976).

3.10 WHO CAN APPEAL

3.11 A party to the record

A party must have standing to appeal. As a rule, this requires that the person or persons be a party in the proceeding below and must be aggrieved by the decision of the lower court. Usually these two requirements present few problems. In most cases, one knows that he or she has been a party to a suit and that the case has been lost.

With regard to the first requirement, appellant must have been a party to the record. Parties to the record include original parties and those who become parties through substitution, intervention or third-party practice. The rule seems simple enough, but substantial amounts of litigation cast doubts. Courts have struggled to define the terms. As a result, there are exceptions to the "party" rule and who can become a party through intervention after judgment.[6] Consequently, a person who is not a named party and has an interest in the outcome (and possible appeal) should endeavor to intervene at the earliest possible time at the trial court level.

Non-party appeals are limited. Primarily they are allowed from consent judgments and certain other final judgments involving class actions and shareholder derivative suits. In addition, certain types of anti-trust actions allow for intervention by a non-party member, as do some bankruptcy proceedings. Other exceptions are discussed in the case of *United States v. Chagra*.[7] If the client is not a party to the record, counsel must be acquainted with the applicable case law and statutes of the jurisdiction to avoid missing an appeal opportunity.

3.12 The aggrieved party

A second requirement for appeal is that the party be "aggrieved" by the decision. Simply put, the appellant must have lost something or have been placed in an adverse position. Usually this results when the appellant is ordered to do something that he or she objects to or is denied the relief requested. This is not limited to outright rejection of the claims but also includes instances in which the appellant receives less than the prayer for relief. For example, if the plaintiff requested $10,000 and the judgment was for $5,000, the party has standing to appeal.

As with the definition of "party," discussed above, the "aggrieved" requirement has prompted litigation. Particularly befuddling are cases in which there are multiple parties. Determining who is aggrieved and to what extent is a challenge. This may result, for example, in different consequences for the various co-parties, such as unequal apportionment of liability among defendants in a damages case.

---

6. Some states specifically allow intervention at the appeals level. *See, e.g.,* Wis. Stat. Ann. § 809.13 (West 1994). Other states specifically prohibit it. *See, e.g., Pearman v. Schlaak,* 575 S.W.2d 462 (Ky.1978).

7. 701 F.2d 354 (5th Cir.1983).

As a general rule then, an appellant must be both a party to the record *and* must be aggrieved by the order from which the appeal is taken. Unless both requirements are met (noting the exceptions of course), there is no right of appeal, and a notice of appeal will be dismissed.

3.20 TYPES OF APPEALS

Prior to a discussion of the various types of appeals, a brief examination of the appellate court structure is instructive. Most states have a two-tier appellate system, similar to the federal court structure. The organization consists of a trial court with original jurisdiction, an intermediate appellate court and a court of last resort or supreme court.[8]

3.21 Review as of right

Most states follow the same pattern. Cases may be appealed as a matter of right to the intermediate appellate court, but the court of last resort selectively chooses the cases it will hear. This is not always the situation. Some types of cases proceed to the high court as a matter of right by direct appeal from the trial court. For example, in several states, death sentence cases go directly from the trial court to the high court. As with other aspects of the appellate process, counsel must be thoroughly familiar with the rules that govern the appropriate body to which the appeal will be taken.[9]

Certain cases decided by the intermediate appellate court also go to the court of last resort as a matter of right and not discretion. This situation has generated differences of opinion among jurists, especially with regard to the United States Supreme Court. Because of the size of the Court's docket, there are those who believe that all appeals should be discretionary.

To permit only discretionary appeals is not allowed within many state court structures. Some states dictate, either by statute or constitutional provision, that certain types of case be heard by the court of last resort as a matter of right.

Non-discretionary cases that go to the high court fall into two categories: cases that deal with a specific subject matter and general

---

8. While the names of the courts may differ somewhat, in most jurisdictions the intermediate courts are titled courts of appeals or appeal and the court of last resort is known as the supreme court. In New York, the highest court is known as the Court of Appeals (the Supreme Courts in New York are the trial courts), and in Massachusetts it is known as the Supreme Judicial Court.

9. Words of caution: the rules of appellate practice are found in various sources and may differ from state to state. For example, in Arkansas, Rule 5–1(j) was enacted following a court opinion which dealt with citing cases during oral argument that were not previously cited in the brief; in Missouri, rules a person would expect to find among the "rules of court" are found in the Constitution (*See* Art. 5 § 10 transfer of cases from court of appeals to supreme court—scope of review); Connecticut allows direct appeals in election disputes and judicial discipline matters as found in Conn. Gen. Stat. Ann. § 51–199 (West 1985).

category cases not based on particular subject matter, but set apart for non-discretionary review by the high court.

The bulk of special subject matter cases are either death sentence questions or constitutional cases. In Ohio, affirmance of the death penalty and an appeal that claims a substantial constitutional question invokes the appellate jurisdiction of the Supreme Court. Other examples of specific subject matter cases include cases arising from the Industrial Commission (North Carolina) and instances in which the courts of appeals have declared a state statute or constitutional provision invalid (Florida). As one would expect, each state has its own provisions on an appeal as of right to the highest court.

As to the second category, or those cases set out for review on a non-discretionary basis, individual states categorize certain types of cases for high court review. For example, in North Carolina, there is an appeal as of right if the appeal is based upon the dissent at the intermediate court level. Some states require two dissents in specific kinds of cases for a non-discretionary appeal (New York).

3.22   Certification review

The certification process for review is available in many state courts as well as the federal system. Through this process, an intermediate appellate court may certify a case, or a specific question within a case, to the court of highest authority. This may be done before or after a decision by the intermediate court. Causes which justify certification generally involve issues of significant public interest or ones in which there is a need for expedited review. The supreme courts of some states have discretion whether to accept certification, while in others, acceptance is obligatory.

In the federal system, 28 U.S.C. § 1254(2) (1994) empowers the courts of appeal to certify to the Supreme Court "any question of law" in a case "to which instructions are desired." Whether to accept certification is a matter of discretion with the Supreme Court. As a result, the process is rarely used and only in extraordinary circumstances.[10]

3.23   Bypassing the court of appeals in the review process

Some cases bypass the intermediate court of appeals in the review process. In most instances, the appeal is not of right but is discretionary. Many state supreme courts, as well as the United States Supreme Court, have provisions that allow them to exercise their discretion to remove a case prior to the intermediate appellate court's decision. The usual grounds for removal at both the state and federal level are to allow an

---

10.   There are two reasons why the certification process is rarely invoked and more rarely granted. First is the basic philosophy that intermediate courts of appeals are supposed to decide cases that come before them and not give over that task to the superior court. Second, by allowing certification, the discretionary aspect of accepting the appeal is eliminated in the higher court. In effect, the intermediate appellate court makes the decision for the higher court, a situation that is not favored, especially in the United States Supreme Court.

expedited decision or because of the public importance of the case. United States Supreme Court Rule 18 provides that certiorari will be granted before judgment in the court of appeals "only upon a showing that the case is of such imperative public importance as to justify the deviation from normal appellate practice and to require immediate settlement in this Court."

Some states provide that cases may be removed for administrative efficiency and the orderly administration of justice. For example, many state supreme courts consider the backlog of cases as a reason to move certain cases to another intermediate court or to accept the case for its own review. Again, the procedures to remove a case and the standards for removal prior to the decision of the intermediate appellate court vary from state to state. Counsel must carefully examine the rules and statutes to determine if it is possible to bypass the intermediate court, and if so, how it is accomplished.

3.24   Discretionary review

The great majority of appeals to the courts of last resort involve cases that are taken on a discretionary basis. Indeed, some states only allow review by the high court by permission of the court (Washington).

The grounds for granting a discretionary appeal vary from jurisdiction to jurisdiction. Some define the grounds narrowly, some broadly, and some not at all. Most consider the importance of the issue to the public, as well as its legal significance. In addition, discretionary appeals often are granted if appeals courts within the system are in conflict with one another on an issue. At times, appeals are granted because the lower court's decision outrages the higher court's sense of justice.

The likelihood of success in obtaining a discretionary appeal, either at the state or federal level, is not good. Nevertheless, counsel should know the grounds for appeal and the successful strategies within the jurisdiction. This knowledge is essential in fashioning the petition.[11]

3.25   Right to appeal lost

The time for filing the appeal is dictated by rule. In over half of the states, the appellant is allowed 30 days to file the notice of appeal or its equivalent. The times vary, however, from 10 days to 90 days for a timely filing.[12] The time is usually computed from the date of entry of the lower court decision, though this too is not always the case.[13]

---

11. The name of the document varies from jurisdiction to jurisdiction and includes: petition or application for certiorari or certification; a petition for writ of error; a petition for leave to appeal; a petition to permit or allow an appeal or a hearing; and a petition for review or to transfer.

12. But see the rules for the State of West Virginia, which has no intermediate appellate court. There the appellant has four months from the date of judgment to appeal to the state supreme court and with good cause shown, an additional two months.

13. For example, in South Carolina, the time runs from the date of receiving the notice of judgment.

Obviously, special care must be taken to ascertain the time frame within which to file the appeal. Failure to do so may well cause the appeal to be dismissed.

Form and substance problems can also defeat an appeal. If the court rule calls for a particular style or format and the appellant is not in compliance, the appeal is subject to dismissal. Likewise, substance problems arise in the notice of appeal. One author relays the story of the attorney who sought to appeal an order denying a motion *for* discovery and inspection, but instead recited that it was an appeal from an order denying a motion for a protective order *against* the discovery and inspection.[14] The mistake was, at best, embarrassing. At worst, it is the type of sloppiness that may well spell defeat.

In money judgments, both the losing and the winning party can defeat a potential appeal. If the losing party voluntarily satisfies the judgment or, as some courts have ruled, a portion of the judgment, that party may have no right to appeal. The issue is deemed moot, because the judgment is satisfied. Likewise, the party who wins a money judgment and accepts payment thereof is deemed to have mooted any challenge to the judgment. However, some courts have held that a party who accepts the benefits can still appeal if a reversal on appeal will not affect those benefits.

Other potential problems for the appellant include failure to perfect the appeal within the appropriate time and failure to post the required bond. To perfect the appeal, court rule dictates the time frame to prepare the record for the appellate court. This includes the portions of the papers on file in the trial court (the trial record), as well as testimony (the transcript) to be included or omitted from the record on appeal.[15] The appellant has a specified time to complete these tasks. Failure to do so may result in dismissal of the appeal.

In many jurisdictions, the appellant in a civil case must post a bond to handle the costs of the appeal and a supersedeas bond or other security to stay enforcement of the judgment from which the appeal is taken. If the appropriate bond is not posted, a motion for dismissal may successfully deprive the appellant of the right to appeal. Note, however, that usually an appeals court will allow the appellant time to arrange for bonds; but once the additional time has passed, the dismissal may be automatic. Again, the court rules of the various states and the federal system vary dramatically. Perusal of the court rules within the jurisdiction will reveal what is necessary to file and perfect an appeal.

---

14. *See* Herbert Monte Levy, How to Handle an Appeal 4–16 (4th ed. 1999).

15. Counsel must check the statutes and rules of the jurisdiction within which the appeal is taken to ascertain if there are parts of the record which are required to be filed by law. Failure to comply with the rules may also lead to dismissal.

3.30 INITIATION AND PERFECTION OF THE APPEAL

3.31 Appeals from the trial court

An appeal used to be a cumbersome and complicated process.[16] But the former requirements at both the federal and state levels have been replaced in most jurisdictions by user-friendly rules for both criminal and civil actions. The appellant now needs only to file a notice of appeal, which gives notice that an appeal is being taken to a named appellate court from the judgment or some portion of the judgment entered on a particular date. In the federal system and many state court systems, the notice of appeal is the only step necessary to validate the appeal.[17] The various state court systems use different names for the notice of appeal, but the substance of the contents of the notice is very similar.

In most jurisdictions, a copy of the notice of appeal must be filed with the clerk of the trial court.[18] This advises the trial court that an appeal has been taken from its ruling. Thus informed, the trial court may knowledgeably act on applications for supersedeas or stay. The notice also alerts the clerk to begin preparation of the record for transmission to the court that will review the decision.

At the federal level and in some states, the clerk of the trial court is then required to transmit the notice to the clerk of the appellate court. Some states require that counsel for the appellant send the notice to the appeals court. Consult the court rules within the jurisdiction to identify who is responsible for this task. It may be prudent for counsel to file with the appeals court as a matter of course, whether or not required by court rule. In any event, a timely filed notice of appeal generally transfers jurisdiction over the case to the appeals court.

In the federal courts and some state courts, the notice of appeal must then be served on the parties by the clerk of the trial court.[19] The appellant is responsible to supply the clerk with enough copies to enable the clerk to serve "each party's counsel of record."[20] In other jurisdictions, the appellant's counsel must actually serve the notice of appeal on opposing counsel and others of interest, with proof of service. Once again, counsel must carefully consult the court rules of the jurisdiction

---

16. *See* Robert L. Stern, Appellate Practice in the United States 105 (2d ed. 1989).

17. *See* Fed. R. App. P. 3(a)(1). Some state court rules require additional information, such as the name of all counsel and parties, their telephone numbers and at times a brief description of the nature of the case and any written or recorded decision in the case. Even in those states, the notice is usually restricted to one page.

18. In many instances, both parties to the suit may decide to appeal some aspect of the decision. This may occur when the trial court decided only partly in favor of one party or the other, or rejects or ignores some contentions put forward by that party. Then a cross-appeal is necessary. The rule in the federal system and most state systems is that a separate appeal or cross-appeal must be filed if any party seeks to change some aspect of the judgment. This concept has come under fire as burdensome and duplicative. Exceptions have been formed by case law. Careful research must be undertaken to ensure that the litigants do not lose their rights to contest the judgment or some aspect thereof.

19. *See* Fed. R. App. P. 3(d)(1).

20. *Id.*

to ascertain who has the burden to transmit the notice of appeal to the higher court and to interested parties.

As one would expect, an appeal requires the payment of a fee. In many jurisdictions, the fee is paid to the clerk of the appellate court when the case is docketed. Generally, a case is deemed docketed when the record is filed in that court. In others, the fee is paid to the clerk of the trial court when the notice is filed. The clerk then forwards the fee to the clerk of the appellate court. The fees vary widely from state to state.

As noted above, many jurisdictions require that the appellant need only file a notice of appeal, or its equivalent, and pay the fee. The higher court then has jurisdiction. This is not, however, the case in all states. Some require other documents to be filed with the notice of appeal.

Many states require one or more bonds to be filed with the notice of appeal. First, in some jurisdictions, the appellant must post a bond to cover the costs of the appeal in the event the appeal is not successful. These costs may include fees to docket the appeal, the cost of the clerk to prepare and transmit the record, and other miscellaneous costs such as printing costs of briefs, appendices and records.

In 1979, Rule 7 of the Federal Rules of Appellate Procedure eliminated the security bond in most civil cases. However, if the appellee believes that the appellant will not be able to pay the costs of the appeal, that issue may be raised by motion with the district court. Per Rule 7, "the district court may require an appellant to file a bond or provide other security in any form and amount necessary to ensure payment of costs on appeal * * *." In state courts, the amount is usually set by rule or statute, though subject to change to secure the potential costs.

In the event the appellant wishes to prevent enforcement of the judgment during the pendency of the appeal, that party will request a stay pending appeal. If the judgment is for money damages, it may be necessary to post a bond in the amount of the judgment. Known as a supersedeas bond, it secures the money judgment for the appellee. Often, these bonds must be filed when the notice of appeal is filed.

Another document that may be required is one that designates the portions of the record the appellant believes are relevant to the appeal. Many times, it is filed with the notice of appeal, though some states allow it to be filed a short time after the appeal is taken. Along with a designation of the record requests, many states require proof that the transcript has been ordered from the court reporter. These matters are discussed in Chapter 1 of this text.

In some states, the notice of appeal must be accompanied by or contemporaneous with the filing of the assignment of errors. This requirement is now somewhat outdated.[21] It used to be a means to

21. In years past, the appellant was restricted to the assignment of errors submitted at the time of the notice of appeal. As a result, every small possible issue that might conceivably arise was raised as a possible error. This practice was cumbersome and

delineate the issues on appeal. Today, increasingly, jurisdictions require the appellant to file an information statement with the notice of appeal or within a short time after the notice is filed.[22]

As with other appellate procedures, if an information statement must be filed, each state has its own requirements. For example, some call for information on the jurisdictional basis for the appeal, the substance of the judgment below and relief sought, information about bonds, stays and whether the record has been ordered. In addition, a jurisdiction may require information on whether oral argument is requested, the names and addresses of all parties to the action, material facts, the issues proposed to be raised and the arguments to be tendered. Many jurisdictions prescribe the number of pages allowable to answer these questions. Some permit a response by the appellee. The required information helps the advocates focus on the important aspects of the appeal. It aids the court to expedite the matter through evaluation for settlement, need for oral argument, issue simplification and possible summary disposition. Note: always be cognizant of the filing requirements for an appeal to the intermediate appellate court. Scrupulous adherence to the rules of the jurisdiction pays great dividends in at least getting the case before the court for resolution.

3.32 Appeals to the highest court after an intermediate court of appeals decision

With a few notable exceptions (as discussed above), most appeals to the highest court must be initiated by filing an application or petition that requests the superior court, in its discretion, to accept the case for decision. The aggrieved party, usually the one who lost in the intermediate appellate court, is the party who files the petition or application.[23] Usually, additional documents are required to be filed. However, it varies from state to state whether they must be filed with the notice requesting review or at a later time. Some states mandate briefing on the merits (Texas) at the time the appeal is filed, while others require only that the notice of appeal be accompanied by a memorandum in support of jurisdiction and a short treatment of the merits (Ohio). The New York Court of Appeals requires a jurisdictional statement be filed within 10 days from the time the appeal is taken which mandates, among other requirements, that it contain the constitutional, statutory, case, or other authority supporting the assertion that the court has jurisdiction to entertain the appeal and to review the questions raised. The United

defeated the purpose for which it was designed, i.e., to alert both the appellant court and the appellee which issues would be argued.

22. A statement of the issues is still required in many jurisdictions. A statement of the issues must be filed by the appellant at the time the record designations are requested in the event the entire record is not requested. The purpose of the provision is to allow the appellee to determine if the record to be reproduced reflects the arguments to be argued on appeal.

23. This document is known by several names in as many states. For example, it may be titled a petition for certiorari, a petition for leave to appeal, or to permit, or to allow, a petition to review, or writ of error, to name a few.

States Supreme Court, along with several states, require the lower courts' opinions, orders, findings of fact and conclusions of law entered in conjunction with the judgment to be attached to the petition or application. Other states require a copy of the record or appendix of the intermediate court to be filed at the time of the notice. This practice was discontinued in the United States Supreme Court because, in the vast majority of cases, the record is not necessary for a decision to grant or deny the petition. It is expected that relevant information about the case will be provided in the initial petition for certiorari.

Before any petition or application is accepted by a high court, that court must satisfy itself that all actions have been completed in the court below. In a number of states, it is actually necessary to document that the lower court has rejected a petition for rehearing or reconsideration. The theory is that if the lower court is required to rule on this petition, the court has the opportunity to change or further elaborate on its decision. Perhaps the theory has merit, but one wonders how often intermediate appellate judges change their minds. The number of times this occurs, while arguably beneficial, is likely more than offset by the time and money squandered by the multitude of unsuccessful petitions for rehearing.

As mentioned above, the main document that is filed with the high court is the petition or application for review. This includes facts showing jurisdiction, reasons why the court should accept the case, and a prayer for relief. In each jurisdiction, the form required for the petition or application either follows the United States Supreme Court form, is prescribed by court rule, or is silent and leaves the matter to counsel. Whatever the rule, one must never lose sight of the goal: to convince the court that the case is right for further review. To that end, if there is no prescribed form, most appellate advocates concur that the best way to proceed is to include the same information as required by the United States Supreme Court.

At the outset, counsel should request the court grant the petition to review the lower court decision. This is known as the prayer for relief. In certiorari requests to the Supreme Court, the next section lists the citations to the opinions below.[24] These include the intermediate appellate court, if available, the district court, and any state court citations. This is for the convenience of the court, because lower court opinions are normally appended to the application. Since this endeavor is duplicative, it often is not required at the state court level. The next section details the jurisdictional basis for the higher court to hear the case. Usually this task can be accomplished in a paragraph and includes the dates of the judgment below, of any rehearing or reconsideration and of any other dispositive action. Also included is reference to the statutory or other basis of the court's jurisdiction. Constitutional, statutory provisions and other authorities to be cited follow the jurisdictional statement.

---

24. But see § 6.41 with reference to the placement of the question(s) presented.

Many state court rules require the questions presented to appear next. This is the logical place, immediately prior to the statement of the case. However, the Supreme Court rule and some state court rules place the question(s) presented at the very beginning of the petition, prior to the table of contents and table of authorities. Wherever the placement, the question(s) should be carefully drafted because most courts will consider only those matters specified in the question(s) presented. Broad questions, however, are deemed to include subsidiary questions which are fairly implied in the general question.

The next section is the "Statement" or "Statement of the Case." Supreme Court Rule 14.1(g) defines it as "[a] concise statement of the case containing the facts material to the consideration of the questions presented * * *." The facts should not be presented in an argumentative fashion. They should be objective, but persuasive. Careful word selection, sentence structure and paragraph development help paint a picture that is favorable, though objective. Present only those facts relevant to the questions presented on appeal. Facts which go against the petitioner's case should also be included, although they should be presented in a way that minimizes any damage they may cause.

The so-called "argument" section of the petition is entitled "Reasons for Granting the Writ." In this section, the advocate details the legal reasons and authorities for the court's review of the case. This section should be succinct and to the point, and demonstrate argumentative writing at its best. Emphasis should be placed on the importance of the case, conflicts within the jurisdiction, and any other reasons to grant review imposed by statute or rule in the jurisdiction.

The "Reasons" section, as well as the previous "Facts" section, present a particularly vexing dilemma for the advocate. The goal is to include all that is necessary to present the full picture, but yet keep it sufficiently concise to allow the justices to make a decision without wading through a mound of material. What to include, then, is of vital importance. A further complication, in many states, is a statutory page maximum for the "Reasons" section. This requires petition brevity. One must check all jurisdictional requirements with respect to contents and length before beginning the petition or application for appeal.

Court documents are always subject to a time frame within which to file. The application or petition for discretionary appeal is no different. In many jurisdictions, the appeal is timely if filed within 30 days from the judgment below. Some states require filing an application for leave to appeal. If granted, the appellant must file a notice of appeal within a requisite number of days (Georgia). A motion for rehearing or reconsideration tolls the statute in most jurisdictions. This is also the case if there is a substantial change in the judgment below. The statute begins to run again at the time the lower court rules on the motion or makes changes in the judgment. Once again, the prudent advocate will carefully check the rules and statutes in the jurisdiction to ensure a timely filing.

Once there is a timely filing of a petition for appeal, the opposing party, in most jurisdictions, is permitted to file a brief in opposition to the petition. As with the petition, there are strict time limits within which this task can be accomplished. In those jurisdictions, the length of the response is usually the same as for the petition.

The contents of the response can follow the form of the petition, or it can be modified in shortened memorandum form.[25] Its function is to convince the high court that the decision below is correct, or at the very least, is not clearly wrong.

Some jurisdictions do not provide for a response brief. Apparently, it is felt the merits of the appeal can be gleaned from the petition and the record from the court below. Though this may be the case in most instances, there are circumstances in which the respondent's position would surely help clarify the issues raised by the petition. In any event, if a response is allowed but not provided in the rules, the fact that no response is filed should not prejudice appellee's counsel. Given the choice, the chance to respond should not be lost, especially if there is room to argue that the issues are not important enough to warrant an appeal.

As noted previously, the reasons to grant a discretionary review vary widely from jurisdiction to jurisdiction. Some are defined by court rule and are extremely broad. Others are narrowly defined. Still others do not specify criteria. For those that attempt to define what cases will be reviewed, the majority of jurisdictions indicate that the resolution of conflicts among the intermediate appellate courts and the importance of the issue as it relates to the populous are primary concerns. In the latter, the language is often sufficiently broad to include any situation that seems ripe for decision by the high court. For example, some states talk of the "gravity and importance" of the case, others talk of "special and important reasons," and still others refer to the "interest of justice." As a general rule, the words are not defined, and allow great latitude for accepting cases. Interestingly, few jurisdictions name error on the merits of the case as a category for accepting an appeal.

In most jurisdictions, a majority of the court is needed to grant review. This is not so in some jurisdictions, including the United States Supreme Court where only four justices must agree that the case is worth hearing. The rationale for the so-called "rule of four" is that if a substantial minority of the Court feels the case is worthy of consideration, it should be "taken and disposed of."[26] Some state courts require three of the seven justices to approve acceptance of the appeal; others require only two votes out of seven. As with the Supreme Court of the United States, most jurisdictions do not regard refusal of the appeal as an affirmation of the merits of the case. Refusing the appeal simply

25. If the respondent agrees with the preliminary matters, such as the question(s) presented and facts as submitted by the petitioner, there is little need to repeat them.

26. *See Ferguson v. Moore–McCormack Lines*, 352 U.S. 521 (1957).

means that the court did not deem the issues sufficiently important to accept the case.

After review of the grounds for granting an appeal and the strength of the case, the careful advocate will also consider the percentage of cases that are taken each year by the court to which the appeal will be taken. Generally, the percentages are fairly low.[27] The chances of success must also be weighed against the added costs to the client and the time that will be expended by all parties.

3.40   HANDLING THE RECORD AND PAPERS ON APPEAL

The main function of appellate courts is to review the decisions of the trial courts. The record made at the trial court level becomes the record of the appellate court. If the appeal is to the court of last resort, the trial court record, along with any additional materials from the intermediate court, become the record. How and what is transmitted to the higher court varies among jurisdictions. The court rules should be studied and carefully followed.

The record generally is conveyed in one of three forms. First, some courts, though fewer each year, require that the entire record be reproduced. This includes all pleadings, motions, orders and other documents filed in the normal course with the trial court clerk. In addition, a transcription of what occurred in the courtroom must be filed. This is usually in the form of electronically recorded material or reporters' notes that are transcribed. To complete the record, any opinions, findings, rulings or other materials that are oral or written giving the reasons for the trial judge's actions must be included. As one can imagine, this is a costly and time-consuming endeavor.

Second, many courts allow the parties to file an abbreviated copy of the record. For example, Federal Rule 10 states that the appellant may order only those portions of the record considered necessary to prosecute the appeal. Of course, provision is made for the appellee to order additional parts deemed necessary to present the appellee's position. The greatest savings to all parties comes when everyone agrees on what parts of the record are important. In that event, only those parts deemed necessary are reproduced and sent to the appellate court. Court rules, even within the federal circuits, vary on the filing necessities. Careful attention must be paid to what must be filed, when it must be filed and by whom.

Third, and perhaps the least cumbersome, are rules of court that allow the parties to file an "agreed statement." For example, Rule 10 of the Federal Rules states:

> In place of the record on appeal as defined in Rule 10(a), the parties may prepare, sign, and submit to the district court a statement of the case showing how the issues presented by the appeal arose and were decided in the district court. The statement must set forth only

27.   See Chapter One for a discussion on the reversal rate for selected jurisdictions.

those facts averred and proved or sought to be proved that are essential to the court's resolution of the issues.

No matter what is required to be filed, advocates must be cognizant of the technical requirements of each court. This includes, but is not limited to, the duties of the parties and the strict time limitations for complying with the rules.

EXERCISES

I.   Don Adams and Mike Edwards are a gay couple who live together. They found the apartment of their dreams, but when they approached the manager/owner of the complex, they were greeted rather coolly. Ultimately, they rented the apartment.

All leases are for three years or longer but allow for periodic increases in rent not to exceed 2.5% of the base rent for the previous year (except in exceptional circumstances). In a footnote to the lease, some examples of exceptional circumstances are listed. They include structural damage to the complex, high incidence of vandalism and other extraordinary occurrences (fire, pestilence, etc.).

Toward the end of the first year, Don and Mike received their lease for year two and noted their rent was going to increase 5%. When they questioned the landlord about the increase, he informed them that it was his prerogative to increase rent and that his "experience" with homosexual couples had not been good. He said there was usually more damage (resulting from domestic violence) and generally more wear and tear on the premises.

Don and Mike refused to pay the additional rent and sued in Federal District Court in Columbus, Ohio. They claimed the manager/owner of the complex infringed on their § 1983 rights. Also, they sought $500,000 in damages. The manager counter-claimed for lost rent, emotional distress and attorney fees.

The matter was tried in the District Court, and the judgment was for the manager/owner in the amount of $50,000. As a result, Don and Mike want to appeal the decision to the Sixth Circuit Court of Appeals. They, of course, want to stay the decision of the District Court.

A.   Assume there is no settlement. What steps must they take to perfect the appeal including the desired stay? Note carefully the time limitations of all activities.

B.   Once the appeal is perfected, explain what their attorney must do at each stage thereafter, through oral argument. Note time limitations for each stage.

C.   If the same case had arisen under state law, i.e., a rent dispute and the matter was lost by Don and Mike in the Franklin County Court of Appeals in Ohio, what steps would have to be taken to perfect an appeal to the Ohio Supreme Court?

Chapter Four

A PRIMER ON PERSUASION

4.00   WORKING TOWARD A DEFINITION

What is it that most influences a court to be favorably influenced by an advocate's argument? It is persuasion, which is a source of multitudinous research studies, papers and books. An entire subculture of communication theory has exhaustively examined what it means to persuade and what it means to be persuaded. Since persuasion is the cornerstone of argumentation, it is little wonder that many of these studies have centered on the law and law related activities. The purpose of this section is to examine a working definition of legal persuasion and its various components as they relate to both written and oral arguments.

Over the years, scholars who have studied persuasion have attempted to determine if there are individual differences in people's reaction to persuasion. For example, in the 1950's, they questioned whether there was one type of person who is generally easy to persuade. There isn't. In the 1970's, some researchers declared that one of the most reliable findings in the field of persuasion was that females are more easily influenced than males. They're not. There is no "one type" of person who is easy to persuade. Rather, people differ because of personality variables, and social and demographic characteristics.

Persuasion, then, has been described as "communication intended to

46

influence choice."[1] In this context, "communication" signifies that the event is symbolic and interactive; "intended" implies the persuasive attempt has a predetermined goal; "influence" suggests some action be taken to move toward that goal; and "choice" suggests the receiver has options available. Other writers define it a bit differently, but all agree it is communication that is meant to influence behavior. In legal argument, the advocate's goal is to influence the outcome of the case. A legal argument delineates the line the advocate asks the court to draw and then attempts to persuade the court that this particular line makes sense and is appropriate.[2]

4.10 PERSUASION AS A PROCESS

Writers in many fields have long suggested that communication is a process. As such, it is dynamic, ongoing and continuous. Because persuasion is a form of communication, the concept of process helps define and explain what takes place in a persuasive argument, whether written or oral.

Process is best described in terms of a model. The purpose of a model is to establish, in simplest terms, the essentials of the ongoing process of argument. It shows how concepts are tied together. It also provides taxonomy, or words, that describe an event. Armed with the model and the descriptive taxonomy, it is possible to dissect the parts. By doing so, how the parts ultimately reconnect is instructive to show how aspects of an argument are important and why.

Any communication between individuals always involves a source or initiator of the message. The message to be transmitted must travel via a channel or vehicle. In written persuasion, the vehicle is normally a document, such as a brief or motion; in oral argument, the vehicle consists of both verbal and non-verbal communication and may also include visual aids.

The second party in a communicative event is the receiver of the message. The receiver decodes or interprets the message based on a myriad of variables such as experience, values, attitudes and prejudices. The receiver has two choices. He or she may respond to the message by some form of feedback or simply continue to listen and watch. In the latter case, the initiator then has two options. He or she may continue with the topic or change topics. During an appellate argument, both forms occur and reoccur. Assuming for a moment that there is some response by the receiver, the simplest model is as follows:

1. Winston L. Brembeck & William S. Howell, Persuasion: A Means of Social Influence 19 (2d ed. 1976).

2. *See* Bradley G. Clary, Primer on the Analysis and Presentation of Legal Argument 44 (1992).

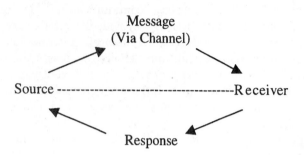

The above model does not take into account the mental activity of either the source, in terms of mental preparation and formulation of the message, or the receiver, in terms of reception and application of motivational incentives. It also does not assume particulars about the message. Each element must be explored.

Perhaps the best starting point are the teachings and philosophy of the rhetorical masters who developed and refined the nature of argument, and more specifically, legal argument.[3] This exercise may seem theoretical and "old fashioned" but, indeed, if one is to understand and excel at the art of persuasion, one must incorporate, either consciously or unconsciously, the principles developed centuries ago. Modern advocates may underestimate the ancients' influence on argument theory as we know it today. In fact, their notions on persuasion provide the underpinnings of the philosophical and the practical, as well as the theoretical and the "how to" manuals. It is, therefore, important to examine the masters' writings and to contemplate their meaning as relates to successful appellate advocacy.

Aristotle and later Roman rhetoricians taught that persuasive presentations, both written and oral, contain three elements. They are: ethos, pathos and logos. The three are inextricably linked, we are told, and a successful argument must take into account their unitary influence as well as their collective importance.

In the succeeding sections, one can observe the trilogy at work. But first, a description:

A. Logos. Logos refers to the argument content exclusive of the participants. Logos describes the logic or reasoning that supports the advocate. Obviously in an appellate argument, either written or oral, the underlying strength of the legal theory is crucial. Having the law on one's side thrusts the advocate ahead of the opposition who struggles with unfavorable legal precedent. But most people have witnessed an advocate lose miserably and yet appear to have all of the law on his or her side. Obviously other aspects of the dynamic "doing argument" are at work.

3. *See* Aristotle, The "Art" of Rhetoric (J.H. Frees trans. Loeb Classical Library ed. 1982); Quintilian, The Institutio Oratoria (H.E. Butler trans, Loeb Classic Library ed. 1980).

B. Ethos. Ethos goes to the heart and soul of the advocate. It speaks to the individual's ethics, integrity and character. Cases are compromised and lost because the bench loses confidence in the advocate, and thus his position. Ethos—the substance of the individual.

C. Pathos. Perhaps the most important, yet least able to grasp and understand, is the notion of pathos. Pathos is the emotional component of persuasion. It cannot be denied that emotions play a central role in decision making. As such, an advocate should maximize those aspects of the argument that emphasize goodness, fairness and the like. Pathos, then, describes the emotion the advocate instills in the reader or listener. While much has been written about pathos and argument, in the end it means the advocate's ability to move the court—to convince its members of the righteousness of the cause.

Armed with the tools of the ancients, modern advocates must be prepared to approach the court with believable arguments, capable of belief because of the argument's strength, the advocate's character and the virtue of the cause.

Subsequent sections in this chapter build on these constructs. The reader is encouraged to reflect on them and fit them into his or her writing and speaking style. A solid argument by a well-respected advocate delivered in a manner that appeals to the fairness and goodness of the cause will go a long way toward winning the day.

4.20 EFFECTS OF THE SOURCE ON PERSUASIVE COMMUNICATION

The model and the discussion of the process of persuasion indicate there are at least two parties to each persuasive event. They are the source of the message and the receiver. Both respond to a message that traverses through a channel. If one adds to the mix the impact of attitudes, beliefs, values and prejudices that each individual brings to the table, plus the impact of the message content, the description about the process tends to be either wildly generalized or drastically compartmentalized. Nevertheless, it is necessary to attempt an explanation. First to be explored is the effect of the source in persuasion.

Together with Aristotle, laymen and scholars alike have attempted to define characteristics that make an advocate effective and persuasive. High on the list is the notion of source credibility. The receiver's perception of trust and confidence in the source emanates from the receiver's belief that the advocate is intelligent, sincere and knowledgeable. Advocates who are viewed as highly credible sources are more likely to sway judges' opinions than advocates who are seen as unprepared, unknowledgeable or unintelligent.

Many factors influence credibility on both conscious and sub-conscious levels. Some of these factors, such as writing mechanics and effective oral advocacy, are explored in greater detail in later chapters. In general, however, the advocate must be scrupulously accurate in all respects in order to maintain credibility. Relevant facts cannot be withheld. Facts cannot be misstated or exaggerated. Opinions cannot be distorted or quoted out of context. Factors that lead to credibility breakdown can be devastating because advocates develop reputations in the legal community. Once an advocate's credibility is tainted, the advocate fights an uphill battle to regain it.

Another factor that influences source credibility is the practicality of the relief sought. The desired outcome must make sense from both a legal and a public policy standpoint. An advocate who asks the court to overstep its judicial bounds (be it in terms of separation of powers, standard of review, overruling established mandatory authority, etc.) will be viewed as unknowledgeable or unintelligent. If the request has far-reaching negative consequences, it may appear the advocate has not devised a workable solution to the problem.

A second concept that is discussed in the literature is source similarity and identification. Similarity refers to those interests, feelings and beliefs that the source and the receiver share in common. For example, if the topic of the argument is the fate of certain lands because of the erosion of the ecosystem, an advocate might direct a comment about the importance of nature preservation to one of the panel members who is an avid environmentalist. In this way the advocate is saying, "I share your views. We have common interests, feelings and beliefs about the continued decay of our environment." As will be discussed later, most experts in the area of advocacy stress the importance of knowing the "judge audience."

Identification is somewhat like similarity, but refers to the ability of the receiver to identify with the source. The advocate wants the judge to identify with the cause at issue. The judge is more likely to side with a particular cause if the judge identifies with the advocate's client. Since it is unlikely that the judge knows the client personally, the task of the advocate is to create a mental relationship between the judge and the client so that the judge is moved to come to the client's aid. Once a relationship is established, it is easier to persuade the judge to rule in the client's favor. Absent an established relationship, the judge has little motivation to help.

The foregoing indicates the importance of the ancients' theories and philosophies. A credible lawyer (ethos) with a good cause (logos) can move (pathos) the judge to the desired position. That is effective advocacy.

4.30   EFFECTS OF FORM AND CONTENT ON THE MESSAGE

To be persuasive, a message has to have meaning. This section examines the qualities that make a message meaningful and persuasive.

Two elements are essential to the success of the message—a central theme and some type of organization. First, the argument must have a central focus, a legal theory or overriding policy reason why the judge should rule in the client's favor. All of the material presented must be tightly organized around this theme. Extraneous material must be deleted so that every sentence advances the theme of the argument.

As Bradley G. Clary notes in *Primer on the Analysis and Presentation of Legal Argument,* "[y]ou have to know where you are going before you can persuade someone else to go there with you."[4] Before the advocate can develop a concrete organizational plan with which to present the legal argument, the advocate must have a clear concept of the theme of the argument and the relief sought. Only then can the advocate fit together all the pieces of the argument to create a unified whole.

Those pieces fit together in any number of ways, as long as there is organization. Scholars have constructed numerous models to help an advocate organize an argument. Whether one works from a time-order pattern, inductive/deductive pattern, or simply a problem solving structure, organization is critical to the outcome of a successful argument.[5]

Organization also has a heavy impact on source credibility. If a written argument is tightly organized and the factual and legal principles logically developed, the reader assesses the writer to be more knowledgeable and credible. The reader perceives the writer has crafted a clear, well-reasoned, reliable argument.

A well-organized brief is also easier to follow. An argument divided into logical steps, with appropriate headings and sub-headings, produces a brief that looks much less daunting. This also helps focus the reader's attention and makes the argument easier to comprehend. If the judge has trouble following the facts or the arguments, he or she will not fully comprehend what the writer is trying to say. With a full schedule, the judge does not have time to mentally rewrite a poorly written brief in order to decipher it. If there is no comprehension, there is no communication. Without communication, persuasion is impossible.

The organization of the brief often serves as the foundation for the organization of the oral argument. Although the original organization may be altered when a panel of judges asks multitudinous questions during an oral argument, the advocate must maintain a firm grasp of the general outline to be able to steer the conversation back to the important issues. This ability will significantly increase the oral advocate's credibility and power of persuasion. Research has demonstrated that listeners may comprehend a disorganized message but they are not persuaded by it. In addition, listeners tend to retain an organized message for a longer period of time. This may be critical to an oral argument if the decision about the case is not made for several days or weeks after the argument.

Appellate arguments usually consist of several issues, some stronger than others. When there is more than one issue to be discussed, the organizational strategy becomes important. Research has shown that

4. *Id.* at 45.

5. For a detailed analysis of several models, see Erwin P. Bettinghaus & Mi-chael J. Cody, Persuasive Communication (5th ed. 1994).

material presented at the beginning and the end of the argument is more likely to affect attitudes and behavior than material placed in the middle. But the real question centers on whether to place the strongest argument at the beginning or at the end. While communications research produces conflicting results, it is generally accepted that the wise decision is to place the strongest argument at the beginning. The rationale for this placement is two-fold. First, by placing the strongest argument first (the one the judges are most likely to agree with legally), the advocate obtains the positive attention of the court. In other words, the court is likely to agree with the position and then is more receptive to the remainder of the argument.

Second, in an oral argument, one takes an enormous risk by delaying the strongest point, because it is possible the point will never be reached. A weak argument may well draw a great number of questions. Time will expire, and the most valuable argument will never be spoken. The only positive reason to leave the best until last is that the strongest aspect of the argument will be the last point the judges hear. However, the loss of this advantage can be ameliorated by a conclusion that refers to the first and strongest argument. This is especially true for the appellee who has no chance at rebuttal.

While *how* the information is ordered is important, *what* information is given is equally crucial. Careful thought must focus on what to select and what to discard. If the advocate includes all background research material, the essential argument is likely to be lost amidst the rubble. In addition, it is usually better to limit the argument to the strongest one or two issues. The advocate who argues these with conviction is more credible than one who takes the "shotgun" approach, splaying every possible argument in hope of winning just one. If the court's focus is on the strongest arguments, the advocate avoids the risk of diluting the strong arguments with several weak or irrelevant ones.

For example, in one oral argument the author examined, the advocate raised "standing." That particular point was not an issue in the lower court. Had it been, it would have been decided in the advocate's favor. So, essentially, the advocate argued a non-issue that would have gone in his favor anyway. Thus he wasted valuable time debating a matter of no consequence. In the end, the judges shook their heads, and the advocate lost valuable time and, most probably, credibility.

More complex issues are raised in dealing with the opposition's argument. Because of the nature of appellate advocacy, there are always two justifiable sides to an appellate argument. If that were not the case, the issues would not have reached the appeals court. How to handle opposing counsel's arguments is discussed extensively in the literature. Oral advocacy experts do not always agree. Some say not to spend valuable time extinguishing the fires of the opponent. Others suggest opposing counsel's arguments should be addressed.[6] For the most part,

6. For a complete discussion on handling unfavorable authority and the oppo- nent's argument, *see* section 6.77 (handling unfavorable authority); section 7.40 (the

the research indicates that advocates should speak to the opposing counsel's argument. Keep it simple: the passwords are discuss, distinguish and deny.

4.40   THE EFFECT OF THE RECEIVER ON PERSUASIVE COMMUNICATION

Communication and rhetorical research indicate that a persuasive model must obviously regard the receiver as a top priority. Persuasion cannot take place if the object of the communicative event is not convinced. The literature is replete with studies leading to information about the importance of audience. Therefore, it is in the advocate's best interest to have as much knowledge about individual members of the bench as possible. An argument to a panel of judges that in the past has opposed inroads into the First Amendment may be quite different than if the panel has exhibited more obtrusiveness toward the subject. The advocate must know the receivers and adapt the message accordingly to have a persuasive effect on the audience.

In analyzing the judicial audience, the advocate should view the judges from all angles.[7] Judges function simultaneously in three capacities—as judicial decision-makers, as trained lawyers, and as human beings. Each role sheds a different light on the issues involved and potentially alters the types of arguments that the judges may find persuasive.

As judicial decision-makers, judges have a job to do. They strive to correct injustices and resolve unsettled issues of law. Judges want to make the "right" decision for many reasons, not the least of which is to avoid being overruled. They endeavor to write a well-reasoned opinion that will stand the test of time and appeal. Judges do not like to appear foolish or appear to misunderstand the real issues. They are also keenly aware of the limitations placed on them. They are wary of paving new roads that break with tradition and well-defined precedent. An advocate who asks the court to overstep its bounds fights an uphill battle. However, an advocate who gives the court the tools needed to write a compelling opinion in the client's favor has a substantial advantage over the opponent.

As trained attorneys, judges recognize there are valid arguments on both sides of the controversy. Many disputes can justifiably be decided either way. Judges are trained to recognize the strengths and weaknesses on each side and to detect faulty inferences and gaps in logic. Therefore, it is often prudent for the advocate to legitimate the judge's doubts, acknowledge the weaknesses in the client's case and provide the judge the tools necessary to overcome those weaknesses.

refutation of appellant's brief and responsive arguments) and section 7.50 (when and if to concede).

7. For an excellent overview of what influences judges, see Jean Appleman, Persuasion in Brief Writing 1–12 (1968).

As fellow human beings, judges are swayed by emotion, by concern for others' well being and, hopefully, by common sense and a belief in what is fair and right. But because judges are also trained attorneys, emotional appeals are more effective if supported by sound logic. As discussed previously, the advocate wants the judge to "identify" with the client. The advocate can do this by emphasizing any similarities that may exist to help forge a relationship between the client and the judge. The advocate who conducts background research into the judge's prior decisions and lifestyle will be able to tailor examples to the judge's interests and viewpoints.

Persuasive research traverses many lines of human communication, from mass media product advertising to political and sociological propaganda. Obviously some constructs are not useful when examining the notion of audience in an appellate argument; however, many are. For example, most advocates assume that appellate judges are highly intelligent. If that is the case, are judges more or less easily persuaded to a particular point of view? Further, are there qualities about an advocate or the argument that may lead to a higher degree of persuasion? Research on these issues, although mixed, substantiates that high-IQ judge-receivers are more likely to attend, comprehend and retain message content and arguments. The downside is that the more intelligent the receivers, the more likely they are to counter-argue and find fault with the advocate's position. Further, many scholars believe that high-IQ receivers are influenced only by strong arguments and evidence.

Therefore, high-IQ receivers pay greater attention to the quality of the argument than do low-IQ receivers. High–IQ receivers are persuaded only when a convincing argument is present in the message. They also recall far more arguments and facts. This explains the tremendous edge a well considered and organized argument has over one that is sloppy and non-authoritative. Not only must the advocate know the argument, but also must know the judge's stance on the issues. If there is genuine opposition to the advocate's position, the arguments must be even stronger and more convincing to persuade the judge.

Judge ideology also can be critical to an argument. Common sense indicates even the strongest arguments are not going to persuade a judge who is firmly opposed to the advocate's position. Knowing that the position exists allows the advocate to craft arguments that are less offensive, even if not totally persuasive. For example, a judge who believes (and has openly expressed those beliefs) that the environment should be protected at almost any cost will not be persuaded by an argument that drilling in the Alaskan arctic will not "really" harm the environment. However, that judge might be mildly persuaded by a well thought-out argument that the U.S. is far too dependent on overseas energy sources. To know the ideology of the audience is a powerful tool.

It is also useful to know the personality of the judges. This notion is supported by research which assesses ways in which people tend to approach ideas, people and beliefs. The research deals in particular with the dogmatic and the authoritarian personalities.

Dogmatism signifies the quality of closed-mindedness. Generally, a dogmatic person resists change, is reluctant to accept new information about a subject, and often relies on the "old" rather than embracing the "new." A judge who demonstrates these characteristics is likely difficult to persuade to adopt a new position or way of thinking. Thus, a persuasive message which suggests changes in the social order and movement away from the status quo probably will be met with resistance. A dogmatic judge, for example, would not be persuaded by an argument that homosexuals should have recognized marital rights if, in fact, the judge views homosexuality as a sin.

Most judges are not dogmatic on all issues or topics. For the advocate, the trick is to determine the values and beliefs of the judge as they relate to specific legal arguments that the advocate intends to make. This is not a new idea. The Honorable John W. Davis suggested that advocates become familiar with the bench. His seminal article[8] invites the advocate to "change places (in the imagination of course) with the court."[9] By doing so, one is able to begin to understand the philosophies, ideas, attitudes and beliefs of the various members of the court. Some authors even suggest the advocate review everything from confirmation hearings (if available), to written opinions, to the judge's behavior in oral argument.[10]

All the above suggest that the personalities of members of the bench are extremely important. A judge's dogmatism, either generally or on specific issues, is definitely an essential characteristic to be discovered and assessed.

Another aspect of personality relates to authoritarianism. Within the communication literature, authoritarianism is defined as that quality in a person that is motivated by power. If prone to do so, judges wield their power in two ways—by domination of the advocate's personality or by imposition of their own ideas on others despite all logic to the contrary.

In the first instance, an authoritarian judge may well enjoy the power that accompanies the title of "judge" and the ability to dominate the courtroom because of that position. If that is the case, the advocate's message may be partially lost because the judge is busy maintaining control and expressing personal views, either outwardly to the advocate in oral argument or inwardly while reading a brief. Anyone who has practiced law has encountered this type of person—one who is engulfed in self-importance.

In the second instance, power comes from imposing personal views on others, despite logical arguments to the contrary. Authoritarians tend

---

8. *See* John W. Davis, *The Argument of an Appeal*, 26 A.B.A.J. 895 (1940).

9. *Id.* at 896.

10. *See generally* Michael E. Tigar, Federal Appeals, Jurisdiction and Practice (3d ed. 1999).

to make absolute judgments based on the values they hold, even if in the judgment of others the contrary argument is rational and logical. The attitude of "my way or no way" is the prevailing theme.

Again, a thorough audience analysis provides an advocate the edge over an opponent who knows nothing about the judge's character and nature. Avoiding the judge's dogmatic values may maintain open mindedness, at least for that judge. Likewise, understanding the motivation of any authoritarian personality may give insight into ways to argue to avoid power plays in which the advocate is likely to lose.

4.50 ESSENTIALS OF A COMPELLING PERSUASIVE ARGUMENT

With the above thoughts in mind, this section explores the essentials for a compelling persuasive argument. The actual process of persuasive communication involves five stages:

1. *The advocate must seize and retain the attention of the judges.* Judges tend to take sides very early. Therefore, from the beginning, an advocate must persuade a judge that the advocate's client should win. To do so, the advocate must start both the brief and the oral argument with the most compelling facts and the strongest argument to immediately seize the judge's attention. But getting the judge's attention is only the beginning. Attention must be maintained during the course of the argument, be it written or oral. Without attention, persuasion will not occur.

A well-written brief or a strong oral argument piques the judge's interest in the advocate's client and in the issues. The judge is compelled to keep reading or asking questions to get to the heart of the matter in an attempt to find a valid reason to resolve the conflict in favor of the client. Judges hear scores of oral arguments and read stacks of briefs each month. The advocate must impress upon the judge the fundamental importance of the issues involved.[11] The judge may be more attentive once the advocate underscores that this is a case of first impression in the jurisdiction or that there is a conflict of laws in lower courts that needs to be resolved. The advocate must also impress upon the judge the injustice of an adverse ruling. In any event, to induce boredom in the presentation is a recipe for disaster. Again, persuasion fails if the advocate's message does not gain and maintain attention.

2. *The advocate must provide language and non-verbals to facilitate the predictable perception of the audience.* To be effective, a message must be meaningful. Advocates and judges may have different perceptions of what certain words mean. The advocate must be certain the words chosen will mean precisely what is intended. Words are the advocate's tools. If precise, they are very effective. When word choice is sloppy, it may be ruinous. The advocate must ensure that both the sender and the receiver are on the same wavelength.

---

11. *See* Clary, *supra* note 2, at 47.

When the subject matter is complex, appropriate use of language is particularly important. One of the functions of a legal argument is to educate the judge concerning the facts, the issues and the relevant law. If the facts are difficult to comprehend or if the law is complicated, the judge may side with whichever advocate can best clarify the issues. Visual aids such as photographs, charts and graphs may be valuable tools to incorporate into both written and oral presentations.

3. *The advocate must have some understanding of the basis of the human desire systems, together with methods of appropriating them to a predictable end.* Communication does not persuade unless there is some desire to believe what is said. The advocate must somehow motivate the judge to decide in the client's favor. As discussed earlier, many factors influence a judge's decision, and the advocate must carefully analyze the audience before attempting to develop an effective persuasive strategy.

4. *The advocate must demonstrate how these desires can best be satisfied by accepting the proposition set forth.* As noted earlier, the purpose of the argument is to convince the court to adopt a particular legal test or draw a line to produce an outcome favorable to the client. Once the advocate has determined the factors that will motivate the judge, the advocate also must convince the judge that the desired result will solve a problem without creating new ones. This task is a challenge, because everyone comes to the courtroom with different values, attitudes and beliefs. To satisfy some need or desire without conflicting with others requires careful analysis of the audience, as well as careful message preparation.

5. *The persuasive messages must produce the desired result.* The goal of the above steps is to guide the receiver of the messages to a predetermined goal. The advocate must lead the judge to the conclusion that a ruling in his or her client's favor is the only logical outcome. No one wins every argument. However, the advocate who has carefully analyzed the audience and spent time devising a strategy before developing an argument will have an edge over the opponent.

4.60 THE PARADOX OF PERSUASION

Anyone who has ever encountered a car salesman knows that the paradox of persuasion is often that: "[T]he harder you push, the more resistance you create. The more you tell the judge what to do and how to think, the more the judge is determined to find the right way on his or her own."[12] For this reason, it is often more effective to lead the judge through the necessary steps to reach a desired conclusion rather than to state one point-blank. By inviting the judge to participate in the development of the argument, the advocate may bring the judge in line with the advocate's train of thought.[13] A judge who has actively participated in

---

12. James W. McElhaney, *How You Argue Will Affect Whether the Judge Sees Things Your Way,* 81 A.B.A.J. 92 (Oct. 1995).

13. *See* James W. McElhaney, *What it Takes to Make Legal Writing Look Persuasive,* 82 A.B.A.J. 84 (Apr. 1996).

formulating a conclusion will be less likely to be swayed from that position.

4.70 DECISION–MAKING STYLES

There are basically two ways a judge may go about making a decision. The judge may look at the facts, determine the relevant law and apply the law to the facts to determine the outcome. On the other hand, the judge may look at the facts, make a preliminary judgment about the appropriate outcome, and then go in search of a legal theory or public policy reason to justify the result.[14]

No matter which decision-making style the judge employs in a particular case, the advocate must provide valid reasons to rule in the client's favor and then provide the judge the tools necessary to write an outstanding opinion.[15]

The aforementioned concepts are not new to appellate advocacy. It makes sense that a persuasive argument must be well organized, contain important information for the reader or listener, and be delivered in a manner conducive to the understanding of the argument. A sloppy unorganized argument that contains little useful information and is poorly written or delivered ineffectively will rarely, if ever, be persuasive. Without persuasion, an advocate cannot expect to change a judge's mind or obtain the judge's vote. The argument will simply fail.

EXERCISES

I. Review the following set of facts: In a criminal case, the defendant was convicted of (1) breaking and entering and (2) theft. He was sentenced to five years probation and ordered to do 300 hours of community service in the county in which he was convicted.

The defendant appealed. Among his claims were: he now lived 170 miles from the county in which he was ordered to do community service, and the judge abused his discretion when he required the defendant to travel that distance to fulfill part of the terms of his probation. The defendant requested the court to order his community service in the county in which he now resides.

The appellate court agreed and ordered the trial court to reassign his community service. The State appealed, stating that to require the trial court to order a new place of community service undermines the sentencing discretion of the trial judge.

The following is the argument presented by the State:

Defendant also argued that the court violated R.C. 2951.02(H) (b) by ordering him to complete the community service in Hamilton Coun-

---

14. Known as American legal realism, it is considered by many to be the predominant interpretive paradigm of 20th century American jurisprudence. For an excellent definition and history of the jurisprudential school known as American Legal Realism, together with an exposition of its basic tenets, see Laura Kalman, Legal Realism at Yale 1927–1960 (1986).

15. *See* Appleman, *supra* note 7, at 6.

ty, since he now resides with his parents who live 170 miles away. He asserted that traveling to Hamilton County created an "unfair burden" upon him.

In reviewing R.C. 2951.02(H)(1)(b), the First District Court of Appeals held that the distance was unreasonable. The court ordered the trial court to correct its sentence to permit the defendant to perform his community service within a reasonable distance from his home in Morrow County.

We contend that this excessively undermines the sentencing court's discretion.

In *State v. McLean* (1993), 87 Ohio App.3d 392, 622 N.E.2d 402, motion overruled 67 Ohio St.3d 1456, 619 N.E.2d 424, the First District Court of Appeals held the R.C. 2951.02(C) grants broad discretion to trial courts to consider and impose any conditions of probation that may be said reasonably to relate to stated statutory ends. The court emphasized the following pertinent portion of the statute:

> In the interests of doing justice, rehabilitating the offender, and ensuring his good behavior, the court may impose additional requirements on the offender, including, but not limited to, requiring the offender to make restitution for all or part of the property damage that is caused by his offense and for all or part of the value of the property that is the subject of any theft offense * * *.

Further, in citing this court's decision in *State v. Jones* (1990), 49 Ohio St.3d 51, 53, 550 N.E.2d 469, the First District recognized the following criteria to determine whether a condition of probation exceeded the scope of the statute:

> In determining whether a condition of probation is related to the 'interests of doing justice, rehabilitating the offender, and insuring his good behavior,' courts should consider whether the condition (1) is reasonable related to rehabilitating the offender (2) has some relationship to the crime of which the offender was convicted, and (3) relates to conduct which is criminal or reasonably related to future criminality and serves the statutory ends of probation.

Defendant, by his criminal conduct, caused the loss of * * * intellectual property consisting of data collected by several professors over * * * time. One of the professors explained to the trial court that the loss "set her back" six months. In fact, much of the data cannot be replaced. Too, the loss adversely affected the careers of the victims in terms of publishing and tenure. (Vol. II./T.p. 14) Many other victims explained their expended time as a result of the actions of * * * the defendant. Additionally, there was a great amount of time spent by law enforcement investigating and prosecuting these crimes.

The state contends that "in the interests of doing justice" and rehabilitating defendant, the trial court properly and justly tailored the sentence to suit the offenses. It is fitting that defendant has excess travel time in light of the loss of an inestimable amount of time and effort he has caused the victims in this case. Further, since the theft of computers occurred in Hamilton County, it seems more than appropriate that defendant should be required to serve this community by working with and sharing his knowledge of computers with inner-city youth. Admittedly, it is not easy for defendant to travel to Hamilton County. However, based on the serious nature of this offense and the inconvenience and "devastating" loss to the victims, the defendant's traveling hardships seem trivial at best.

A. Evaluate the excerpt for persuasiveness, using the constructs of Chapter 4.

(1) What are the main contentions of the advocate?

(2) What is the theme?

(3) How is it organized?

(4) Does it appear to appeal to any aspect of the judges' values?

(5) Are there other potential arguments that come to mind?

(6) Does the advocate present both sides?

(7) Is there another side and, if so, how might it be countered?

(8) Are there policy arguments?

(9) If you knew that at least two of the judges were tough on crime, how would you take advantage of that fact?

(10) Based on the excerpt, are you convinced the trial judge should be able to order community service in the county in which the felon was convicted?

B. Rewrite the excerpt in a more convincing and persuasive manner.

II. *Brentwood Academy v. Tennessee Secondary School Athletic Association* is a United States Supreme Court case decided in 2001. In that case, a private high school sued the state interscholastic athletic association under sec. 1983, seeking to prevent enforcement of a rule prohibiting the use of undue influence in recruiting student athletes. More particularly, when the Association penalized Brentwood Academy for violating the rule, Brentwood sued the Association and its executive director under 42 U.S.C. sec. 1983, claiming that the rule's enforcement was state action that violated the First and Fourteenth Amendments. The District Court granted Brentwood summary judgment and enjoined the rules enforcement. The Sixth Circuit found no state action and reversed. The issue before the Supreme Court was whether state action existed for purposes of the Fourteenth Amendment.

Throughout the book, the notion of persuasion is developed as each section of the brief and the oral argument are analyzed and discussed. For purposes of this exercise, specific brief sections are used to illustrate the power of persuasion.

A.   In a Supreme Court brief (unlike most lower court and state court briefs), the first section is entitled Question Presented. This is the first chance to inform and persuade the reader-judge to the point of view espoused by the brief. Analyze the following two Questions Presented for persuasiveness. Be prepared to discuss why each is or is not persuasive. To help you evaluate each question, consult 6.45 that provides a checklist for an effective question presented. Together with the information in this chapter, you should be able to evaluate each question. Note: Both comprise the Question Presented from briefs in support of the petitioner filed in the *Brentwood Academy* case.

1. Whether the regulatory conduct of a nominally private secondary school athletic association, which "establishes and enforces all of the rules by which high school teams and players, at both public and private schools, compete throughout the state of Tennessee," *Brentwood Academy v. Tennessee Secondary Sch. Athletic Ass'n.,* 190 F.3d 705, 706 (6th Cir.1999)(Merritt, J. dissenting from the denial of petition for rehearing denied *en banc*) and whose "membership consist[s] entirely of institutions located within the same State, many of them public institutions created by the same sovereign," *NCAA v. Tarkanian,* 488 U.S. 179, 193 n. 13 (1988), constitutes state action under the Fourteenth Amendment and under 42 U.S.C. sec. 1983.

2. Whether an athletic association's regulation of inter-scholastic athletic competition constitutes state action under the Fourteenth Amendment and activity under the color of state law for purposes of 42 U.S.C. 1983 (1994 & Supp. III 1997), when the association is controlled by representatives of public schools located in the same State.

B.   The second opportunity to present the advocate's views is in the Table of Contents discussed in 6.12. The Table of Contents is nothing more than the Point Headings which appear at the beginning of each section of the brief and serve as an introduction to the various sections. Taken together, in the Table of Contents the advocate can effectively provide a roadmap for the reader by indicating the important topics, expressed in a persuasive manner, that will be discussed. Examine the following Point Headings, individually and collectively, for persuasiveness and effectiveness. Do they inform the reader what the case is about? Are you persuaded to the writer's position? In each of the two examples, can you offer suggestions to improve the point headings based on the notions of persuasiveness?

"Argument:

Respondent is engaged in state action because it is controlled by its public school members and it serves state educational objectives.

A. Public schools and their officials are state actors.

B. Government controlled entities that serve government objectives are state actors.

C. Athletic associations that are composed primarily of public schools in a single state are state actors.

D. Respondent's regulation of interscholastic athletic competition constitutes state action."

"ARGUMENT

A. PARENTS' RIGHTS AND SCHOOL CHOICE

B. UNCONSTITUTIONAL TREATMENT OF NONPUBLIC SCHOOL CHOICE

C. STATE CONTROL OF ATHETIC (sic) PROGRAMS

D. UNCONSTITUTIONAL DISCRIMINATION WITHOUT REMEDY"

C. In section 6.50, the Statement of the Case (facts) is discussed. The facts are meant to inform but also to persuade. This is the advocate's best opportunity to tell the court the client's side of the story. They must be scrupulously accurate BUT can and should be favorably worded. Often, the petitioner's rendition of the facts is much more extensive and documented because it is the first presentation to the justices.

Examine the following two excerpts from the facts portion of the briefs. The first excerpt explains the recruiting rules and the violation from the perspective of the petitioner Brentwood Academy.

"The Recruiting Rule Violation. The district court held the Recruiting Rule unconstitutional on its face and as applied. The "as applied" violation stemmed from a letter sent in April 1997 by petitioner's head football coach to all new incoming male students. *Id.* at 13–B. The letter was purely informational; it set forth the dates in May for spring football practice and invited the students to attend if interested. The letter was sent only to new students who had already applied, had been accepted for admission, and had signed a contract to attend petitioner the next fall. *Id.* The letter was followed by a telephone call to the parents of each of the students to reaffirm that participation in spring practice was entirely optional. *Id.* at 14–B. The students who received the letters were entering high school and, therefore, had to change schools as they were graduating from middle school ... Sending the letters and making the telephone calls, however, constituted a Recruiting Rule violation."

The second explains the recruiting rules from the respondent's perspective.

"The TSSAA recruiting rule serves two important purposes. First, it prevents unscrupulous individuals from treating athletically gifted children as commodities and luring those children to attend particular schools because they are athletically gifted, without regard to whether they will be well suited to the academic and social climates of the school. Second, the recruiting rule is a means that the member schools of TSSAA have chosen to keep the playing field level among competitors. Brentwood Academy, on the other hand, has no apparent interest in a level playing field. Brentwood Academy understandably likes its view from the top and the recruiting of athletically gifted 13–and 14–year-old kids is one way for Brentwood Academy to remain there."

Having read both excerpts, identify what makes each persuasive. Are you more persuaded by the first or the second excerpt? Why?

D. The Argument section of a brief is the chief vehicle used to persuade the judges to the advocate's position. Each argument must be considered in its totality but turning a phrase or composing a persuasive passage is always useful to the cause. Examine the following excerpt from the petitioner's argument and from the respondents' argument, each discussing whether TSSAA is a private or public entity.

For the Petitioner:

"TSSAA is organized, controlled and governed by public entities and by public officials acting ex officio. *See West v. Atkins*, 487 U.S. 42, 49–50 (1988)("[G]enerally, a public employee acts under color of state law while acting in his official capacity"). TSSAA pursues "governmental objectives," *Lebron*, 513 U.S. at 400, by exercising regulatory authority over an important component of Tennessee's education system—interscholastic athletics. See Petition for Writ of Certiorari at 18–19 U Appendix E (submission of Chester E. Finn, Jr. and Daniel Casse). TSSAA is not a private organization structured by private parties unrelated to the state or local governments. It is not a privately owned and operated institution that sells services to the state. Nor is it a private company with a private board and a nongovernmental character whose relationship with government is limited to a character whose relationship with government is limited to a commercial interaction such as the sale of services.[1] Rather TSSAA is primarily composed of and controlled by,[2] and exclusively governed by public entities and public officials whose single mission is the regulation of interscholastic athletics of Tennessee's schools."

For the Respondent:

"TSSAA is a private entity in all respects. It operates from privately owned property. Its day-to-day operations are conducted by privately employed citizens. It receives no government funding. While its employees are permitted to participate in the Tennessee Consolidated Retirement System, the private corporation pays the employer contribution from its own private funds. For government employees who are members of the TCRS, the employer contribution is paid by the government from

---

1. *Contrast Blum v. Yaretsky,* 457 U.S. 991, 1011 (1982)(privately owned nursing home with state Medicaid contract not a state actor).

2. See notes 32–35 and accompanying text, *infra*.

public funds. [R. 42 Ronnie Carter Dep. Pp. 271, 291–92, Apx. Pp. 264–65, 266].[3]

"TSSAA's power to enforce its rules as to Brentwood Academy does not flow from the State of Tennessee or from any statute or valid regulation of any state agency or any other act of the state. TSSAA's power to enforce its rules as to Brentwood Academy flows directly and solely from the voluntary membership contract which Brentwood Academy signed, under which it agreed to comply with the TSSAA rules and decisions in order to receive the opportunity to proclaim itself a TSSAA champion.[4] Brentwood Academy's contract is with a private entity, not the state."

Having read both excerpts, which one is the most persuasive and why. Do you think the use of footnotes in the respondent's argument is a good idea? Why or why not?

3. TSSAA is one of three private associations, along with the Tennessee Education Association and the Tennessee School Boards Association, whose employees are statutorily permitted to participate in the Tennessee Consolidated Retirement System. Tenn. Code. Ann. Sec. 8–35–118. Although the employees of those three organizations are not employees of the government, the General Assembly has recognized that the three organizations often draw employees from the teaching profession. The availability of participation in TCRS is a means by which the General Assembly has permitted members of the teaching profession to leave government employment and go to work for one of these associations without losing the ability to continue accruing retirement benefits under TCRS. However, the government does not pay any portion of the employer contribution for employees of those three associations who continue to participate in TCRS.[R.42 Ronnie Carter Dep. P. 271, Apx. pp.264–65].

4. *Lebron v. National Railroad Passenger Corporation,* 513 U.S. 374 (1995), relied upon extensively by the Petitioner in its brief, did not involve a determination that a private entity was acting under color of state law. Instead, the Court in *Lebron* concluded that Amtrak was in fact a government entity or agency. Amtrak was established by Congress, its structure and powers statutorily decreed by Congress. *Id.* at 383–87. Its directors were government appointees. *Id.* at 385. The Court held: "We hold that where, as here, the Government creates a corporation by special law, for the furtherance of governmental objectives, and retains for itself permanent authority to appoint a majority of the directors of that corporation, the corporation is part of the Government for purposes of the First Amendment." *Id.* at 400. TSSAA was not created by special law for the furtherance of governmental objectives, nor does the state have permanent authority to appoint a majority of the Council or Board members. *Lebron* has no application here.

Chapter Five

PREPARATION FOR BRIEF WRITING

Analysis

5.00 INTRODUCTION

5.01 The importance of the brief

The brief has been described as the most important component of a successful appeal. It gives the judges the first and, many times, the last impression of the merits of the case. Judge Goodrich of the United States Court of Appeals for the Third Circuit said:

> It is hard to overstate the importance of the brief on an appeal. Oral argument will be discussed later. It is important too. But it is made only once in nearly all instances and it is inevitable that some of its effect will be lost in the interval between the time the argument is made and the court opinion appears * * * . But the brief speaks from the time it is filed and continues through oral argument, conference, and opinion writing. Sometimes a brief will be read and reread, no one knows how many times except the judge and his law clerk.[1]

Over the years, the brief has assumed ever-increasing significance. As discussed in Chapter 8, the emphasis of appellate practice used to be the oral argument. Many oral arguments lasted for days, and the decision of the case was pronounced upon completion of the argument or shortly thereafter. As court dockets grew, the time for oral argument

---

1. Herbert F. Goodrich, *A Case on Appeal—A Judge's View*, in A Case on Appeal   1, 10–11 (4th ed.1967).

was shortened.[2] In the United States Supreme Court, instead of days for an argument, such as the renowned orations of Daniel Webster, arguments were limited to hours and eventually to thirty or less minutes. At present, several arguments are often heard during the course of a day. As a result, judges find themselves in the position of rendering their decision long after the arguments take place. There is no place to turn, except to the brief, to refresh the recollection of the argument, days or even weeks after it occurs. This situation is only exacerbated as the number of appeals grows yearly.

The intermediate appellate courts also face the pressure of too many arguments to be heard in too little time. To meet the increased burden, time limitations are also imposed in these courts. While some circuits routinely hear arguments in all cases, many circuits now hear oral arguments only in exceptional circumstances. Interestingly, it is often the court's initial examination of the brief that helps determine whether the questions raised are sufficiently substantial to justify oral argument.

The importance of the brief is obvious. It may be the only vehicle by which the advocate presents his or her argument. Even in instances in which oral argument is granted, with "hot courts"[3] the brief is the first impression of the appeal and likely will be the last. Therefore, sloppy thinking and writing may well produce the only perception that members of the bench have of the advocate, the client and the case.

In sum, the importance of the brief is best stated by Justice Thurgood Marshall, who wrote:

> Regardless of the panel you get, the questions you get or the answers you give, I maintain it is the brief that does the final job, if for no other reason than that opinions are often written several weeks and sometimes months after the argument. The arguments, great as they may have been, are forgotten. In the seclusion of his chambers the judge has only his briefs and the law books. At that time your brief is your only spokesman.[4]

5.02   The role of the brief

The chief role of the brief is to present to the court the issues in controversy and, based on the law and facts, how those issues should be decided in order to reach a just conclusion. Properly done, the brief states the specific grounds for affirmance or reversal based on supporting authority. The operative words are *supporting authority*. No amount of opinion without authority will sway the judges to the advocate's position. Pure opinion and speculation do not make a winning brief.

---

2. See Chapter 8, § 8.00 in which the time limitations for oral advocacy are discussed.

3. A "hot court" is described as one in which all the judges have read and studied the briefs in advance of the oral argument. The members of the bench come to the argument with very specific concerns about the merits of the case.

4. Thurgood Marshall, The Federal Appeal, in Counsel on Appeal 141, 146 (Arthur A. Charpentier ed., 1968).

A brief is a persuasive document that is meant to inform the appellate court of:

(1) the facts that gave rise to the litigation and subsequent appeal;

(2) the specific issues raised in the appeal based on the alleged errors committed in the court below;

(3) the questions of law raised by the issues as defined;

(4) the principles of law that the advocate believes govern the outcome of the issues raised;

(5) the advocate's view of the appropriate application of those principles to the client's case; and,

(6) the specific relief requested by the advocate.

Remember the appellate brief must demonstrate that the advocate is correct and that the relief requested is appropriate and just. How these tasks are accomplished is the topic of the next several chapters.

5.10 FAMILIARITY WITH THE COURT RULES

The formal requirements for briefs are rule-driven and vary from jurisdiction to jurisdiction. The Federal Rules of Appellate Procedure will be examined to explicate the types of rules the advocate must know and follow as to the content and form of the briefs and appendices, as well as how and when they must be filed and served.[5]

The contents of briefs are fairly narrowly defined.[6] The appellant's brief must contain, under appropriate headings and in order, a table of contents, statement of the issues, statement of the case, the argument and a short conclusion.[7] The appellee's brief is likewise defined, as well as any reply brief that may be filed. There is a specific section which admonishes counsel not to discuss the parties in terms of appellant and appellee but rather to use actual names or descriptive terms. How to refer to the record is carefully explained, as well as what to do if there is specific reference to statutes, rules, regulations, etc. Of course, the length of the brief is carefully controlled.

The form of brief is regulated by Rule 32. In this rule, the type of paper and print, size of type, spacing of type and even the color of the cover is dictated. The appellant's brief shall be blue, the appellee's red, and an intervenor or amicus curiae, green. The information on the cover of the brief is strictly defined. The amended rules now detail print size, line spacing and margin requirements to reflect computer use in the preparation of briefs. It is little wonder that attorneys at times fail to follow the rules for the form of the brief.

5. See Appendix B for the full text of the Federal Rules of Appellate Procedure.

6. Fed. R. App. P. 28.

7. Each of the sections is described in some detail. For example, the statement of the case shall first indicate briefly the nature of the case, the course of proceedings and its disposition in the court below. There shall follow a statement of the facts relevant to the issues presented for review, with appropriate references to the record.

Rule 31 deals with filing and service of briefs. In the federal courts, the appellant has 40 days after the date on which the record is filed to file and serve the brief. Then the appellee must file and serve the response brief within 30 days after the service of the opening brief. Reply briefs must be served within 14 days after service of the appellee's brief. There are some noted exceptions to this rule.[8] Rule 31 also dictates the number of copies to be filed and served, as well as the consequences of failure to file briefs.

The Federal Rules of Appellate Procedure specify the general requirements for content, form, filing and service. However, they also provide that each circuit may establish additional requirements or even change the rules as described.

Likewise, in state courts there is usually a set of appellate rules that govern appellate procedure. And, like the federal rules, generally state rules may also be supplemented or replaced. The United States Supreme Court has a separate set of rules that regulate filing and serving briefs.[9] Therefore, as usual, the procedural rules of each court, whether federal or state, must be checked to determine the precise requirements for the briefing process.

There may be a high cost for non-compliance with procedural rules. In the most egregious cases, failure to comply results in dismissal of the case.[10] Some courts assess costs to the offending party. Failure to file a brief by the appellee may result in loss of the right to be heard at oral argument.

Courts regard the rules of procedure seriously. Without them, valuable court time is lost assessing the issues and arguments related to the appeal. As stated in one case,

> [T]here is no excuse for the failure of any member of the bar to understand or to comply with the rules of this court. They are promulgated so that causes coming before the court will be presented in a clear and logical manner, and any litigant availing himself of the jurisdiction of the court is subjected thereto. Not to be minimized is the necessity of compliance as an accommodation to the correct dispatch of the court's business.[11]

5.20 FAMILIARITY WITH THE CASE

As the advocate begins review of the case, it is essential to compile notes. Nothing is more frustrating than to know that a fact, a case, a

---

8. But see Rules 25 and 26 as they interact with Rule 31(a)(1). These rules raise timing issues. They are very tricky when taken together.

9. *See* Appendix A.

10. *State ex rel. Queen City Chapter of Society of Professional Journalists v. McGinnis,* 461 N.E.2d 307 (Ohio 1984). In this case, a document entitled Brief in Support of Relators' Complaint consisted of a one-page document that simply stated

"[r]elators here adopt by reference their memorandum previously filed in support of their first motion for summary judgment." This document was filed with the Supreme Court of Ohio. The court's reaction was to dismiss the action *sua sponte,* saying that the relators failed minimal compliance with the Rules of Practice.

11. *Drake v. Bucher,* 213 N.E.2d 182, 184 (Ohio 1966).

statute or any other aspect of the appeal has been reviewed, but be unable to locate the material. Notes need not be extensive. Short excerpts will serve the researcher well to provide a roadmap of where the review has gone and where it needs to go.

5.21 Review of the record

An important step in preparing to write the brief is a thorough review of the record. Before in-depth study is undertaken, however, the best approach is to get a general idea of the totality of the case. This is no problem if the appellate counsel tried the lawsuit in the trial court. Nevertheless, if a considerable amount of time has elapsed since the case was tried, perusal of counsel's trial court file will be beneficial.

For new counsel brought in to take the appeal, this type of review is crucial. It is impossible to comprehend the issues without understanding the facts. Likewise, any attempt to assess facts in a vacuum without benefit of the legal theory or theories of the case will be just as frustrating. For new counsel, a solid appreciation of the case is obtained only after review of trial court materials, such as the opinion, findings of the court and judgment, any auxiliary briefs or memoranda filed with the trial court, charges to the jury and testimony.

If the appeal is taken to the second tier of the appellate process, that which transpired during the first appeal is particularly helpful. The briefs filed and the court's opinion lay a good foundation to understand the basics of the case.

With a firm comprehension of the issues that gave rise to the appeal, counsel is now in a position for extensive review of the record. This means reading all materials which will be before the appellate court, except those matters that are clearly irrelevant.[12] A systematic approach to record review will facilitate digesting and summarizing its content.

First, make an accurate history of the case. Explore both its factual and procedural history. All facts, whether favorable or unfavorable, should be noted and recorded. It is not enough just to read the facts. One must summarize them with page references. Counsel will want to note where in the record (1) the pleadings appear, (2) testimony of the witnesses can be found, (3) specific evidentiary points are located, (4) exhibits are found, and (5) other potentially important information such as procedural matters are located. Eventually, if this information is readily locatable, multitudinous hours will be saved in writing the brief. Also, there is a theory that the actual process of physically recording material, either by recording on a computer disk or putting pen to paper, aids in assimilation of the material. Further, at the conclusion of this exercise, it is easier for the attorney to appreciate how the different parts of the record fit together. Remember: this is not the stage to begin

---

12. One such example of irrelevant material might be *voir dire* when there is no claim of error as it relates to jury selection.

sorting through the facts to determine the issues. That task will come later.

With the facts and the procedural postures identified, counsel can now identify the positions asserted by the opposition at the trial. They may well appear in some form on appeal.[13] Determining the opposition's potential arguments places counsel in a better position to evaluate the opponent's case, as well as formulate arguments in response to those claims.

Having identified the positions taken at trial, the reviewer is now ready to look for any concessions, implicit or explicit, that appear in the record. Concession may come by way of pleadings, testimony or the actions of opposing counsel.[14]

One last step many attorneys find helpful is to rearrange digests or notes as they relate to a single subject. If the notes are recorded on a computer, it is a simple task to reorganize them. If the notes are by hand, cutting and pasting may be necessary. This technique gives a better idea of the emphasis placed on the positions taken at trial. For example, a matter identified in the pleadings and the subject of a motion and testimony needs careful examination. It may well appear on appeal. The information in digest form, in one place on a particular topic, is very useful.

5.22   Review of the law

5.22–1   Introduction

It is axiomatic that comprehensive research is essential to an effective legal argument. Through research the advocate discovers the principles upon which to develop a sound and logical theory for the appeal. In addition, careful research assists the advocate to gain insight into not only the law, but also social and policy implications.

Strategies for the conduct of legal research are the subject of numerous legal research publications. Most law schools cover the topic in the first year of law study. Since each publication has individual characteristics and approaches, the use of each publication is beyond the scope of this book. Nevertheless, some pointers are worth mentioning, if only for purposes of review.

---

13. For example, assume a state in which negligence, contributory negligence and last clear chance are still the law. During the course of the trial, assuming the case is one in which the three elements are a factor, testimony will probably be introduced to prove all three. Also there will be a request for jury instructions on the elements. If the judge refuses to give an instruction on last clear chance, one issue on appeal might be the correctness of that decision and whether it constitutes reversible error.

14. For example, take the case of a sports agent who fails to inquire into the financial stability of a team and signs his player to a contract with that team. If the agent claimed in both the pleadings and testimony, he did not know of the financial woes of the team, there may be an implicit concession that the agent is negligent for failing to make the proper inquiry pursuant to his fiduciary duty.

The main purpose of legal research is to find primary mandatory authority to support the position the advocate intends to espouse. Mandatory authority is that which must be followed. For example, the intermediate court in any state is bound by the decisions of the court of last resort of that state. This characterization is overly simple. Obviously the facts of the decided case and the law as applied must be similar to the case being researched. Primary authority includes the constitution, statutes, and case law from the highest court, as well as rules, regulations and decisions of administrative agencies in the jurisdiction.

The initial approach to research is generally dictated by one's knowledge of the subject matter. If little is known, the best approach is to obtain background information. Legal encyclopedias, hornbooks and practice manuals provide the necessary tools to introduce the topic. These sources are also excellent for locating primary source materials, such as cases and statutes. Many researchers feel that reading of a general nature often helps put the issues into perspective. However, if the advocate is already familiar with the material and feels comfortable with the issues, a more focused research plan should be devised.

Whatever the level of knowledge, thoughtful review of the hierarchy of the law is essential. This review suggests to the researcher how and where to search and helps evaluate the authority to later make the final decisions about which sources best promote the argument.

5.22–2 Hierarchy of our legal system

5.22–2–a Constitution and case law interpretation

The United States Constitution is the supreme law that articulates the principles that ultimately bind governmental bodies at the federal, state and local levels. It creates the bodies that formulate legal rules. These include the legislature, the judiciary and the executive branches of government. The constitution dictates their powers, the exercise of which must not contravene constitutional principles.

The early judicial history of the United States established the notion of judicial review.[15] The judiciary became the ultimate interpreter of the constitution. Cases that deal with constitutional issues are accorded special status. If there is a question, for example, about the constitutionality of an enacted law and the judiciary declares the law unconstitutional, the provision is invalid. Conversely, neither the executive nor the legislative branch of government can overrule a judicial constitutional decree.

Therefore, the first matter to be resolved by the researcher is whether there is a constitutional question involved in the appeal. If the answer is affirmative and the Supreme Court has ruled on the matter, there is little room for argument.

15. *See Marbury v. Madison,* 5 U.S. (1 Cranch) 137 (1803).

5.22–2–b   Statutes and their interpretation

Statutes enacted by the legislature are second in status to constitutional provisions and their interpretation. Under our system of government, they take precedent over judicial determinations and administrative rulings. This is true unless the particular court or agency has been given constitutional authority to decide the issue.

Because of the importance of statutes in our legal system, the researcher must determine at the outset if the issue on appeal is controlled by statute. This approach may save hours of fruitless research. An entire line of cases stretching over decades can be obliterated by a single stroke of the legislative pen.

Like constitutions, statutes are generally interpreted by the judiciary. To properly interpret legislative enactments, it is often necessary to ascertain the intent of the legislators, particularly when the words of the statute are ambiguous or vague. The role of the courts is to determine the meaning of the words.

How this is accomplished has been a controversy that has spawned volumes in the legal literature. Generally, the legislative history is instructive. A legislative history includes, but is not limited to, committee reports, hearings and their resultant reports and floor debates. Other tools that courts use to determine meaning include use of the canons of statutory construction, the historical context surrounding the passage of the statute, and comparison of analogous statutes from other jurisdictions, with special emphasis on their interpretation by courts.

In the end, the goal of the judiciary is to give meaning to the statute as written or, in the event the statute oversteps its constitutional boundaries, declare it invalid. Once again, this is a classic example of our legal system's checks and balances.

5.22–2–c   Administrative rules, regulations and decisions

Many researchers consider administrative rules, regulations and decisions to be on the same level of the hierarchy as statutory law. This is certainly true if the outcome of the controversy is controlled by the administrative agency. That determination should be made at the outset.

Administrative agencies are generally created by statute, but, in some instances, by state constitution or the executive branch. Administrative agencies exercise various degrees of power with a variety of functions. The statute or constitutional provision that creates the agency defines those powers. For example, many agencies are empowered to make their own procedural rules. These rules may define how and when papers must be filed to commence an action, procedures for pre-hearing, hearing and post-hearing activities, appeal procedures and the like.

Given power by the enabling statute or constitution, many administrative agencies act both as a legislative and a judicial body. These agencies promulgate regulations that establish the substantive legal rules in the field that the agency controls. For example, the Internal

Revenue Service establishes regulations which define the requirements that must be met for forming and maintaining a Sub-chapter S corporation.[16] Regulations of this nature resemble statutes and have the same power and effect as statutes. They are also equally vulnerable to constitutional challenge.

In their judicial capacity, agencies adjudicate disputes. The controversy may involve two parties, such as the case of an employee and employer disputing whether worker's compensation benefits should be paid for an injury. On the other hand, a dispute may arise which involves just a single regulated party who has broken some rule of the agency. Although the process resembles a court adjudication in that evidence is garnered and parties are examined and cross-examined with a resultant decision, the whole process is much less formal. The rules of evidence are more relaxed as to admissibility. Most importantly, agency determinations are accorded substantial deference as long as the decision is supported by evidence and the agency has complied with procedural fairness. If a matter is appealed to a court, the review usually considers only the result as to whether the decision is arbitrary, capricious or unreasonable, based on the evidence.

5.22–2–d   Case law

Some controversies are controlled only by judicial decisions that have evolved over time. While this is increasingly rare, these matters are not controlled by statutes, constitutional provisions or agency rules or regulations. In other words, mandatory precedent is found only in case law that generally has been decided by an appellate court.

The controlling doctrine which gives weight to case-made precedent is known as *stare decisis*. The doctrine holds that once a court has formulated a rule that governs a set of facts, that rule will be applied to controversies involving similar facts. The operative words are *similar facts*. While they do not have to be mirror images, the closer the fact pattern, the more likely the court will apply the rule previously enunciated. However, the researcher must be prepared to face the possibility that the facts in the present case are elusively distinguishable from those in past cases. Creative analysis may be required.

Having established the importance of the facts, the researcher must carefully ascertain the rule of law that controls the controversy. This is known as the *ratio decidendi* of the case, or that legal principle upon which the case turns. If the court had not applied that principle, the case would not have been decided as it was. Confusion arises because judges often discuss auxiliary legal rules to explain some portion of the opinion. Such discussion is not paramount to the decision and is known as *obiter dictum*. Care must be taken not to cite dicta as authority. The rule of

---

16. Promulgated over several years, the first set of revised regulations was so bad that the whole process was started anew. The second set was deemed to be better, but not much better.

law upon which the case is resolved is what constitutes the mandatory precedent.[17]

5.22–2–e   Rules of court and their interpretation

There are a variety of court rules. Their authoritative value depends on the nature of the rule. For example, the Federal Rules of Civil Procedure describe and define how a civil case moves through the federal system. The rules are subject to review for constitutional concerns. Likewise, the Federal Rules of Appellate Procedure describe the procedural aspects of cases brought before the federal intermediate appellate courts.

Individual courts within both the federal and the state systems promulgate rules by which attorneys must abide.[18] These rules vary widely but are determinative of actions within the particular court in which they are formulated.

5.22–3   Secondary sources

To this point, the sources of the law discussed are primary in nature; in other words, those sources that contain the law. Secondary sources are not authoritative, but rather summarize, explain, analyze and comment on the law. They are valuable research tools and may be persuasive if there are no primary sources to determine the issue. They are used in a variety of ways. The researcher must know how and when the sources may be used successfully.

As previously discussed, if one is unfamiliar with the area of law to be researched, secondary sources may be used to provide background. The best places to begin are a legal encyclopedia, a hornbook or a practice book. These offer the reader a comprehensive view of the law and are objectively written. Secondary sources are also excellent "finding tools" to aid the researcher in locating primary authorities. American Law Reports Annotated, digests and looseleaf services are especially helpful to find primary authority.

If there is no mandatory primary authority, some secondary sources may be persuasive. While there is some question as to which sources are most persuasive, the various Restatements are high on the list. The Restatements cover a variety of topics and attempt to restate the common law of the various jurisdictions. They are drafted by the American Law Institute, a consortium of legal scholars and practitioners who are widely respected and known for their expertise. While the Restatements provide an excellent source of the law, they also are excellent case-finders.

---

17. For example, if the issue of the case is whether to grant an injunction to prevent a party from using another party's material that has been copyrighted, the court may well discuss the law of copyright. The *ratio decidendi*, however, will center on the law as it relates to the issuance of an injunction. The copyrighted material may help explain the decision, but should not be cited as authority for the law of copyright.

18. See generally the discussion at § 5.10, wherein the high cost of non-compliance is discussed.

Law reviews and other legal periodicals are sources often cited as persuasive authority. These journals provide in-depth information with extensive footnotes to supporting authority. Journal authors provide research that is usually exhaustive. Hours of research may be eliminated if an article on point can be located. One cautionary word: legal periodicals often contain the views of the author, who may or may not agree with the actual law. However, the author's own views are usually discernable and thus do not detract from the source's usefulness.

Treatises are also sources that may be cited. Treatises may be either multi-volume or a single-volume work. They are normally written by experts in the field and provide explanations and footnotes about a single topic. They provide authoritative citations and extensive explanations of the law.

The weight to be accorded secondary sources is often dependent on the status and reputation of the author of the work. For example, a law review article written by a recognized tax policy expert is more persuasive than an article written by a second year law student who has a view on tax policy. The same is true of treatises. Therefore, care must be taken in selecting secondary sources to cite to a court. Since primary mandatory authority always ranks first, judges consult secondary sources only as a way to understand and interpret the law. Hopefully, it will be in a light most favorable to the advocate who utilizes the secondary source.

5.22–4   Other materials not of a legal nature

At times, a case presents itself that cannot be answered by strictly legal analysis and argument. Non-legal sources may be appropriate and effective. Perhaps the most famous practitioner to employ this approach was Louis D. Brandeis in his brief in the case of *Muller v. Oregon.*[19] In that case, the Court considered "extracts from over ninety reports of committees, bureaus of statistics, commissioners of hygiene, inspectors of factories, both in this country and in Europe" to decide the issue of how many hours an employed woman could work in a day.[20] The use of extra-legal materials in briefs became known as a "Brandeis style brief." Since *Muller*, others have employed the technique. For example, the Supreme Court found social science studies helpful when considering the case of *Brown v. Board of Education.*[21] The Court examined studies that explored the detrimental effect on the education of black children under the "separate but equal" doctrine. The landmark abortion case of *Roe v. Wade,*[22] also considered studies that were not legally based. In that case, the Court considered various data on abortion when making its decision. Information examined included medical practices and mortality rates.[23]

19. 208 U.S. 412 (1908).

20. *Id.* at 420 n. 1.

21. 347 U.S. 483 (1954).

22. 410 U.S. 113 (1973).

23. Indeed, some briefs are based almost entirely on extra-legal material. In the case of *Nancy Beth Cruzan v. Director of Missouri Department of Health,* 497 U.S. 261 (1990), the respondents in their brief argued against withholding food and hydra-

The basis for considering these types of materials lies in the notion of *judicial notice*. The court will take judicial notice of materials outside of the record which are, for example, of a scientific nature such as studies, surveys and conclusions of experts in fields outside of the law. This type of information is most helpful when the court is trying to decide matters that involve general questions that are not fact specific. The *Brown* case and the *Roe v. Wade* case are illustrative of the types of questions that are aided by this type of data.

A key element for a successful proffer of extra-legal material is that it emanates from an expert. Uncorroborated opinion is not persuasive and leads to loss of confidence in the advocate. In summary, the advocate must ask the following questions:

1. Is the issue one that is not fact specific?

2. Will understanding of the issue be aided by material that is not legal in nature?

3. Is the material authoritative, i.e., are the studies, statistics and general data generated by a recognized source?

4. Are the materials persuasive?

If the answer to the four questions is yes, the argument may be a candidate for a Brandeis-style brief. One case comes to mind. What sources could an advocate use to support an argument that lung cancer is caused by cigarette smoking? The possibilities are almost limitless.

5.22–5   Too much research

There are pitfalls to over-researching. First and foremost is the likelihood of duplication. Most researchers are driven to continue their research by the overpowering thought that somehow something has been missed. Usually it is the "big" case that is right on point, or it may be the uneasy thought that there is precedent that simply has not been found. Even worse is the fear that what has been found is obsolete. As a result, far too many hours are spent needlessly going over material that simply echoes what has been located. The trick is to know when to stop. A good rule of thumb is to move on to the writing process when the same cases, statutes, theories and the like begin to repeat themselves. Chances are the "magic" case that will be overpoweringly persuasive and decisive of the appeal simply does not exist.

Pitfall number two is that matters of little importance may seem relevant when, in fact, they simply cloud the main issues. Usually the

tion from a comatose patient and relied heavily on materials not of a legal nature. Many items were opinions of experts with respect to patients in a vegetative state. Studies of comatose patients were introduced. Aristotle and Cicero were quoted and at one point in the brief the following appeared "God spoke, and these were His words '[T]hou shall not kill.' Exodus 20." It should be noted that the latter quotes were to introduce or emphasize a point developed in the brief. Caution must be used to ensure that the court has enough primary authority to make an informed decision. Extra-legal materials help persuade the court to make that decision based on other than straight legal theory.

researcher has a fairly good idea of what issues are going to be important to the appeal. Of course, during the process of research, the issues come more sharply into focus. That is a positive. However, it is also possible during this time to begin second-guessing what originally seemed important. It is easy to be distracted by collateral matters and spend an inordinate amount of time on issues that prove to be inconsequential. At best, time is again wasted, and at worst, small insignificant matters may creep into the final product. Clarifying issues is constructive, but second guessing the issues may be damaging.

All researchers have a finite amount of time to complete the project. Too much researching significantly reduces the valuable time needed for outlining, drafting and redrafting. Most people find it far more enjoyable to explore the law in the library than to put pen to paper to create the written product. The third pitfall of over-researching then is to cut short the time for writing a high quality brief. The advocate may have impeccable research, but if the final product is poorly written and unpersuasive, the research will have been for naught.

To avoid the pitfalls, a research plan must be devised that includes not only an outline of the issues to be researched but also a time frame within which to complete the project. Even though both elements will be subject to revision as issues develop, there is at least an initial plan. The construction of a plan and attempting to stick to it will yield better results than simply beginning the research willy-nilly with no course of action in mind.

5.30   SELECTION OF A THEME

Before selection of the issues and how they will be argued, the advocate should decide on a theme. The theme is the overall unifying notion upon which the argument is based. It is the single idea which, if accepted by the court, will likely result in a favorable decision. The theme can be a moral or philosophical notion, preferably one with which the members of the court will identify. The theme may be based on equity or policy considerations. It may be based on the notion of not disturbing long-standing precedent. But whatever is chosen, it should be evident throughout the brief. The advocate should consider what the court must think and believe if the decision is to be favorable. For example, assume the issue before the court is whether the state should allow same-sex marriages. The theme of the brief for the state may be to maintain the underlying notion that marriage is a union between one man and one woman. The theme for the brief of the same-sex partners might be constitutional discrimination.

Selection of a theme requires a great deal of thought. Often, lawyers simply begin to write without determining exactly the message the judges are supposed to receive. The result is likely to be a document that just doesn't "hold together." This document may be passable, but it will not be persuasive.

5.40   SELECTION OF ISSUES TO BE ARGUED

After a thorough review of the record, the law, the equity and the policy arguments, it is now time to select the issues to be argued on appeal. There may be choices. The natural tendency of most lawyers is to include every issue and every argument that can be raised, fearing that something will be missed. The prudent advocate, however, should carefully include only the most important issues in the brief. Remember: a brief is not like the pleadings of a case in which all possible matters are included. Briefs are meant to be persuasive, and the art of persuasion favors quality, not quantity.

Weak points dilute strong ones. As one commentator noted:

> Appellate advocacy on civil appeals calls for courage in the lawyer: the courage to forego, the willingness to pass alluring grounds that may exist in the record. The lawyer must make difficult choices. He must make calculated judgments in abandoning points for appeal. The compendious effort that throws everything erroneous or even everything reversible at the court runs the risk of pegging the strength of the appeal to the weakest link. Selectivity then is the key.[24]

5.50   THE PRELIMINARY OUTLINE

An outline is essential in the creation of any document of length. The preliminary outline is just that—preliminary. It will change as the advocate proceeds through the process of organization of the issues and determination of how best to present them.

5.51   Reasons to outline

An outline provides the most efficient way to draft a document. By outlining, the attorney will discover weaknesses in the argument that may need to be reinforced with additional research or issue development. There is nothing more disruptive than the need to return to the library halfway through writing the brief. Valuable time is lost, and the momentum of the task is jeopardized.

The outline helps organize the actual drafting of the arguments. Without one, it is difficult to see how the arguments fit together into the whole. Poor organization leads to poorly structured arguments that may need to be redone and, in some cases, discarded because they don't fit. Again, valuable time is lost.

A good outline is like a road map for a traveler. Without one, it is possible to get lost or wander aimlessly. The entire writing process is much easier if there is a master plan, so there is never a question about what comes next.

24. Milton Pollack, *The Civil Appeal*, in   ed., 1968).
Counsel on Appeal 29, 39 (A. Charpentier

In addition, a strong outline adds to the clarity and conciseness of a brief. With each argument in its proper place, the reader will more easily follow the points. Thus, an outline adds clarity. An outline also promotes conciseness. The writer is more likely to march purposefully through the points to be made rather than to search for words to express ideas not adequately developed.

An outline should add substance to the brief. As the attorney outlines, the arguments to be included are appraised. It is easier at this stage to evaluate their strengths and weaknesses. It is also easier to decide whether the arguments need to be enhanced, or, if illogical, discarded. Once the time is invested in actually writing the arguments, it is more difficult to truly evaluate them. This is especially so if time is of the essence. Thus, the actual substance of the brief should improve if there is a strong outline.

In the end, the final written document will be sharper. The attorney has taken the time to think about the substance, the flow, the weak points, the strong points, and whether further work must be done before the actual writing process takes place. There is a solid organization that "hangs" together, with little chance that ill-thought-out tangents will be interjected.

Time spent on developing a good outline will more than compensate for the time that is wasted on poorly crafted arguments that do not flow. But remember: an outline is a starting point. It may well be altered during the writing process. This is as it should be. Use it as a tool for organization and as a starting point. Let the writing progress from that point.

EXERCISES

I. The following is a partial transcript of a record. The names of the documents are indicated, but the formal captions on most documents have been eliminated. The name of the case is The State of Texarkana, ex. rel., Jane White, Relator, vs. The Industrial Commission of Texarkana, Respondent.

BEFORE THE INDUSTRIAL COMMISSION OF TEXARKANA

Question: Allowance of Claim

On August 7, 1997, the claimant was working as a Home Products salesperson. She had worked in this capacity for approximately four months prior to the date of the injury. Home Products, Inc., is in the business of manufacturing cookware and tableware. The products are distributed by six different regional distributors which are wholly independent from Home Products, Inc. The products are sold through home parties during which a dealer demonstrates the products and takes orders. The claimant was such a dealer. The claimant received her goods from Home Distributors, the regional distributor for the State of Texarkana.

There was no written contract between Home Distributors and the claimant identifying the relationship. The claimant was free to book her own parties when and where she wished. Brochures showing the available goods and suggested retail prices were provided by the manufacturer of the goods. The claimant submitted an order to Home Distributors and received the goods seven days later. She paid wholesale price for the goods. The claimant then delivered the goods to the customers and collected the suggested retail price from them. Her compensation was the difference between the wholesale and retail prices. In addition, she received a 5% bonus from Home Distributors if her monthly order was in excess of $1,500. No taxes were withheld from these bonus checks. Home Distributors did withhold $25/month from the claimant's check to cover the cost of a voluntary hospitalization program.

Each Wednesday morning, Home Distributors held dealer meetings at which successful sales techniques were discussed. These meetings were not mandatory, but attendance was strongly suggested. Recognition of successful sales personnel was made during the meetings. Suggested formats for the demonstration parties were also discussed.

At approximately 8 p.m. on August 7, 1997, the claimant was demonstrating an omelet pan at a party at the home of Joyce Withers who lives at 59 Oak Street in the City of Metropolis, Texarkana. There were 14 other people who were present and watched the demonstration. During the demonstration, Robert Withers, the husband of Joyce Withers, burst through the kitchen door, screaming, "I told you I'd never let you go to another man!" He pulled a gun and shot his wife in the head. The claimant was standing beside Mrs. Withers at the time. The claimant immediately fainted. Since that date, she has been totally disabled due to a psychoneurotic condition.

The Supreme Court of Texarkana has never addressed the questions involved in this claim. Specifically, the court has not developed criteria for determining whether an individual is an employee or an independent contractor for purposes of worker's compensation. Nor has it determined if a mental injury is considered the same as a physical injury under the meaning of Texarkana Rev. Code § 3142.01(C).

Recommend:

That the Industrial Commission find from proof of record the claimant is not an employee within Texarkana Rev. Code § 3142.01(A);

Further, the claimant did not suffer an injury within Texarkana Rev. Code § 3142.01(C).

DEPOSITIONS

The following is a portion of the deposition of Jane White.

Q: Ms. White, what was the nature of the work you performed for Home Distributors?

A: I was their employee.

Q: Please Ms. White, answer the question. It is for the court to determine your legal status with Home Distributors. Let me be more precise. Did you ever discuss advancement with any officer of the company?

A: No.

Q: Have you ever suffered from depression?

A: Yes, but not for awhile.

Q: Were you treated for depression?

A: Yes, I took pills.

Q: Do you still take medicine?

A: No.

The following is a portion of the deposition of John Dowle, representative of Home Distributors.

Q: How many employees do you have in this region?

A: None. They are all independent contractors except for the management. There are two of us, so yeah, I guess there are two "employees."

Q: So you don't have to pay benefits, is that correct?

A: No. That's just the way the company has always operated—cleaner, more efficient.

Q: Have you ever had a worker's compensation claim before?

A: Not since I've been with the company.

Q: How long have you been working for them?

A: Approximately six months.

Q: In your opinion, why is this arrangement advantageous to your independent contractors?

A: It allows them total flexibility. They can work or they don't have to. Obviously, we want them to and that's why we give a bonus. But they can use their own best time—nights—weekends.

APPEAL TO THE COMMON PLEAS COURT

1. Relator Jane White is the claimant in a worker's compensation claim resulting from an industrial injury suffered on August 7, 1997, which occurred in the course of and arising out of her employment with Home Distributors, known as claim number 94321.

2. On said date, Home Distributors had in its employ more than one regular employee and was qualified to pay compensation benefits to its employees for any compensable injury arising out of and in the course of employment.

3. On August 10, 1997, Jane White filed her application for compensation and said application was disallowed on September 13, 1997.

4.   Jane White is entitled to participate in the workers' compensation fund as set forth by the law of the State of Texarkana.

5.   A jury trial is hereby demanded.

Wherefore, relator demands judgment that she is entitled to participate in the workers' compensation fund.

IN THE COURT OF COMMON PLEAS
STIPULATION

The parties hereby agree that the Statement of Facts in claim number 94321, before the Industrial Commission of the State of Texarkana, shall be admitted as the facts relating to the alleged injury of Jane White in the case pending before the Court of Common Pleas.

IN THE COURT OF COMMON PLEAS
ORDER

The court finds that Jane White is not entitled to participate in the workers' compensation fund of the State of Texarkana for the reasons that she did not sustain an injury arising out of and in the course of her employment and that she was not an employee of Home Distributors.

IN THE SUPREME COURT, STATE OF TEXARKANA
NOTICE OF APPEAL

Notice is hereby given that Jane White appeals from the order of the Common Pleas Court denying her the right to participate in the worker's compensation fund of the State of Texarkana.

THE STATUTE

3142.52   Compensation in case of injury

Every employee who is injured in the course of employment wherever such injury has occurred, provided the same was not purposely self inflicted, is entitled to receive * * * such compensation for loss sustained on account of such injury.

3142.01   Definitions

As used in Chapter 3142 of the Revised Code:

(A) "Employee" or "worker" means:

(1) Every person in the service of any person, firm, or private corporation, including any public service corporation, that employs one or more workers regularly in the same business or in or about the same establishment under any contract of hire, express or implied, oral or written, including aliens and minors. * * *

(B) "Employer" means:

(1) Every person, firm, and private corporation, including any public service corporation, that has in service one or more workers

regularly in the same business or in or about the same establishment under any contract of hire, express or implied, oral or written.
* * *

(C) "Injury" includes any injury to the physical structure of the body whether caused by external, accidental means or accidental in character and result, received in the course of, and arising out of, the injured employee's employment.

3142.59   Appeal to court of common pleas.

The claimant or the employer may appeal a decision of the industrial commission in any injury case, other than a decision as to the extent of disability, to the court of common pleas of the county in which the injury was inflicted or in which the contract of employment was made if the injury occurred outside the state.

    A.   Representing Jane White, examine the record as given.

        1.   What are the facts that gave rise to the case?

        2.   What potential legal questions will be raised?

    B.   Do a preliminary outline of the record.

    C.   Devise a research plan to answer the legal questions involved in the case. Consider:

        1.   Constitutional issues;

        2.   Statutes involved;

        3.   Case law;

        4.   Administrative rules and regulations;

        5.   Rules of court;

        6.   Secondary sources.

    D.   Pick a theme for the brief.

    E.   Do a preliminary outline for the brief.

II.   Rarely is a case on appeal ever one-sided. Having examined the record in depth, take the respondent's side of the argument and:

    A.   Pick a theme for the respondent's brief;

    B.   Do a preliminary outline.

III.   Is the outline different for the respondent's brief and the petitioner's brief? If so, why or why not?

Chapter Six

WRITING THE OPENING BRIEF

Analysis

6.00 INTRODUCTION

Before the actual task of writing the brief begins, the advocate should carefully consider the primary audience for whom the brief will be written—the judges of the appellate court. First and foremost, remember that judges are both lawyers and human. As such, they react from both perspectives to what is presented to them. They must first become interested in the case and then convinced that justice and equity favor the advocate's side. Cold, lifeless syllogisms will not succeed. Instead, the goal is to spark their interest at the outset and hold that interest throughout the reading of the document.

As a lawyer, the advocate should consider what would arouse one's own interest in a brief. For most people, the human features of the case command the greatest attention. Therefore, sterile legal issues unconnected to the "people" aspect likely will not seize the reader's interest or attention.

Judges have little patience with poorly written documents. Inadequately written briefs distract the reader and divert attention from the real issues. Incompetent writing comes in many forms—poor grammar, improper sentence and paragraph structure, misspellings, and sloppy organization are constant offenders. The limitations on judges' time make it difficult from the outset to get a comprehensive reading of one's brief. Do not make the task even more daunting than it needs to be. Make the brief interesting, and easy to read.

6.01   Brief writing goals

The writer should formulate several goals when planning and writing the brief. The following concepts are essential to a good brief:

Accuracy. All aspects of the brief must be scrupulously accurate. This applies from the statement of the facts to the use of authority. Because the facts are at the beginning of the brief, the judge will quickly assess the truthfulness of the advocate. As discussed in § 5.56, although it is in the client's interest to portray the facts most favorably, distorting them asks for trouble. Legal authority must reflect accurately the meaning of a case. Misrepresenting the holding, or any aspect of a case, will result in loss of confidence by the court.

Clarity and precision. Persuasive writing must be clear and precise. Long garbled sentences often result in complex and unclear long paragraphs. These are the antithesis of good legal writing. Judges want to read and understand the content of the brief. They do not have time to decipher ambiguous structures, either in word or syntax. There will be no second or third reading. Ambiguous words also provide ammunition for the opponent, who will construe them to his or her advantage.

Brevity and conciseness. As explored in § 1.20, most judges are overworked. They appreciate briefs to the point, not rambling, redundant or regressive. A good brief presents the most important issues with the least amount of verbiage. A strong outline promotes both brevity and conciseness.

Simplicity. This quality is appreciated by all. Far too many lawyers assume that judges are experts in all areas of the law. This may be a fatal error. With the rising complexity of the law, the need for simplicity is paramount. Do not assume a judge understands the intricacies of the Internal Revenue Code or the complicated regulations that drive many aspects of environmental law. Step back and ask, "[a]s a lawyer, who is unfamiliar with this topic, what is it that I must explain so that the issue is understood?" At times a simple paraphrase of the section or regulation is helpful. Keep the writing and constructs as simple as possible.

Creativity. A creative argument is more likely to be read with interest. Imagine a slightly different twist to present the material. Many times, equity and policy arguments can be creative. A novel theory or way of thinking about a topic is welcome. Again, do not distort the issues, but do present them with some flare.

Conviction. The appellate lawyer is an advocate. As such, he or she must believe in the cause. That should be abundantly clear throughout the brief. Persuasion of others is highly improbable if the writer is unconvinced. Lack of conviction will be discerned.

6.02   Component parts of the brief

Court rules govern the form and content of the brief. The body of the brief always contains four main parts.

1.   Question(s) Presented or Statement of the Issues

2.   Statement of the Facts or Statement of the Case

3.   Argument

4.   Conclusion

Most courts require other elements as well. It is not uncommon for the court rules to call for a Table of Contents, an alphabetized Table of Cases, a Table of Statutes and Other Authorities, a Summary of the Argument and the like. To illustrate the divergence of the requirements, a comparison of the rules for brief content in the Second Circuit and those of the Fifth Circuit is instructive. The Second Circuit generally follows Rule 28 of the Federal Rules of Appellate Procedure, with the addition of two local rules that read:

1.   Briefs must be compact, logically arranged with proper headings, concise, and free from burdensome, irrelevant, immaterial, and scandalous matter. Briefs not complying with this rule may be disregarded and stricken by the court.

2.   Appellant's brief shall include, as a preliminary statement, the name of the judge or agency member who rendered the decision appealed from and, if the judge's decision or supporting opinion is reported, the citation thereof.

Another local rule specifies the size type to be used and mandates that the cover indicate on whose behalf the brief is filed.

The Fifth Circuit, on the other hand, devotes several pages to additional rules peculiar to that circuit. The length is carefully controlled, and the contents are very specific. All briefs must contain: a "certificate of interested persons"[1]; a summary of argument which should not be a "mere repetition of the headings under which the argument is arranged" and should seldom exceed two and never five pages; record references; request for oral argument; statement of jurisdiction; and the standard of review. The rule then states the order in which the contents are to appear, as governed by Rule 28 of the Federal Rules of Appellate Procedure and this local rule:

Certificate of interested persons, if required

Statement regarding oral argument

Table of contents

Table of authorities with page references

Statement of jurisdiction

---

1.   A certificate of interested persons is to be filed on the first page of each brief before the table of contents or index and certifies a complete list of all persons, * * * who or which are financially interested in the outcome of the litigation * * *.

Statement of issues

Statement of the case

Course of proceedings and disposition in the court below

Statement of facts

Summary of the argument

Argument including standards of review

Conclusion

Certificate of service

Fortunately, for the beleaguered lawyer who is trying to comply, a note following the rules states that upon request the clerk will loan counsel sample briefs and appendices which comply with the form prescribed and a copy of the checklist used by the clerk to examine the briefs to determine if they are acceptable. Once again, the password is examine the rules. The consequences of noncompliance may be disastrous. Judges have little tolerance for attorneys who fail to comply with the court rules. Failure to comply may result in disciplinary sanctions against the attorney, striking the brief from the record, taxing costs to the errant attorney, and outright dismissal of the appeal, to name a few. Careful attention to the court rules is time well spent.

6.10 PRELIMINARY REQUIREMENTS

Several parts of the brief help organize the material, set a context and generally inform the court what is requested of it. Many of these parts are required by court rules.[2]

6.11 The cover page

The cover page provides the court valuable information. It must conform to the rules of court. Rule 32 of the Federal Rules of Appellate Procedure indicates generally the colors for the cover of the brief. The information found on the cover page usually includes:

(1) the name of the appellate court to which the brief is addressed;

(2) the name of the court or agency that rendered the decision below;

(3) the names of the parties involved in the appeal with their appropriate designation, i.e. appellate, appellee, petitioner or respondent;

(4) the docket number of the case;

(5) the term in which the court is to consider the appeal;

(6) the nature of the proceeding (e.g., Appeal; Petition for Review);

2. *See* Fed. R. App. P. 28.

(7) the title of the document (e.g. Brief for Appellant);

(8) the names and addresses of counsel representing the party on whose behalf the document is filed.

Because the cover page is the first impression that the judge has of the brief and the case, care should be taken to make it as attractive as possible. Appendices C and D present excellent cover page examples.

6.12 Table of contents

Most people think of a table of contents as a list of the topics that will be covered with the appropriate reference to the page on which the topic begins. Few think that argument points can be made in this section of the brief. Not so.

The table of contents is either the second or third element of the brief seen by the reader. First is the title page or cover. Then, depending on whether the question(s) presented precede the remainder of the brief, the table of contents appears. The table of contents is the advocate's first opportunity to begin arguing the case. It consists of all of the point headings and sub-headings that appear throughout the brief. One circuit makes it mandatory that the point headings and sub-headings be reproduced in full in the table of contents. This is the standard in most appellate courts.

The point headings precede the actual argument and serve to introduce the reader to the issues about to be argued. These point headings are succinct argumentative statements that relate to the specific legal principles that follow in the argument. As such, they present the entire argument in capsule form. After reading the table of contents, the judge should understand the client's position and have good reason to decide the issues favorable to that position. See Appendices C and D for an illustration of the power of the table of contents.

6.13 Table of authorities

The table of authorities presents the citations to the legal materials used in the brief and the page or pages on which they appear. The table should be scrupulously accurate as to citation form and page number cites. A judge will often return to the table for a reference to the page in the brief where a specific case or statute is discussed. If the page number is incorrect, the judge will be forced to search through the brief. This quickly becomes irritating.

The key is to make the table of authorities user-friendly. The best approach is to first list the cases, in alphabetical order. Constitutional provisions are next, followed by any statutory provisions. The last section should include those materials that are not primary in nature. These may include citations to treatises, law review articles, empirical studies, restatements and the like. Each section should be carefully labeled and highlighted in some fashion. Remember: the reader is still forming a first impression of the brief. The table of authorities is one of the first items encountered in the brief.

6.14 Statement regarding oral argument

Rule 34 of the Federal Rules of Appellate Procedure is the basic rule for the federal circuit courts but specifies it is subject to local rule. Increasingly, circuits are requiring that counsel specifically state that oral argument is requested and why it is necessary. A typical rule appears in the Fifth Circuit local rules and reads:

> Counsel for appellant must include in a preamble to appellant's principle brief a short statement why oral argument would be helpful, or a statement that appellant waives oral argument. Appellee's counsel must likewise include in appellee's brief a statement why oral argument is or is not needed. The court will give these statements due, though not controlling, weight in determining whether to hold oral argument.[3]

Other circuits require that each party "file a statement not to exceed one page providing a summary of the case, the reasons why oral argument should or should not be heard, and the amount of time * * * necessary to present the argument."[4] State court rules likewise differ. Care must be taken to ascertain if it is necessary to request oral argument, should counsel deem it necessary. Failure to make the request in the brief may result in waiver of the oral argument component.

6.15 Special requirements

In addition to the foregoing, many courts mandate other specific requirements. For example, the District of Columbia Circuit requires that the brief contain a glossary of terms that define each abbreviation if the abbreviation is not well known.[5] In the First Circuit, case citations must include both the State or Commonwealth cite, plus the national reporter citation.[6] The Third Circuit is very specific about citations. If, for example, a United States Supreme Court case is cited, the citation should be to the official reports; if not available, the cite should be to the West reporter, and if not available in West to the Lawyers Cooperative reporter.[7] If the case is found only in Law Week, specific information is required to be shown in the citation.[8]

The Fourth Circuit advises the parties that if the name of an attorney appears on the brief, that person must argue the case in the event that the lead counsel cannot.[9] The Seventh Circuit cautions that no argument or comment is allowed in the statement of the facts—just a fair summary.[10] The Eighth Circuit does not allow a party to incorporate by reference the contents of a brief filed elsewhere.[11] while the Eleventh Circuit requires counsel who adopts by reference to include a statement describing in detail the portions so adopted by reference.[12]

---

3. 5th Cir. R. 28.2.4.

4. 8th Cir. R. 28A(f)(1).

5. *See* D.C. Cir. R. 28(a)(3).

6. *See* 1st Cir. R. 32.2.

7. *See* 3d Cir. R. 28.3(a).

8. *Id.*

9. *See* 4th Cir. R. 28(c).

10. *See* 7th Cir. R. 28(c).

11. *See* 8th Cir. R. 28A(g).

12. *See* 11th Cir. R. 28–1(f).

Many of the circuits have specific rules that relate to particular kinds of cases. For example, bankruptcy, patent and Tax Court cases have other special requirements.

6.20 STATEMENT OF SUBJECT MATTER AND APPELLATE JURISDICTION

In the federal system, all circuits require that the parties indicate the court's jurisdiction to hear the appeal, as specified by the Federal Rules of Appellate Procedure.[13] Most of the circuits require a separate section that is specifically entitled "statement of subject matter and appellate jurisdiction." Some circuits, such as the Eleventh Circuit keep it simple: "Each brief shall include a concise statement of the statutory or other basis of the jurisdiction of this court, containing citations of authority when necessary."[14] Still others specify, in great detail, what must be incorporated in the jurisdictional statement.[15] Failure to include all that is necessary may result in the brief being stricken from the record.

6.30 PRELIMINARY STATEMENT OR NATURE OF THE PROCEEDING

Most appellate courts do not require a separate Preliminary Statement, which is also labeled as The Nature of the Proceeding. At the federal level, the requirement has been eliminated in all circuits. The information formerly contained in the Preliminary Statement is essentially the jurisdictional statement required by the Federal Rules of Appellate Procedure.[16]

For those courts that require this statement, the information contained in it is basically the procedural history of the case and the general nature of the proceeding. It is the first account of the case that members of the court read. It informs them of the cause of action and provides them a quick overview of what transpired below. If there is no preliminary statement, as is the case in the United States Supreme Court, that information should be included at the beginning of the Statement of the Case. Information contained in the preliminary statement includes:

1. the party taking the appeal;

2. the court from which the appeal is being taken;

3. whether there was a trial in the matter;

4. whether the matter was tried to a judge or jury;

5. the disposition of the case below; and

6. other relevant information that would indicate the nature of the proceeding.

13. *See* Fed. R. App. P. 28(a)(4).

14. *See* 11th Cir. R. 28–1(g).

15. *See* 7th Cir. R. 28(a).

16. *See* Fed. R. App. P. 28(a)(4).

6.40 QUESTIONS PRESENTED AND STATEMENT OF THE IS- SUES

6.41 Placement

Court rules may dictate where the question(s) presented are placed. For example, in briefs to the Supreme Court of the United States, the questions presented precede all other matter, including the table of contents.[17] The general rule for the various federal circuits is that the "statement of the issues presented for review" follows the table of contents, table of authorities and the jurisdictional statement.[18] If there is no court rule with respect to placement, the general rule of thumb is to put the questions presented early in the brief. If a preliminary statement is used, the questions presented should follow that statement but appear before the statement of the facts. By placing the issues to be decided by the court in this position, the court is better able to appreciate the significance of the statement of the facts. In other words, the questions presented develop a context within which the court can more easily understand the importance of the facts. Remember: the judges want to know quickly what the issues are and what they are called upon to decide.

6.42 Purpose of the questions presented

The questions presented actually have three purposes. First, they identify and describe the legal issue raised by the case on appeal. They specify what must be decided by the appellate court. They emphasize to the court the matters that are vital to the case.

Second, the questions presented serve to inform the court about the case. Because the questions are strategically placed, they introduce the essence of the case. The statement should provide the broad picture so that the facts and arguments can be more easily understood. To that end, it is necessary to provide sufficient factual information to describe the issue. An abstract legal issue must be given substance and solidity. For example, "[d]id the complaint state a cause of action?" lends little assistance to a judge's understanding the issue. A better approach is to interweave the facts that prompted the dismissal of the complaint, the wording of which will subtly suggest the answer desired by the advocate. It might read: "Did the complaint state a cause of action when the contract between the plaintiff-lessee and the defendant-lessor specifically required the lessor to make repairs to the property in the event of fire?"

Third, as suggested by the previous sentence, while the questions presented must be scrupulously accurate, they can serve as a persuasive device. Subtle wording that suggests a favorable outcome is the hallmark of a good question. In the following two examples, each fairly states the issue, but each might induce a judge to come to a different answer. The matter at issue was whether the President of the United States is entitled to postpone litigation on a private matter that preceded his

---

17. *See* Sup. Ct. R. 24.1(a).   **18.** *See* Fed. R. App. P. 28(a)(5).

presidency, during his term of office. Counsel for the petitioner, President Clinton, stated the question as follows:

> Whether the litigation of a private civil damages action against an incumbent President must in all but the most exceptional cases be deferred until the President leaves office.

This wording suggests that the answer to the question should be "yes" because (1) the case deals with an incumbent President and (2) such an action would be only in "the most exceptional cases," a situation that counsel will argue is not present.

The counsel for the respondent, on the other hand, stated the question as follows:

> Whether the court of appeals erred in holding that petitioner was not entitled as a matter of law to a postponement or a stay of all proceedings for the duration of his presidency, when such a postponement or stay would effectively operate as a grant of official immunity for acts beyond "the outer perimeter of [the President's] official responsibility," the limit for presidential immunity set forth in *Nixon v. Fitzgerald,* 457 U.S. 731 (1982).

This language suggests the matter not be postponed, because it would amount to giving the petitioner immunity beyond the scope established in a previous case that considered presidential immunity.

6.43   The length of the question presented

Many times in an attempt to get "everything" in the question presented, the entire question collapses of its own weight and becomes meaningless. The idea is to include enough facts to explain the legal issue. Too many facts clutter the question and cloud the issue. Too few facts leave the reader with no context. For example, in the follow question presented, most readers will be totally perplexed and simply quit reading in the middle of the text.

> Should the judgment of the district court setting aside the order of the state Corporation Commission dated October 3, 1957 denying the application of Alfredo Gonzales, transferor and Bekins Van and Storage Company, Inc., transferee, of a portion of certificate of public convenience and necessity No. 739, be reversed for the reason that said order of the Commission is in all respects reasonable and lawful, having been entered pursuant to the Commission's power to approve or disapprove a proposed transfer as the public interest may require, and upon a finding that said transfer would not be in the public interest?

That question would better be replaced by the following:

> Was the state Corporation Commission's order denying permission to transfer the certificate of convenience and necessity lawful, reasonable and supported by substantial evidence, and therefore, did the district court err in setting it aside?

If need be, use more than one question, especially if there are two very distinct issues. Rarely should more than two questions be used.[19] If there appear to be four or five questions presented, ways to tie one or more of them together should be examined. Often, several questions or sub-points can be combined to address a basic issue. For example, from the Clinton case, the respondent had to deal with several issues that include the following:

1. Did the court of appeals err in holding that petitioner is not entitled as a matter of law to a postponement or stay of all proceedings for the duration of his presidency?

2. If such a stay is allowed, would it effectively act as a grant of official immunity to the suit?

3. Should such a stay be allowed when the question involved in the lawsuit is one which had nothing to do with presidential responsibilities?

4. Would such immunity be beyond the scope set forth in *Nixon v. Fitzgerald*, 457 U.S. 731 (1982)?

In the end, the respondent presented one succinct question presented as set out in § 6.42.

The best way to write an effective question that takes into account several facts and points of law is to make a list of what should be included. In the question above, the four listed components needed to be included. By reducing them to their component parts, it is easier for the writer to see the big picture and then put together a comprehensive yet understandable question presented.

Unfortunately, this section of the brief is often a shear waste of paper. Brief writers, unaware of the potential for powerful advocacy, simply toss them together in the final stages of assembling the brief. The previous sections have alluded to some of the problems.

To review, many questions presented are too general and do not include sufficient information to be useful. Some questions are so long and cumbersome that the reader will give up in mid-question and turn to the opponent's brief to ascertain the issues. At times, there are too many questions. If counsel discovers that four or five issues appear important, he or she should look for a common thread to tie some of the issues together. And, of course, avoid the rhetorical question that is really a non-question. If there is only one obvious way to answer the question, it is likely either too general or a rhetorical question.

6.44   The use of "whether" questions

This author has long advocated that the use of "whether" questions should be avoided. However, the fact that the practice is wide spread

---

19. Large complex cases that present multiple claims may require more questions   presented.

indicates that "whether" questions are accepted and, in many instances, are the preferred form.

There are two reasons why "whether" questions are problematic. First, beginning the question with "whether" results in an ungrammatical sentence. When one of the first sentences of the brief (in the Supreme Court of the United States, the first sentence) is ungrammatical, it potentially sets a distasteful tone for parties who adhere to the rules of grammar. Second, questions that begin with "whether" suggest there may be more than one outcome. The purpose of the question presented is to advocate the client's position through persuasive wording. A "whether" question is neutral or objective.

Compare the following two questions that illustrate the difference between a question beginning with "whether" and one that begins with a verb.

Question 1

Whether a district court, as a proper exercise of judicial discretion, may stay such litigation until the President leaves office.

Question 2

Should a district court, as a proper exercise of its judicial discretion, stay litigation until the President leaves office?

The first question appears weaker and more tedious than the second. For persons offended by ungrammatical constructions, the first question becomes even more ineffective.

6.45 A check list for an effective question presented

In the formulation of the questions presented, one will make this portion of the brief more meaningful by adherence to the following checklist:

     1.   The question must be understandable on a first reading;

     2.   The question must be fact specific;

     3.   The question must eliminate excessive detail (keep it simple);

     4.   The question must accurately state the issue; and

     5.   The question should be worded to suggest a positive answer for the position advocated.

6.50 THE STATEMENT OF THE CASE

6.51 The importance of the facts

The importance of the facts is best expressed by the Honorable John W. Davis in his now famous article *The Argument of An Appeal* when he said, "[i]n an appellate court the statement of the facts is not merely a part of the argument, it is more often than not the argument itself. A case well stated is a case far more than half argued."[20] It is, in many respects, the most important part of the brief. Too often, however, the facts are relegated to the last part of the brief written, usually at crunch time and with little consideration of their ultimate impact. As Wiener stated "[t]he greatest mistake any lawyer can make, after he has written a fine brief on the law, is to toss in a dry statement of facts and send the thing off to the printer."[21]

The importance of a well conceived and written set of facts cannot be over-emphasized. The expression *ex facto jus oritur*—the law arises out of the fact—expresses the basic tenet. A case is never decided on "the law" but rather if and how "the law" is applied to a set of facts. Justice Robert H. Jackson underscored the role of the facts when he stated:

> It may sound paradoxical, but most contentions of law are won or lost on the facts. The facts often incline a judge to one side or the other. A large part of the time of conference is given to discussion of facts, to determine under what rule of law they fall. Dissents are not usually rooted in disagreement as to a rule of law but as to whether the facts warrant its application.[22]

The court has only the advocates' recitations of the facts by which to formulate the law of the case. The power of a well-stated set of facts is formidable.

6.52 Identification of the facts

Facts come in two varieties—substantive and procedural. Both are important to the decision in the case. Procedural facts inform the reader how the case made its way through the court system. Substantive facts relate what happened prior to the litigation. As discussed in § 6.30, many courts require that the brief writer separate the procedural facts, i.e., the preliminary statement or nature of the proceeding, from the statement of the substantive facts. If the court rules do not require a separate procedural statement, care should be taken to include both the substance and procedure of the case.

6.53 Choice of facts

The record of the case may well consist of hundreds of pages of material. From that, the advocate must pick which facts to present and which facts to omit. Those chosen should be relevant to the issues and equities of the case. Only the pertinent facts which will have an impact on the issues on appeal should appear in the Statement of the Case. Within the bounds of accuracy, the most favorable facts should be chosen and stressed.

---

20. John W. Davis, *The Argument of an Appeal*, 26 A.B.A.J. 895, 896 (1940).

21. Frederick Bernays Wiener, Briefing and Arguing Federal Appeals 44 (1967).

22. Robert H. Jackson, *Advocacy Before the Supreme Court: Suggestions for Effective Case Presentations*, 37 A.B.A.J. 801, 803 (1951).

Perhaps the best way to determine the pertinent facts is to list those facts that are essential to support the advocate's theme or theory of the case, including facts the court must have before it to make a determination favorable to the advocate's case. Usually other explanatory facts are necessary in order for the story to be coherent. Those can be added. What one must avoid are facts that add nothing to the narrative and confuse the story line.

Consider for example the case of *James Kirkland Batson, Petitioner, vs. Kentucky, Respondent* in which the prosecutor exercised four of his six peremptory challenges to strike all black veniremen from the panel of a black defendant.[23] What follows is the Statement of the Case as presented by the Petitioner, Batson. Which facts are necessary, which are explanatory, and which simply are not needed and perhaps confuse the matter?

This case commenced by the return of Indictment No. 82–CR–0010 by the Jefferson County, Kentucky, Grand Jury on January 6, 1982. (Transcript of Record (TR, p. 1–3). That Indictment alleged that Batson committed the offenses of second degree burglary and receipt of stolen property valued at more than $100 (TR, p. 1)). The Indictment charged also that Petitioner was a second-degree persistent felony offender and liable to enhanced punishment upon conviction for the two substantive offenses.

In support of the first charge, the prosecution introduced a Mrs. Spencer who lived in the house where the break-in occurred. She saw Petitioner Batson crouched down in another room of her house. Then Batson and her purse containing watches, rings and cash disappeared. (Transcript of Evidence (TE, p. 19–22). The second charge was supported by the testimony of a pawnbroker who said that Batson and another pawned property taken from Mrs. Spencer. This was done shortly after the break-in. (TE, p. 135–139; 140) Trial was had in Jefferson Circuit Court on February 14–15, 1984. (TR, p. 211) Batson was convicted both of burglary and of receipt of stolen property. (TR, p. 212). Because he was found to be a persistent felony offender (TR, p. 212), Batson was sentenced to a term of 20 years imprisonment by Judgment dated March 20, 1984. (TR, p. 222–223)).

The error complained of here occurred after the jury had been examined and challenged on voir dire and after the peremptory strikes had been made by counsel. (TE, p. 5; TR, p. 119–120). Batson's trial lawyer moved to discharge the panel on the ground that all four black jurors who had been included in the venire had been struck by the prosecutor's preemptory challenge and that an all white jury resulted. Under those circumstances, counsel continued, Petitioner was denied "his right to an impartial trial [sic], a cross-section of the community under the Sixth and Fourteenth Amendments. He's also being denied equal protection of the law

---

23. *Batson v. Kentucky,* 476 U.S. 79 (1986).

under the United States Constitution. And he's also being denied a fair impartial trial." (TE, p. 6; App., p. 3).

In a colloquy with the prosecutor and with the trial judge, Batson's lawyer elicited the following statements:

> Does the Court agree—essentially, the facts I'd want to establish at a hearing are, number one, that there were four black jurors on the panel and that the Commonwealth exercised its pre-emptories [sic] as to those, all four black jurors.
>
> THE COURT: We, they can do it if they want to.
>
> Q: Do you accept that as true? Is that accurate, Mr. Gutmann?
>
> A: Yeah, during this particular—yeah. I struck four blacks and two whites.
>
> Q: Okay. And that this left an all-white jury. Is that right?
>
> A: In looking at them, yes; it's an all-white jury. (TE, p. 7–8; App., p. 3.) (Footnote: Batson of course is a black man)

To Batson's renewed arguments about denial of equal protection of the law, of fair cross-section of the community and fair and impartial jury, the trial judge stated that those complaints were relevant only to the selection of the panel, not to the selection of the petit jury for a particular case. (TE, p. 7; App., p. 3–4). The objection to swearing the jury and the motion to set aside the panel were overruled. (TE, p. 8; App., p. 4). The jury was sworn and returned verdicts of guilty as to all three charges contained in the Indictment. (TE, p. 9; App., p. 4; TR, p. 211).

An examination of this set of facts is probative. The material contained in Paragraph I is explanatory in nature. While those facts appear dry and somewhat lifeless, they are procedural and necessary to understand the background of the case. Much of paragraph II however, except for the information about the trial and its outcome, contains facts that are not necessary to the outcome of the case. One sentence requires more than one reading to understand and makes little sense as written.[24]

The heart of the case is stated in paragraph III. There the attorney asserts the basis of his claim. How effectively he makes his points will be considered later in this section. The colloquy the attorney describes is interesting, but not necessary. It appears its purpose was to emphasize the point that the judge and opposing counsel were little concerned with the outcome of the jury selection. The last paragraph gives the trial judge's rationale for the decision and, though not handled particularly well, is necessary information about the case.

Again, to maximize the impact of the facts, the advocate must decide what facts the court must have to make a decision, what facts help set a context or explain those that are necessary, and what facts can be

---

24. In the middle of the paragraph the writer says "[t]he second charge was supported by the testimony of a pawnbroker who said that Batson and another pawned property taken from Mrs. Spencer."

eliminated. The facts to be included should be outlined. The advocate can then decide how best to organize and present them.

6.54   Organization of the facts

Facts are usually presented either chronologically or topically. There are champions of both methods. The truth is, the case will dictate which approach to take. Remember: the advocate must try to tell a convincing story.

If dates and times are important to the story line, a chronological approach probably is best. Judges, like most of us, understand linear development. Chronology lends itself to this approach. For example, if the case involves a worker's compensation claim, the circumstances of the injury along with dates are important to establish a valid case.

If, however, the case is a complex one in which chronology plays a minimal role, the facts are best developed topically. A topical arrangement allows the advocate to separate the relevant material into easily assimilated sections. For example, in a corporate takeover, pre-takeover facts may set the stage. The takeover effort may follow. The resultant litigation constitutes the last part of the facts. This type of scenario often requires the use of subdivisions within the facts. This approach allows the reader to assimilate the facts in chunks. However, care must be taken not to overuse sub-headings, because the result can be a choppy, unconnected set of facts that leaves the reader confused.

Word to the wise: never march through the record simply summarizing the testimony of each witness as he or she appeared at the trial and the facts as they appear in the transcript.[25] At times, the facts developed at trial do not lend themselves to either a chronological or a topical approach. Without careful reconstruction, facts simply become a mishmash that quickly sends the judge to the opponent's brief to determine what really happened.

6.55   Presentation of the facts

The most important part of the Statement of Case is its opening few lines. The writer should capture the reader's attention in the beginning passages. Never begin with unimportant, unfavorable or uninteresting facts. A good example of how NOT to begin a Statement of Case is illustrated above in the *Batson* case. Recall that the opening line was "[t]his case was commenced by the return of Indictment No. 82–CR–0010 by the Jefferson County, Kentucky Grand Jury on January 6, 1982." A reader's first reaction is probably "so what?" A better opening is "[t]his case presents a collision of two important criminal concepts: the right of a prosecutor to make peremptory challenges versus the right of a defendant to be tried impartially by a fair cross-section of the community." This opening tells the judge the nature of the case and the

---

25. Check the court rules with respect to reproducing the witnesses' testimony in the brief. Some states actually require an abstract or summary of the pertinent testimony. This is, however, the exception.

facts to consider later. Hopefully, the first sentence makes a lasting impression.

Once the advocate has a strong start, the momentum must not be lost. It is essential to a good set of facts that the story be interesting. Many advocates lose the judges by a recitation of boring facts. Keep the pace lively. Paint a picture easy to visualize, much like an author who crafts an unfolding scene of a story. Remember: a judge's acquisition of knowledge is ongoing and cumulative. The advocate should consider how the judge would best assimilate the story. Set a context, develop the main theme and fill in the details later.

Consider once again the earlier portrayal of facts from the *Batson* case. After a dull beginning, the second paragraph also leaves much to be desired. Recall it begins with:

> [i]n support of the first charge, the prosecution introduced a Mrs. Spencer who lived in the house where the break-in occurred. She saw Petitioner Batson crouched down in another room of her house. Then Batson and her purse containing watches, rings and cash disappeared.

The first mistake is to refer to the witness as "a Mrs. Spencer," a term that dehumanizes her and suggests she is one of many Mrs. Spencers.[26] With respect to the second sentence, one is left to wonder how she happened upon Mr. Batson, how he entered the house, where he was crouched, and what happened then. The last sentence suggests total mystery. How, if Mrs. Spencer was watching a crouched Batson, did her purse, Batson and all the contents of her purse disappear?

Perhaps the aim of the Petitioner was to minimize the break-in and the theft, though that matter was not at issue. But the writer risks losing the reader by a confusing and uninteresting narration.

The following is offered as a substitute. It does not place Mr. Batson in a worse scenario but merely clarifies what happened.

> In support of the first charge, the prosecution introduced Nancy Spencer, who lived in the house where the break-in occurred. She testified that when she exited her kitchen, she saw Mr. Batson crouching in the dining room behind the credenza. She returned to the kitchen to call 911. Upon reentering the dining room, she discovered that Mr. Batson and her purse were gone. Her purse contained watches, rings and cash.

In deciding which facts to use and how to present them, try always to accentuate the positive and de-emphasize the negative, all within the bounds of accuracy. Take for example the following case:

---

26. Take care not to refer to the parties as appellant or appellee, plaintiff or defendant. The designations may be very confusing. The Federal Rules of Appellate Procedure limit such designations in the body of the brief. *See* Fed. R. App. P. 28(d). Always humanize the client. Make him or her a live body with a story to tell. The facts will be easier to follow and much more interesting.

Two college students live next door to each other in a dormitory. Bob is a morning person, and Jim is a night person. Jim studies best late at night with sound in the background. Bob, the early riser, is a light sleeper. Therein the problem.

On the night of May 10, 1998, Jim was studying next door with Axel Red, a heavy metal band, playing in the background. Bob was trying to sleep with little success. Finally, Bob went next door and asked Jim to turn his music down. A scuffle ensued and, Jim's jaw was broken.

If one represents Bob's interests, the facts might be stated in the following manner:

During the course of the year, Bob and Jim have been next-door neighbors in Caldwell Hall on the Old Drake campus. Jim is known to study late while playing music. Most of Jim's classes are in the afternoon, which allows him to sleep late in the morning. Bob, on the other hand, attends early morning classes. He is a light sleeper.

In the past, Bob and Jim have had words about the loud music late at night. On the night of May 10, Bob was trying to get to sleep, having spent most of the evening in the library studying for an 8:00 a.m. exam scheduled for the following day. Next door, Jim was loudly playing a heavy metal album. The loud "music" made it impossible for Bob to sleep.

After 45 minutes of enduring the noise, Bob knocked on Jim's door to request that he turn the "music" off or at least lower the noise. Jim informed Bob that he had the music turned down as much as possible and demanded that Bob leave. When Bob did not immediately respond, Jim pushed him into the door. To defend himself against further assault, Bob raised his right arm, striking Jim under the chin.

Jim is suing for damages from the injury.

An attorney representing Jim might state the facts in the following manner:

During the course of the year, Bob and Jim have been next-door neighbors in Caldwell Hall on the Old Drake campus. Jim usually studies late with the aid of background music.

On the night of May 10, Jim was studying in his dorm room. He was listening to a new album when Bob knocked on the door. He insisted that Jim turn down the music because it was keeping him awake. Jim explained that the music was turned as low as possible for him to hear it. Bob again commanded that the music be turned down. Jim, seeing that the conversation was going nowhere, asked Bob to leave. When Bob did not start for the door, Jim nudged him in that direction. Bob swung at Jim, struck him in the chin and broke his jaw.

Jim is suing for damages as a result of the attack.

Each set of facts tells basically the same story. Bob's lawyer details more facts to paint a more sympathetic picture of his client. Jim's attorney, on the other hand, chooses facts that are more positive for his client and eliminates or de-emphasizes those facts that are potentially harmful. Keep in mind, however, all essential facts pertinent to the issues must be presented. To omit facts that are unfavorable is to invite trouble. As Wiener has said "[g]rasp your nettles firmly."[27] Tell the court what it needs to know to make a fair and just decision.

6.56 The essentials of a good statement of the case

A cardinal rule for stating the facts is that the writer must maintain objectivity. The Statement of the Case can still be persuasive, but must also be objective. The use of value-laden terms that over-emphasize some facts and minimize others is not appropriate.

The facts must be scrupulously accurate. If the court discovers misstatements or omissions, it will turn to the opponent's brief to determine what really happened. Confidence in the advocate will be lost, and the remainder of the assertions may be discounted. As Wiener noted "[t]he mark of really able advocacy is the ability to set forth the facts most favorably within the limits of utter and unswerving accuracy."[28]

While commentators agree that the Statement of the Case must be objective, not argumentative, and scrupulously accurate, all assert that an advocate should make every attempt to persuade through favorable wording. The choice of words may have a powerful effect on how the facts are interpreted. For example, in a brief advocating abortion rights, an advocate likely will refer to the unborn as a "fetus." The term is fairly neutral. On the other hand, anti-abortionists likely will call it a "child," a term which suggests a very different connotation. In a right-to-life case in which the issue was whether to discontinue sustenance, the pro-life party spoke of "starving" the comatose woman. The opposition referred to the same act as "withholding fluids."[29]

One word of caution: the use of connotations to produce a more favorable spin on the facts is perfectly acceptable; the use of pejoratives is not. By using value-laden words, usually adjectives, the facts take on a subjective characterization. This is to be avoided.

While choice of words is important to paint a favorable picture, choice of facts is equally important. Not all facts can be included in the Statement of the Case. The trick is to choose the most pertinent facts with care, then accurately and objectively portray them.

Consider, for example, the case of *William Jefferson Clinton v. Paula Corbin Jones*.[30] The first line in the Statement of the Case for Mr. Clinton reads "[p]etitioner William Jefferson Clinton is the President of the United States." The first line in the Statement of the Case for Ms.

27. Wiener, *supra* note 21, at 50.

28. *Id*. at 49.

29. *Cruzan v. Director, Mo. Dep't of Health*, 497 U.S. 261 (1990).

30. 520 U.S. 681 (1997).

Jones reads "[i]n Arkansas on May 8, 1991, respondent Paula Corbin Jones was a $6.35–an-hour state employee, and petitioner William Jefferson Clinton was the Governor." As illustrated in Appendix D, Jones' Statement of the Case details what allegedly transpired in the hotel room on the day in question. Further, it develops in detail events after the alleged meeting. Mr. Clinton's Statement makes no mention of any of these details. His attorneys concentrate almost exclusively on the procedural aspects of the case.[31] This is a classic case of two briefs, two fact statements, each with very different emphasis but both dealing with the same issues.

In summary, a good Statement of the Case is accurate, objective and persuasive. It tells an interesting and informative story. Because the facts *are* the case, a solid Statement of the Case is of paramount importance.

6.57 Citation to the record

Each fact requires a record cite. This is mandated by most court rules when citing within the Statement of the Case and the Argument.[32] In addition, careful citation to the record indicates thoroughness on the part of the advocate who prepared the facts.

Cites to the record can be a type of persuasive tool. Each cite tells the reader that there is support in the record for that fact. Careful citation gives the advocate and the Statement of the Case credibility. When in doubt as to whether a citation is necessary, err on the side of over-inclusion rather than under-inclusion.

6.60 SUMMARY OF THE ARGUMENT

Several jurisdictions require that a Summary of the Argument precede the actual argument. The Supreme Court of the United States specifically requires a Summary of the Argument. Rule 24(1)(h) states that the summary "should be a clear and concise condensation of the argument made in the body of the brief; mere repetition of the headings under which the argument is arranged is not sufficient." In 1994, Rule 28 of the Federal Rules of Appellate Procedure was amended to also include the requirement of a summary of the argument. The amendment reflects the previous practice in many of the circuits.

One might question the purpose of the summary. By this point in the brief, the judge will have read the point headings reproduced as the table of contents, and the facts. The issues should be obvious. While this may often be the case, the summary may nonetheless be important, especially in a complex case. It gives a capsule or bird's-eye view of the entire argument in a few short paragraphs. The summary is strategically placed immediately before the main body of the argument. This provides a unique opportunity to present the entire argument before the neces-

---

31. *See* Appendix E.

32. *See* Fed. R. App. P. 28(a)(7) and (a)(9)(a).

sary concentration on detailed argument development within the confines of the point headings.

The summary is not solely for issue identification. It is a tool for persuasion. It is the only time the entire argument is presented in compact form. By its nature, the summary should be a succinct, accurate and clear condensation of the argument developed in the body of the brief. While numerous citations are not necessary, the most compelling authorities should be included for persuasive effect.

The summary's length is, of course, dependent on the number of issues raised and somewhat on the length of the brief. Commentators disagree on how much is too much. Some suggest the summary be no more than 5% to 7% of the total argument portion. Others believe 10% is a good "ballpark" figure. Some jurisdictions specify the appropriate length. One noted writer suggested not more than two or three pages.[33]

The summary is an excellent tool for use by judges at various stages of the controversy. It introduces the judge to the issues on appeal. It acts as a refresher of the case just before or during oral argument. For judges who do not read the entire brief, the summary may be the only section that is thoroughly read. In any of the above scenarios, the Summary of the Argument is important, and should be carefully crafted.

Because of its contents, the summary must be the final portion of the brief to be written. Its preparation comes at a time when most brief writers are ready to call it quits, having spent hours, days, even weeks on the main sections of the brief. But this is not the time to slacken. The summary must be a powerful beginning that sets the scene, introduces the main theories of the case and persuades the reader to think positively about the issues.

The following Summary of Argument stands as a good example of a successful summary:[34]

> This brief is premised on the belief that the concept of the jury as a fair cross-section of the community announced in *Taylor v. Louisiana,* 419 U.S. 522 (1975), was designed to secure a trial jury that is representative of the community and not simply to create a representative panel or venire from which the prosecutor can exclude groups of people by means of peremptory challenges. Petitioner here proposes a remedy for improper use of peremptory challenges similar to that found in *People v. Wheeler,* 148 Cal.Rptr. 890, 583 P.2d 748 (1978), which permits a defendant to question the prosecutor's peremptory challenges when it appears that those challenges are being used to exclude a particular group of people. The remedy is required because none of the previous approaches to

---

33. *See* Robert L. Stern, Appellate Practice in the United States 284 (2d ed. 1989).

34. Interestingly, this Summary of Argument comes from the same brief that

presented the facts so poorly. In the quoted summary, some sentences are overly long. However, the substance of the summary is on point and effective.

ending discrimination in the selection and empanelling of the jury has been satisfactory.

The remedy proposed is based on a simple and well-known principle of evidentiary inference which at once provides a solution to the problem of discrimination by exclusion of groups and prevents undue restriction on the use of peremptory challenges by the prosecutor. As shown here, the remedy proposed is simply to apply Wigmore's "doctrine of chances" on a reasonable scale to discern the intent of the prosecutor when he exercises his privilege of peremptory challenges. Where, as here, the prosecutor uses all or most of his peremptory challenges to remove black people from the jury, a reasonable inference arises that he may be excluding only on the basis of race and is thus defeating, by means of state statutory privilege, the defendant's constitutional right to a representative jury. Present practice under *Swain v. Alabama,* 380 U.S. 202 (1965), forecloses any action on this inference. It is, therefore, necessary for the Court to declare that state practice with regard to peremptory challenge may be questioned by a criminal defendant in order to assure trial by a representative jury.

In this short summary, the author sets the theme of the argument and tells the reader the main theories and cases upon which he will rely. It sets a context within which to place the arguments to follow because it is positioned immediately prior to the first point heading and argument.

6.70   THE ARGUMENT

The argument portion constitutes the bulk of the brief. Its function is to persuade through logic and reasoning that the result requested is correct and just. This section is meant to show, through persuasion, that the facts fall within the scope of the controlling authorities and that policy requires a favorable outcome. Gone is the objective style of writing. Accuracy is still required, but the emphasis shifts to fashioning a persuasive and convincing argument. After reading this section, the judge should be convinced, intellectually and emotionally, that the client's case is a winner.

6.71   Selection of the points to argue

One of the most difficult tasks for an appellate advocate is the choice of the issue or issues to argue in the brief. Often, the trial record presents many alternatives. Generally speaking, most judges and authorities on the subject suggest less, rather than more. Judge Herbert F. Goodrich said:

> There should not be too many points on appeal. A case with two or three points clearly stated and vigorously argued is much better than one filled with a dozen bases of complaint. If a court goes through a half dozen points which it regards as too small to be material it is likely to become a little impatient concerning the possibilities of the rest. Furthermore, a long, long list of points to be

urged on appeal is in danger of creating the impression in the judges' minds that "the trial couldn't possibly have been so bad as that."[35]

Simply put, if the advocate argues too many points, especially those of minimal importance, the stronger points will be diluted and thus weakened.

However, as with all generalization, there are exceptions. If, for example, the lower court has adversely ruled on a number of alternative grounds, the appellant must deal with all these issues or risk losing the appeal. Likewise, if a number of errors during trial raise an issue of cumulative prejudice, the totality of errors must be addressed. The best way to handle that type of case is to introduce the issue of cumulative effect and discuss the errors under one heading. Separate headings for each error are cumbersome and confusing.

Selectivity, then, is the password. The appellate lawyer must evaluate all arguments and select only those that have a reasonable chance of persuading the court. Counsel should resist the urge to include minor points that are non-essential to the argument. This so-called "shotgun" approach to brief writing will result in a loss of confidence in both the advocate and the cause.

6.72   Organization of the points to be argued

As a general rule, the most effective brief usually begins with the strongest point first. The idea is to make a powerful impression on the judges at the outset. As stated by Justice Tate:

> Generally, a point that goes to the very heart of the case should be argued first. An experienced judge will usually select the strongest issue for [sic] study first. But the judge initially may not know what is counsel's strongest issue, unless counsel, based on his knowledge of the facts and his legal research, so directs the court.
>
> As a psychological matter, appellant's counsel should force the court early to face head-on his strongest argument; otherwise, the judicial impression of its forcefulness may be lessened, if its study is not reached until after the judge has half-decided on affirmance, having rejected counsel's previous arguments.[36]

Judge Goodrich makes another excellent point when he says:

> For the appellant the best rule is to bring up the strongest point first and hit it as hard as it can be hit. It is the first point which necessarily gets first attention of the men in the black robes while their attention is at its highest. If unimpressive and small points are discussed before the biggest ones are taken up, the impression will be that this case does not amount to much. But if a good strong

---

35. Herbert F. Goodrich, *A Case on Appeal—A Judge's View*, in A Case on Appeal 1, 7 (1967).

36. Albert Tate, Jr., *The Art of Brief Writing: What a Judge Wants to Read*, 4 Litigation 11, 14 (Winter 1978).

point is effectively presented, the smaller ones may fall into place as clinching arguments to support the conclusions already indicated by the strong first point.[37]

As usual, there are exceptions to this rule. In some cases, the strongest argument may logically fall after lesser arguments are made. For example, if the petitioner prevailed in the trial court, but was reversed in the court of appeals on a technicality, counsel will likely have to place the technical point first to convince the court it needs to consider the merits of the case. And, at times, the logical flow necessitates discussion of minor points in order to appreciate fully the most important issue or the one that is likely to be decisive. It may be inadvisable to fracture the natural flow of an argument in order to place the strongest argument first. Understanding the argument in its totality is vitally important. Nevertheless, if there is a choice, the strongest argument should be presented first.

6.73   Writing the point headings

6.73–1   Contents of a good point heading

Having decided the issues to be argued and their order of presentation, the next task is to draft the point headings. A "point" is a specific ground for a ruling in favor of counsel's position on appeal. Each point is developed under a relevant point heading. If there is only one legal theory or ground that supports the question raised by the appeal, it is likely there will be only one major point heading. Sub-headings can be used to further organize a single heading. Often there is more than one legal contention and thus more than one major point heading.

Point headings are more than just titles to specific sections of the brief. They also appear as the Table of Contents at the beginning of the document. Solid point headings both organize the brief for the reader *as well as* make the initial argument of the brief when the reader peruses the Table of Contents. The advantages to be realized by utilizing this latter opportunity should not be lost because of ineffectual point headings.

Point headings should be forceful, declarative, argumentative sentences. They should contain a conclusion that naturally follows from the principle of law as applied to the facts of the case. As such, they should not be abstract concepts of the law, or simply a factual statement, or just a conclusion. A properly drafted point heading contains facts, law and a conclusion. In addition, point headings should be interesting, informative and easily understood. Strategically placed, they introduce the argument and need to seize the attention of the reader. A poorly drafted point heading does not induce further reading.

As previously mentioned, a major point at times suggests minor points that need development. In that case, sub-headings may be em-

37.   Goodrich, *supra* note 35, at 14.

ployed. The advocate must use caution with sub-headings. Too many will fragment the argument and disrupt the flow of the text.

6.73–2   Problematic point headings

6.73–2–a   The point headings are not informative

Point headings that do not enlighten the judge of the facts, law and logical conclusion are uninformative. For example, "the complaint should be dismissed," does not tell the court, legally or factually, why this action should occur. It is a mere conclusion that does not help the judges focus on the argument. There is little incentive to continue reading. More needs to be added about the case. A better point heading might read "the complaint should be dismissed because it does not state a cause of action based on contract law." Now the reader knows that the issue to be discussed in the main body of that section of the brief centers on the fact that the complaint did not state a cause of action (the legal issue) in contract law (the factual issue) and, therefore, should be dismissed (the logical conclusion). It is even stronger if the contract principle is more defined, such as "the complaint should be dismissed because it does not state a cause of action based on the contract theory of fraud."

6.73–2–b   The point heading is not argumentative

Equivocal points headings that merely suggest an action are ineffective. Consider a point heading that reads: "The evidence should not be considered sufficient." This suggests that maybe it is and maybe it isn't, but it probably should not be considered sufficient. First, this point heading is far from electrifying. It does not grab the reader and move him or her to read on. Second, while the advocate's position is expressed, it is weak. A judge will be left wondering if the advocate is really convinced. Finally, as with the previous example, it does not relate enough facts to form a conclusion that should inevitably follow from the law and facts.

6.73–2–c   The point heading is too cumbersome

Cumbersome point headings usually result from an attempt to include too much in the heading. In a previous example, it was illustrated how a question presented can overwhelm the reader. Using the same case,[38] the point heading for the brief might read:

> The judgment of the district court setting aside the order of the state Corporation Commission dated October 3, 1957 denying the application of Alfredo Gonzales, transferor and Bekins Van and Storage Company, Inc., transferee, of a portion of certificate of public convenience and necessity No. 739, should be reversed for the reason that said order of the Commission is in all respects reasonable and lawful, having been entered pursuant to the Commission's

---

38. *See* § 6.43.

power to approve or disapprove a proposed transfer as the public interest may require, and upon a finding that said transfer would not be in the public interest.

This is cumbersome and ineffective, and the sentence structure does not allow an easy identification of what the advocate seeks from the court. The advocate asks that the judgment of the district court be reversed, but between the words "judgment of the district court" and "should be reversed," appear 39 words. By the time the judge gets to what the advocate really wants, to-wit, that the court reverse the judgment, it is necessary to start over to see what it is that is to be reversed. A better point heading would read:

> The judgment of the District Court should be reversed because the state Corporation Commission's order denying permission to transfer a certificate of convenience and necessity was lawful, reasonable and support by substantial evidence.

In this heading, the judge knows immediately what is requested of the court and why. The heading is short and to the point.

6.73–2–d   The point heading omits important information

A point heading which omits information necessary to form a complete picture of the facts, law and conclusion is ineffective. For example, in a capital punishment case, the following is confusing.

> Capital punishment is acceptable punishment since ratification of the Eighth and Fourteenth amendments.

The judge is left to wonder in bewilderment how the advocate got from "acceptable punishment" to the "Eighth and Fourteenth amendments."

A better point heading is:

> Capital punishment is historically a constitutionally acceptable punishment as reflected in the common law of England, its incorporation in plain language into the Constitution of the United States, and the decisions of American courts since ratification of the Eighth and Fourteenth amendments.

6.73–2–e   The point heading is just a bare announcement

Point headings that merely announce the topic of the section are perhaps the most useless of all. They give no guidance to the judge when reading the Table of Contents and little guidance during the course of reading the brief. The following point headings appeared in a brief to the United States Supreme Court in the case of *Woodson v. North Carolina*.[39] This example is taken from the brief for the petitioner.

---

39. 428 U.S. 280 (1976).

The respondents brief, on the other hand, used extensive headings and sub-headings. In addressing the matter of plea bargaining, jury discretion, and clemency, the point headings read as follows:

THE EXERCISE OF HUMAN JUDGMENT, IN GOOD FAITH, PURSUANT TO THE OBLIGATIONS OF THE CONSTITUTION, STATUTES AND OATHS OF OFFICE BY PROSECUTORS, JURORS, JUDGES AND THE GOVERNOR ARE NOT VIOLATIVE OF THE EIGHTH AMENDMENT.

(a) The prosecutor, in evaluating his cases and his chances of conviction success, and in plea bargaining to strengthen his chances of conviction, is acting consistently with his constitutional duty and his oath of office.

(b) The judgement exercised by jurors, individually and collectively in a criminal case is permissible and required by the Constitution.

(c) There is no constitutional infirmity in the jury's being informed that the consequences of a guilty verdict for first degree murder is the death penalty, with no jury option for sentence recommendation.

(d) The trial judge's action in submitting lesser-included offenses to the jury where the evidence warrants their submission is not violative of the Constitution.

(e) The exercise of executive clemency by the Governor is properly an unfettered, independent and judicially unreviewable act of mercy.

These comparisons emphasize the importance of solid point headings. There is little doubt which brief judges will find most useful. As noted previously, a review of the Table of Contents capsulizes the entire theory of the case and the main arguments of the brief. Little can be gleaned from the Table of Contents of the petitioner's brief in the above example. About the only help that petitioner's brief gives is to indicate the page number on which the point is discussed. There is little else to indicate the theory or theme of the case.

6.74   Standard of review

The standard of review for appellate cases was discussed in Chapter One, § 1.10. The standard used determines both the nature and degree of error the appellant must prove in order to obtain a reversal of the trial court. It tells the attorney how much deference the appeals court will give to the action of the trial court.

Many appellate courts, including all Federal Circuit Courts of Appeal, specifically require that the appropriate standard be delineated in the brief.[40] Even if there is no rule, an appellate brief should indicate the standard of review. Thus, the appropriate standard must be carefully researched.[41]

If the standard of review is controversial, it should be argued along with the other points in the brief. It may be included as a separate heading or subheading. It may appear as a separate section between the Statement of Facts and the Argument. It may also be discussed in the opening part of the first argument. The prominence it receives will depend on how favorable the standard is to the particular issues of the case on appeal.

6.75 Types of arguments

Basically there are four types of arguments: arguments of law, of fact, of equity and of social policy. A superior brief will effectively use all four types in varying degrees, depending on the strengths of each and the theme that is chosen.

6.75–1 Arguments that are law-specific

Most cases at the appeals level have strong legal arguments focusing on legal precedent. If the interpretation of a case, statute, administrative regulation or the like is dispositive of the matter, the argument will largely be law-specific. For example, in the case of *Zalud Oldsmobile, Inc. v. Limbach,*[42] the issue was whether demonstrator vehicles registered to a dealership qualify as personal property for tax purposes. The answer to that question centered on the interpretation of Ohio Revised Code § 5701.03 and attendant sections that define the terms within § 5701.03. Much of the brief concentrated solely on the interpretation of the various statutory sections. Little else was relevant for the issues presented in this appeal.

6.75–2 Arguments that are fact-specific

All arguments have facts, but some cases are more fact driven than others. For example, a recent case involved homeowner's insurance coverage for a young babysitter who allegedly molested his charges. Suit was brought for money damages against the insurance carrier. The first point argued by the parties against the insurance company was worded as follows:

---

40. *See* Fed. R. App. P. 28(a)(9)(B).

41. This task is challenging because cases present questions of pure law and mixed questions of fact and law. Different standards are required for each of the foregoing types of cases. To further complicate matters, the courts have been inconsistent in their use of terminology when assessing the standards as they apply to the issues.

42. 628 N.E.2d 1382 (Ohio 1994).

For purposes of determining liability coverage under a policy of insurance that excludes coverage for bodily injury "which is expected or intended by the insured," the conduct of each insured must be separately analyzed against the terms of the insurance contract to determine the existence of coverage.[43]

Obviously, legal principles will be applied in determining the merits of this case. Even so, the issues on appeal are far more fact-specific than the previous tax example. Throughout the briefs of both parties, the attorneys demonstrated and argued facts.

6.75–3 Arguments of equity and policy

Of necessity, an advocate must argue that the law applies to the facts. Often that is not enough. The judges want to believe the decision they make is a just decision. Accordingly, judges may be uncomfortable with an argument based strictly on precedent unless it is clear where the equities lie. The advocate must explain why justice will be done if the court finds for his or her client.

Policy arguments illustrate why the result requested will promote a societal good. In a recent case involving the so-called 75/25 rule[44], the advocate for the Health Plan argued:

> This translates into a saving of over $500,000 annually. DAHP (the Health Plan) also has programs in place to address one of the biggest problems/risks facing its members—prenatal care and premature births. A full-time educator on DAHP's staff works with all pregnant members. DAHP's Baby's Birth Right program gives women incentives to seek early and regular prenatal care. The result has been babies with higher birth weights and fewer complications.[45]

Health issues surrounding mothers and children have long been of paramount interest to society. By showing the court that those interests are part of the on-going program of DAHP, the attorneys gave the court a reason to hold for their position (though without apparent success).

If feasible, the most persuasive briefs use all four types of arguments. These should be interspersed throughout the brief. The advocate should not separate the equity and policy arguments from the arguments of fact and law. All too often lawyers make their legal arguments and then, almost as an after thought, add a section that sets forth the equity and policy arguments. To do so assumes that the reader is able to connect the legal arguments, presented pages before, with the policy arguments which appear at the tail end of the brief. This makes it

43. *Cuervo v. Cincinnati Ins. Co.*, 667 N.E.2d 1234 (Ohio 1996).

44. 42 U.S.C. § 1396b(m)(2)(A)(ii) requires that HMOs, as a condition of receiving federal matching funds, have no more than 75% of its enrolled individuals insured under Medicare or eligible for Medicaid.

45. *Dayton Area Health Plan, Inc. v. State, Dep't of Ins.*, 668 N.E.2d 999 (Ohio Ct. App. Montgomery County 1995), *appeal dismissed*, 663 N.E.2d 1301 (Ohio 1996).

difficult to understand all aspects of the argument. Equity and policy should be discussed in the context of the facts and law.

6.76   Use of authority in the brief

6.76–1   Primary authority

The choice of authority and its use is crucial to an effective brief. The advocate must attempt to use favorable precedent, preferably mandatory primary precedent, if available. Cases from the highest court in the jurisdiction that address the legal issues and are factually similar to the advocate's case are the most prized. If arguing to an intermediate appellate court, cases decided by that tribunal are useful. If there is no law defined in the jurisdiction, well reasoned cases from other jurisdictions that are factually and legally similar may be persuasive.

Recent cases are generally preferable to older cases, but there are exceptions. If an old case establishes the law of the jurisdiction and has been followed over time, the advocate should include that case to show a continuing trend. If the old case is especially well reasoned and on point, it should be included.

In most instances, if the case has reached the appeals court, there is no precedent that is directly controlling. In that situation, the advocate must convince the court that precedent from other jurisdictions and secondary authority provide an equitable result, are based on sound policy, and are compatible with the jurisdiction's existing body of law.

The battle is only partially won when the advocate finds solid precedent. The treatment and development of the precedent is critical to a good brief.

If case law is the basis for authority, each case that supports a main proposition must be carefully analyzed for the judges. It is unacceptable merely to cite a case and boldly assert its black letter law. The judges will have no means to assess its value. With the press of heavy caseloads, few judges take the time to examine a cited case to determine its relevance to the argument. Instead, judges will probably dismiss it out-of-hand as unimportant. In the same vein, some brief writers state a proposition of law and then follow it by a cite or several cites. In this situation, the reader will question why the cases are cited in the first place. For example, in the following excerpt, a reader is left with the question of the relevance of the two cases that follow the quote: "The scheme of taxation here thus fails the compensatory tax test. *Fulton Corp. v. Faulkner*, 116 S. Ct. at 855–60 & n. 6; *Henneford v. Silas Mason Co.*, 300 U.S. 577 (1937)."

In presenting the analysis to the judges, the advocate must first sketch the facts as they relate to the point of law for which the case is cited. Keep this short and to the point. Auxiliary facts from a case only confuse the issue and prolong unduly the discussion of the case. The holding must appear early in the discussion, usually followed by the rationale for the holding. Make certain reasoning or rationale of the case is the point upon which the case turns. This is known as the *ratio decidendi* of the case, as opposed to *dicta*.[46] The last step, if it is not readily apparent, is to draw the parallels between the two case, the one that is under review and the cited case.

Of course, not every cited case need be detailed in this fashion. If, for example, the advocate needs to define a legal term, extensive analysis does little good. The point for which the case is cited is only the definition contained in it. Also at times the fact patterns are very similar for a number of cases. In that event, reiteration of the facts, the holding and the rationale for all these cases is redundant. The password is to maintain flexibility in how the various authorities are handled. Do not feel locked into a pedantic pattern of case analysis and discussion. Vary the writing style and the material presented to enhance the effectiveness of the presentation. In the end, one must ask if the discussion provides sufficient information to allow the judges to understand why the case is cited and its precedential value.

If the case on appeal rests on a statutory section, it may be necessary to examine the history of the statute. Repealed portions and amendments are particularly important. A comparison of the present statute's wording with its past form is often instructive. If time permits, examination of the legislative history may provide insight into the reasons for the law's passage and to the kind of cases it was meant to apply.

If the statutory section is explained through regulations, how the statute was meant to function may be ascertained. Regulations involving the Internal Revenue Code, as well as other federal administrative agencies, may be useful to show the application of the statute to the case on appeal.

6.76–2 Pitfalls in the use of authority

Chief among the pitfalls in the use of authority is string citing. There is little or no reason to string cite. Usually one citation with an explanation of its value is sufficient. The exception is the instance in which several cases with similar facts and rationale are virtually the same and are equally persuasive. Showing the judges that there is more than one authority may be helpful. The operative word is *may*. Some judges simply are not impressed with a show of power. Others find it annoying. If more than one cite is used, it is advisable to include a parenthetical after the cite to indicate the relevant aspects of the holding or reasoning.

Equally problematic are lengthy quotations. This is true for both case opinions and quotations of sections of the record. The latter practice is especially egregious and should be avoided. At times, there is a passage that simply cannot be paraphrased with the eloquence and grace of the

46. *Dicta* has been described as incidental information provided by the writer of the opinion. It is not necessary for the holding but may provide additional insight into the rationale.

original writer. In that instance, capture the essence and eliminate material that is not relevant. A memorable quote will add emphasis and persuasiveness to an argument, but brief writers tend to overuse quotations. The practice leads to choppy, uneven writing. This is especially true with long block quotes that are likely to be skipped by the reader. When in doubt, paraphrase.

6.76–3 Citation of dicta

Commentators caution against citing dicta in a brief. That notion needs examination. In § 4.22–2–d it was noted that dicta is incidental comment made by the judge that is not dispositive of the issue before the court. Does that mean it is useless to the advocate? The answer to that question is a resounding "no." Dicta can be very persuasive.

The late scholar Karl Llewellyn in his famous book The Bramble Bush, observed the following:

> *The court can decide only the particular dispute which is before it.* When it speaks to that question it speaks *ex cathedra*, with authority, with finality, with an almost magic power. When it speaks to the question before it, it announces *law*, and if what it announces is new, it legislates, it *makes* the law. But when it speaks to any other question at all, it says mere words, which no man needs to follow. Are such words worthless? They are not. We know them as judicial *dicta*; when they are wholly off the point at issue we call them *obiter dicta*—words dropped along the road, wayside remarks. Yet even wayside remarks shed light on the remarker. They may be very useful to him or to us.[47]

In this passage, Professor Llewellyn suggests there are two forms of dicta—judicial dicta, or that which has some relationship to the issues under consideration, and obiter dicta, that which is akin to an aside with little relevance to the issues. The former is likely more persuasive than the latter.

For example, consider a case in which the issue is whether an injunction should be granted because of a possible violation of the copyright laws. The question centers on the principles underlying the issuance of injunctions. Development of the constructs of copyright may well be instructive when considering whether to issue the injunction. This development is not, however, necessary to the decision of the case, but it is relevant to it. It may be deemed judicial dicta. Should an issue later arise about an aspect of copyright that was discussed in detail in the case, the language could be persuasive. If, on the other hand, the judge strays into a discussion about an unconnected topic, such as general property damages unrelated to copyright, the subject is likely to

---

47. Karl Llewellyn, The Bramble Bush: On Our Law and its Study 40–41 (Oceana Publications, 7th prtg. 1981).

be deemed *obiter dicta*. As Professor Llewellyn would say, they are "words dropped along the road, wayside remarks."[48]

The persuasiveness of dicta then is directly proportional to the relationship of the words to the issue of the case. This relationship must be analyzed. The bottom line is to exercise caution when citing legal concepts that do not constitute the law upon which the case is decided. Dicta can be persuasive; but always indicate that it is, in fact, dicta.

6.76–4   Use of secondary authority

Secondary authority is used when no primary authority exists. At times, it is also used to bolster weak primary authority. Not all secondary authority is of equal persuasiveness. If, for example, there is no domestic statutory or case law on point, a well-reasoned case from another jurisdiction may be highly persuasive. This is especially true if the law articulated in the case fits comfortably in the body of law already in existence in the state in which the appeal arises. However, statutory law of another jurisdiction is not persuasive.

Dissenting opinions may also be persuasive. While not the general rule, cases from time to time are overruled. Should that occur, the reasoning of a dissenting opinion will often be adopted by the majority. As stated by Chief Justice Hughes:

> A dissent in a court of last resort is an appeal to the brooding spirit of the law, to the intelligence of a future day, when a later decision may possibly correct the error into which the dissenting judge believes the court to have been betrayed. Nor is this appeal always in vain. In a number of cases dissenting opinion have in time become the law.[49]

Always indicate that the decision cited is to a dissenting opinion. An advocate who neglects to apprise the bench that the cite is to a dissent risks loss of confidence or worse. Opposing counsel is sure to point out the omission.

If a dissenting opinion is to be used, choose it carefully. A strong dissent in a case that was decided within the last two years probably will not be persuasive. Most, if not all, of the Justices are probably still members of the court. If they weren't convinced then, they won't be convinced now.

There are other sources that can also be cited to an appellate court. Well-reasoned law review articles written by outstanding scholars may be persuasive. However, this authority should be cited only if there is no primary authority or to bolster the primary authority. Care must be exercised in the choice of both the law review and the author. A well-reasoned article written by a former Justice of the Supreme Court that appears in the Harvard Law Review likely will have persuasive qualities. An article by an unknown may be useful, but its worth is questionable.

---

48. *Id.* at 41.

49. Charles Evans Hughes, The Supreme Court of the United States 68 (1928).

Treatises by well-known authors are at times cited in briefs, as are the various Restatements of the Law. But again, caution should be used in choosing any secondary source. If possible, it should be well-known, on point and, generally accepted in the legal literature.

6.77 Handling unfavorable authority

During the course of research, the advocate probably will find unfavorable case law. "Why" and "how" to deal with it are two questions that must be addressed. "Why" deals with the authority that flows from the advocate's ethical obligation as a lawyer. The Model Rules of Professional Conduct, Rule 3.3, provides in part: "[A] lawyer shall not knowingly; * * * fail to disclose to the tribunal legal authority in the controlling jurisdiction known to the lawyer to be directly adverse to the position of the client not disclosed by opposing counsel." The reason for this rule is to assure that a just result is reached.

Another reason for disclosure is tactical. If the advocate has found the case, the opponent likely has discovered it also. By its inclusion in the context of the advocate's argument, the case may be minimized or undermined. One should use every opportunity to explain why the authority should not be followed.

A word of caution is in order. Some advocates spend their entire briefs "putting out the fires" of their opponent. Do not make that mistake. Each side has an argument to make. If the advocate spends an inordinate amount of time dealing with adverse cases, the theme and argument in his or her case will not be developed.

"How" best to deal with adverse authority is a second concern for most advocates. Wiener suggests that in some instances, it is best to "ignore the offending precedent—always provided, of course, that it is not a square holding—and to deal with it *sub silentio*."[50] This suggestion may be considered, but the foregoing discussion of the ethical and tactical issues must also be weighed. It may be good advice if the precedent is not particularly strong or particularly important. Otherwise, ethics and tactics may dictate a straightforward approach.

A second way to deal with unfavorable authority is to attack it "boldly and frontally."[51] That can be dangerous unless there have been clear signs that the precedent is weak and about to fall.

The third and probably the best way to deal with an offending case is to distinguish it. The facts provide the most fertile basis to distinguish authority. One may argue: the facts of the two cases are not sufficiently similar to apply the adverse precedent; the policy goals of the two cases are different; an application of the law of the offending case will create negative consequences not compatible with existing law; the adverse authority makes "hard law" not in keeping with the needs of society; and, if all else fails, that the offending case was wrongly decided and needs rectifying. This final suggestion is a last resort argument, especial-

50. Wiener, *supra* note 21, at 152.   **51.** *Id.*

ly if more than one case espouses the same legal principle. It basically tells the appellate court that there is no way to harmonize the two cases.

When distinguishing cases, stick to the main issues of the offending case. Don't get mired in minor details. The appellate court will see this as knit picking and generally a waste of time and paper.

6.80   THE CONCLUSION

The Conclusion is the last section of the brief the members of the court will read. There is a wide range of opinion as to what the Conclusion should contain.[52] Some writers categorically assert that it is a waste of time and paper merely to say "[f]or all of the above reasons, the decision of the trial court should be reversed." Others disagree and espouse the view that the Conclusion should specifically state the relief sought and nothing more.[53] The latter group believes that the Conclusion as stated above will do nicely. Others take a slightly different approach. They suggest that the request for relief may be enough, unless the arguments are numerous and complex. In that situation, the writer might want to do a brief summary to remind the court of the main contentions of the advocate.

This author believes the conclusion presents the last opportunity to persuade the court of the rightness of the advocate's arguments. To that end, a good conclusion will accomplish two objectives. It will provide the court with a brief summary of the theme of the brief, and it will succinctly state the action of the court requested by the advocate.

The conclusion should not rehash the arguments, but it should gently remind the court of the essence of the arguments. Think about the theme of the argument when formulating the conclusion.

The best way to write the conclusion is to begin with the strongest point. Remember: the best or strongest argument was the first one that was read. Presumably the least important argument was the last one read. State the strongest point first so that, once again, the judges are reminded of the strength of the case.

The last portion of the Conclusion should specifically state a description of the requested relief. Do not make the court guess what is requested. While some requests are straightforward and uncomplicated, others may be more complex. For instance, in a case in which the appellant wants the court to order a new trial and provide specific

---

52. Always check the court rules to see if there are guidelines on what should be included in the conclusion.

53. The United States Supreme Court Rule 24(j) states that the brief includes: "A conclusion specifying with particularity the relief the party seeks." Therefore, most briefs to that Court include a very brief one or two sentence summary just prior to the Conclusion. For example, in the case of *General Motors Corp. v. Tracy,* 519 U.S. 278

(1997), the Petitioner's final sentence just before the conclusion read "In sum, the tax not only violates the Commerce Clause; it also violates GM's equal protection rights." That sentence was followed by the Conclusion that read "[f]or the foregoing reasons, the judgment of the Supreme Court of Ohio should be reversed." See also Appendices C and D for the conclusions in both the Jones and Clinton briefs.

directions for the conduct of the trial, that relief must be precisely specified.

The Conclusion should be no longer than one or two paragraphs. Often, it can be handled in a few sentences. A guide for drafting the Conclusion is to remember that less is far better than more. It should provide a solid closure of the brief, nothing more.

Following the Conclusion, the signature of the brief writer(s) appears. It is customary and proper to use the following form:

> Respectfully submitted,
>
> JONES, VAUGHN & SLATE
> Amy C. Jones
> 1460 H. Street, N.W.
> Washington, DC 20005
> (202) 950–6500
>
> *Counsel for Petitioner*

July 31, 2002

6.90   THE APPENDIX

The Appendix appears in the brief after the Conclusion. The purpose of the Appendix is to include pertinent documents that may be of use to the court. This saves time, since members of the court will not have to specifically search for those materials. In describing what is to be contained in briefs to the United States Supreme Court, Rule 24(f) states:

> The constitutional provisions, treaties, statutes, ordinances, and regulations involved in the case, set out verbatim with appropriate citation. If the provisions involved are lengthy, their citation alone suffices at this point, and their pertinent text, if not already set out in the petition for a writ of certiorari, jurisdictional statement, or an appendix to either document, shall be set out in an appendix to the brief.

This list is not exhaustive. In a contract case, for example, it may be prudent to include the contract in question. Thus, lengthy quotes from it in the body of the brief will not be necessary.

When discussed in the body of the brief, reference should be made directly to the page on which the language appears in the appendix.

EXERCISES

I.   Review the following set of facts:

Edward Winters was an elderly man who entered the emergency room at St. Francis–St. George Hospital (SFSG) with heart related complaints. He was stabilized, but during his stay, he executed a "No Code Blue" order which was written by his physician and entered in the hospital records. (A "No Code Blue" means do not resuscitate in the event of a life-threatening occurrence). He claimed he did not want to "end up" like his wife.

He suffered ventricular tachycardia (V-tach) and was defibrillated by a nurse, in contravention of his order. One day later, after another episode of V-tach which ended spontaneously, Mr. Winters asked to be removed from monitoring equipment and asked not to be defibrillated again. He was moved to another room in accordance with his wishes. The following day, he suffered a stroke that left him paralyzed. Two years later, he died.

His family brought suit basically on the theory of wrongful life. The claim was that he had requested not to be coded, the hospital ignored the claim and as a result, Mr. Winters stroked, thus encountered enormous expense for nursing care during the remaining years of his life. The hospital should, therefore, shoulder the responsibility for those expenses. There is no claim that the defibrillation caused the stroke.

The hospital claims there is no such cause of action as "wrongful life." Health care providers can be held liable only for nominal damages for providing life-saving care.

After trial, the matter was appealed to the court of appeals. That court held "Mr. Winter cannot recover general damages for 'finding himself alive after unwanted resuscitative measures.' * * * [H]e can still recover all other consequential damages 'caused by the unwanted resuscitative efforts and the express violation of his wishes.' "

The court determined that Plaintiff would not be able to establish that the defibrillation caused Mr. Winter's stroke. It did conclude that the damages sought may be recovered if the jury finds that it was reasonably foreseeable that unwanted resuscitative measures would cause adverse health consequences to him. The Court of Appeals entered judgment in accordance with its opinion and SFSG now appeals to the Supreme Court.

  A.   Write a Question(s) Presented for each side of the issue.

  B.   Write a point heading for each side that deals with the issue of compensable damages. Remember: the family seeks damages for Mr. Winter's infirmities and their related expenses because they claim the hospital wrongfully kept him alive. The hospital claims all that are owed is nominal damages, because there is no such cause of action as "wrongful living."

  C.   Write the facts for both sides of the case.

II.   Analyze the following questions presented based on the information contained in the chapter. State the pluses and minuses for each question. Is there additional information that should be given to make the question more understandable and persuasive? Rewrite the questions. You may assume names, if identifying the parties would be helpful. Respond to the following:

A.   Whether the imposition and carrying out of the sentences of death for the crime of murder under the law of Georgia violates the Eighth and Fourteenth Amendments to the Constitution of the United States.

B.   Whether Ohio Rev. Code § 1742.12 as applied to Dayton Area Health Plan is in conflict with and, therefore, pre-empted by federal Public Law 102–276.

C.   Whether the trial court judge erred when he ordered a defendant who pleaded guilty to two felonies to serve 300 hours of community service.

III.   The following are point headings. Analyze them for persuasiveness and completeness. How could they be improved? You may assume names, if identifying the parties would be helpful. Rewrite the point headings to obtain maximum persuasiveness.

A.   Petitioner/Appellant 5th Amendment Constitutional rights to due process of law were violated relative to his liberty to execute beloved and deceased brother's will.

B.   The Petitioner/Appellant was not confronted with the witnesses against him or to have compulsory process for obtaining witnesses in his favor.

C.   The constitutional violations are a derivative of abuse of judicial discretion by the Common Pleas Court pursuant to Revised Code 2921.45(A) by the Appeals Court to restore Petitioner's rights as a matter of law of which they erred by not providing a remedy.

IV.   The facts and the summary of the argument in the *Batson v. Kentucky* case appear on page 96 and page 103 respectively. As noted, the facts could be improved. Rewrite the facts. The text provides suggestions for those that appear in the brief. The question you must ask is whether those facts are even pertinent to the issue of the case.

Chapter Seven

APPELLEE AND REPLY BRIEFS

Analysis

7.00 INTRODUCTION

The principles for writing a good appellant brief are equally applicable to the appellee brief. Persuasive techniques are basically the same. The content, however, may be slightly different. For example, Federal Rule of Appellate Procedure 28(b) states:

> The appellee's brief must conform to the requirements of Rule 28(a)(1)—(9) and (11), except that none of the following need appear unless the appellee is dissatisfied with the appellant's statement: (1) the jurisdictional statement; (2) the statement of the issues; (3) the statement of the case; (4) the statement of the facts; and (5) the statement of the standard of review.

However, a decision to leave the statement of the issues and the facts to the appellant is a questionable tactic as discussed in § 7.30. There are other essential differences between the opening brief and the appellee's brief.

7.01 The purpose of the appellee brief

Unlike the appellant brief, the appellee brief has a two-fold task. First, it sets forth the affirmative position of the appellee. Second, it responds to the arguments of the appellant. The strongest appellee brief primarily develops an affirmative presentation that supports the lower court decision, and secondarily, refutes the appellant's claims.

121

The brief is not a defensive document. All too often, appellees make the mistake of arguing almost exclusively in the negative. This is not a recommended strategy. The appellee brief should be strong and affirmative. It should delineate with firm conviction the correctness of the lower court decision. The tone should be positive. It is ineffective to use appellant's contentions and merely insert a negative term. For example, assume that the appellant's point heading reads "[t]he complaint stated a cause of action in contract." The wise appellee will not respond simply with "[t]he complaint did not state a cause of action in contract." Reasons should be given why this is the case. The court should not have to guess why the appellee makes this claim. Seize the opportunity to inform and persuade the court.

7.02   The appellee's advantages

The appellee has several advantages in an appeal. First and foremost, the appellee won in the trial court. This means the appellant must convince the appellate court that prejudicial error was committed. The operative word is *prejudicial* error. If the error was "harmless" or if it was corrected later in the trial, there may be no prejudicial error. In addition, appellate courts are slow to overturn trial court decisions[1] because that court had the advantages of evaluating, first-hand, the witnesses and complainant, the evidence, and all other aspects of the case. Also, the standard of review may be difficult to overcome. Finally, the decision of the trial court carries the presumption of correctness.

Strategically, the appellee is also in the superior position. The advocate writing for the appellee has studied the opponent's opening contentions and pondered their ramifications before committing to a plan of action. However, the wise advocate will begin to write the answering brief long before appellant submits the opening brief. The factual statement, issue formulation, potential point headings and arguments to be raised should be formulated in advance. This exercise prevents two things from occurring: first, it forces the advocate to think affirmatively about the issues and not simply fall into a defensive mode once the opening brief has been received; second, it prevents the age-old tendency to procrastinate.

Once the appellant brief is received, the issues and arguments can be examined to assess the modifications needed in the advocate's draft. Answers to the following questions will help determine what to include in the appellee's brief.

● With respect to the appellant's facts, can some facts in the appellee's brief be omitted, summarized or strengthened?

● Are there gaps and omissions in the appellant's facts that need attention?

---

1.   See § 1.03 for a discussion about the number of decisions that are overturned on appeal.

● Should any arguments be abandoned because they are weak, untenable and unpersuasive because of appellant's arguments?

● Should other arguments be expanded due to gaps in appellant's reasoning or omissions in the law?

● Should new arguments be formulated because of accidental concession by the appellant?

● Have new lines of reasoning been submitted by the appellant that need to be answered?

Simply put, the advocate must reassess the previously written preliminary drafts to reply to the appellant's arguments and stress affirmative elements that strike at vulnerable points in the appellant's position. This task is made far easier once the appellant's brief is analyzed, a luxury not enjoyed by the writer of the opening brief.

Another advantage in responding to the opening brief is that the appellee can assess the organization of the brief. Commentators differ as to whether the appellee's organization should follow that of the appellant's brief. This author believes the appellee, while refuting all tenable points made by the appellant, should organize the brief to create the best possible impression. This strategy depends on the strength of the appellant's various points. If the appellant has one major argument, with auxiliary weaker arguments, the appellant probably will address the strongest argument first. The appellee is not obliged to discuss that point first. However, strategically attacking the appellant's major point can itself become the appellee's strongest argument. This is especially so if the point is contentious, the equities questionable and the law somewhat uncertain. The auxiliary weaker points can then be discussed in more summary fashion.

On the other hand, if the appellant for example has three solid arguments, the appellee may want to put his or her strongest argument first. It is mostly a matter of evaluating the equities and the law of each argument and presenting a document that both refutes the arguments of the opponent and presents affirmatively the arguments of the appellee that favor upholding the trial court decision.

One important consideration should be kept in mind. The appellee's argument must be carefully crafted both to integrate the affirmative points and refute the appellant's contentions. It is not effective to attack the opponent in one point heading and make an affirmative argument in the next. Rather, integrate the material for maximum effect. At times one can best destroy the adversary through one's own argument.

7.10 ANALYZE THE OPPONENT'S BRIEF

7.11 Make an outline

The first step in analyzing the opponent's brief is to make a thorough outline of it. Each significant point should be noted with its supporting arguments and authorities. These contentions must be summarized, an exercise that allows appellee's counsel to analyze all-important arguments even if appellant's brief is poorly organized and written. For example, if point one and point four make basically the same statement, that fact should be noted. A concise response can then be made to that issue and ultimately strategically placed in appellee's brief for the maximum persuasive effect.

With an outline, the advocate must now consider each point and examine the strengths and weaknesses. There is no substitute for this type of analysis, particularly the weaknesses in the appellant's brief.

7.12   Look for weakness in the appellant's brief

The best initial way to assess weaknesses in the opponent's brief is to go through the following inventory, though there may be other weaknesses to note as well. These inquiries are starting points.

7.12–1   Errors of fact

Has the opponent omitted important facts that distort the information conveyed to the court? If so, that matter must be drawn to the attention of the court in the appellee's statement of facts. While it is never wise to engage in personalities, it is perfectly acceptable (and necessary) to inform the court that the appellant has omitted facts pertinent to the case. Sarcastic remarks are not acceptable, but the appellee may use persuasive language that effectively discredits the appellant. Remember: the first rule of good brief writing is to write a fact statement that is scrupulously honest. Compare the facts as stated by the appellant with the record. This is the easiest way to discover errors of fact.

7.12–2   Errors of law

Has the appellant erroneously applied the applicable law to the case on appeal? Is the law that was applied the *ratio decidendi* of the case or is it *dicta*? In other words, does the case cited as authority support the proposition for which it is espoused? Look for inaccurate quotations, taken out of context, that do not support the appellant's proposition.

A second and more subtle form of error of law occurs when the argument espoused by the appellant is correct, but simply inapplicable to the case on appeal. This occurs when the appellant fails to analyze the exceptions or limitations of the doctrine. For example, assume a case in which the appellant has applied the law of several cases to the case on appeal. As discussed, the analysis is correct. However, the problem arises because there is an exception to a minor, though critical, point. This is potentially fatal to the appellant's argument. If this occurs, the appellee should acknowledge the correctness of the analysis, *as far as it was taken,* and then explain to the court why the limitation or exception calls for a decision in favor of the appellee.

Spotting errors in the law requires both careful analysis of the arguments and extensive research and preparation. There are no substitutes. Never assume the appellant's research is complete and accurately stated. Appellee's research must be thorough to uncover any weaknesses.

7.12–3 Errors of logic or reasoning

Errors of logic and reasoning are probably the most common among brief writers. Often they stem from a failure to discuss each step in a process. It is a "linking" problem. Instead of logically proceeding from A to B to C and then to D, the advocate establishes A, and then perhaps B, but skips C to jump to D. Causation is a particularly fertile area for this type of linking problem. The following example illustrates the point.

In a contract action, the trial court finds for the defendant Smith. The plaintiff Brown appeals, arguing there was a contract between Smith and Brown, Smith breached the contract and, as a result, Brown suffered damages. Brown lost at trial. On appeal, Brown argues the trial court erred in finding for Smith because the breach was proven and he was damaged. On appeal, in his brief, Brown presents an array of authority that supports his position—contract-breach-damages. However, on close review, counsel for Smith finds the issue of causation unclear. There is a gap in the logic. Reviewing the case: there was a breach, Smith was the party who breached; and Brown was damaged. Missing is why the breach caused damage to Brown. Perhaps other forces ultimately caused the damage. Perhaps Brown was actually responsible.

This is an extremely simple example, but the idea is clear. Leaps of logic can be the undoing of the appellant, but appellee bears the responsibility to show the reasoning or logic is erroneous. It is not effective simply to make the claim without illustrating how the logic failed.

7.12–4 Inconsistent arguments

Inconsistent appellant arguments are often difficult to detect, but if detected, they are quite helpful to the appellee. By definition, if one argument is correct, the other inconsistent argument must be in error. The inconsistencies are usually discovered after appellee has done a thorough job of analyzing the theories and reasoning contained in appellant's brief. Sometimes in the zeal of advancing many arguments, the opponent fails to realize that opposite claims have been made. If the inconsistencies are important, they must be addressed and presented to the court.

For example, consider a contract case in which there are competing theories of recovery. If one seeks to recover under the reliance theory, the damages should return the party to where the party was before the contract was entered. If, on the other hand, the plaintiff seeks recovery under the expectation theory, the damages will be the difference between that promised and that received. The following case illustrates how competing interests may arise in an appellate proceeding.

Jones entered into a contract with Smith for Smith to construct certain machinery. In preparation, Jones first expended $10,000 to build the foundation. Use of the machinery would have produced revenues of $50,000 in the first year of operation, but Smith breached the contract. For purposes of this illustration, assume that no one else can build the machinery. Jones sued to recover $60,000. The trial judge's instructions were unclear, and Smith prevailed. On appeal, Jones argues he is entitled to the $60,000. In the appellant's brief, counsel for Jones argues for $10,000 out-of-pocket expenses for building the foundation and $50,000 in lost revenues during the first year. Smith's lawyer counters with the argument that, in effect, Jones is seeking double recovery for the foundation. In order to realize revenues of $50,000, $10,000 would have had to be expended for the foundation. If recovery is based on anticipated revenues, the $50,000 recovery includes compensation for the cost of the foundation. An extra $10,000 puts the appellant in a better position than he or she ever expected to be.

The example illustrates inconsistent arguments. The appellee's counsel must be ever vigilant to scrutinize each argument to uncover inconsistencies in the opposing counsel's brief. If there are inconsistencies, material to the case, they must be carefully analyzed and forcefully expressed to the appellate court.

7.12–5 Concessions

As with inconsistent arguments, concessions usually are accidentally made by the opponent. The advocate who discovers a concession must capitalize on it. The best way to discover a concession is to search the record and appellant's brief. These provide the most fertile grounds to locate points that have been conceded.

Concession may be implicit or explicit. The explicit concession is the easiest to discover. If there simply is no argument that can be made, the opponent may have little choice but to concede the point. If that occurs, appellee's counsel should point out the concession and explain, in detail, its importance.

Implicit concessions are less obvious. They may occur when opposing counsel accidentally makes an argument contrary to his or her position. They may also occur if appellant's counsel misjudges the importance of an issue and fails to develop it.

Concessions in the brief or in oral argument can be disastrous to the other side. The advocate who identifies and then capitalizes on a concession may turn the case in the appellee's favor.

7.20 BASES THAT SUPPORT THE APPELLEE

Defense of the judgment below is the theme of appellee's argument. The posture should be one of quiet reasonableness. Overstatement has no place in the appellee's brief.

While there are many bases to support the lower court opinion, the following are some of the most common.

1.   Deference to the factual findings of the trial court is primary because the trier of fact has weighed the physical evidence, observed the witnesses and evaluated their credibility.

2.   Harmless error provides another basis to support the lower court decision. Rarely is there a trial without error, but that error, if it exists, is usually not reversible. The question is whether the error prejudiced the appellant. If rights were not impaired, there is no need to disturb the lower court decision.

3.   If counsel for appellant raises an issue to which there was no objection at trial, the appellee has a solid basis of support in the appellate court. The failure to object by appellant generally is deemed to waive the right to later claim an appealable issue.

4.   Appellee should emphasize that appellant had his or her day in court and lost. There must be an end to litigation because of the ever-burgeoning court dockets.

The list is not exhaustive, but it does represent reasons to support affirmance of the trial court decision.

7.30   WHAT TO INCLUDE IN THE BRIEF

The appellee's brief should contain all aspects of a well-written appellant brief. The summary should be strong, and the point headings should be powerful. Remember: if the appellant fails to inform the court about the issues, facts or the law applicable to the facts, the judges will turn to the appellee brief for guidance. Thus, a poorly written, uninformative appellee brief may be equally counterproductive.

As previously mentioned, the Federal Rules of Appellate Procedure do not require that the appellee make a jurisdictional statement, or a statement of the issues, case, facts or applicable standard of review. Careful thought must be given, however, whether to eliminate any of the foregoing five statements. Least likely for controversy is the jurisdictional statement, though there certainly is room for error by the appellant. Rule 28(a)(2) addresses the requirements of the jurisdictional statement. Both legal and factual recitals must be made, any of which could be misstated or misconstrued.[2] The appellant's statement of the standard of review must also be examined. Some circuits are very explicit about

---

2. Fed. R. App. P. 28(a)(4) states in relevant part that the jurisdictional statement should include:

(A) the basis for the district court's or agency's subject-matter jurisdiction, with citations to applicable statutory provisions and stating relevant facts establishing jurisdiction; (B) The basis for the court of appeals' jurisdiction, with cita-tions to applicable statutory provisions and stating relevant facts establishing jurisdiction; (C) the filing dates establishing the timeliness of the appeal or petition for review; and (D) an assertion that the appeal is from a final order or judgment that disposes of all parties' claims, or information establishing the court of appeals' jurisdiction on some other basis.

stating the appropriate standard.[3] The appellee's counsel must carefully analyze whether the appropriate standard has been articulated by the appellant.

The appellee's greatest risk is to allow the appellant to dictate the statement of issues and the statement of facts. With respect to the issues on appeal, the appellant and the appellee rarely see eye to eye on the issues. For example, in *Clinton v. Jones*,[4] the lawyers for President Clinton couch the second issue in terms of whether the district court, as a proper exercise of judicial discretion, may stay such litigation until the President leaves office. The lawyers for Paula Jones question whether the court of appeals erred in reversing the grant of immunity for acts beyond the outer perimeter of the President's official duties. The former stress the rightness of the district court (suggesting it acted within the proper exercise of judicial discretion), while the latter suggest there is no error because the acts are beyond the President's official duties. As an appellee, do not simply accept the appellant's view of the issues.

Still rarer yet is the time that the appellant's statement of facts reflects the theme of the appellee. First, subtle words with very different connotations probably will be used by each party. For example, if one argues an aspect of an abortion case, the party who favors abortion will call the entity a "fetus." The party opposing abortion may well say it the "unborn child" or the "baby." Second, the order and manner in which the facts are presented may make a difference in their subtle persuasiveness. Consider the *Clinton v. Jones* briefs for example. President Clinton's counsel presented the facts in a topical manner. The procedural aspects of the case were stressed, which is a topical approach. Ms. Jones' counsel used a chronological approach, more story-like than Clinton's brief. Third, facts not critical to the decision may be omitted by the appellant. Appellee's use of those facts can be very persuasive. Also, since facts more favorable to the appellant will be stressed, appellee may choose to ignore those facts entirely.

Returning once again to the *Clinton v. Jones* briefs, Clinton's counsel began his recitation of the facts in the following manner:

> Petitioner William Jefferson Clinton is President of the United States. On May 6, 1994, respondent Paula Corbin Jones filed this civil damages action against the President in the United States District Court for the Eastern District of Arkansas. The complaint was based principally on conduct alleged to have occurred three year earlier * * *.

---

3. As noted in Chapter One, the Federal Rules of Appellate Procedure require only that the appellant's brief state the standard of review applicable to each issue on appeal. Some circuits, however, specify more specific standards. For example, in the Fifth Circuit, a standard articulated is "that the district court erred in formulating or applying a rule of law." *See* 5th Cir. R. 28.2.6. It is unlikely that both the appellant and the appellee will agree this standard is the correct one on review.

4. *See* Appendices C and D.

Ms. Jones' lawyers, on the other hand, after an initial paragraph that introduced how Ms. Jones got to the President's hotel suite, continued in paragraph two by stating:

Mrs. Jones, who had never met the Governor before, entered his suite at his invitation. Small talk followed. Mr. Clinton asked Mrs. Jones about her job. The Governor noted that David Harrinton, his appointee who served as the director of Mrs. Jones's agency and her superior there, was his "good friend." The Governor then made a series of verbal and physical sexual advances toward Mrs. Jones, and undressed himself from the waist down. Horrified, Mrs. Jones moved away from Mr. Clinton and said, "Look, I've got to go."

A complete reading of the facts leaves one to wonder if the two parties were actually arguing the same case.

In summary, appellee should carefully review the statement of jurisdiction, the statement of the standard of review, the statement of the issues presented on appeal, and the statement of the facts. In most instances, the appellee will strive to articulate these portions of the brief in a manner most persuasive to appellee's positions. To allow the appellant to dictate the entire stage for the appellee's case on appeal is foolhardy.

7.40   THE REFUTATION OF APPELLANT'S BRIEF AND RESPONSIVE ARGUMENTS

The primary goal of the appellee's brief is to refute the appellant's points and, at the same time, make solid responsive arguments. The two cannot be separated. They should be woven into a substantive whole. There are, however, areas in which the appellant may be weak. Special attention must be directed to the areas where appellee can make direct refutation to build solid arguments. The following are examples.

1. *Evidence of faulty logic.* Faulty logic may stem from numerous problems in the argument. Do the facts of the authority cited relate to the law so that the conclusion drawn can effectively be applied to the case on appeal? Does the authority stand for the proposition espoused? Is the authority dispositive of the issue? Is the authority cited easily distinguishable? Leaps of faith generally signal faulty logic.

2. *Faulty logic that leads to inadequate support for conclusions.* The end result of faulty logic usually is that the conclusions are simply unsupported by the cited authority. The advocate must ask: are there missing premises upon which the conclusion is based? Do omissions in fact or law lead to a different conclusion? Is the basic underlying theme or theory ultimately unsupported by the legal and factual presentation of the appellant? If so, there is inadequate support for the conclusions stated. These deficiencies may be difficult to spot because of their subtlety, and only through careful and diligent analysis are errors such as these discovered.

3. *Unintended results if the opposition's position is accepted.* If the position espoused may result in potentially unfair implications for other cases, courts are unlikely to agree with that position. For example, if the appellant argues that a particular privilege should be extended in the case under appeal, the appellee can perhaps show that the extension of that privilege will prejudice the rights of others not a party to the lawsuit. Therefore, extending immunities may fall within this type of argument. Counsel for the appellee must emphasize to the court that appellant's argument would result in future unfair consequences. Counsel must then offer a better solution, thus refuting the appellant and building a responsive argument.

4. *The strength of competing arguments.* Appellants often have solid arguments. Thus, the appellee must show that appellant's arguments, though legally and factually sound, are not as significant in resolving the issue as those of the appellee. This approach has risks. It admits that the appellant has good arguments. However, if this is the case, the appellee must convince the court that there are preferable, sounder, and better policy justifications for the appellee's position.

In similar fashion, the appellee may convince the court that counsel's arguments are not only more important to the resolution, but also that appellee's ultimate resolution is preferable to the one offered by the appellant. The argument proceeds by admitting appellant has tenable arguments, but appellee's are better. Once again, the approach is vigorously to respond.

7.50 WHEN AND IF TO CONCEDE

The matter of conceding is a sticky issue. Some commentators suggest if there is an argument that cannot be confronted, the best way to handle it is to ignore it. Their contention is that to draw further attention to the point only makes it seem more important than it is. Better to make one's own argument and let the judges determine the strengths and weaknesses of the two opponents.

This is a mistake. If the authorities and arguments are on point, the advocate should confront them and practice "damage control." As one author stated: "To admit nothing and concede nothing may satisfy one's aggressive instincts, but it is not a persuasive posture for an advocate."[5]

Damage control is best practiced by admitting or conceding the argument; but one should then immediately indicate to the court the limits of the concession and argue its relative insignificance. The concession must emphasize that the decision should still be in favor of the appellee. For example, in a case potentially involving hurt or damaged feelings, appellee may concede that the appellant will not be compensated if the court finds for the appellee, but the appellee should quickly establish that there is no cause of action for that type of damage. This technique is especially useful if the cause of action claimed by the

5. Girvan Peck, Writing Persuasive Briefs 145 (1984).

appellant does not neatly fit into the existing common law, or fall within the jurisdiction's statutory scheme.

To conclude, at times it is strategic to concede a point, especially if it is incontestable. However, counsel must then argue the limits of the concession and guide the court to what is important and decisive in the case.

7.60 THE REPLY BRIEF

Court rules usually provide that the appellant has a finite number of days to file a reply brief to the appellee's brief. The main question is whether a reply brief is necessary. In most cases, it is not.

7.61 The necessity of filing a reply brief

By the time the judges get to this point in the controversy, the last thing they want is more paperwork, especially if the document does nothing except rehash old arguments or quibble about inconsequential arguments raised by the appellee. The test always is whether the appellee has either raised new matter or muddied the positions so dramatically as to require the appellant to clarify the issues.

7.62 The contents of a reply brief

A good reply brief should be short, powerful and to the point. It should not attempt to deal with every conceivable error or omission contained in the appellee's brief. This will be viewed as a sign of weakness. The reply brief should answer new issues raised only if they could substantially affect the outcome of the case. Nit picking at the appellee's points is counter productive. Also, this is not the time to raise new issues that should have been contained in the opening brief.[6]

Reply briefs need not be divided into major sections like the opening brief, e.g., Statement of the Case and Argument. Nevertheless, the points must be set out with specificity. A point heading that reads "Reply to Point II" is totally unhelpful.

The appellant may attack any portion of the appellee's brief. For example, while generally not fertile grounds for misstatement or omission, even the Questions Presented may call for a reply. Usually, however er reply briefs take aim at some portion of the appellee's main arguments. Matters most likely to necessitate a reply are:

(1) The appellee raises a new issue. This is a clear case in which the appellant must file a reply brief. This is especially so if the issue raised could be dispositive of the case.

(2) The appellee misstates the record. If this should occur, identify the misstatement and direct the court to the place in the record where the correct version may be found.

---

6. Generally, the rule is issues cannot first be raised in the reply brief. *See Mississippi River Corp. v. FTC,* 454 F.2d 1083 (8th Cir.1972). Some courts overlook this rule while others deem the issue to be waived.

(3) The appellee misstates or omits some aspect of a case. This may involve a misstatement or omission of facts that distort the case, such as: misapplying a cited case to the case on appeal; distorting the holding; distorting quotations or taking quotations out of context that change the meaning; or, otherwise improperly interpreting the appellant's case.

This list is not exhaustive. At times the entire theory and theme of the appellee's brief requires a response. For example, at the federal level, if the appellee's theme suggests the court adopt a position contrary to the one in place in the home circuit, a reply brief should be filed. In the reply brief, the appellant should explore the policy of avoiding inter-circuit conflict, when possible, and remind the court that it is this type of decision that triggers Supreme Court review.

Court rules differ dramatically among the jurisdictions. Thus it is important to read carefully the rules relating to reply briefs. Many of them specify form, substance, and filing times.[7]

EXERCISES

I. In Chapter 6, you were given the facts and the summary of the argument written by the Petitioner in the case of *Batson v. Kentucky*. Write the facts for the Respondent, State of Kentucky.

II. The brief for Respondent Paula Corbin Jones is found in Appendix D. Review the brief and answer the following questions:

    A. The facts are lengthy. Are they effective as written? If so, why. If not, why not? If you think they could be more effectively presented, what would you include and what would you omit?

    B. Does the Summary capture the essence of the argument? Is there anything you would add to the Summary?

    C. Are the point headings effective? If so, why? If not, how would you draft them to maximize their effect?

III. Does the respondent's brief utilize any of the "bases that support the appellee (respondent)" found in § 7.20?

IV. Does the respondent's brief refute any of the arguments espoused by the President's counsel, Mr. Bennett?

V. Are there any concessions made by the petitioner on which the respondent capitalized?

VI. The Petitioner filed a Reply Brief. (See Appendix E).

    A. Does it reply to issues raised by the Respondent?

    B. Does it reiterate old arguments?

    C. Does it raise new issues?

    D. Is it effective? If not, why not?

---

7. *See* Fed. R. App. P. 28(c).

Chapter Eight

PRELIMINARY CONSIDERATIONS BEFORE ARGUMENT

Analysis

8.00 ORAL ARGUMENT THEN AND NOW

Oral advocacy in England was long a cornerstone of appellate review; indeed, appellate review developed as an oral process. Barristers preferred oral argument, partially because the cost of printing written ones was prohibitive. Oral arguments often lasted days. It is not surprising that the English tradition found its way to the United States. In the famous case of *Gibbons v. Ogden*,[1] the Supreme Court of the United States, headed by Chief Justice John Marshall, began hearing oral argument on February 4, 1824. The first oralist was Daniel Webster who spoke for two-and-one-half hours. Thomas J. Oakley, counsel for Ogden, followed for an hour on that day and for the entire court day on February 5. Thomas Emmet spent the whole third day, February 6, and two hours on February 7 delivering his oratory. The arguments finally concluded on the 8th when William Wirt closed for the appellant Gibbons. This was oral advocacy in the grand fashion. It must be noted, however, that in the term in which *Gibbons* was decided, the United States Supreme Court handed down only thirty-six opinions. In recent years, the Court averages about ninety opinions per year.[2]

---

1. 22 U.S. (9 Wheat.) 1 (1824).

2. During the 2000 term, 86 cases were argued and 93 cases were disposed of by full

As modern printing mechanisms developed, the written brief gained greater importance. Many judges preferred to have a written document to ponder before deciding a case. The brief became more important as the court dockets became busier with each passing year. Time limits on oral argument began to appear. Some critics of oral argument have suggested that the tradition should be eliminated altogether. They claim that it is unnecessary and time consuming; better that the time is spent studying the briefs. Fortunately, while the argument time has been substantially reduced and some courts retain the right to eliminate argument in some instances, the oral argument still is a mainstay in appellate advocacy. The role of the advocate, however, is decidedly different.

As noted by one author[3] the shift from oral argument to the brief was gradual. The oral component remained important and often decisive for many appellate judges. It was more the practice than the exception that appellate judges came to the argument "cold," that is without having read the briefs. They, therefore, knew nothing about the case. It was up to the lawyers to educate the judges, not only about the facts and issues, but also about the applicable law. It was the custom in many courts to preliminarily decide the outcome of the case immediately following the argument. Obviously, in a close case, the oral skills and acumen of an attorney could win the day for the client.

As caseloads grew, appellate courts began to handle oral argument in a different fashion. In most courts, argument time was shortened to one hour and then later was slashed to thirty minutes per side. In addition, oral argument was not automatic in all circumstances. More judges began to prepare for the cases by reading the briefs. Thus, the function of the argument moved from educating the bench about the basic facts and issues to one of sorting out troublesome points of law, inconsistent facts and policy concerns. Gone are the days when attorneys had hours to hold forth, and dazzle the Court with pure eloquence. While persuasion remains the key to a good oral argument, the approach to advocacy has changed.

Today, the advocate must converse with the court members and answer their concerns. As Chief Justice Rehnquist has stated, the more the advocate's tone is conversational, rather than oratory, the better the case will fare. The advocate should regard the exercise as an intellectual discussion, where concerns are aired in an attempt to realize a just conclusion.

8.10 WHO SHOULD APPEAL AND ARGUE THE CASE

The matter of who should handle the appeal is debatable. There are differing and conflicting conclusions. On one side are those who say it

opinions. This seems to be about average for the past several years with 83 cases argued and 79 disposed of during the 1999 terms.

3. Robert J. Martineau, Appellate Practice and Procedure 401 (1987).

should be the attorney who tried the case. They suggest that to bring in a specialist is a vast waste of time and money. That lawyer will not be familiar with the case. In addition, they argue, the trial lawyer better appreciates and remembers the nuances of the case, as well as the substance of the evidence. This is especially so if the trial lawyer wrote the brief on appeal.

Others dispute these arguments. Judge Paxton Blair, once Solicitor General of the State of New York and Chief of the Division of Appeals, Corporation Counsel, City of New York wrote:

> I have always held that the trial man is *not the best man* to handle the appeal, but may even be the worst * * *. The appeals specialist views the case precisely as does the appellate court, through the little square window of the record, so to speak, and not as something viewed from the great outdoors. The trial man's mind cannot free itself of matters which entered in during preparation for trial but which did not get into the record * * *. Then, too, the style of oratory a trial man develops through his constant appeal to a jury less learned than himself is out of place in an appellate court * * *.[4]

Simply put, the trial attorney may be too close to the case to see the issues from an appellate court's point of view. This is particularly true if the trial was an emotional one. In addition, appellate attorneys are more familiar with the appellate rules, procedures and the applicable precedents in the appellate courts.

In some instances, there is no choice with respect to who handles the appeal. For example, in some government agencies and law firms, it is a senior attorney who becomes the oralist. Many times, that attorney has neither tried the case nor written the brief. In that situation, the oralist must rely on briefing memos from those who are familiar with the issues.

One matter upon which most experts agree is that there is no perfect answer for all cases. If time allows, financial concerns manageable and appellate expertise advantageous, outside counsel might be the answer. In other instances, if finances are tight and time is limited, the trial lawyer, of necessity, may be pressed into appellate service. Ultimately, the most important points to consider are the comparative abilities of the available lawyers and the best interest of the client.

8.20 THE IMPORTANCE AND BENEFITS OF ORAL ARGUMENT

The notion that most appeals can be submitted on the briefs, without benefit of the oral argument, is a practice that is discouraged by both the bench and the bar. The American Bar Association, in its 1977 Standard Relating to Appellate Court, § 3.35, states:

---

4. Judge Paxton Blair, *Appellate Briefs and Advocacy,* 18 Fordham L. Rev. 30, 46– 47 (1949).

Oral argument is normally an essential part of the appellate process. It is a medium of communication which for many appellate counsel and many judges is superior to written expression. It provides a fluid and rapidly moving method of getting at essential issues. It contributes to judicial accountability, enlarges the public visibility of appellate decision-making and is a safeguard against undue reliance on staff. * * *. [W]hen an appeal is considered on its merits * * * oral argument should never be discouraged routinely and should be denied only if the court is convinced that the contentions presented are frivolous or that oral argument would not be useful.

Former Supreme Court Justice Brennan once stated:

[O]ral argument is the absolutely indispensable ingredient of appellate advocacy * * *. [O]ften my whole notion of what a case is about crystallizes at oral argument. This happens even though I read all of the briefs before oral argument; indeed, that is the practice now of all the members of the Supreme Court * * *. Often my idea of how a case shapes up is changed by oral argument * * *. Oral argument with us is a Socratic dialogue between Justices and counsel.[5]

Mr. Justice Harlan, who also has spoken to the issue, echoes his sentiments.

[O]ral argument gives an opportunity for interchange between court and counsel that the briefs do not give. For my part, there is no substitute, even within the time limits afforded by the busy calendars of modern appellate courts, for the Socratic method of procedure in getting at the real heart of an issue and in finding out where the truth lies.[6]

There are other pragmatic reasons why an advocate argues before an appellate tribunal and why it can be said *never ever* waive oral argument. The following observations are illustrative.

If courts of appeal have discretion to choose which cases will be heard orally, it indicates that any case so chosen, in at least some judicial minds, raises troublesome questions or concerns. Therefore, if the case is set for oral argument, counsel should assume that the case is getting special attention and that the outcome may well be in doubt. In few instances is oral argument set in a case that clearly can be decided on the briefs.

The oral argument is the last chance to make a strong argument for the case. The briefs have been read. The oral argument allows the advocate the opportunity to develop a central theme upon which the judges can make their decision. It takes the case from a formal, detached written form to something that is more personalized and living, and susceptible to persuasion.

5. Harvard Law School, Occasional Pamphlet No. 9, pp. 22, 23 (1967).

6. Ralph M. Carson, *Conduct of the Appeal—A Lawyer's View*, in A Case on Appeal 74 (1967).

Even a judge who has taken a position on a case will probably at least listen to the arguments. That judge may rethink his or her original opinion if the opponent fails to make a convincing argument because of ineptitude, lack of preparation, or simply because resolution of the issues is unsettled. A door is opened where before it was closed.

Assume the following three scenarios. In the first, the case is straightforward, the issues are relatively few in number and the advocate is convinced that the argument will prevail. One might ask: why chance defeat and jeopardize victory by requesting oral argument? There are two solid answers. First, a member of the panel may have thought of troublesome issues that counsel had not addressed in the brief. The oral argument will allow the advocate the opportunity to confront the confusion and resolve it. Second, even if one assumes a winning case from the outset, the argument may well serve as a tool, later used by the judges, to mold the written opinion to that precisely requested by the advocate.

In the second situation, assume that the advocate has a difficult case. A written brief may not suffice. This is the time oral argument is most important. The advocate has an opportunity to persuade the court that policy requires a change, that the law has been misinterpreted or that the law as enunciated makes "hard" law under the circumstances of this case. It may also be a time to minimize or even undermine a position taken by opposing counsel.

In the third scenario, suppose a judge, after reading the briefs and thinking about the issues, develops a new line of inquiry different from that espoused by the advocate in the brief. A perspicacious advocate can seize the moment, respond to this inquiry, develop a new line of reasoning and answer the concerns of the judge. Absent oral argument, this cannot occur.

Additionally, it is a known fact that some people more easily understand and relate better to the spoken word rather than the written word. For those individuals, the oral argument would be a better communicative device than the brief.

Chief Justice Rehnquist makes two excellent points about the importance of oral argument. First, he notes that the argument is the only time an advocate has to confront face to face the nine members of the Court who will decide the case. Second, it may well be only one of two occasions when the justices convene to consider the case. In short, this is an excellent opportunity to be present with the Court when it collegially concentrates on the advocate's case.

Several years ago, Judges Myron H. Bright and Richard S. Arnold of the Eighth Circuit Court of Appeals examined the effects of oral argument on the results of their decisions. During a ten-month period, they asked themselves three questions about the cases orally argued before them. The questions were: (1) Was oral argument necessary? (2) Was oral argument helpful? (3) Did it change my mind about the case? The results are as follows:

1.	Was oral argument necessary?	Yes	No
	Judge Bright	85%	15%
	Judge Arnold	75%	25%
2.	Was oral argument helpful?		
	Judge Bright	82%	18%
	Judge Arnold	80%	20%
3.	Did it change my mind?	Yes	Maybe
	Judge Bright	24%	7%
	Judge Arnold	15%	2%

While these figures are impressive, other judges say that oral argument is not that influential. Nevertheless, in view of what has been written about the importance of oral argument, much by judges themselves, an advocate given the chance should *never ever* waive the opportunity for a face to face conversation with an appellate bench.

8.30   OBTAINING ORAL ARGUMENT

8.31   Rationing oral argument

Many appellate courts do not hear oral argument as a matter of course. In the federal courts of appeals and the United States Supreme Court, however, cases are scheduled for argument unless the court, on its own initiative, determines not to hear oral argument. The circuits vary widely as to when to allow argument and for how long. Thirty minutes per side is slightly above average among the circuits, with some allowing as little as 10 to 15 minutes for each advocate. There remains the possibility of greater time allocations should the court deem discussion of the issues to require additional time. One-hour arguments, which were the rule rather than the exception, have long disappeared. The sheer number of appeals simply has eliminated this luxury.

Because of the wide divergence among the circuits as to which arguments to hear and which to accept on briefs, an amendment to the Federal Rule of Appellate Procedure 34(a) to set minimum standards to decide this issue was passed in 1986. This rule allows the courts of appeals to dispense with argument in certain instances. However, the parties may request oral argument and state why oral argument is necessary. Rule 34(a)(2) provides that oral argument will be allowed unless:

(A) the appeal is frivolous;

(B) the dispositive issue or issues have been authoritatively decided; or

(C) the facts and legal arguments are adequately presented in the briefs and record and the decisional process would not be significantly aided by oral argument.

8.32   Considerations for granting argument time

Courts generally have wide discretion to allow or deny oral argument. Once the decision has been made to deny oral argument, however, there is little or no recourse to challenge that determination. Even so, the process of making the decision varies from circuit to circuit. Some circuits use staff attorneys to screen cases. In other circuits, there is a greater amount of judicial involvement. In any event, whoever makes the decision must be convinced to hear oral argument. "This is a case of first impression" is not likely to stir the imaginations of the brief reviewer. A better approach is to explain "this is a case of first impression because it involves * * * "and then fill in the blank as concisely and convincingly as possible. Counsel should consider what it is that is particularly interesting about this case and why it needs to be presented live rather than only in written form.

Of course, the parties may notify the court that counsel wishes to submit the case on the briefs rather than to argue. As noted previously, this can be a dangerous move, one not recommended by most lawyers and judges.

Likewise, rules governing oral argument differ from state to state. For example, in some states, the advocate must inform the court that it does **not** want to be scheduled for oral argument; in others, those who wish to argue must so state on the title page of the brief. In still others, an explanation must be given as to why oral argument is necessary. The bottom line is that all advocates must know and carefully follow the rules of the court in which the oral argument will take place.

8.40 FAMILIARITY WITH COURT RULES—A SHORT SURVEY OF SOME DIFFERENCES AMONG THE FEDERAL CIRCUITS

Court rules vary dramatically from jurisdiction to jurisdiction. For purposes of writing this section, the rules for all of the federal circuit courts of appeal were examined. The results are quite remarkable.

First, there are the actual rules of each circuit. In addition, most, but not all, of the circuits have what are called Internal Operating Procedures. In many instances, these procedures describe more precisely what the court uses as guidelines for oral advocacy. For example, the Tenth Circuit informs the advocate how to prepare and present the oral argument, as well as what to argue. Judge James K. Logan used to suggest that advocates "[t]ry not to read the argument unless necessary to read opening lines to keep from passing out from fright."[7] The Fifth Circuit specifically forbids reading. The Sixth Circuit discloses the names of the judges who will hear the case two weeks before the date of the argument (that information is posted on the Court's computer bulletin board system). The Third Circuit sends out the names of the panel members 10 days prior to the argument. The First Circuit "holds the view that seldom is counsel well served by an advance reservation of

---

7. Patrick Fisher, Clerk of the Tenth Circuit Court of Appeals tells this writer that this particular pithy advice has now been written out of the Practitioner's Guide which was formerly found in the Internal Operating Procedures, 10th Cir., VII Oral Argument (C)(2)(c)(ii), in Federal Local Court Rules (Law. Co-op 2d ed. 1995). It remains good counsel.

time for rebuttal * * *. Counsel are expected to cover all anticipated issues in their arguments in chief."[8] The Tenth Circuit, on the other hand, suggests that it is "good practice for appellant to reserve a few minutes of the allotted time for rebuttal."[9] Some circuits require oral argument unless waived by the panel and some do not allow it unless approved by the panel. The Third Circuit suggests criteria for accepting oral argument. More specifically, it advises that "[e]xperience discloses that judges usually find oral argument unnecessary when:

(a) the issue is tightly constrained, not novel and the briefs adequately cover the arguments;

(b) the outcome of the appeal is clearly controlled by a decision of the Supreme Court or this court; or

(c) the state of the record will determine the outcome and the sole issue is either sufficiency of the evidence, the adequacy of jury instructions, or rulings as to admissibility of evidence, and the briefs adequately refer to the record."[10]

Further, the Third Circuit states: "Experience discloses that judges usually vote for oral argument when:

(a) the appeal presents a substantial and novel legal issue;

(b) the resolution of an issue presented by the appeal will be of institutional or precedential value;

(c) a judge has questions to ask counsel to clarify an important legal, factual, or procedural point;

(d) a decision, legislation, or an event subsequently to the filing of the last brief may significantly bear on the case; or

(e) an important public interest may be affected."[11]

The likelihood is that these criteria are shared by most if not all of the circuits. The Third Circuit was helpful in making explicit what is useful for advocates in cases in the other circuits as well.

The District of Columbia Circuit tapes the arguments and the tapes may be purchased by the advocate after the case has been completely closed. The Fifth Circuit tapes the arguments, but no one can hear them. Its procedures suggest that, with the advanced approval of the Court, the advocates may arrange at their own expense for a qualified court reporter to be present to record and transcribe the oral argument should the advocate desire a copy of it (after the transcript is prepared, the tapes must be destroyed). How time is signaled varies from court to court. Likewise, counsel's suggested time of arrival varies together with how to check in, where to sit, when the arguments begin, the days on which arguments are heard, the length of the argument and who

8. 1st Cir. R. 34(c)(2).

9. Internal Operating Procedure, 10th Cir., VII Oral Argument (C)(2)(e), *in* Federal Local Court Rules (Law. Co-op, 2d ed. 1995).

10. Internal Operating Procedure, 3d Cir., 2.4.1, *in* Federal Local Court Rules (Law. Co-op, 3d ed. 2001).

11. *Id.* at 2.4.2.

determines the length of the argument to name others. In short, some circuits are more user friendly than others.

8.50 FAMILIARITY WITH OPPOSING COUNSEL, THE COURT-ROOM, AND EXPECTATIONS OF THE COURT

8.51 Know the opposing counsel

It is helpful, if possible, to know opposing counsel. Everyone has strengths and weaknesses. To evaluate those in advance can only benefit one's preparation of both the brief and the oral argument.

Here are some questions one should pursue: First, is the trial lawyer arguing the appeal? As discussed previously in this chapter, there are some potential problems with the trial counsel making the argument.

Second, whether or not the trial lawyer is now appellate counsel, is he or she experienced in appellate advocacy? The skills needed for arguing an appeal are very different from those needed in the trial courtroom. An experienced trial lawyer does not necessarily make a good appellate advocate.

Third, does opposing counsel have any known idiosyncrasies? Different people have different styles. Knowing these can work to one's advantage. For example, if opposing counsel tends to be loud and flamboyant, the advocate may want to choose a style that is deliberate, thoughtful, well reasoned and calm. If opposing counsel is laconic, a more aggressive posture may be advantageous. However, one must still use one's own strengths. What is suggested here is to consider how the opponent's strengths can be neutralized and weaknesses exposed.

8.52 Know the tribunal

Who the judges are, how they think, and why they think the way they do are important considerations for the prospective advocate. Judges, as others, are the products of their education, background and life experiences. The advocate who understands those aspects of the panel can better fashion arguments that will be the most productive. Note: the operative word is *help* the advocate fashion an argument. Obviously, there is no certain way to know how any one judge will react to any given issue on any specific day; but to know some background and the personalities of the bench allows the advocate to have a better chance to predict potential positions on issues.

If the advocate is appearing before a state Supreme Court or the United States Supreme Court, the judges will be known. If the advocate is before a court of appeals, information about the panel is usually available from the clerk's office. At times, the names of the judges and the cases they will hear are posted on public bulletin boards or sent to the advocates.

Having that information, the advocate is well advised to research the backgrounds and propensities of each panel member. A helpful resource for this exercise is the Almanac of the Federal Judiciary.[12] Contained in this publication are biographies, extracts from the judge's most important opinions and lawyer evaluations of the judge's performance on the bench. Armed with that information, one might contact attorneys who have argued before the prospective panel. Opinions written by panel members give the advocate an idea of judicial positions on issues. One definitely should study selected opinions, especially if they cover an issue or issues relevant to the advocate's appeal. A careful search on a legal database is the easiest method for locating opinions and law review articles penned by members of the appellate panel.

Knowing how the panel members act while engaged in oral argument is also helpful. The author recalls one crusty appellate judge who often appeared to torment advocates about tangential issues, just to be contrary. One must ask: does the judge ask questions on tangential issues? Are the questions generally helpful in nature, meant to draw out the issues? Is the judge courteous? Or is the judge aggressive, to the point of rudeness? Are the questions at times hostile? The advocate who is unprepared for the type or style of questioning may be prey to catastrophe. Usually one of two events occurs: the advocate withers and collapses under pressure; or the advocate becomes hostile and defensive. Either is a recipe for disaster. In the former, the advocate is likely to make serious concessions; in the latter, the advocate risks being considered disrespectful and thus forfeits credibility.

8.53 Know the courtroom and environs

Know the location of the courthouse and its surroundings. If the advocate intends to drive, is there adequate parking and how far is the parking from the courthouse?

All advocates should be familiar with the physical attributes of the courtroom in which they will present their oral argument. The chambers of the United States Supreme Court have been described as large, with a massive bench stretching the entire width of the room. The acoustics are terrible, and everyone speaks into a microphone. Surely an advocate who is to appear before this august body should be forewarned about the physical attributes of the room. To name but two concerns, this will allow the advocate to adjust the speaking voice and consider how to maintain eye contact, as discussed in Chapter Ten.

There are other logistical concerns. These seem simple, but a failure to know their dimensions in advance can be harmful. Consider the following:

- Is there ample lighting in the courtroom? Some courtroom podiums have their own personal light. Imagine a situation in which a young advocate struggles through an oral argument, unable to see clearly, only to discover he failed to turn on the light.

12. Almanac of the Federal Judiciary   Business 2002).
(Megan Chase et al. eds., Aspen Law and

- Are time signals given? Many courts routinely do not give time signals. It is up to the advocate to assume that responsibility.
- Is there room on the podium for a watch or a stop watch? Is the watch large enough to see?
- Does the appellant's counsel sit at a particular table? If so, which one?

Of course, many of these questions are answered after one argues in a particular courtroom. But one time may be the only time. Anything an advocate can do to alleviate the trauma inherent in oral advocacy is time well spent.

8.54　Time to arrive

The general rule is: *always sooner than later*. Some courts require that counsel be present when the court opens on the day of argument; others schedule a time certain. In the latter, counsel usually is requested to be in court a certain number of cases ahead, in the event that those cases conclude sooner than expected. The clerk of the court can be very helpful with respect to the policies of the court.

In the United States Supreme Court, counsel is requested to be in the courtroom when the preceding argument begins.[13] There are two advantages to this rule. First, counsel has time to collect and sort items that will be used during the argument. Second, this affords an opportunity to observe an argument in progress. Knowing the routine before beginning one's argument is especially important if counsel is a novice. Even experienced advocates should observe in advance the court to which they will make their argument. If possible, this should be done more than once.

Out-of-town lawyers are especially advised to arrive early—a day early. One never knows when an unexpected event will delay the trip. The last thing an advocate needs is the additional stress of arriving just in time to race to the podium unsure of whether all is in order for the argument.

8.55　Courtroom etiquette

As previously mentioned, an advocate must be familiar with the court's rules and its practices. For example, the appropriate opening for addressing the entire court is usually "May it please the court." However in some courts, the rules or simply the traditions may require a different salutation. In the Supreme Court of the United States, the salutation is "Mr. Chief Justice _____ and may it please the court."

Tradition usually dictates, unless governed by court rule, that the appellant sits on the left of the bench as he or she faces it. And of course, whenever spoken to, the advocate must stand. This is especially true at the outset when the Judge or Justice asks the parties if they are ready to proceed. It is considered proper etiquette to address individual judges as

---

13. *See* Guide to Counsel, United States Supreme Court, 2001.

Your Honor rather than using that person's last name. The worst case scenario is that the advocate calls the judge by the wrong name. Also, using last names suggests familiarity with the judges, a practice to be discouraged. Collectively, when referring to the entire bench, it is probably less awkward to refer to them as "The Court" rather than "Your Honors," though either is acceptable.

Chapter Nine

PREPARATION FOR THE ORAL ARGUMENT

Analysis

9.00 PRELIMINARY THOUGHTS

For most advocates, no matter the degree of experience, oral argument is an exercise fraught with anxiety. The good news is that a certain degree of anxiety is helpful because it enhances the advocate's sharpness when the adrenalin starts pumping. The bad news is that too much anxiety leads to clumsiness and a perception, by the bench, of unpreparedness. This in turn creates a lack of credibility.

9.01 Importance of preparation

To be effective and credible, one must prepare. There is no substitute for long hard hours of preparation. As one seasoned lawyer so aptly states:

> Ah, preparation! There is where the magic begins! Yet young lawyers seem disappointed when I tell them so. They yearn for an easy formula that will permit them to bypass the stodgy stuff called work. I wish I could explain to them that true preparation is not work. It is the joy of creating.[1]

Not all lawyers experience exhilaration in the preparation for argument. But it is true that, for many advocates, the amount of time spent preparing is directly proportional to the ultimate quality of the oral

---

1. Gerry Spence, How to Argue and Win
Every Time, 128 (1995).

argument. Further, it is only through thorough preparation that the advocate will feel a degree of confidence necessary to deliver a top quality argument.

How one prepares depends on several factors, not the least of which is the age-old problem of time. If an advocate is called upon to do an appellate argument just hours or days before the argument is scheduled, time is of the essence and its use must be rationed.

9.02 Preparation is an individual exercise

No matter what the circumstances dictate, preparation is the key to confidence and a good argument. There is no such thing as a good "winged" argument. Anyone who claims to have "winged" an argument with success is probably a fool in advocate's clothing.

How one prepares is, however, a very individual exercise. For the novice, even total immersion may seem insufficient. This may or may not be true. Previous experience with public speaking or appellate advocacy may help to define the level of preparation necessary prior to argument. One's self confidence in the knowledge of the case prior to beginning preparation also plays a role. In short, the amount and type of preparation is dependent upon an individual's honest conception of self, as well as the time frame within which to work.

The method that is useful to one advocate and not another depends on the individual. The essential task is to discern a methodology that best prepares the advocate for the ultimate goal of a successful oral argument. Whatever choices are made, there are always three components to preparation. First, the advocate must be totally familiar with the record, the briefs, the facts and the law. Second, the advocate must determine how best to cover the most salient points within the confines of the time limitations of the argument. In other words, the advocate must analyze the best way to organize the argument to get the important points before the court. Third, the advocate must decide the type of notes to take to the podium and prepare them accordingly. Each of these has vital sub-components. All must be examined and resolved.

9.10 FAMILIARITY WITH THE BRIEFS AND RECORD

There are divergent views on how to begin preparation for the oral argument. Some writers suggest review of the record first, followed by review of the briefs and then of the pertinent law. Obviously, all of the review components are interrelated. In time, all must be mastered.

Many seasoned advocates believe the best way to begin the entire process of review is first to reread the appellate briefs. This sharpens the conception of the issues thought to be important to each side of the case. Also, any brief worth its weight in paper will set forth a persuasive (if one-sided) set of facts. Some authorities believe that the facts in a brief are the *most important component*. Brief writers are instructed to recite the facts in a scrupulously candid manner but, in doing so, should use language most favorable to the client's position. Having read the facts in both the appellant's and the appellee's briefs, the advocate should have a sound understanding as to the basis of the appeal. Armed with issue and factual information, aspects contained in the record that support or contradict the arguments raised can be noted and thoroughly reviewed.

Various authorities have suggested numerous ways to acquaint oneself with the record. For example, if the oralist also wrote the brief, an abstract of the record is generally constructed to help organize the major points of the brief. In some situations, a review of the abstract is sufficient. This, however, entails significant risks. Since oral argument may well come months after the briefs are filed, even the best memories may fade. Abstracts, then, are not adequate either to familiarize oneself with the record or to advise an inquiring judge where a document or piece of evidence can be found. Even worse than relying on abstracts is a review only of an index of the record. This can be disastrous.

Realistically, there is no substitute for rereading and then tabbing important components of the record. These may include the major pleadings, key evidence, the lower court opinion, findings and the final decree—to name but a few. One can expect the tabs to change somewhat during the formulation of the oral argument depending upon the importance of emerging issues. In addition, key points in the record that prove to be pivotal to the argument, should also be tabbed.

More than one expert has stressed the importance of "geographic familiarity" with the record. Geographic familiarity means that the advocate can articulate where in the record specific information can be found. This includes, but is not limited to, documents, pleadings, testimony and the like. The only way to achieve that degree of knowledge of the record is to reread it, outline it, and tab it. During oral argument, it is not effective for the advocate to shuffle through the record to answer a simple question. For example, assume a case in which the advocate is asked about a jury instruction, but he or she cannot locate the instruction. This undermines confidence in the advocate, stalls the argument and wastes everybody's time. Most judges are not impressed by such ineptitude.

9.20 FAMILIARITY WITH THE PERTINENT LAW

9.21 How to become familiar with the law of the case

The first step in a review of the law is to Shepardize all citations in the briefs. There is obviously little need to review case material that is no longer good law. In addition, if the case hinges on a statutory provision, any amendments or deletions to the statute need to be located and put into the calculus. A search should also be made for any new or replaced regulations, if applicable. In short, a complete check needs to be made of all authority that has been cited by each side. With that task complete, step two may be undertaken.

It is axiomatic that good advocacy requires a thorough understanding of the issues and the law pertinent to those issues. How one acquires familiarity with the law generally depends on the experience of the advocate and whether he or she wrote the brief. In that case, the advocate likely has a working knowledge of the law. Nevertheless, a thorough review of the materials covered in the brief is still necessary. Some authorities suggest that every citation should be reread. If the brief is relatively fresh, however, examination of the main cases, statutes, and other auxiliary material will suffice for an adequate review. On the other hand, if the advocate was not the brief writer, the principal authorities should be reviewed. No amount of distillation by another person takes the place of reading and rereading the pertinent materials.

The level of experience of the attorney must be considered. A seasoned advocate probably will feel comfortable reviewing the main authorities upon which the case turns. But for the novice, nothing substitutes for reading and rereading all of the materials cited in the briefs. In short, the "first timer" must eat, sleep and breathe all aspects of the case. Total immersion is the only way to prepare.

With the issues and authorities in mind, the advocate should then briefly outline the arguments. This puts the issues into perspective. Ask the question: "What is dispositive of those issues?" If the answer is the interpretation of a case or cases, then the application of those cases to the facts of the case on appeal must carefully be evaluated. What are the similarities? What are the differences? Was there a statute that has an impact on the issues? Is that statute driven by a regulation? Do other auxiliary materials come into play?

For example, suppose the issue on appeal deals with a tax matter. There probably is a statutory provision that will influence the outcome of the case. In addition, a regulation or regulations likely indicate how the provision should be interpreted. But is the regulation legislative or interpretive? There may also be other IRS materials that could have an impact on the case. These may include revenue rulings, private letter rulings or technical advice memoranda. Each document forms a part of the puzzle and should be examined individually. At this stage, one begins to think about the theme of the argument. But, before deciding on a theme, all aspects of the case must be mastered.

The last check of the case law is to determine whether any new law has emerged since the briefs were filed. Do not disregard this possibility. More than one advocate has been embarrassed by failure to research the most recent decisions. For example, perhaps another circuit has recently decided one or more of the issues in the case. This is extremely useful information, positively or negatively, in preparing for oral argument. It is likely that the judges will know of this case and the theory upon which it was decided. A probing inquiry often emanates from a recently decided case not covered in the briefs. It provides fertile ground for questioning. A well-prepared advocate should have located that case and be ready to address the result and reasoning. The alternative scenario is that the advocate "discovers" the case and, by appropriate procedures, is able to call this to the court's attention. In truth, the advocate hopes for such good fortune—if the holding is favorable.

It is difficult to imagine that an advocate will over prepare for an oral argument. There is, however, one word of caution. In the process of reviewing all authority, be careful to stay focused on the main issues to be argued. This is not the time to venture into tangential matters that will cloud the vision of the law upon which the case turns. Continue to question probable topics for discussion during the oral argument. If a new-found issue seems far from the mainstream, it likely will not be of much interest to the judges.

9.30 ORGANIZATION OF THE ARGUMENT

With a clear understanding of the record and the legal authority upon which the case is based, it is now time to determine the organization of the argument. These imperatives should be observed:

9.31 Evaluate the case

The first step is an accurate evaluation of the case as a whole. The task is to determine which issues are legally the strongest, which issues are ancillary, and which issues are inherently weak. Both sides of the argument should undergo this scrutiny. Honest and penetrating analysis of one's own weaknesses is absolutely required. When examining the issues, the opponent probably will argue and explore potential responses to those arguments. Evaluate the persuasiveness of all arguments for both sides, based on factual support, legal underpinnings and policy considerations. In addition, one should consider the vulnerability of issues, and whether they should be raised at all. Likewise, some points simply may not lend themselves to oral argument.

For example, some authorities feel that in-court exhibits are distracting and a waste of time. But what if an issue requires the use of graphics? The advocate must decide whether the point can be made without an exhibit, whether to chance an exhibit, and whether the issue is crucial to the outcome of the argument. While this exercise is mostly one of thinking, notes should be made of the various arguments as they occur to the advocate. Eventually the notes will be turned into a rough outline. Basically, this is the time for selection and appraisal of all potential arguments, both pro and con, in the case.

9.32 Choose carefully the issue(s) to argue

Armed with a list of arguments, it is now time to pick the issue or issues that will be the most persuasive. All issues cannot be covered in the short period of time allocated for the oral argument. Nor should they be. Rather, the wise advocate carefully chooses the issues to be presented based on the now-completed evaluation of the case as a whole.

Sometimes it is helpful to get the opinion of others about issue evaluation. Do not hesitate to discuss the case with other lawyers or anyone who will listen. Occasionally an advocate who is completely immersed in a case fails to spot an issue that can be highly persuasive; even worse, the advocate does not see potentially troublesome points or weaknesses in the reasoning. It is commonly known as the "can't see the forest for the trees" syndrome.

In the end, simplicity is the key. Leave the complex issues that are best understood if read and studied to the brief. If they are crucial, the best approach is to sketch them broadly and then be prepared to answer questions should they arise. Mr. Justice Jackson once wrote, "[t]he impact of oral presentation will be strengthened if it is concentrated on a few points that can be simply and convincingly stated and easily grasped and retained."[2]

9.33   Outline in broad strokes

The list of salient points to be covered in oral argument is the first step in the process of organization. Next comes an outline crafted, at first, in broad strokes with the focus on reconciling and coordinating major ideas. It is here that the rudiments of the argument are born. Now the advocate can begin to think in logical patterns. Minor issues that can be woven into primary issues take form. As the outline becomes more sophisticated, the legal authorities to support the contentions can be inserted. In the end, the outline should describe the major premises, the minor premises and the supporting authority.

9.34   Choose a theme

The next step for successful organization is to pick a theme. This crucial element of organization is often overlooked. Basically, the theme is the common thread that runs through the argument and describes the rightness of the case. It may center on one legal issue that is critical to the case, or it may be a combination of several issues with a common bond. For example, the legal issue or issues may be whether the application of a statutory provision was proper, but the theme may be the harshness of the result should the provision apply. Think of the theme as being the foundation of the argument upon which the issues are built.

9.35   Prepare in detail

Once all aspects of the factual, legal and policy considerations are reviewed, and a theme determined, the advocate is now ready to prepare in detail the argument that he or she plans to deliver. The question then is: what exactly is it that one prepares? A written text? A detailed outline? A simple outline? There is merit in each of the above and, in the end, individuality will dictate what is best for an advocate. Remember: this is the final *preparation* stage. What is written at this point is not necessarily or wisely taken to the podium during the delivery of the argument. That remains for further discussion.

2.   Robert H. Jackson, *Advocacy Before the Supreme Court: Suggestions for Effec-*   *tive Case Presentations,* 37 A.B.A.J. 801, 803 (1951).

Some advocates feel it is best to write the argument in its totality. This reasoning maintains that writing one's argument in detail confirms that the argument is sufficiently important to allocate precious time and effort to the process of putting it on paper. In addition, the exercise allows the advocate to explore what he or she knows, and divulges weaknesses as well as strengths in the argument. It can disclose gaps in transitions between issues. And it helps organize and strengthen the main point or points that need to be stressed in the argument. As one lawyer says:

> [W]hen we engage in the physical act of writing, a connection is struck between the hands and that portion of the brain where our creative powers are stored, so that we are more likely to produce a new idea while we write or type than while we engage in the simple act of thinking alone.[3]

Other authors advise not to write the complete argument. A review of those sources, however, indicates that the concern is that once it is written, the advocate will take the text to the podium and read it to the court—a horrific mistake. The other concern is that once the argument is written, it will be memorized. Once memorized, the advocate risks a loss of flexibility if the court interrupts with questions. The advocate may forget where the memorized argument was interrupted and become unnerved. An otherwise good argument may unravel. Although the problems that potentially arise from reading or memorizing a written argument are real ones, it is important to remember that these problems are avoidable.

Assuming for a moment that the argument is written, the advocate must now distill what is in the draft. Many advocates annotate the text with notes, catchwords, highlighting or underlining. Some take this draft version to the podium, but this author has long observed that if a draft is sitting in front of the person, some portion of it will be read, with disastrous results.

There is uniform agreement that some type of written notes should be used during oral argument. One author suggests that the first and last sentence be written in full.[4] The first sentence assures that the advocate gets a good start. It also helps overcome some of the anxiety of actually beginning the argument. Equally important are the final words the advocate leaves with the court—perhaps a reiteration of theme or a reminder of the request for relief. Between the first and last sentence, some lawyers prefer to use catchwords to remind them of the central ideas to be conveyed to the court. Others prefer topic sentences as a reminder. Still others use the point headings or the table of contents of the brief. Whatever technique is used, it is universally agreed that some form of notes should be consulted. As one author stated "[o]nly a few

---

3. Spence, *supra* note 1, at 24.

4. Edward D. Re, Brief Writing and Oral Argument 145 (8th ed. 1999).

brilliant and audacious advocates have the temerity and ability to argue without having in front of them notes of any sort * * *."[5]

While there is no single "right" way to prepare for an oral argument, there are a multitude of pitfalls that can doom an argument. These include:

• failure to master all aspects of the case, including the opponent's case, as they relate to the record (facts and procedure), the law and potential public policy;

• failure to select the most pertinent points for argument;

• failure to organize the argument into a cohesive whole; and

• failure to prepare totally and completely for the argument itself.

The last step is an ongoing process. One does not simply make notes about what is to be said. Rather, one must review and revise to improve the substance that comes with rethinking strategies. Through this process, the advocate gains greater familiarity with the contents, which ensures a reduced need for notes and greater flexibility to respond to the court's questions.

One last note about preparation should be considered. After the theme has been determined, the points for discussion have been defined and the outline is complete, the advocate must consider that the argument may develop in one or more of three very different ways, depending on the activity of the court. Each possible variant must be anticipated in order to respond to the concerns of the court and, at the same time, to develop the argument theme.

First, assume that the judges ask very few questions. Obviously, the advocate should use this to full advantage to make all major points and whatever minor points that will help further the cause. This takes careful planning. All too often, advocates with minutes to fill will simply repeat arguments. This practice will undoubtedly bore and frustrate the judges. Thus, the long argument should be developed with the advocate ever mindful of the totality of time that may be available.

A second situation is one in which the advocate is bombarded with questions that do little to develop the theme of the argument. If this occurs, it is necessary to have firmly in mind the essential points necessary to make a convincing argument. Some like to describe this as the "short form" argument.

Third, one may be questioned in a manner that is helpful to develop one's theme. This is the best of all worlds. But the advocate must be thoroughly prepared to recognize and take full advantage of this scenario.

A strong likelihood exists that, during the course of the argument, the advocate will encounter all three forms, i.e., no questions, many questions that do not help develop theme, and other questions that are

5.   Robert L. Stern, Appellate Practice in the United States 391 (2d ed. 1989).

useful. Likewise, the bench may shift from active to passive or *vice versa* during the argument. This requires the advocate to be so thoroughly prepared that it is possible to accommodate the judges' questions and still make the arguments necessary to carry the day.

9.36   Approach the podium prepared and confident

Once the argument has been prepared and outlined, the advocate must decide the form of notes to take to the podium. The case for and against a written argument has already been made.[6] Under no circumstances should a written text, if there is one, be taken to the podium. One author has suggested that, if the argument is written, one method is to highlight the writing and have it available to jog one's memory. This technique is fraught with peril. As noted, many advocates, with the best of intentions, read a text if it is in front of them. As mentioned earlier and explored later, reading to the court is not only discouraged, it is forbidden in some courts. Equally troubling is the advocate who takes copious notes to the podium. The likelihood is that the advocate will, for all practical purposes, read to the bench. The net effect is that the argument that could have been is never made.

Some authors suggest that the advocate outline the important points to be made and place them on large index cards. They suggest that only one side of the card be used and that each card contain only one point and its subpoints. Therefore, so goes this suggestion, one need not look at a printed page and search for the points one wishes to make. Finally, it is recommended that when each argument is completed, the advocate should turn over the index card. This practice could be a disaster, for several reasons.

First, assume the argument seemingly progresses as planned. Suddenly, a question is asked that is to be covered very late in the planned argument. The advocate is then forced to shuffle through a mound of index cards in an attempt to locate the point pertinent to the judge's question. As once described, the oralist takes on the appearance of a Las Vegas gambler as he or she shuffles away. And then what? Does one reshuffle to try to relocate the point of interruption? What if the cards get hopelessly out of order? This is a prescription for chaos. The advocate will probably be frustrated, forget important points and possibly thereafter argue in a sequence that is totally confusing.

Second, the situation may occur where the advocate is asked a question toward the end of the argument that pertains to materials originally covered at the beginning. At that point, all or nearly all of the cards are turned face down. Once again, the shuffling begins. Once again, potential chaos!

Other authors suggest that the argument be outlined and written on a yellow legal pad. In this scenario, instead of shuffling cards, he or she must flip pages back and forth over the top of the podium. Thus, instead

---

6. *See* § 9.35.

of shuffling cards, one is creating yellow waves. Is this distracting to the bench? Of course it is.

The best approach, after outlining, is to list the key points that need to be made. Indicate the strongest authority for each point in the argument. This information should then be placed on a file folder, regular or legal. The front page of the folder should contain the introduction, the nature of the case (in one or two sentences), the essential or key facts (one word reminders to jog the memory) and the specific issue or issues to be decided. The inside two pages of the folder are reserved for the key points of the argument. They should only be short notes to maintain the argument's flow. Should the court question point four when the advocate is only on point one, he or she can locate point four without shuffling cards or turning pages. The concluding remarks are placed on the last page of the folder. As the argument concludes, one simple page turn is all that is required.

The key to success is to keep the points concise. It is absolutely essential that the oralist knows the points to be developed. The file folder must specify key concepts that will jog the memory together with the legal authority to support these propositions, should the bench inquire. Record cites should also be noted for facts that gave rise to the key concepts.

This technique will not work if the advocate attempts to put all details on the folder. The tendency then is to read from the folder, and the method becomes self-defeating.

In summary, the advocate takes to the podium a short outline, preferably on a file folder, the tabbed record, (should the court inquire about a specific fact not included on the folder) and a tabbed brief for quick reference to key arguments or citations.

9.40 REHEARSAL OF THE ARGUMENT

How one rehearses, with whom, and where are matters of personal preference. However, one thing is certain. Rehearse one must. Mr. Justice Jackson, himself a consummate advocate, once said:

> Do not think it beneath you to rehearse for an argument. Not even Caruso, at the height of his artistic career, felt above rehearsing for a hundredth performance, although he and the whole cast were guided and confined by a libretto and a score.[7]

Another famous writer and advocate, Frederick Bernays Wiener made this astute observation:

> No lawyer would dream of filing with the clerk the first rough draft of his brief. Why then present to the court the first draft of your oral argument? Many lawyers, too many of them, do just that— which is why such a lot of sorry oral arguments are heard in Federal appellate courts throughout the land * * *.

---

7. Jackson, *supra* note 2, at 861.

Preparation and rehearsal will save you from going off on unprofitable or even untenable side issues, will spare you the waste of precious minutes on nonessentials, and will substantially assist you in eliminating unhappy turns of phrase.[8]

One suggestion is to first rehearse the argument with no notes—just to get the feel of it. This, of course, should be in a quiet place with no help and no distractions. The arguments in support of this technique are that this reveals the needed areas of concentration, it overcomes the mountainous hurdle of "doing" it a first time, and it may provide the lawyer some positive insights into the case. Despite these arguments, this author does not think that this rehearsal is very effective. It is too foreign to what will actually take place. Instead, it is suggested that more preparatory work be completed before the first rehearsal takes place. The following practices are encouraged.

Discussions with associates or friends during the brief-writing stage and beyond are helpful. It allows the advocate to explore and discuss the issues before any attempt is made to formulate the oral portion of the appeal. New insights may be garnered through this exercise.

After thorough preparation, which includes choice of theme and choice of issues, a preliminary outline should be formulated. Rehearsals can then begin in earnest. Initially, a run-through alone with no judges is desirable. This technique indicates to the advocate how much time it will take should the bench ask no questions. Then, of course, it is necessary to modify the argument for the expected contingency that questions will be asked, which may be few or may be many. In addition, questions of law or fact that need more exploration come to the forefront and should be addressed at this point. The various arguments' strengths and weaknesses become evident.

Some authors have suggested that one should rehearse the argument to anyone who will take the time to hear it—a nice idea but extremely time consuming. And, in truth, most lawyers have neither the time nor the inclination to search out unsuspecting associates or friends upon which to practice.

Like every other form of preparation, the amount of rehearsal needed to polish an argument is proportional to experience and natural talent of the advocate. But even the most talented suggest that a rehearsal be argued before two groups. The first group should be a well-versed group of lawyer associates who closely resemble real judges. They will probably ask the type of questions that will be raised by the court. The best of all worlds is actually to have this group subdivided in a "cold" and a "hot" group. The mock "cold" group will be unprepared on the issues of the particular case, will understand the constructs, but will have no particular expertise in the law of the case. It is likely they will address more tangential issues than a panel of "hot" lawyers, who may

---

8. Frederick Bernays Wiener, Briefing   (1967). and Arguing Federal Appeals 295, 296

have worked on the case, read the brief (perhaps participated in its writing), and have an intimate understanding of the issues.

In the ideal world, the second group of people who will be helpful are lay people, with only a limited or no knowledge of the law. The rationale for this technique is that the argument should be understandable even to those who do not otherwise comprehend the legal underpinnings of the case. Again, this is a good idea and somewhat workable if there is a parent, a spouse or a significant other who is willing to hear the argument. Non-legal personnel of any variety are helpful.

Finally, an audiotape of the argument is useful. A videotape is even better. Irritating and distracting mannerisms are revealed on camera and can be corrected. As with this and other preparation techniques, time is the enemy. In the end, the attorney must rehearse as much as possible in order to feel comfortable and confident with the argument. How much is enough is most assuredly a very personal thing; but all experts agree, rehearsal is a critical part of delivering a successful argument.

9.50   HOT BENCH—COLD BENCH

Prior to presenting the oral argument, the advocate should attempt to determine whether it is the custom of the court members to read the briefs and record prior to argument. As previously discussed, information about the panel that will hear the case may be obtained by discussions with other lawyers, inquiry of past or present clerks or simply the general knowledge about the customs of the judges. This is important, because final preparation of the argument may well depend on whether the panel has read the briefs and the record.

The so-called "cold court" comes to the argument with little or no knowledge about the case. This often results when the final opinion to be written has been pre-assigned to a particular judge prior to the oral argument. Oftentimes, that judge prepares for oral argument to a greater degree than the other members of the bench, who may depend on the memoranda circulated by the judge who has drawn the case assignment or from clerks familiar with the case. For those who are not familiar with the case, the advocate's job is to educate them about the facts and the issues. As a result, questions may well center more on facts and basic issues than on searching questions of policy. One cannot be certain of this, but the advocate will surely have to spend more of the allotted time on the basics.

On the other hand, if the bench is known to be "hot," the judges have read and digested both the record and the briefs. Usually, the final opinion is not pre-assigned to any particular judge prior to oral argument. This type of panel has little patience with listening to the facts or a lengthy oration about the issues that surround the controversy. Usually if the advocate begins to recite the facts, an icy stare is accompanied by an equivalent of, "counsel, rest assured we have read the briefs and understand the issues. What I want to know is what we do about the interaction between the Fourteenth Amendment guarantees of equal protection and due process and the rights of privacy arising either under the Ninth or Fifth Amendments in this case, and why." The advocate is thrust into full throttle within approximately thirty seconds of beginning the argument. Details that the advocate had planned to discuss must now be discarded. The advocate must be prepared for this, particularly with a "hot" bench. Otherwise, there may be several minutes of allotted time left with nothing to say. The advocate should always have contingency plans to take advantage of the full time allocated.

With most oral arguments, some members of the panel will have read the record and the briefs, others will have read their clerk's distillation of the record and the briefs, and others will know nothing about the case. The advocate should come prepared to recite the essence of the case on the assumption that the judges are hearing it for the first time. It is better to err on the side of too much information than not enough, because one can be assured that the court will inform counsel if the facts and issues are known. Judge Bright of the Eighth Circuit Court of Appeals relates the story of a young lawyer who began his presentation: "Your Honors, this is a contract case. A contract represents a mutual manifestation of mutual consent, usually supported by consideration." The presiding judge interrupted: "Counsel, you may assume that this court is generally familiar with the rudimentary principles of contract law." Counsel then promptly replied: "That's what I thought in the court below."[9]

The key to success is flexibility. The advocate must be ready to discuss the facts and issues because counsel "must assume that the judge has never heard of the case or of his situation."[10] On the other hand, counsel must also be prepared to delve into the heart of the argument at the outset because the bench may ask questions in an order that was not planned by the advocate.

Careful planning for different alternatives is not easy, but it is essential. As this chapter began, it concludes: there is no substitute for preparation.

EXERCISES

I. In order to complete the exercises for this chapter, you must be intimately familiar with the briefs in the *Clinton v. Jones* case. They are found in Appendices C and D. In addition, you have the benefit of the actual oral arguments that are contained in Appendix F. The author suspects that the oral arguments *did not* go according to plan.

Based on the material in this chapter, organize and prepare the oral argument you would make in the petitioner's case or the respondent's case. As you organize the argument, provide the following analysis:

9. Myron H. Bright, *The Ten Commandments of Oral Argument*, 67 A.B.A.J. 1136–37 (1981).

10. Milton Pollack, *The Civil Appeal*, in Counsel on Appeal 45 (Arthur A. Charpentier ed., 1968).

A.   Evaluate the case as a whole. What are the strengths, and what are the weaknesses?

B.   Choose the best issue or issues to argue. Remember: you cannot include each small segment of the brief. What issue or issues do you plan to argue?

C.   Outline the argument in broad strokes. Having picked the issues, what information is critical to get before the court? Are there cases that should be discussed? If so, which ones and what is important about each case?

D.   Choose a theme. This is a critical part of the argument. Remember: the theme ties the entire argument together. It should be evident throughout the argument.

E.   Prepare the argument in detail. Do you plan to write it out? Do you plan just to make notes? As presented in the text, the choice is a personal one. Be prepared to articulate why you have chosen the method of preparation you have used.

F.   Once the argument is prepared, what do you plan to take to the podium? Index cards? A legal pad? A piece of paper? A file folder? Be prepared to explain why you have chosen the vehicle to be used at the podium.

Chapter Ten

PRESENTATION OF THE ARGUMENT

Analysis

10.00   INTRODUCTION—A NEW THEORY TO EXPLAIN AN OLD PHENOMENON

Experts suggest that the advocate have a conversation with the court. Lecturing and reading are strongly discouraged as previously discussed. The notion of conversation is not a new concept. The Honorable John W. Davis in his address to the Association of the Bar of the City of New York, a now eminent piece on oral advocacy, relates that Justice Hughes once said:

> It is a great saving of the time of the court in the examination of extended records and briefs, to obtain the grasp of the case that is made possible by *oral discussion* and to be able more quickly to separate the wheat from the chaff. (emphasis added)[1].

Justice Jackson spoke to the use of dialogue with the court when he stated, "a lively dialogue may be a swifter and surer vehicle to truth than a dismal monologue."[2] Chief Justice Rehnquist, then Associate Justice Rehnquist, flatly states the same principles govern questions and

---

1. John W. Davis, *The Argument of an Appeal*, 26 A.B.A.J. 895 (1940).

2. Robert H. Jackson, *Advocacy Before the Supreme Court: Suggestions for Effec-* *tive Case Presentations,* 37 A.B.A.J. 801, 862 (1951).

answers in oral argument as in ordinary conversation. He also suggests the advocate keep the tone conversational and not of an oratory nature.

The idea that appellate courtroom advocacy is a type of conversation, or should be, strongly suggests an examination of the notions of persuasion and effectiveness. That was precisely the research this author undertook in a linguistics study of appellate advocacy and consequent Ph.D. dissertation.[3] The research quickly uncovered that many authors have directives for advocates, e.g., maintain eye contact, don't read, and the like, but with no explanation for the **why** or the **how** of the directive. The following sections explore "how" to make an effective oral argument and explain "why" it is effective. Many of the constructs that follow, are drawn from the aforementioned research and subsequent dissertation. The thesis is that the oral argument is a *special* kind of conversation. It is a subset of general face-to-face interaction, in that it is constrained, formalistic and suasive in nature.

10.10   FORMALITIES

Prior to an examination of the mechanics of the oral argument, attention must be focused on certain formalities in the process of *doing* argument. The first impression, and perhaps the last, is based partially on the appearance of the advocate. Also, the advocate's attitude that is brought to the courtroom can act as a plus, or if inappropriate, a very large minus. The next two sections explore the importance of attire and attitude.

10.11   Attire

While it may seem a trivial matter, one's attire for an oral argument is, in fact, important. Justice Jackson remarked that one of the questions most asked of the clerk's office centers on what the advocate should wear.[4] One must realize that judges, either consciously or unconsciously, notice how advocates dress. Justice Jackson stated "[y]ou will not be stopped from arguing if you wear a race-track suit or sport a rainbow necktie. You will just create a first impression that you have strayed in at the wrong bar."[5]

Common sense should dictate that the advocate dress to avoid an adverse impact on or distraction from the persuasive content of the argument. Shabby, sloppy or even overly casual dress suggests, rightly or wrongly, that one's thinking may mimic one's dress. To avoid this perception, conservative is the prescription for courtroom attire. This suggests business suits for both men and women. While formal morning attire is no longer required before the United States Supreme Court, many practitioners still adhere to that dress code. Again, to quote Justice Jackson, "[t]he lawyer of good taste will not worry about his dress, because instinctively it will be that which is suitable to his station in

3. *See* Carole C. Butler (nee Berry), A Study of Effective Appellate Advocacy (1990)(unpublished Ph.D. dissertation, The Ohio State University).

4. *See* Jackson, *supra* note 2, at 862.

5. *Id.*

life—a member of a dignified and responsible profession—and for an important and somewhat formal occasion."[6]

10.12 Attitude

Along with proper attire, the advocate must approach the courtroom with an appropriate attitude. Some attorneys berate the court and orate much like one would cross-examine a hostile witness. Others defer to the court as if to apologize for bringing the case before it. Some are flip and appear annoyed at the questions from the bench. Others are so in awe of the bench that paralysis sets in at the first question. All these attitudes are to be avoided.

Wiener suggests that an attorney's attitude should be one of respectful intellectual equality. This does not mean the advocate shows no deference. Think of it as a discussion between a first-year lawyer and the senior partner. Both bring a perspective to an issue and both attempt, through discussion, to come to some resolution of that issue. A satisfactory resolution cannot be achieved if the young lawyer is so fearful of the senior partner that he or she does not speak up when asked a question. A resolution also cannot be realized if one party is flippant, irascible, or condescending. Simply put, the oral argument is a conversation. As such, the rules of etiquette that govern a conversation must be followed if the conversation is to succeed.

Attitude applies to opposing counsel, as well as members of the bench. Wiener cautions that a display of personality clashes is dangerous. Lawyers should never criticize each other before the court. While the temptation may be great, respect must be shown to opposing counsel in both word and deed. When an argument is reduced to raw emotion, the party provoking the emotionalism will likely be regarded with disfavor.

10.20 OPENING THE ARGUMENT

The opening sentences of the argument are essential. They set the context of the argument and, if effective, seize the court's attention. As in any communicative event, a good first impression is important. For the appellant, counsel should describe the essence of the case in two or three sentences. For the appellee, the opening should center on the central theme of the argument in a manner that refutes what the appellant has just argued. For both sides, the opening tells the court what is to be argued in the most interesting possible manner.

The formal introduction of oneself and co-counsel, if there is one, usually opens the argument.[7] It can be as simple as: "May it please the court, my name is Mary Smith. With co-counsel James Jones, I represent the Widget Company of America, appellant in this matter."

---

6. *Id*. at 862–63.

7. But note the beginning of the arguments before the United States Supreme Court, which are found in Appendix F.

Or it may be a little less formal and more personal, if allowed by rule or tradition. One such opening might be: "Good morning and may it please the court, my name is Mary Smith, etc."

If the advocate must request rebuttal, that request is made following the introduction. However, in some courts, the appellant must reserve rebuttal at check-in at the clerk's office. This matter should be determined prior to or at the time of arrival for the argument.

As a matter of form, the advocate should then deliver a short statement describing the nature of the case. If not obvious, the appellate jurisdiction of the court should be specified. While not particularly exciting, a simple statement like: "This case comes here on appeal from the Franklin County Common Pleas Court, which set aside a jury verdict for the plaintiff." Granted, the judges will not hang on every word but hopefully it will stave off an apocryphal answer to a question once posed by Justice Holmes—"[h]ow did you get here?" to which the advocate allegedly responded "[o]n the Baltimore & Ohio."

It is suggested, however, that a livelier opening might be in order. For example, the opening few lines of Attorney Gilbert K. Davis' argument on behalf of Paula Jones is illustrative:

> Mr. Chief Justice, and may it please the Court: William Jefferson Clinton, the citizen, who holds the office of the presidency of the United States, advances the novel claim of immunity from the progress of litigation while he is President. This immunity, he derives, he says, from the separation of powers doctrine of our Constitution and he further contends that the judicial branch of Government must suspend the processing of Paula Corbin Jones' lawsuit until he is out of office, potentially for a period of seven years after the date of her filing of the suit. This novel proposition has three fundamental errors. (Counsel then began to articulate the errors, but was interrupted with a question after stating the first error)[8]

If the outcome of the lower court has not been articulated, and usually it has, that must now be specified.

Perhaps the most important part of the opening is the recitation of the issue or issues central to the case. Many times, the issues suggest the theme of the argument that forms a framework upon which the bench may now focus. It is important to remember that the judges may have heard several arguments before the one counsel is arguing. Their attention must be seized immediately.

In sum, the opening should not span more than thirty seconds. But they are a crucial thirty seconds. In that short time, the advocate introduces oneself, reserves rebuttal time if appropriate, states the nature of the case, the outcome in the lower court, and the issues that will be addressed. In doing so, the advocate sets the theme and provides a context for the argument.

8. The full text of the three arguments may be found in Appendix F.

The following is an example of a good opening to the appellant's argument and comes from *Michelin Tire Corp. v. Wages,* 423 U.S. 276 (1976):

Mr. Chief Justice, and may it please the Court: This is a case which involves the import clause of the Federal Constitution and the proper interpretation and application of that clause to imported tires and tubes. The sole issue is whether tires imported without packaging and held for the sale by the importer in his warehouse in the original form in which imported are immune from local *ad valorem* taxes by reason of the import clause. The trial court upheld the importer's claim of immunity with respect to both tires and tubes. The Supreme Court of Georgia affirmed with respect to the tubes but reversed with respect to the tires notwithstanding the fact that both the tires and the tubes are handled precisely in the same manner while in the importer's warehouse.[9] Here, counsel included a salutation, described the nature of the case, the issue before the court and gave a brief history of the proceedings.

Compare the following mishmash that constitutes the opening statement in *Runyon v. McCrary,* 427 U.S. 160 (1976). The issue was private discrimination.

Mr. Chief Justice, Honorable Justices: I represent the Bobbe's School, which is Mr. and Mrs. Runyon, who are operating it; and I will limit my argument to the narrow area of what I consider the crucial issue in this case and, if necessary, will rebut on the point of the statute of limitations on the right of attorneys' fees.

Now, first let me touch on the facts a little bit as to the reason why we are here. The Bobbe's School is a small school in Arlington Virginia–Fairfax Virginia; it is right on the line—that operates a private school. It has been stipulated in the facts that the school is not supported in any way by any Federal or state money and it depends entirely in its support upon the student enrollment.

Insofar as the Bobbe's School is concerned—now, this case was consolidated with the Brewster School—but insofar as the Bobbe's School is concerned, Mr. and Mr. McCrary and Mr. and Mrs. Gonzales testified—and, of course, this is unrebutted—that, as a result of a telephone call—that is, by both parties, one in '69 and one in '71 or '72, as I recall—and no further contact and no formal application—as a result of a telephone call, it brought into play Section 1981 of the Civil Rights Act that we are now here under * * *.

Further examination of the transcript shows that the argument, following this stumbling beginning, further deteriorated. At the end, the advocate did not appear to know what he was arguing. The Justices

9. 83 Landmark Briefs and Arguments   Constitutional Law 285, 287 (1977).
of the Supreme Court of the United States:

must have been totally bewildered. The bottom line: A good beginning is essential to establish the tone for the entire presentation.

10.30 STATEMENT OF FACTS

Most experts agree that a concise statement of facts immediately follows the opening. Great care should be taken with their preparation. John W. Davis expounded on the importance of the facts when he stated:

> [f]or it cannot be too often emphasized that in an appellate court the statement of the facts is not merely a part of the argument, it is more often than not the argument itself. A case well stated is a case far more than half argued.[10]

The court will decide the issues based on the facts. If the facts are unclear, the argument will founder on the issues, and the advocate will be far less persuasive, if persuasive at all. In the end, the atmosphere created by the statement of the facts often prevails throughout the argument.

As in the brief, the facts should be stated objectively. The time for intense advocacy is near, but at this juncture, objectivity still is the password. Favorable, forceful wording should still be used. As long as the facts are honestly detailed, language to promote the client's case is essential. At the end of the advocate's recital of the facts, the bench should understand the equities of the case and be receptive to counsel's arguments.

Prior to composing the facts, the advocate should carefully consider what the judges need to know in order to understand the case. This can be dicey. Advocates have the tendency either to go into great detail (having lived with the case for months or perhaps years) or, because of the great familiarity with the case, sketch the facts too briefly. The former can be disastrous, because time is precious and an advocate can little afford to spend valuable minutes on detail that will probably only confuse the bench. The latter is also dangerous because, in order to comprehend the arguments, the bench must have a clear understanding of what brought the case to the appellate court. Therefore, the decision as to what to include and in how much detail are a priority in formulating the facts.

The facts should always be rehearsed before a live audience, preferably one that has little knowledge about the case. If boredom or puzzlement sets in, the advocate knows something is wrong. The depictions are either too long or too short or too obtuse. Adjustments must be made. This is the time to listen to what lay persons have to say. Their reactions must be noted and changes in the recital of facts must be made.

How best to present the facts obviously depends on the depth and detail needed to ensure their understanding. A narrative best paints the picture. Remember: comprehension is cumulative. The facts should work from the major points to minor or detailed points. Most agree that a

---

10. Davis, *supra* note 1, at 896.

chronological presentation is best. That is the way life presents itself and is best understood.

Simply tell the story. Do not unduly add cumbersome, nonessential information. For example, in the following excerpt, the information is basic and unencumbered:

> Mr. Brown ran the red light and crashed into the Jones' automobile. The force of the crash propelled the Jones' car into a telephone pole. Mr. Jones died instantly.

Compare the following, in which nonessential facts simply get in the way of meaning:

> The record states that the appellee Carl Brown ran the red light. Testimony by witnesses LuAnn Dean and Catherine Smith indicates that Carl Brown's car then crashed into the auto driven by David Jones. Both Dean and Smith testified that because Brown's car hit Jones' car, the Jones' car was propelled into a telephone pole that was opposite the Jones' car. The coroner testified that it is almost certain that David Jones died instantly.

The first excerpt tells a fast moving story, one that the members of the court can remember. The picture is clear, succinct and not cluttered with auxiliary information that inhibits the picture.

A chronological presentation of the facts is usually the most effective, but not always. At times, facts are best presented topically.[11] If this latter method is chosen, one recites facts as they relate to the issue being discussed. This can be a useful way to proceed if there is more than one issue and the issues are not conveniently linked together. In other words, if issue one revolves around a set of facts that has little or no bearing on issue two, the best approach may be to talk about the facts of issue one and then move on to the facts of issue two.

Whatever the choice of organization, the hallmark of a good set of facts is accuracy. Accuracy suggests three concepts. First, the facts must not be distorted in an attempt to paint a picture that is favorable to the advocate's client. Distorting the facts will surely lead to the court's loss of confidence in the advocate and the cause. Second, and in a similar vein, the advocate should not over zealously characterize the facts. Having lived with the case can lead to painting the picture in shades more vivid than are deserved. Again, loss of credibility can result. Score one for the opponent. The court may look to that side to get a more balanced view. Third, facts that are important though unfavorable, to the client's position, should be addressed. Not to address these facts is a lost opportunity to bring them into the open to dispel their importance. It may appear to the bench that there is an attempt at evasion. The importance of accuracy can never be overstated.

The best approach is to outline the facts that are necessary to understand the issues to be argued. Outline in broad strokes. Then begin

---

11. *See* Jackson, *supra* note 2, at 803.

to fill in the blanks with detail that will help develop the picture completely. Always strive for favorable wording, but do not overstate the case. Include unfavorable material, but mention it briefly. Practice to ensure the right amount of time has been allotted and to smooth out the presentation.

In the end, the advocate should have "virtually a 'canned' factual statement,"[12] that includes precisely the facts the advocate wants to include, stated just the way they should be stated and in exactly the time allotted to them.

It is not uncommon, however, for the court to waive the facts. If the members of the bench have read and studied the briefs, recitation of the facts wastes valuable time. If the court waives the facts, be prepared to launch into the meat of the argument. Judge Engel relates a particularly humorous segment of an oral argument that occurred in the Sixth Circuit. Apparently one Sixth Circuit judge interrupted a long-winded recitation of the facts and reminded the attorney that the court had read the briefs and was well acquainted with the facts. "I want to believe that, Your Honor," was the rejoinder, "but that's the mistake I made in the district court."[13] One can only hope the advocate then began his argument.

10.40 BODY OF THE ARGUMENT

10.41 Introduction

The body of the argument calls for a very different form of communication. Up to this point, in both the brief and the oral argument, the watchword has been "objectivity." This does not suggest that the advocate has avoided favorable wording, or a structure and organization that puts the client's case in the best light. What it does mean is that the advocate should set the context to inform the court accurately and objectively of the facts and issues to be discussed during the argument.

Once through the preliminaries of the argument, the advocate must concentrate on a presentation of the points in the most persuasive and positive manner. Gone is objectivity. The aim is to convince the members of the court that the position taken is the best and only position that makes sense under the circumstances. This is accomplished through strong arguments, both legal and policy oriented, proper emphasis, and careful answers to the court's questions. Vital to the success of an oral argument is to remember that the advocate is arguing *to* the court, not *with* the court. This is a great difference; the prudent advocate is careful not to slip from one mode to the other. This is especially critical if the advocate encounters a particularly aggressive and/or hostile judge.

---

12. Henry St. John Fitzgerald & Daniel Harnett, *Effective Oral Argument*, in 18 Prac. Law., No. 4, 51, 57 (A.L.I.-A.B.A., Apr. 1972).

13. Albert J. Engel, *Oral Advocacy at the Appellate Level*, 12 U. Tol. L. Rev. 463, 468–69 (1981).

10.42　Types of questions

This section examines both the type of information that is sought by the judges and the style of questioning. For example, a question may be asked in a hostile or adversarial way about an issue of policy. The information sought is how the argument promotes a certain policy, but the style of questioning indicates that the judge either is not convinced, disagrees or is playing devil's advocate.

10.42–1　Information sought

Most questions are asked in search of information. The information sought may be about certain facts of the case. Usually these facts are not readily perceivable and have not been addressed in the statement of facts. Often these questions center on either a procedural issue in the lower court or facts that precipitated the suit. They may be background questions that require record clarification or verification. In the following example, a specific record cite is requested. If this question is asked, the advocate should have that information available through tabs of the record. Otherwise, distracting page shuffling will ensue.

> Advocate: The Cable Company has never made direct application to the City of Stewart and therefore * * *.

> Judge: Counsel, where in the record do you find that information?[14]

The questions may seek information about the authorities cited. They may ask for a citation to specific cases or the application of a particular case to the one under consideration by the court. In the following excerpt, the judge wants the advocate to name a specific case that is similar to the one under consideration. Note that the advocate did not relate a specific citation in this instance. Apparently that was acceptable to the judge, because he did not pursue a citation.

> Judge: What is the closest case that is akin to this case in your judgment?

> Advocate: Actually the closest case would be the *Red Line* case which does uphold the fairness doctrine.

Generally, the judges do not want to hear simply the issues and holding of the case. They want an analysis of why the prior case should apply and how it fits into the existing framework of the law. This is evidenced by what followed the above.

> Judge: That's interesting. And the *Red Line* case is applicable? I don't see it.

Policy considerations make up another type of question that an advocate should anticipate. Appellate courts are especially interested in the ramifications of their decisions. They want to know how their decision will have an impact on society. Often, judges ask questions

---

14. Some of the examples used are extracts from oral arguments that were studied and became the basis of the author's Ph.D. dissertation. *See* Butler (nee Berry), *supra* note 3.

regarding how the advocate's position will promote some desired public good. For example:

> Judge: One of the express purposes of the 1984 amendment to the 1934 act was to promote competition. Creating a monopoly by the municipality, how does that promote competition?

Questions about the opponent's argument should be anticipated. This is especially so if the matter before the court is a close one. Counsel should always be prepared to rebut the opposition's cases, arguments and authorities. In the following excerpt, the advocate makes an argument, and the judge abruptly changes topics to pursue a line of questioning which departs from what the advocate is arguing. This pattern of questioning is especially challenging, because the advocate must totally switch gears.

> Advocate: They exert no editorial control and that is why this act does not infringe on the editorial control of the cable operator.

> Judge: Then how do you distinguish the decision in *Quincy Cable*?

Now and then, a member of the bench will ask a collateral question. These questions do not move the case forward because usually the issue raised is not squarely on point. It may be a troublesome side issue that the judge is bothered by, or it may be the judge's way of testing the depth of knowledge of the advocate. A question that seems collateral must be answered, but the advocate should then strive to return to the issues of importance. In the following example, the judge asks a question about the constitutionality of a piece of legislation. The advocate answers quickly and then returns to theme.

> Judge: Well, what Congress has decided and what's constitutional are sometimes two, a little different, aren't they?

> Advocate: That's correct but respondent urges this court to not ignore the decision of the legislature in this matter.

> In *Columbia Broadcasting Systems v. Democratic National Committee*, the court recognized that cable television does provide a potential for a great deal of public discussion.

Occasionally a member of the court will ask a question that has absolutely no relevance to the case. These questions can be tough to handle, as is illustrated in the following example.

> Judge: Is there a standing issue here?

> Advocate: Well no your honor. That was never raised in the lower court.

The advocate was taken back a bit, and the answer did not represent one of his best efforts. This may be unavoidable, but one must attempt to anticipate even the occasional irrelevant question.

10.42–2 Style of questions asked

The style of questioning is closely related to the information that is sought. Often these cannot be differentiated. But one must be wary. An advocate can be mistakenly lulled into thinking that he or she has the court in hand if the bench is asking only "friendly" questions; or the advocate can be intimidated if the court shows signs of hostility or aggressiveness. The style of questioning may set an important tone to which the advocate must respond.

Most judges claim that questions that they ask are "friendly" in nature. There are two kinds of friendly questions. First, the judge may attempt to assist the argument's progression. That does not mean that the information sought is necessarily helpful to the cause. It may raise an issue that is troublesome for the advocate, but it is not meant to irritate or belittle counsel. In the following excerpt, the issue of interfering with editorial discretion is a matter critical to the advocate's argument. While the answer is "no," it gives the advocate the opportunity to explain why not.

Judge: Doesn't that in fact interfere with editorial discretion?

Advocate: No because in this instance, cables are merely conduits and as conduits the programmers do not exercise the same degree of discretion that they do when they originate their own programming and that is in keeping with this Court's decision in *Pittsburgh Press v. Pittsburgh Commission on Human Relations.*

The second type of "friendly" question is one that is designed to rescue a faltering argument. The author recalls an argument in which the advocate was under horrific fire by a judge known to ask questions that were less than helpful. Finally, as time was running out, a sympathetic judge, who somehow managed to intercede, said to the advocate, "[y]ou know, counsel, ever since law school I have never understood the difference between contributory negligence and assumption of the risk. Could you explain that to me?" This, of course, was exactly the distinction that needed to be made in order to have a chance at winning the case. As the advocate's time expired, he managed finally to explain how his client's case fit within the doctrine of contributory negligence and not assumption of the risk. That was a friendly question!

The hostile questioner presents a genuine challenge to the advocate. A hostile and aggressive judge can unnerve even the best of advocates. The reason for the hostility may stem from a basic dislike for the case or a frustration at being on the minority side of the case. In either event, the advocate must carefully answer the question in a non-judgmental way, exhibiting neither sarcasm nor irritation. The more frustrated the advocate becomes, the less effective the argument will be for the duration of the advocate's time. Personalities must not intrude into the argument.

As frustrating is the hostile judge who insists on bantering or debating with the advocate. If the questions center on an important part of the discussion, the banter is useful. This is, however, rarely the case. Usually, if the judge insists on debating the issue, the points gradually stray further and further from the mainstream of the argument. Clearly, counsel cannot cut off the dialogue, despite the belief it is going down a path to nowhere. The best approach is to attempt to answer the question and tactfully return to the main points. With luck, the advocate will be rescued by a "friendly" question. Fellow members of the bench know the personality of this kind of judge and, more often than not, will attempt to steer the argument back on course.

Now and then, counsel will encounter a judge who interjects humor into the argument either through questioning or observation. How to respond to this type of judge can be dicey. The best approach is to enjoy the moment and get on with the argument. One never knows how the bench will respond to a humorous retort. If the comment falls flat, the atmosphere of the courtroom can become a deep freeze. Better safe than sorry.

For example, in the next excerpt, the judge was trying to introduce a little levity. The advocate had been making an economics argument that hinged on territorial and geographic issues.

> Judge: So the geography and economics and maybe a little sociology and psychiatry thrown in, whatever we have, somehow we can limit First Amendment rights depending on which we have before us, is that right?

The advocate acknowledged that the judge was being somewhat facetious and answered with a broad smile:

> Advocate: No, your honor. This is not a limit of the First Amendment rights. This is a limit of how a business is going to carry on its operations within the City of Stewart.

10.43   Response to questions

The often-quoted John W. Davis said it best when he stated:

> Rejoice when the Court asks questions. And again I say unto you, rejoice! If the question does nothing more it gives you assurance that the court is not comatose and that you have awakened at least a vestigial interest. Moreover a question affords you your only chance to penetrate the mind of the court, unless you are an expert in face reading, and to dispel a doubt as soon as it arises.[15]

If the exercise is to be a conversation and one that is meant to persuade, a dialogue is absolutely necessary. Without the question-answer sequence, the oral argument becomes a lecture. Nevertheless, there is no doubt that questions from the bench can be a frightening experience. The advocate must remember that the questioning process allows judges to obtain information and to clarify elements of the case. Through questions, matters come to the court's attention that may not be perfectly clear from the briefs. From the judges' perspective, answers to their questions are the foremost purpose of the oral argument. Likewise, from the advocate's perspective, answering the concerns of members of the bench is the reason for "doing" argument. Terror should

---

15.   Davis, *supra* note 1, at 897.

strike at the heart of the advocate who gets no questions. If there are no concerns by the judges, they obviously have made up their minds. Considering the dismal reversal rate, this is hard on the appellant. It is far easier for the court simply to affirm than to reverse and plow new ground.

10.43–1 Listen, think and answer

The keys to successful response to questions posed during appellate argument can be expressed in three words—listen, think and answer. These indicia are axiomatic to good advocacy, but many advocates do little or nothing to heed these suggestions. Perhaps the least appreciated of the three concepts is *listening*.

Listening carefully to the questions posed through the course of the argument lends great insight into the types of concerns of the individual judges. This is especially so for the appellee, who has the benefit of observing the questioning patterns of the various judges during the appellant's argument. An advocate can identify the judge who is concerned about public policy, or one who is concerned about the specifics of the legal argument. One can also learn the style of the judges. With this information, the advocate can adjust the arguments to fit the concerns of the individual judges. This applies whether one is the appellant or the appellee.

More important than following the questions asked of others is paying attention to those asked of oneself. As Chief Justice Rehnquist noted:

> If you are going to be able to intelligently answer a question, you must first *listen* to the question. But it is surprising how often appellate advocates, just like many people in private conversation, seem to hear only part of the question, and respond to the part of it they heard even though the answer they give may not be an adequate response to the entire question. (emphasis original)[16]

A classic example of not listening to the court's question is relayed by Judge Peck who was a former presiding judge of the Appellate Division, First Department, of the New York State Supreme Court. He stated:

> We recently had before us a lawyer for an appellant in a criminal case whom we had never seen before. The presiding judge asked him, 'Did you come here *pro hac vice?*' to which he responded, 'No, I came by taxi-cab.'[17]

Rule number one, then, is listen to the question.

Rule number two is think before answering. Lawyers frequently misinterpret the question asked by the judge. This will occur far less often if the advocate listens carefully and then thinks through the question before answering. In the following sequence, the judge asks the

16. William H. Rehnquist, *Oral Advocacy*, 27 S. Tex. L. Rev. 289, 302 (1986).

17. David W. Peck, *Time for Oral Argument*, 4 Litig. 39, 54 (Winter, 1978).

advocate what a newspaper must provide consumers who want to advertise. The advocate obviously didn't listen and think, because her answer began with the notion of advertising but ended in a discussion about cable operations, a matter that the judge was not addressing.

> Judge: Aren't newspapers required to provide an opportunity to put something in the medium, such as in terms of advertising? You buy a full page and you put in your block.

> Advocate: Newspapers provide certain forms of advertising but then cable operators provide certain people with the option of putting on their own publications on the cable systems; that is producers are allowed to come on to the cable and use their shows.

Equally as problematic as answering half the question or misinterpreting the question is the advocate who answers the question he or she wishes had been asked. In the following sequence, the advocate was asked a question but preferred to answer quite a different question.

> Judge: Supposing a municipality decided not to grant any franchises?

> Advocate: Well your honor, in the case at bar we have this exclusive franchise policy that we assert, because the government can bring forth no compelling governmental interest that is narrowly tailored to achieve that end * * *.

Rule number three is answer the question. A subset of this rule is never postpone a question. Justice Jackson spoke to that issue when he said:

> I advise you never to postpone answer to a question, for that always gives an impression of evasion. It is better immediately to answer the question, even though you do so in short form and suggest that you expect to amplify and support your answer later.[18]

If a short form is used, it is important to cover the issue, before the close of the argument. However, the better strategy may well be to answer the question fully when it is posed. This approach takes more finesse because it requires the advocate to skip to another part of the argument and then return to reassemble the pieces of the argument that were left behind. The advantage to an answering in full is that the point then has been covered and a repeat of even a part of the argument need not be done. Another advantage is that there is no risk that one will forget to return to the point later in the argument. And finally, the advocate has answered the concern of at least one member of the court.

Jurist John W. Davis long ago summed it up:

> If you value your argumentative life do not evade or shuffle or postpone, no matter how embarrassing the question may be or how much it interrupts the thread of your argument. Nothing I should think would be more irritating to an inquiring court than to have

---

18. Jackson, *supra* note 2, at 862.

refuge taken in the familiar evasion "I am coming to that" and then to have the argument end with the promise unfulfilled.[19]

An advocate who evades the question runs even greater risks than one who postpones. A judge's reaction is likely either to be skeptical of the advocate and the argument, or to pursue the matter with a vengeance. In the following sequence, the advocate attempts to evade the question. The judge forces an answer. The advocate loses credibility and becomes frustrated, thus disrupting her argument.

Judge: Well, as I understand it, city utility poles can handle only three particular cables. Is that correct?

Advocate: The cities

Judge: Is that correct. Yes or no!

Advocate: Yes your honor. (voice drops off)

10.43–2   Confusing, irrelevant and unanswerable questions

In the preceding examples, the questions were ones that could be expected by the advocate. The problems encountered were ones of a failure to listen, to think or to answer. But what of the situations in which the question presented is confusing, irrelevant or the answer is unknown? Each will be considered separately.

For most advocates, the likely scenario is one in which the question asked is simply not clear. Many times, this situation arises when a judge attempts to apply a body of law, as he or she understands it, to some new fact that is raised either by the advocate or another member of the bench. In the following sequence, the advocate has been arguing what will happen *if* the cable company in question is forced to bow to the city's franchise scheme. The judge asks a question based on his understanding of new facts raised by the advocate and attempts to fit them into his understanding of the Fourteenth Amendment.

Judge: That's all in futuro, right?

Advocate: Pardon me, sir?

Judge: All in the future, is that correct?

Advocate: Your honor, we have not participated in this auction process so in that sense, yes, it is in the future. But because we have a threatened injury which affects a First Amendment right, we have standing to raise this issue.

Judge: How can you take something in futuro?

Advocate: In relation to the Fourteenth Amendment claim your honor?

Judge: That's correct.

Sometimes the problem of understanding arises due to a hypothetical that the court poses to the advocate. In the following sequence, the

19.   Davis, *supra* note 1, at 897–98.

advocate has argued that because the city has telephone poles that would accommodate three cable companies, all three companies ought to receive franchises. Based on that information given to the bench, the following ensued and the advocate became confused.

> Judge: Suppose there were room for three on all but half a dozen poles in the city where there was only room for one. Would that mean that the city could grant a license only to the one or would the city have to construct extra space on those six deficient poles?

> Advocate: I'm afraid I don't understand your honor.

> Judge: You have suggested (advocate's new factual scenario) that because there is space for three, the city ought to franchise at least three. Suppose that for half a dozen of the poles in the city, there was space for one. Would the city then be justified in limiting the franchise to one cable company?

In both of these excerpts, the advocate was unsure what the judge was asking. Should that situation arise, it is perfectly acceptable to request clarification of the question. A response such as "I'm afraid I don't understand the question your honor" is preferable to "[y]our question is not clear." As seen in the first excerpt, the advocate asked for clarification of the question. He got to the heart of the matter by simply asking if his honor wanted him to address the Fourteenth Amendment issue. This is the only occasion in oral argument in which the advocate should question a judge. Sometimes the approach can be along the lines of "[i]f I understand the question, your honor, you are asking * * *." The important point is that counsel be prepared so that this ploy is not used frequently. It should only be used when there is genuine confusion that results from a question that could not have been anticipated. If the advocate is continually asking for clarification, the bench will suspect that the advocate is either stalling or is unprepared.

Equally troubling, however, is the advocate who should ask for clarification and does not. This pattern of answering appears to be more problematic than simply to ask if the judge would repeat the question or to state that clarification is needed. In the following sequence, a rather complicated question is asked. The advocate, rather than accept the judge's question "do you understand?" tries to answer with disastrous results.

> Judge: Suppose that the City had invited bids and accepting the fact that they could only accommodate three sets of cable on the existing utilities and suppose that they said they were going to award a franchise to any one of the bidders but that once it was installed, there would be three cable companies that could successfully compete in the market place. Would you have a different argument and would we have then filled the scarcity argument? Do you see what I mean?

Advocate: You're saying that if there were eventually three companies on the poles that that's would how it would be that there's where the scarcity would be?

Rather than utter complete nonsense, it is better to request that the judge clarify the question. Remember, the oral argument is a dialogue. Conversants in free conversation request clarification from others on a regular basis. It is expected in a conversation if there is misunderstanding as to meaning.

Another and somewhat dicier situation arises when a judge asks a question that seems totally irrelevant to advancing the argument. This could be a misunderstood point on the part of the judge, a hypothetical that misses the mark or simply a question that is tangential to the argument. If the situation arises, the advocate should attempt to answer the question, and, in the process, show why the issue has no impact on the outcome of the case.

In the following excerpt, the judge asks for the advocate's reaction to a hypothetical proposition. It is up to the advocate to answer the question and dispel the notion that, even if this had been the case, it would make no difference.

Judge: I'm interested in your reaction or answer to the position taken by the trial court saying that in doing this the city was merely assuring the widest possible diversity of information sources and then suggested this is consistent with the congressional intent and object of the First Amendment. Do you agree or disagree with that conclusion?

Advocate: I disagree with that, your honor.

Judge: Why?

Advocate: In so finding, the district court first of all went outside the scope of its 12B6 review for there is nothing in the complaint to indicate a compelling governmental interest to allow impingement on Lanstel's First Amendment rights.

Judge: If, all right. Suppose that had been presented. What is your answer to that contention?

Advocate: Still your honor, this court has always engaged in a balancing test where a compelling governmental interest must be shown and weighed against the First Amendment rights alleged and even if that was a salutary objective to gain diversity of information we submit * * *.

The trick in situations such as this is not to appear to be put off by the question. Even if the advocate knows that the line of questioning is not dispositive of the case, a respectful attitude must be maintained. Counsel must remember that members of the court have every right to pursue whatever direction they wish. Simply answer the question and move forward.

One of the most disconcerting situations is one in which the advocate finds that he or she does not know the answer to the question. This, of course, should happen rarely and only in circumstances that could not have been anticipated. Should this dilemma arise, the worst possible approach is to try to "wing it." This posture most surely will result in loss of credibility of both the advocate and the argument. The best approach is simply to admit not knowing the answer and offer, if the point is at all significant, to reply in a supplemental memorandum following the oral argument. Note that the operative word is *significant*. If the advocate is fully prepared, most issues will have been considered in advance, and questions relating to them can be answered. It is the question that is not anticipated and totally tangential to the argument that may confuse the advocate. For example in the next segment, the unsuspecting advocate has just completed her introduction—exactly one sentence long.

> Judge: Excuse me counselor. Before you get on to that subject, I note in the complaint a reference to the provision of private telecommunication service to interstate customers. Is there any further information as to the nature of that service provided.

> Advocate: At this time your honor, I apologize, I am unable to provide that information.

Her answer was completely honest and forthright. She continued her argument as if nothing had happened and no one followed up on the errant question.

If the question posed strikes at a weak section of the argument, there may be nothing to do but concede the point. If the advocate is prepared, the question will have been anticipated. The best approach is to admit the weakness, state that there really is no good answer to the question but urge that the issue is not dispositive of the case. Be prepared to point to facts or legal theories that diminish the effect of the weakness and support the strengths of the case.

In the next sequence, the judge poses a devastating question to the advocate. After some stumbling, he tries to divert attention away from his initial response, which appears to be a concession, by pointing to a strength in his argument.

> Judge: You don't think this is a First Amendment case at all do you?

> Advocate: Oh it's a First Amendment case, your honor or rather the petitioner would ask this court to *believe* that it is a First Amendment case. However, the complaint fails to state a claim under the First Amendment because it has no right of access to the utility poles. It has no constitutional right to be a franchise cable operator. There is nothing in the record to lead this court to believe that the petitioner necessarily has a right to be an operator or to possess this medium.

As one can see from the above, concessions can come via a slip of the tongue or as shown in the sequence that follows, by the request of the court to admit a weakness in the argument.

> Judge: Here, unlike the *Miami Herald* case, all the city is doing is requiring that certain channels be set aside for public, education and governmental use. Totally content neutral. Wouldn't you concede that they are totally content neutral.

> Advocate: That may be correct your honor, but aside from that fact, in *Miami Herald*, this Court was particularly concerned with the chilling effect that such a right of access may have on editorial discretion. But here we do not have a chilling effect on editorial discretion; we have a total usurpation of editorial discretion.

Here the advocate partially admitted that the judge was correct but then quickly pointed out that, notwithstanding that fact, the real issue centers on editorial discretion and not on the contents of the message. Damage control is at the heart of making a concession.

One last point. Most cases that come to the appeals courts have at least one key question that poses difficulty and/or embarrassment to the advocate. Many lawyers come to oral argument with the fervent hope that the question will not be asked. It will be. If the matter has not been thought out carefully, counsel can easily be caught off balance and appear to the judges to be unprepared. The court likely will assume that the advocate has not taken an important point seriously or is not willing to attempt to resolve problems with which the judges are wrestling. Should this happen, a valuable opportunity will be lost to guide the judges' thinking as it relates to the matter. A well prepared and well reasoned answer that acknowledges the difficulties of the case, yet leads the court in the advocate's direction, is the best that can be hoped for.

10.44   Development of the theme of the argument

As previously discussed, the advocate must have a theme upon which the entire argument is built. The theme helps define the issues to be discussed and lays the basic groundwork. Because it is the central point of the argument, it is necessary to develop the concepts embodied in the theme. If the advocate gets taken too far off course by an inquisitive judge, the theme will never completely materialize. It is important, then, to be ever cognizant of getting the main points across that thoroughly develop the theme. To do this is one of the trickiest aspects of oral argument, in no small part because the judges, through questioning, have the superior power to dictate the content of the discussion.

10.44–1   Qualities that help develop theme and argument

There are several characteristics that help the advocate develop the theme of the argument. They are cohesion, use of the judge's question to return to the theme, use of the judge's own words to return to the theme and use of a short conclusion at the end of the answer to a question. Each will be discussed.

9.44–1–a   Cohesion

Theme cannot be developed if the argument lacks cohesion. Conversations, whether in the appellant courtroom or in everyday life, are not random strings of words. Words are spoken for a variety of reasons but always in an attempt to make meaning of what has just been said or is about to be said. The concept of cohesion recognizes the thematic relationship between present words as well as words across a series of talk. Within the appellate oral argument, theme development depends on the ability to see relationships within and between messages. If the argument lacks cohesiveness, the theme disintegrates and meaning is lost.

Cohesion occurs within the appellate argument in many different forms. Linkages exist between and across various forms of conversational units. This means that there are individual message units which adhere to one another to make a whole, as well as entire segments between the advocate and the judge which form a complete topic within the argument. For example in the following sequence, there is a clear case of breakdown between the message units.

> Advocate: We are before the Court today challenging the constitutionality of the respondent's franchise and auction precondition requirements as I as Lanstel has is has its First Amendment right being violated.

Quite obviously, the grammar structure is a disaster, which contributes to the general breakdown of the sentence. In addition, the advocate begins by saying "we" are before the court, then turns to "I" and finally to "Lanstel" before getting to the reason for the court challenge. The sentence itself is not cohesive and, as a result, leaves the listener wondering why the advocate is before the court.

Breakdown in the question-answer sequence likewise is costly with respect to the overall thematic development. For example:

> Judge: Could you tell me how you would handle four applications, if you were the city, in this particular context?

> Advocate: Well your honor, undeniably, the city does have an interest in insuring that fly-by-night cable companies do not come in, install their lines, experience financial demise and then collapse, leaving the city with the repairs to be made to the public facilities.

Here, there is total breakdown in theme development. The judge asks a straightforward question, and the advocate simply addresses another issue.

In order to fulfill theme, there must be continuity and purpose, which is cohesion. For example, if the advocate proposes to develop a certain theme in the argument and then fails to do so, there was a lack of cohesion between the introductory phase of the argument and the body of the argument. Likewise, if the concluding remarks do not relate to what has come before, there is a breakdown between development and conclusion.

10.44–1–b   Use of the judge's questions to return to theme

Because the questioning process is central to the oral argument, the advocate's use of the judges' questions to return to the argument and hence develop theme is important. Various authors have offered advice about how to return to the argument. Some suggest that the advocate return to the main point, while others counsel to answer the question and then return to the patterned outline. Still others advise the advocate to integrate the question into the argument. While there are pros and cons to all these suggestions, none address the difficult question as to just how the advocate either returns to the main point or outline, or integrates the question into the argument. The next several examples should help an advocate who attempts to use the judge's question to return to theme.

One successful technique is to use some type of transition from the judge's question back into the argument. The transition may come in the form of a semantic tie with the answer or a substantive tie within the answer. In the following sequence, the judge asks a question, the advocate answers the question and immediately returns to her discussion of Congressional intent as it relates to the act in question. There is a clean transition from question to answer to return to theme. In this instance, the tie from answer to return to theme is semantic in nature.

> Judge: You assume that necessarily this operator is going to make money?

> Advocate: It is the City's hope that the company will make money *and* that is why Congress enacted this act. Prior to the act, cities were left with no cable operator when they couldn't make money and in hopes of having a cable operator who will not dismantle their system and leave the city with nothing * * *.

In the next sequence, the judge asks a tangential question. The advocate answers the judge's concerns and then uses the answer as a springboard back into the argument. In this instance, the tie within the answer is substantive in nature.

> Judge: You are not taking a position that the act of 1984 is itself unconstitutional?

> Advocate: That is correct your honor. We are not facially challenging the statute because it is capable of constitutional application. *However, the city in this case has applied it unconstitutionally.*

While the above two responses appear to be similar, in fact there are subtle differences. In the former pattern, the advocate uses only the answer to return to theme. In the latter, the advocate uses both the question and the answer to return to theme. Both result in a solid answer and the advocate's return to theme.

10.44–1–c   Use of the judge's own words to return to theme

A third technique to return to theme is to use the judge's own words when answering the question. This technique appears to enhance the advocate's argument. The answer to the question presented is restated using the actual words that formed the question in the first place. For example, in the next sequence, the judge has said "the express purpose of the 1984 amendment to the 1934 act was to promote competition." The remainder of the judge's question and the advocate's beginning words are as follows:

Judge: Creating a monopoly by the municipality, how does that promote competition?

Advocate: It promotes competition in that * * *.

Likewise, this same technique may be used to respond in the negative. For example:

Judge: * * * so somehow we can limit First Amendment rights depending on what we have before us?

Advocate: No your honor. This is not a limit on First Amendment rights. (The advocate then tells the court why this is not a limit on First Amendment rights, an issue crucial to his argument)

By using the judge's own words, the advocate not only ties directly to what has just been discussed, but also shows deference to the choice of words the judge has used.

10.44–1–d   Conclusion at the end of the answer

One of the most successful strategies to promote cohesion and hence theme is the use of a concluding sentence within the answer. The concluding sentence ties to the beginning of the answer sequence. In effect, the advocate introduces the topic, develops the topic and then concludes the topic. Consider the following:

Judge: Well, what Congress has decided and what's constitutional are sometimes a little different, aren't they?

Advocate: That's correct but respondent urges this court not to ignore the decision of the legislature in this matter.

In *Columbia Broadcasting Systems v. Democratic National Committee,* the court recognized that cable television does provide a potential for a great deal of public discussion. But to cap that potential, to maximize the facilities of a cable operator, this court also recognized that mandatory access was desirable and practical. In that case, this court stated that the value of our legislature's opinion should not be undermined merely because a cablecaster has set its claim under the umbrella of the First Amendment.

That is why the respondent urges this court to take heed to warnings of Congress and what they have set forth for the city.

Prior to this sequence, the advocate argued that Congress had studied the issues surrounding the needs of both cablecasters and cities with respect to the 1984 act. The judge then questioned the advocate about possible tension between acts of Congress and the Constitution. She answered his question directly but then suggested that Congress not be ignored, a point necessary for her development of theme. She strengthened her argument with a case cite and explanation and finished by reiterating the point that the court be cognizant of Congressional intent.

In the following sequence, the advocate not only introduced, developed and concluded but also used the judge's own words in the concluding sentence.

> Judge: But they have control in that sense, do they not, over what is transmitted over their own cables. Under the ordinance, they would be required to set aside certain channels, including channels for commercial use by others, over which they have absolutely, utterly no control as I understand it. Doesn't that in fact interfere with editorial discretion?

> Advocate: No because in certain instances, cables are merely conduits and as conduits they do not exercise the same degree of discretion that they do when they originate their own programming. This is in keeping with this Court's decision in *Pittsburgh Press v. Pittsburgh Commission on Human Relations*. In that case, this Court stated that when a newspaper, which is afforded the greatest protection by the First Amendment, acts as a receptacle or a conduit for the information of others, they have no constitutional protections in that capacity. *They exert no editorial control and that is why this act does not infringe on the editorial control of the cable operator.*

10.44–2 Potential impediments to theme development

Just as there are qualities that enhance an argument, there are problematic qualities that impede its development. They include step skipping, the need for the judge to re-ask a question and changing topics in mid-sentence.

10.44–2–a Step skipping

Just as there are strategies for successful theme development, there are also patterns of argument that can inhibit theme. One such pattern is step-skipping. Simply put, the advocate omits chunks of the conversation that may or may not be important for the judges' understanding of the theme. This phenomenon is especially troublesome if the bench is "cold" and unfamiliar with the arguments. In complex legal arguments, if information is missing, there may be no shared context between the advocate and the bench. If that occurs, the argument may be confusing at best and not understood at worst. Either reaction will require clarification by the advocate. This costs valuable time and possibly loss of credibility.

For example, in the following sequence, the court asks a question, the advocate answers but appears to have skipped a couple of steps in getting to the answer.

Judge: There are no local governments or Federal government regulating the number of newspapers are there?

Advocate: No, your honor, but in *Miami Herald Publishing Company* for example, a Florida statute attempted to have a right of access to the newspaper medium and this court absolutely rejected that possibility.

Here, the question centered on whether the court could regulate the number of newspapers in a particular region. The advocate's response was "no" but that in a case that even attempted to regulate the right of access, *which is a far less intrusive type of regulation than the number of newspapers*, this Court would not allow such a statute. The italicized portion was not articulated in the argument.

In this instance, it is possible to understand the argument, but in order to garner the impact of what was said, the judges would have had to understand the implications of the italicized portion. Obviously, when all parties to the argument do not readily understand the matter discussed, problems can develop in establishing meaning. This is especially true in a situation in which one party, for example the advocate who is engaged in the step-skipping process, has superior knowledge of an issue.

In the next segment, large portions of the argument are left out and meaning is consequently difficult to comprehend.

Judge: But isn't this the same situation here where there is limited physical availability—one to three cables—and the city has decided that because of that physical limitation and because of the burden that is involved in digging up conduits and so forth, they're going to select one rather than three? Isn't the parallel very close?

Advocate: Well your honor, I think the important distinction to be made is that in the hypothetical you posited, what we don't have is a total ban on communicative activities, which is what we have in the case at bar.

Played out in its entirety, with the italicized portion connoting the steps that were skipped, a better response is, "Well your honor, I think the important distinction to be made is that in the hypothetical you posited, *there would be one cable operator*. What we don't have is a total ban on communicative activities. *But because of this unconstitutional auction process, in which we have chosen not to participate, there is a total ban on communicative activities*, which is what we have in the case at bar." In this segment, the advocate must have assumed that all members of the bench followed the argument and, therefore, there was a shared context. That is a dangerous assumption. If there is no shared context, the judges may well conclude the advocate has not responded to the question because the answer proffered does not make sense, given what the court has asked. Taken together with the fact that the words are uttered in a matter of a few seconds, with no time to ponder the meaning before the next utterance, the entire exchange becomes problematic.

In the following segment, the court is virtually baffled as the advocate takes gigantic steps without a shared context.

> Judge: Was it the right of only your client to decide what should go over those airways or does the governmental interest here on behalf of all citizens who might be involved, and therefore has a right to take those channels.

> Advocate: Your honor, in this situation, we have no indication of any compelling governmental interest on the face of the complaint.

Here, the argument would be "Your honor, in this situation, *in order for the government to have a right to those channels, and therefore to broadcast its programs, the government must have a compelling interest. A compelling interest would be shown if * * * and* we have no indication of any compelling governmental interest on the face of the complaint." Basically, the listener must fill in the blanks in order to understand the advocate's argument. In the above exchange, there was apparently no shared context, because members of the bench, in fact, posed clarifying questions about the points he made. Step skipping can lead to time-consuming additional questions. This is to be avoided, as the following section illustrates.

10.44–2–b   Need for the judge to return to a former question

A second theme development inhibitor occurs when the judge has to re-ask a question, either because the advocate is not responsive to the question or the judge is not satisfied with the advocate's answer. Obviously, this pattern consumes valuable time that could better be spent developing the argument. In addition, the advocate risks the judge's frustration and a possible loss of credibility. For example:

> Judge: As I understand it, city utility poles can handle three cables, is that correct?

> Advocate: The cities

> Judge: Is that correct, yes or no.

While on its face, this exchange is not particularly disruptive—but when the argument is examined in its totality, it is evident the advocate had previously engaged in similar non-responsive answers. Apparently the judge simply wanted one straight answer and did not get it. The judge's frustration is expressed pointedly.

Not all re-asked questions are this dramatic. Nevertheless, they are time consuming and potentially disruptive. The following segment illustrates the potential pitfalls of not directly answering a question.

> Judge: I would like to know whether or not you believe that the Cable act of 1984 is constitutional?

> Advocate: Your honor, we are challenging the constitutionality of that act as applied. On its face, the act is very permissive. It says such things as a municipality may do this or may do that. It doesn't mandate anything and thus we are challenging the city's rules as applied from that statute.

> Judge: So I am clear you are not taking a position that the act of 1984 is unconstitutional?

> Advocate: That is correct your honor.

In addition to confusing the judge, this segment, when studied on paper, is difficult to understand. Imagine hearing the passage and trying to fit it into the argument as a whole.

10.44–2–c   Changing topics in mid-sentence

Another pattern that hampers theme development are instances in which the advocate gets ahead of him or herself in the argument. This can result in changing topics before the topic under consideration is exhausted. The following illustrates the point:

> Advocate: However, cable has evolved far beyond that and what cable has become is the electronic print media in that newspapers, we give newspapers a high degree of freedom because newspapers have been seen traditionally as operating as the fourth estate someone called it, but must operate to give people that information and allow people to speak without the restraint of government.

While the passage suffers from grammatical errors, changing topics is probably the most confusing. The advocate begins by the assertion that cable is really an electronic print media. Then, apparently she intends to make some reference to the press but loses track of her line of thought and launches instead into a discussion of newspaper freedom. Simply put, the advocate changes topics with no warning to the listener and with no way to put the comments in context.

In the next sequence, the advocate is misunderstood when he makes a mid-sentence topic change. Here, the judge has just asked a question about whether all of the alleged harms will occur in the future. The advocate responds to that question and then makes a mid-sentence shift.

> Advocate: Your honor we have not participated in this auction process so in that sense, yes, it is in the future, but because we have a threatened injury which affects a First Amendment right, we have standing to raise this issue.

Here, the advocate propounded two different arguments. They apparently effected a comprehension overload, because in the next sequence the same judge said:

> Judge: That was your associate's argument—the First Amendment. How can you take something in futuro?

His co-counsel's argument did center on the First Amendment; the point that the advocate was making was that there was standing to raise the issue because of a First Amendment harm. That is one of his arguments, but it is virtually lost because of his mid-sentence topic change.

The foregoing details some problematic patterns for theme development. There are other patterns that damage a good argument as well. In the following section, citation use within the argument is discussed. Failure to follow some practical guidelines when citing materials during the oral argument can lead to an unfavorable result.

10.45   The citation of authority during oral argument

Citing authority in open court raises three issues: how to cite; when to cite; and, what to cite. Obviously, the oral argument requires a very different use of case citations than the brief. Some advocates insist on multitudinous case citations and extensive, even excruciating detail of their facts. These advocates believe an explication of minutia will impress the judges. This most assuredly is not the case.

As previously discussed, in the brief each important issue is supported by complete case citations, with an explanation of why particular cases are not only applicable but dispositive of that issue. If the judge does not understand the use of a case in a brief, the written words allow for another reading and time to think. Those luxuries do not exist in oral argument. Cognitive overload is always a potential problem in a speech/hearing situation. Simply put, the meaning is likely to be lost on long citations with accompanying factual detail. The best plan is to leave the details for the brief.[20]

The honorable John W. Davis explains it well.

There is a cognate fault of which most of us from time to time are guilty. This arises when we are seeking to cite or distinguish other cases bearing on our claims and are tempted into a tedious recital of the facts in the cited case, now uncommonly prefaced by the some awkward phrase "That was a case where," etc. Now the human mind is a pawky thing and must be held to its work and it is little wonder after three or four or half a dozen such recitals that not only are the recited facts forgotten but those in the case at bar become blurred and confused. What the advocate needs most of all is that his facts and his alone should stand out stark, simple, unique, clear.[21]

Davis makes good points. One, the judges will lose track of the various facts of the cited cases. Two, the judges will confuse the facts of the case at bar with the cited case. There are two other potentially devastating results. The advocate may become confused with the facts of the cited cases (either individually or as they relate to one another) and the case at bar; or, in the worst possible scenario, the advocate may confuse the

---

20. A more comprehensive discussion of the case may be necessary if the case cited appears to be on point and goes against the oralist position. Then a certain amount of dissection of both the facts and the law may be necessary in order to distinguish the case and reduce its impact.

21. Davis, *supra* note 1, at 898.

facts of his or her own case. Rule one is: do not bog down on the facts of cases one cites.[22]

In rare instances, however, one may find a quick recitation of the facts is necessary. This occurs in situations in which (1) the judges likely have not read the briefs, or (2) all of the judges may not be familiar with the cited case,[23] or (3) the case is of special importance, and (4) a short recitation of the facts likely will not confuse the judges.

Rule two is: keep it simple. If a case is cited, just the name of the parties will usually suffice. It is awkward and unnecessary for the advocate to provide the entire cite, unless it is requested. The judges won't remember it anyway. The best approach is to name the case and note where in the brief the case is cited and developed.

The foregoing assumes that the advocate will cite authority during oral argument. Oral argument experts disagree on whether case cites are necessary during an argument, but most authorities believe there are instances in which a proffered case cite is beneficial. Wiener offers his suggestions on the appropriate time to cite a case.

> Where, however, the immediate subject-matter of a principal heading had not come up recently or involves a somewhat obscure point, it is well to cite a few of the leading, landmark cases as you go along, by way of reassuring the court that you are not just spouting law by ear but have solid authority to support you. Remember—just a few, not the sort of collection you may properly set out and discuss in your brief.[24]

There are, however, instances in which a case cite or series of case cites are important and others where they are detrimental. Justice Jackson, observes that most judges cannot recall the exact words of a statute or document, but do remember the Court's own precedent. He states:

> * * * I should make the contrary assumption about the Court's own precedents, particularly its recent precedents. I can think of no more dismal and fruitless use of time than to recite case after case, with explanations why each is, or is not, applicable.[25]

He also notes that if one or two good solid precedents fail to convince the court, a host of weaker ones only further undermines the argument. In other words, he and probably most judges view with skepticism citations to several authorities that presumably make the same or similar points.

---

22. It is perfectly appropriate and probably desirable to detail facts of a case when requested by a member of the court to distinguish it or show its applicability. Should that occur, the advocate can be fairly certain the bench shares the same foundation and familiarly with the concepts of the authority.

23. This may occur if there are several panels within the particular court. For example, it is unlikely that all of the judges of the 2d Circuit are familiar with all of their associates' opinions. This is certainly true across federal circuits and within the various appeals courts at the state level.

24. Frederick Bernays Wiener, Briefing and Arguing Federal Appeals 322 (1967).

25. Jackson, *supra* note 2, at 804.

Occasionally the advocate will discover that, in order to make a cogent argument, it is necessary to cite to other primary authority. This may include constitutions, statutes or administrative materials. If this is the case, great care must be taken to present only the most relevant information as it relates to the case. Sometimes a succinct quote is necessary. This is not preferable, but if the argument depends on such authority, the advocate must deal with it. Again, simplicity is the password. Be careful not to muddy the waters by bogging down in lengthy orations that are little understood through an oral litany and are best read and studied.

History and legislative intent may also become important for interpretive purposes. Legislative histories can be compelling in the brief, but in oral argument they are often cumbersome and confusing. If the recital of a legislative history is needed to make a crucial point in the argument, and if it can be easily summarized, then a short summary is permissible. Otherwise, the temptation to use it should be ignored. Instead, mention of its location in the brief is helpful to the court.

Other secondary authority at times may be cited. Great caution should be exercised. The advocate should turn to secondary authority only when primary authority likely is not dispositive of the issue. Selection of secondary authority must be carefully chosen. Only authors or works of great stature should be considered. Appellate courts are not receptive to secondary authority, unless the issue is open to interpretation and primary authority does not foreclose a decision of the matter.

10.46   Reading and quoting to the court

Frederick B. Wiener advanced the best advice to oral advocates when he said "[n]ever read your argument. *Never read your argument.* **NEVER READ YOUR ARGUMENT**."[26] The purpose of the oral argument is to have a dialogue with the court, a conversation of sorts. Reading to the court quickly results in boredom. An oralist cannot hope to obtain, much less keep, the attention of the court if his or her eyes are affixed to a piece of paper perched on the podium. The last thing an advocate needs is a bench that is either dozing off or simply not attentive.

10.46–1   The importance of eye contact

One who reads cannot maintain eye contact. As John W. Davis said "[t]he eye is the window of the mind and the speaker does not live who can long hold the attention of the audience without looking it in the face."[27] Eye contact is a signal that the communication channel is open. If one reads, conversation is discouraged because the channel is closed.

In normal face to face communication, one does not expect a person to read a prepared text if the latter is trying to convince someone that Sony is a better TV set than Zenith. Further, a written presentation

---

26.   Wiener, *supra* note 24, at 282.   **27.**   Davis, *supra* note 1, at 898.

destroys all semblance of spontaneity, as well as flexibility. Judges are less likely to voice their concerns if the advocate reads the argument with eyes turned away from the bench. If there are questions, a scripted presentation discourages development of points that interest the judges because the advocate is intent on returning to the script. Valuable opportunities to enhance a point important to the court are lost.

Reading to the court is unprofessional, and many courts have banned reading by court rule. Rule 34(c) of the Federal Rules of Appellate Procedure provides that "[c]ounsel must not read at length from briefs, records or authorities." The Supreme Court of the United States in Rule 28.1 states: "Counsel should assume that all Justices have read the briefs before oral argument. *Oral argument read from a prepared text is not favored.*" In his discussion about reading to the court, Chief Justice Rehnquist tells the story of an advocate who began reading his brief early in the argument. The presiding judge reminded him of the court rule which prohibited reading; he persisted, albeit in a dramatic way. The presiding judge finally interrupted to say: "Counsel, I think you may be sure that we have read your brief." The attorney replied: "Yes, but you have not heard it with gestures."[28] An oral argument is most assuredly not a brief with gestures.

Justice Thurgood Marshall once commented on reading the brief. He said:

> I don't know of a single judge who doesn't strenuously object to the rehashing of a brief. The judge has read the brief. Once you have prepared your brief, use your argument to prepare yourself for the questions. It is not what is in your brief. I have seen instances in which rehashing has been tried. I have seen instances in which it has been done. I have seen no instances in which it has worked.[29]

The foregoing does not suggest that reading short passages or quotes are inappropriate. If the case turns on the language of the statute or the terms of a written document, it may be necessary to read it to the court. However, keep the excerpts short and do not overly rely on quotations. The bench will soon lose interest in the argument.

If an advocate finds it necessary to read a short quote, it is imperative that the quoted language be at hand. An advocate who cannot find what it is that he or she wants to read risks the court's annoyance. If the quote is lengthy, try to summarize. Be careful, however, that the summary does not distort the meaning by selective inclusion or exclusion. It is important to inform the court that only part of the quotation is being read and where in the brief the remainder can be found.

Finally, when reading, most advocates have a tendency to speed up their speech pattern. This practice results in confusion as to the significance or meaning of the quoted material. Make a specific effort to slow

28. Rehnquist, *supra* note 16, at 298.

29. Thurgood Marshall, *The Federal Appeal,* in Counsel on Appeal 139, 155 (Arthur A. Charpentier ed. 1968).

down so that the judges can follow the material and grasp its importance.

10.47   The importance of voice

The long hours of preparation will be for naught if the advocate is unable to speak effectively before the panel of judges on the day of oral argument. Start with the fundamentals of good public speaking as a foundation for a good performance. Remember, this is a conversation, albeit a formal conversation, with the court. In this conversation, the advocate must be heard and must place proper emphasis on what is described below as the "punctuation" of oral presentation.

10.47–1   The advocate must be heard

One of the first tenets of either an oral argument, a speech or a conversation is that the oralist must be heard. This seems like an obvious point, but its importance is underscored by the fact it is discussed in most major treatises that deal with the argument of an appeal. The tendency to be timid afflicts many advocates who appear before an appellate panel. This must not occur, because a counsel, who cowers and is unable to be heard, undermines the argument from the beginning. Some judges simply will not strain to listen but rather choose to ignore what the advocate tries to say. Other judges ask for clarification, usually in the form of a request of the advocate to repeat the statement. Justice Jackson offers some excellent advice:

> If your voice is low, it burdens the hearing and parts of what you say may be missed. On the other hand, no judge likes to be shouted at as if he were an ox. I know of nothing you can do except to bear the difficulty in mind, watch the bench, and adapt your delivery to avoid causing apparent strain.[30]

The effective speaker becomes so by trial and error. The only way to learn good speaking skills is to do it, practice, and do it some more. Some people succeed by practicing before a mirror; some succeed by practicing before a live audience; and still others find that videotape provides the best method for spotting speech patterns not conducive to effective advocacy.

10.47–2   Proper emphasis

Research shows that the manner in which the words are spoken can be critical to the success of the argument. In order to avoid problematic speech traits, one must be aware of them. All experts agree that *proper emphasis* is critical to understanding. Therefore, speech patterns that interfere with emphasis are to be avoided. Think of emphasis as the punctuation of the oral presentation. Using no punctuation with the written word can lead to confusion—likewise with the spoken word.

---

30. Jackson, *supra* note 2, at 861.

Several speech patterns interfere with proper emphasis. Chief on the list is the monotone voice. As Mr. Wiener observed, the best way to illustrate a monotone in print is to reproduce a written piece with no punctuation.[31] In the following sequence, one should note the number of times that the passage must be read before the meaning is determined.

Actually the closest thing would be the *Red Line* case which does uphold the fairness doctrine and which does state that viewers and listeners do have a right of reply and that should prevail here because there is scarcity and that's why the use of this petitioner's property does not constitute a permanent physical invasion but is merely a use which is mandated to subserve a compelling interest and to enhance diversity and moreover even if that is considered a taking in this case it has been duly compensated.

This run-on sentence, at first unintelligible, becomes understandable when correctly punctuated. The same problems exist if made in this way at oral argument, and they can be similarly overcome if there is proper punctuation in the oral presentation.

Closely related to the monotone is the reading voice, because by definition, reading is a monological form of speech. A reading voice is defined as one that has little pitch, stress or tempo changes within a set of speech units. If an advocate and the judges are engaged in a conversation, reading is counterproductive. The common signaling, shifts or transitions from one activity, such as telling, to another, such as responding, is potentially lost. In addition, when an advocate reads, the pace of the talk usually increases. Valuable questions that may help develop the argument will not be asked because, by the time the question can be formulated, the advocate is long past that point and on to another topic. The reading voice, with its attendant gaze downward, simply is not conducive to good advocacy.

Very similar to the reading voice is the memorized voice. Intonational patterns are like the reading voice. This pattern may be a problem for two reasons. First, as with the reading voice, the advocate tends to speed up the talk. Second, memorized oratory can become a lecture of sorts, thus the potential for conversation diminishes.

The halting voice presents yet another problem for emphasis. An advocate's voice is halting if he or she has a series of one or two word speech units in which there is no marked intonational drop or rise that indicates either that the unit is over or, conversely, that more is to come. Members of the bench, if waiting for an indication of closure to ask a question, may be confused with respect to when that particular message unit is concluded. In addition, halting speech may be interpreted as unsure speech with respect to the content of the message being transmitted.

To illustrate in print, think of each one of the words in the next sequence uttered with no inflection and very hesitantly.

31. See Wiener, *supra* note 24, at 285.

First the criteria that is used in selecting the cable franchise permits that a cable operator's speech is chilled.

An argument delivered in this fashion quickly becomes boring. Members of the bench simply lose interest.

Mumbling through an oral argument presents two problems for the advocate. First, the argument will lack emphasis. Second, credibility will be lost. For example, in the following sequence, one wonders if the advocate is unprepared, inarticulate or both.

Advocate: Um, if I if I could restate it. What I am what I am saying is that the city is um taking is uh looking to um determine what the determining what the proper franchisee is looking to the character of that franchisee.

To avoid a lack of emphasis and to punctuate the argument, the advocate must use the pause. Short pauses indicate a verbal comma. Longer pauses, with a dropping intonation, signal the end of a sentence. An even longer pause emphasizes a thought unit is complete. As in ordinary conversation, judges may be distracted from the argument. Should that occur, a pause may be used to regain the attention of the bench. Silence invites members to look up to see what is happening.

10.48 Nonverbal communication

Nonverbal communication or body language helps explain what is said in a conversation. This applies whether the conversation is over a cup of coffee or in the appellate courtroom. While non-verbals provide a potential for aid, they also raise the risk of damage. Non-verbals can enhance the discussion but also can distract. Therefore, advocates must recognize the signals they transmit through body movements.

Hand movements are probably the number one problem for advocates, especially those who have, by nature, an animated personality. Hand movements can be successfully used to drive home a point, but the advocate must be wary of repetitious movements that do not add meaning to the argument. One example is taking one's glasses on and off and waving them in the air. One advocate who was observed had the unpleasant habit of adjusting his glasses every time a question was asked. After a short while, observers became so interested in how far up his nose he could push his glasses (under heavy questioning), that the meaning of the question/answer sequence was lost. Waving or pointing is another annoying habit. Avoid at all costs taking a pencil to the podium. Before long, the pencil becomes a tool for shaking or worse, pointing at the judges. Drawing imaginary pictures in the air is problematic. In a key point of one argument, the advocate, in describing a television set, drew an imaginary box in the air, when referring to "that little box." Air quotation marks are also annoying.

Facial expressions are revealing. A grimace or an apparent pained expression to a judge's question suggests that one either doubts the relevance of the question or is unsure of the answer. The so-called poker face that shows interest and deference is probably best when listening to a question. The flip side is never sneer or assume a derisive smirk when the opponent is struggling with a tough argument. It is just bad manners. If the judges see it, they will not be impressed.

Other gestures to avoid include scratching one's ear, stroking one's hair, and fumbling with papers on the podium (thus the reason to take only a file folder to the podium). Some advocates have the habit of always glancing downward each time a judge asks a question. It is as if the advocate is in search of the answer before the question is asked, a mannerism unlikely to conjure images of confidence.

Body language is an important positive in an argument. The key to success is to identify annoying mannerisms, eliminate them and begin to work on positive body language and facial expressions.

10.50 USE OF PHYSICAL EXHIBITS

In limited circumstances, physical exhibits such as maps, charts, diagrams or pictures aid the oral argument. The decision whether to use physical materials involves several considerations. A primary factor is whether the exhibit will enhance or detract from the argument. For example, if the point to be amplified is a minor one, the use of an exhibit may well evoke more discussion than the point deserves. As a result, valuable time is lost that could be used to advance more important points of the argument. To be mired in non-essential conversation is counter-productive to a good argument.

If known, the composition of the panel should also be considered. If an advocate is arguing before a panel of judges well known to "split hairs," use of physical exhibits may prompt extensive discussion. If the point is important, its use may be significant. If not, the exercise will be a waste of time. Also, judges who best assimilate material visually will probably welcome the exhibits. Those who learn best from the written word may find the material superfluous, even irritating. If the panel is not known, either personally or before the commencement of the argument, the password is flexibility. One must determine the best course of action based on previous knowledge of the bench and adjust it, as necessary, to the actual development of the argument. Remember: once before the court, the exhibit may draw comment from opposing counsel.[32]

Another concern is that an exhibit may appear to expound on a relatively simple point. This may be perceived as an insult to the intelligence of the panel. Risking the alienation of the panel is definitely not recommended.

Nevertheless, some facts are better understood if the judges can visualize the problem, as well as hear about them. An example might be boundaries in a real estate dispute, or diagrams and charts that relate to

---

32. It is recommended to discuss any proposed exhibits with opposing counsel prior to argument to determine if there is any objection to its use. If there is, the matter can be resolved prior to argument instead of using valuable time to make that determination during the argument.

a patent issue. If physical evidence is used, that evidence must either be in the trial court record, be based directly upon some fact in the record, be an appropriate subject for judicial notice, or be a combination of these elements.[33] The same material should also be presented in the main body or appendix of the brief so that the judges may later peruse it at their leisure during deliberations. It is, however, a profound error to present each judge with a copy of the exhibit. One advocate tells the story of a lawyer who tried to distribute maps to the Justices at argument. The Chief Justice then informed the lawyer that there were plenty of atlases in the Supreme Court library and to proceed promptly with his argument—not an auspicious beginning to be sure.[34] In addition, having material before each judge invites distraction during the remainder of the argument.

There are some rules to remember if physical exhibits are to be used. First, the exhibit **must** be large enough for all members of the court to see. The entire exercise will be futile if the judges must strain to see the exhibit. Second, use a pointer and stand to the side so as not to interfere with the judges' line of vision. Third, large numbers of exhibits should not be used. One visual aid usually is the most effective. More exhibits clutter the courtroom and the judges' minds. When counsel has finished with the exhibit, it should be covered or removed from the courtroom. To leave it in place serves as a distraction during the remainder of the argument. In addition, remember that the advocate must provide all necessary auxiliary materials. Do not assume that easels, pointers or any other materials can or will be provided by the officers of the trial or appellate court.

A major exception to the use of physical exhibits is an appellate argument before the Supreme Court of the United States. The length and shape of the Bench makes it very difficult for all of the Justices to see an enlargement, no matter the size and where it is placed. Because microphones are used in that chamber, the advocate who steps away from the podium to explain the diagram, likely loses the impact of his explanation. As Chief Justice Rehnquist noted, the acoustics in the Supreme Court are terrible. The best advise is for counsel to test both the visibility and the acoustics in the courtroom before the oral argument—another reason to come early.

10.60 SUMMATION AND CONCLUSION

The importance of the summation and conclusion has been debated over the years. Wiener states that the "advocate's closing words are important, and they should leave an impression of combined strength and dignity."[35] Stern states that, unless the conclusion adds something of

---

33. *See* Owen Rall, *The Use of Visual Aids in Courts of Review,* 52 Nw. U. L. Rev. 90, 97 (1957).

34. *See* William F. Jung, *Effective Appellate Advocacy: Lessons Learned at the U.S. Supreme Court,* 60 Fla. B.J. 17 (July/August

1986). Further this author says never use physical exhibits. Just put them in the brief.

35. Wiener, *supra* note 24, at 332.

substance, it is probably not persuasive. More particularly, he says that "[t]here rarely will be time to summarize at any length what one has said before, and to attempt to do so in a few sentences or in a punchy short conclusion, resounding as it may be, is not likely to convince judges who have not already reacted favorably to the reasoning in the substantive argument."[36] Nevertheless, if time has not expired, most authors suggest that some kind of conclusion is desirable if only for the purposes of closure. If the advocate's time has elapsed, a request for time to conclude is risky. It is most embarrassing to have the court tell one that its members have heard quite enough. This ending leaves the advocate with neither strength nor dignity. Investigation of a court's general response to additional time requests should be made in advance. Some courts simply do not allow additional time. Other courts are quite lenient and allow the advocate to conclude after time has expired. Determine the probable response by a court to this possible request *before* the actual argument.

Basically, advocates find themselves in one of three situations as the argument nears its end: (1) the argument has gone as planned and there is time for a summation and conclusion; (2) time is elapsing and the advocate is rushed; or (3) there is time to spare. Each requires a different approach to concluding the argument.

The best of all worlds is one in which the advocate delivers a summary and a concluding peroration just as time expires. In this instance, the summary should reflect the theme and thus the most important points of the case. The conclusion makes clear what is desired, i.e., a new trial, reconsideration of specific issues on remand, etc. Both the summary and the conclusion should have been carefully planned ahead of time. Some people feel comfortable writing this portion of the argument. If so, it must not be read or appear to be memorized.

The most common scenario is one where time is fast evaporating. Hopefully the most important aspects of the argument have been covered, and all that remains is a closing. In this situation, a skeletal summary and conclusion, again reiterating the theme, should be offered. Avoid the ever popular "for the aforementioned reasons, the judgment below should be reversed." While the statement provides closure, it does little else. Take the theme of the arguments previously discussed, and state something akin to the following:

> To conclude, regulations such as these impede not only cable operators' First Amendment rights but the viewers' rights as well. (the theme) As this court has noted, the viewers' rights are paramount. In the interest of preserving First Amendment freedoms of the cable operator as well as the viewer, we ask that this court reverse the decision below and rule in appellant's favor.

The time-to-spare scenario poses the greatest problem for the advocate. For some reason, oralists feel they must use all the allotted time.

---

36. Robert L. Stern, Appellate Practice in the United States 431 (2d ed. 1989).

This simply is not so. If the points of the argument have been properly developed and covered, then all that remains is to deliver a short summary and conclusion, thank the court and sit down. The court will appreciate the gesture. The worst approach is to argue issues that were not planned. The risk is getting caught in inconsistencies, contradictions, or misstatements.

To fill the time, some advocates reiterate issues already discussed. Do not do this. First, it takes the matter out of the context within which it was previously discussed. Second, it may appear the advocate lacked material to discuss, which might evidence lack of preparation. And third, it may appear to be merely filling time. Remember: the summary and conclusion are the last pieces of information to be conveyed to the court. It is most effective if the court pays attention and is not distracted by extraneous matters.

10.70 THE APPELLEE'S OR RESPONDENT'S ARGUMENT

Most of what has been said about the formulation and delivery of the petitioner's argument applies equally to the respondent's argument. Statistics favor respondents, because they have already won in the court below. It is the petitioner who must convince the court to overturn the lower court decision. Additionally, the respondent has had the advantage of observing members of the court with respect to their concerns, questioning style and demeanor. This can be an invaluable asset to the discerning respondent.

The respondent's argument must develop the advocate's chosen theme, but it also must be a rebuttal to the petitioner's theme. This is a challenging assignment because it demands the ultimate of flexibility. Clearly, the respondent's argument can and should be planned in the same manner as the petitioner's argument. But the respondent must also be prepared to selectively abandon the prepared argument in favor of developing issues raised either by the petitioner or by the court. In other words, during the petitioner's argument, close attention must be taken of the sticky points raised. This must be balanced with the respondent's own argument. It is a mistake to spend the entire time putting out the fires of the opponent, point by point.

At the outset, the respondent should inform the court of the issues to be discussed. There is no need to reiterate the facts. However, a good beginning may be to stress some aspect of the facts that have been glossed over or forgotten by the petitioner. In the following sequence, the respondent calls into question a fact that has been raised by the petitioner.

May it please the court, my name is "X" and on behalf of the respondents, I will establish that the mandatory access provisions of the City of Lanstel do not constitute a violation of this petitioner's First Amendment rights and do not constitute a taking in violation of this petitioner's Fifth Amendment rights.

The petitioner has alleged that paragraph eight states that under-
ground conduits are a viable alternative to this petitioner's setting
up a cable system. That is not true.

Likewise, if a question has not been answered satisfactorily, offering
a better explanation than proffered by the petitioner is an excellent
strategy. It has the dual purpose of both answering a question posed by a
judge (who obviously was interested in the answer) and, if handled
carefully, discrediting the opponent if the original answer was off the
mark.

In the following sequence, the advocate refers to a previous question
posed by one of the judges during the petitioner's argument. The
petitioner had compared the case under consideration to the previously
decided *Quincy* case. The respondent, who disagreed with the assessment
of that case said:

> In relation to the question posed by Justice "Y" about the *Quincy*
> case, there are many features that distinguish it. In that case, the
> city requested that the cable operator use all of its channels because
> they were requesting that all local programming be aired by the
> cable operator. So in effect the cable operator would have used all of
> its channels to disseminate information which it did not originate.
> In this case, only six out of a minimum of 52 channels will be used
> by the city or by the public.

Here, the advocate both made an important point and somewhat discred-
ited the petitioner by a delineation of a major factual difference in the
two cases. The petitioner, in his argument, had simply misinterpreted an
important case, and the respondent was able to "seize the day," thus
scoring points for her argument.

One last point. While emoting is likely not persuasive, a little
righteous indignation can be effective. Do not be afraid to refer briefly to
the sanctity of the jury system, the crowded court dockets, the length of
time that the case has already consumed, etc. For example:

> This case has been in the judicial system for 13 years. First filed in
> 1982, the defendant moved for dismissal based on failure to state a
> claim. The motion was denied. Next defendant moved for judgment
> on the pleadings, which was also denied. Heavy discovery followed
> and the defendant moved for summary judgment. Denied once
> again. Two years ago, the jury, which had all of the facts before it,
> awarded the plaintiff, Linda James, $250,000 because the defen-
> dant's negligence maimed her for life. The defendant appealed.

10.80 THE REBUTTAL

The petitioner faces a number of dilemmas with regard to a possible
rebuttal. Some experts suggest that rebuttal time should always be
reserved and then used. Others suggest that it should be used very
sparingly. Justice Jackson, in his seminal article on appellate advocacy,
stated:

I would not say that rebuttal is never to be indulged. At times it supplies important and definite corrections. But the most experienced advocates make least use of the privilege. Many inexperienced ones get into trouble by attempting to renew the principal argument. One who returns to his feet exposes himself to an accumulation of questions. Cases have been lost that, before counsel undertook a long rebuttal, appeared to be won.[37]

As one author put it, "[d]on't snatch defeat from the jaws of victory."[38]

The first decision then, is whether to reserve rebuttal time. Proponents of rebuttal suggest it is the opportunity for the petitioner to make important points. Further, they suggest, rebuttal should always be reserved in case a reply is needed. Then, if not needed, simply waive the time. Usually the reservation of two to three minutes in a 20–minute argument is sufficient.

There are several cardinal rules with respect to rebuttal time. First and foremost, this time should be used exclusively for rebuttal. It is not a time to rehash the argument or raise new theories. The judges will either tune out or, worse, become annoyed with the advocate. After a long argument, the last thing they want to hear is what has already been said, albeit in shortened form. Rather, rebuttal is used to correct misstatements of law or fact and major omissions. A correction of the respondent's version of the record, if in error, is especially important, since the court may not otherwise realize the error. Rebuttal also provides the petitioner an opportunity to comment on questions asked by the court during the respondent's argument. Remember: don't waste the court's time on insignificant errors when they will have no impact on the outcome of the case. As one observer noted "[a]n insipid, note-cluttered, nit-picking rebuttal statement is far worse than none at all."[39]

One word of caution: the rebuttal should be aimed at only two or three major elements of the respondent's argument. Many lawyers try to score as many points as possible on rebuttal. In the end, they score none at all. Rebuttal issues are, by their nature, taken out of context. To muddy the waters by wading through five or six issues, which may be difficult to follow, invites trouble. Hit the main point or points and finish in a forceful manner.

Once the advocate has decided to rebut, the next question is *how* or *if* to prepare in advance. Authorities differ. Some suggest it is foolhardy not to prepare, while others say it is impossible to prepare in advance when one does not know what will evolve in the argument. Both sides of this issue will be presented below. It is then for the individual to determine what works best.

37. Jackson, *supra* note 2, at 804.

38. Myron H. Bright, *The Ten Commandments of Oral Argument,* 67 A.B.A.J. 1136, 1139 (1981).

39. William D. Mitchell, *Wiener: Effective Appellate Advocacy,* 64 Harv. L. Rev. 350, 351 (1950) (book review).

The argument for an unprepared rebuttal suggests that the rebuttal be given extemporaneously based on one's memory and on notes made during the course of the respondent's argument. The issues deemed most important, and thus worthy of rebuttal, should be highlighted in some way. Sometimes a catchword to remind the advocate of the answer might also be included in the notes. Again, those chosen for inclusion should be only those most important to the petitioner's case.

Proponents of the prepared, or partially prepared rebuttal, note that the advocate should think about the arguments that he might make if he were the respondent. Likewise, the questions the court is likely to ask as it relates to that argument should be forecast. Anticipating what issues will be raised allows the advocate to evaluate how best to answer those arguments. Even so, flexibility must be uppermost in the advocate's mind. It is entirely possible that the respondent's omissions, misstatements and unanticipated arguments will consume all the rebuttal time. If this is the case, a prepared rebuttal will not be useful.

There is wisdom in both methods. Obviously, a rebuttal cannot be "canned." The advocate must always be cognizant of what is transpiring in the respondent's argument. It is essential to listen carefully and take notes for later use. One must also determine how to respond if specific issues are raised, either by the respondent or the court. One successful way to prepare is to note possible questions or issues on the left hand part of the page and the answer to the questions or issues on the right hand side. When an issue is raised, the advocate merely has to check it off. In the end, the matters to resolve will be: (1) which issues to rebut—the answer being the most important ones; and (2) if there are other matters that were not anticipated, upon which notes were taken during the respondent's argument. The decision of what to raise is then one of choice based on the assessment of those issues.

As mentioned, the preparation for rebuttal is an individual matter. Some preparation is advisable, if only to determine most of the possible issues and questions that might come up. Remember: rebut only contentions raised in the respondent's argument, including omissions and misstatements. If nothing can be added to enhance the petitioner's case, waive rebuttal. If that is the situation, by this time in the argument, the gesture will be appreciated.

10.90   THE ARGUMENT THAT SHOULD HAVE BEEN MADE

Justice Robert H. Jackson of the United States Supreme Court offers some encouragement to those advocates who appear before appellate tribunals. Recognized as one of the most competent appellate advocates of his time, he said:

I used to say that, as Solicitor General, I made three arguments of every case. First came the one I planned as I thought, logical, coherent, complete. Second was the one actually presented-interrupted, incoherent, disjointed, disappointing. The third was the utterly devastating argument that I thought of after going to bed that night.[40]

Simply put, arguments in an appellate court are unlikely to develop as the advocate had planned. Nevertheless, they still may be very good arguments. Sound thought and preparation will assure that the argument, even if not devastating, will be perfectly acceptable.

EXERCISES

I. In the Exercise for Chapter 9, you prepared an oral argument for one or all of the parties. During that preparation, you determined, pursuant to the contents of Chapter 9, that certain points had to be expressed in order to potentially obtain a favorable judgment.

A. Did the Petitioners attempt to articulate those concepts?

B. Did they succeed?

C. In examining the arguments, do you see a possible opening to interject one or more of the points that needed to be communicated to the Court?

D. Did the Respondent attempt to articulate those concepts?

E. Did he succeed?

F. In examining the argument, do you see a possible opening to interject one or more of the points that needed to be communicated to the Court?

---

40. Jackson, *supra* note 2, at 803.

Chapter Eleven

POST–ARGUMENT MEMORANDA, BRIEFS AND PETITIONS FOR REHEARING

Analysis

11.00   POSSIBLE FURTHER ACTIONS AFTER ORAL ARGUMENT

The conclusion of oral argument usually signals the end of the advocate's direct actions on appeal. The briefs were filed and the arguments made. Nothing else remains except for both sides to await anxiously the decision by the appellate court. This is the usual scenario. There are exceptions.

The following sections explain possible post-argument actions that must, should or might be undertaken by counsel. These include the necessity or, in the alternative, the desirability of a supplemental brief or memorandum. The second possibility is the advisability of filing a petition for rehearing. The sections which follow explore supplemental briefs, memoranda, and petitions for rehearing.

11.10   MEMOS AND BRIEFS AFTER ORAL ARGUMENT

At times, the court requests supplemental information to consider before a final decision is rendered. This request can come during or after oral argument. Usually, counsel will file either a supplemental brief or a supplemental memorandum, but the court may request counsel to file the desired information in letter format. Whatever the form, counsel should always indicate that the material filed is pursuant to a request by the court.

If the request comes during oral argument, it is likely to arise from one of two circumstances. First, if counsel is unable to answer a question that appears bothersome to the court, it is acceptable for counsel to inquire whether the court desires additional information after the argument. If the issue is truly perplexing, most judges will welcome further insight into the matter. A second situation is one in which a member of the court specifically requests a supplemental memo on an issue. This can come by direct request such as "[c]ounsel, I'm confused about this issue, and it doesn't appear to be addressed in either brief. Could you enlighten me in a post-argument memo?" Counsel should respond to this specific request at the earliest moment and file the memo with the desired information. A slightly less obvious comment from the bench might be "[c]ounsel, do you intend to file a memo on this point?" This should be taken as a command.[1] At any rate, counsel should always indicate that the memo or brief is filed pursuant to a request by the court. The document should cover only material that specifically addresses the matter to which the court requested clarification.

11.20 REHEARINGS

The losing side on appeal is often tempted to file for a rehearing. Caution is advised. There usually is little reason to file a request for rehearing, except for one last desperate chance to snatch victory from defeat. Rehearings are, for the most part, a lost cause. This is especially true when the issue raised in the petition for rehearing was addressed in a dissent to the majority opinion. In that situation, the majority has considered the issues and rejected them. If the dissenters were unsuccessful in conference, it is highly unlikely that an abbreviated petition filed by the losing party will be persuasive. To ask for a rehearing usually wastes time and money.

This is not to suggest that all rehearings are denied. At times, a rehearing is justified. For example, if there has been a new decision that seems to control the issue or an intervening statute that is retroactive, a petition for a rehearing will probably be successful. In addition, the principle of appellate mistake recognizes there must be a means to correct errors. If, after a careful reading of the decision, the losing counsel determines that the court "overlooked" or "misapprehended"[2] material points raised on appeal, counsel may have good grounds for a rehearing. Simply put, "if the court is persuaded it has or may have blundered, it will grant rehearing to avoid an unjust result or to correct material error."[3]

With respect to a rehearing of any judgment or decision on the merits, Rule 44.1 of the United States Supreme Court says that "the

---

1. *See* Frederick Bernays Wiener, Briefing and Arguing Federal Appeals 263 (1967).

2. See below, § 11.22, for an explanation of the words overlooked or misapprehended.

3. David W. Louisell & Ronan E. Degnan, *Rehearing in American Appellate Courts,* 44 Cal. L. Rev. 627, 635 (1956).

petition shall state its grounds briefly and distinctly * * * ." Rule 44.2 addresses grounds for a rehearing when certiorari is denied. It states that grounds "shall be limited to intervening circumstances of substantial or controlling effect or to other substantial grounds not previously presented." Rehearings do not occur often, but special circumstances may warrant their consideration.

One rule is paramount. Counsel should not file a petition for rehearing merely because of dissatisfaction with the outcome of the case. In some jurisdictions, including the United States Supreme Court, the attorney is required to certify that the petition is filed in good faith and not for delay. Even if there is no certification requirement, the ethical attorney does not file a rehearing petition simply to delay the outcome of the appeal.

11.21 Filing the petition

The time-frame for filing a petition for rehearing differs widely from one jurisdiction to another. For example, Rhode Island allows only five days within which to file a petition.[4] Other states allow 30 days. Fourteen days are allowed in the United States courts of appeals[5] and 25 days in the United States Supreme Court.[6] Carefully check the time within which to file the petition.

The contents of the petition are prescribed by court rule and vary in degrees of detail. For example, Federal Rule of Appellate Procedure 40(a)(2) requires:

> The petition must state with particularity each point of law or fact that the petitioner believes the court has overlooked or misapprehended and must argue in support of the petition.

However, many court rules limit the number of typed pages that can be submitted. As specified in the above Federal Appellate rule, the petitioner may present whatever he or she desires, except the page limit is 15 pages.[7]

Obviously, the petition or supporting brief should deal only with new material. It is pointless to attempt to reargue the case that has already been decided. The court will consider only new or overlooked material that might change the result of the decision.

Court rules must also be examined to determine the actual physical aspects of the petition for rehearing. Some prescribe the method of printing or duplicating, as well as the cover content and color. In addition, there are rules that regulate the number of copies that must be submitted. As always, time spent inspecting the rules results ultimately in time saved.

---

4. *See* R.I. Sup. Ct. R., Art. I, R. 25(a).

5. *See* Fed. R. App. P. 40(a)(1).

6. *See* Sup. Ct. R. 44.1.

7. *See* Fed. R. App. P. 40(b).

11.22   Reasons to grant or deny petitions for rehearing

As previously explained, courts are loath to grant petitions for rehearing. As court dockets skyrocket, advocates cannot hope to reverse this trend.

In some states, statutes indicate the reasons to grant a rehearing. In others, each case is decided on an *ad hoc* basis. As previously noted, the United States Supreme Court does not specify standards for a rehearing except that the grounds must be stated "briefly and distinctly."[8] Many states that specify grounds use the words "overlooked" or "misapprehended" as it relates to arguments in the case. Most do not explain the meaning of those words. Although losing parties usually believe their arguments have been overlooked, misapprehended or misconceived, this is insufficient. The exact standards various courts employ is difficult to discern, but there are some guidelines.

The most solid reason for rehearing is a new judicial decision or statutory change which is at odds with the decision of the case that was appealed. A decision by a higher court or the same court which is in conflict with the holding or reasoning of the case may provide grounds for reversal without reargument. Rehearing is appropriate if application of the new case or statute is not clear.

Another court of equal rank that has decided the issue and is in conflict with the case provides another possible basis for rehearing. This holds unless the court in the instant case knew of the decision and rejected the authority as not applicable or persuasive.

At times, if it appears a ruling may have an unanticipated impact, a court will grant a rehearing. For example, a ruling may seem ultimately fair in one case, but prove to be illogical when applied to others. Though courts do not like to recall their decisions, a rehearing is superior to overruling the case at a later date.

Reasons to deny rehearings are more numerous than those to grant them. Crowded dockets present a logistical problem to rehearing cases on a regular basis. If the case has been carefully considered, it is unlikely the judges will change their minds when the matter is reargued. Thus, the exercise will be a waste of time. In addition, judges, like most people, prefer not to admit their decisions are wrong. As Wiener put it "[m]ost persons do not like to change their minds once they have made them up—and most judges share that well-nigh universal reaction."[9]

11.23   Response to petitions for rehearing

While a petition usually requires a response by opposing counsel, this does not necessarily apply to a petition for rehearing. In the words of Federal Rule of Appellate Procedure 40(a), which echoes most state rules and the United States Supreme Court:

---

8.   Sup. Ct. R. 44.1.   **9.**   Wiener, *supra* note 1, at 367.

Unless the court requests, no answer to a petition for panel rehearing is permitted. But ordinarily, rehearing will not be granted in absence of such a request.

The rule makes good sense, because most petitions for rehearing are denied. To require a reply to a petition that is likely to be denied is a waste of time for counsel and the court and a waste of money for the client. On the other hand, if the court finds merit in the petition, a response is helpful to emphasize, albeit for different reasons,[10] why the court was correct in the first place.

States that allow a reply to be filed, have a rule that usually states that failure to respond shall not be considered an admission that the motion should be granted. If, however, a state's rules give no indication of the consequences of failure to reply, counsel should file a reply to the motion.

11.24 Rehearing en banc[11]

Some courts, notably the Federal Circuit Courts of Appeal, do not use all members of the court to hear each case. Instead, cases are usually heard and decided by a three-judge panel. Normally, a rehearing petition is directed to the three judges who originally decided the case. Now and then, a rehearing en banc may be sought by the losing party or by any active member of the court. In the federal system, Federal Rule of Appellate Procedure 35(a) governs the practice. It provides in part that:

> An en banc hearing or rehearing is not favored and ordinarily will not be ordered unless:
>
> (1) en banc consideration is necessary to secure or maintain uniformity of the court's decisions; or
>
> (2) the proceeding involves a question of exceptional importance.

The language allows some leeway, but very little. On the subject of courts sitting en banc, the Second Circuit has stated that the procedure is "often an unwieldy and cumbersome device generating little more than delay, costs and continued uncertainty that can ill be afforded at a time of burgeoning calendars."[12] The Eighth Circuit goes a bit further. Its Rule 35A(2) warns:

> The court may assess costs against counsel who files a frivolous petition for rehearing en banc deemed to have multiplied the proceedings in the case and to have increased costs unreasonably and

---

10. Advocates are cautioned never to simply repeat arguments made. Rather, a petition for rehearing should emphasize new reasons to justify a rehearing. Presumably, the respondent would reply to those reasons in an effort to thwart a reconsideration.

11. It appears that the latest amendments to the Federal Rules of Appellate Procedure now use the "en banc" instead of "in banc." Whether the new phrase will be italicized is yet to be known.

12. *Green v. Santa Fe Industries,* 533 F.2d 1309, 1310 (2d Cir.1976), *reversed on other grounds,* 430 U.S. 462 (1977).

vexatiously. At the courts's order, counsel personally may be required to pay those costs to the opposing party.

In summary, grant of a rehearing en banc is unlikely and, in some circuits, may prove costly. This is especially true if only the losing party makes the request. There is a better chance if a member of the court is also sufficiently concerned about the outcome to move the court for a rehearing en banc.

As with most aspects of appellate practice, post oral argument proceedings are dictated by court rule. Read and study them. Great amounts of time, energy and money will be saved by this simple, but necessary, exercise.

*

Appendix A

RULES OF THE SUPREME COURT OF THE UNITED STATES

I have included the United States Supreme Court Rules for two reasons. First, there are several references throughout the material to the rules. Having easy access to the rules is helpful in understanding the text. Second, some Professors require their students to craft their briefs based on this set of rules. Handy access is advantageous to this endeavor.

Table of Contents

PART I. THE COURT

PART I.   THE COURT

Rule 1.   Clerk

1. The Clerk receives documents for filing with the Court and has authority to reject any submitted filing that does not comply with these Rules.

2. The Clerk maintains the Court's records and will not permit any of them to be removed from the Court building except as authorized by

the Court. Any document filed with the Clerk and made a part of the Court's records may not thereafter be withdrawn from the official Court files. After the conclusion of proceedings in this Court, original records and documents transmitted to this Court by any other court will be returned to the court from which they were received.

3. Unless the Court or the Chief Justice orders otherwise, the Clerk's office is open from 9 a.m. to 5 p.m., Monday through Friday, except on federal legal holidays listed in 5 U.S.C. § 6103.

Rule 2. Library

1. The Court's library is available for use by appropriate personnel of this Court, members of the Bar of this Court, Members of Congress and their legal staffs, and attorneys for the United States and for federal departments and agencies.

2. The library's hours are governed by regulations made by the Librarian with the approval of the Chief Justice or the Court.

3. Library books may not be removed from the Court building, except by a Justice or a member of a Justice's staff.

Rule 3. Term

The Court holds a continuous annual Term commencing on the first Monday in October and ending on the day before the first Monday in October of the following year. See 28 U.S.C. § 2. At the end of each Term, all cases pending on the docket are continued to the next Term.

Rule 4. Sessions and Quorum

1. Open sessions of the Court are held beginning at 10 a.m. on the first Monday in October of each year, and thereafter as announced by the Court. Unless it orders otherwise, the Court sits to hear arguments from 10 a.m. until noon and from 1 p.m. until 3 p.m.

2. Six Members of the Court constitute a quorum. See 28 U.S.C. § 1. In the absence of a quorum on any day appointed for holding a session of the Court, the Justices attending—or if no Justice is present, the Clerk or a Deputy Clerk—may announce that the Court will not meet until there is a quorum.

3. When appropriate, the Court will direct the Clerk or the Marshal to announce recesses.

PART II. ATTORNEYS AND COUNSELORS

Rule 5. Admission to the Bar

1. To qualify for admission to the Bar of this Court, an applicant must have been admitted to practice in the highest court of a State, Commonwealth, Territory or Possession, or the District of Columbia for a period of at least three years immediately before the date of application; must not have been the subject of any adverse disciplinary action

pronounced or in effect during that 3–year period; and must appear to the Court to be of good moral and professional character.

2.   Each applicant shall file with the Clerk (1) a certificate from the presiding judge, clerk, or other authorized official of that court evidencing the applicant's admission to practice there and the applicant's current good standing, and (2) a completely executed copy of the form approved by this Court and furnished by the Clerk containing (a) the applicant's personal statement, and (b) the statement of two sponsors endorsing the correctness of the applicant's statement, stating that the applicant possesses all the qualifications required for admission, and affirming that the applicant is of good moral and professional character. Both sponsors must be members of the Bar of this Court who personally know, but are not related to, the applicant.

3.   If the documents submitted demonstrate that the applicant possesses the necessary qualifications, and if the applicant has signed the oath or affirmation and paid the required fee, the Clerk will notify the applicant of acceptance by the Court as a member of the Bar and issue a certificate of admission. An applicant who so wishes may be admitted in open court on oral motion by a member of the Bar of this Court, provided that all other requirements for admission have been satisfied.

4.   Each applicant shall sign the following oath or affirmation: I, _____, do solemnly swear (or affirm) that as an attorney and as a counselor of this Court, I will conduct myself uprightly and according to law, and that I will support the Constitution of the United States.

5.   The fee for admission to the Bar and a certificate bearing the seal of the Court is $100, payable to the United States Supreme Court. The Marshal will deposit such fees in a separate fund to be disbursed by the Marshal at the direction of the Chief Justice for the costs of admissions, for the benefit of the Court and its Bar, and for related purposes.

6.   The fee for a duplicate certificate of admission to the Bar bearing the seal of the Court is $15 and the fee for a certificate of good standing is $10, payable to the United States Supreme Court. The proceeds will be maintained by the Marshal as provided in paragraph 5 of this Rule.

Rule 6.   Argument *Pro Hac Vice*

1.   An attorney not admitted to practice in the highest court of a State, Commonwealth, Territory or Possession, or the District of Columbia for the requisite three years, but otherwise eligible for admission to practice in this Court under Rule 5.1, may be permitted to argue pro hac vice.

2.   An attorney qualified to practice in the courts of a foreign state may be permitted to argue pro hac vice.

3.   Oral argument pro hac vice is allowed only on motion of the counsel of record for the party on whose behalf leave is requested. The

motion shall state concisely the qualifications of the attorney who is to argue pro hac vice. It shall be filed with the Clerk, in the form required by Rule 21, no later than the date on which the respondent's or appellee's brief on the merits is due to be filed, and it shall be accompanied by proof of service as required by Rule 29.

Rule 7. Prohibition Against Practice

No employee of this Court shall practice as an attorney or counselor in any court or before any agency of government while employed by the Court; nor shall any person after leaving such employment participate in any professional capacity in any case pending before this Court or in any case being considered for filing in this Court, until two years have elapsed after separation; nor shall a former employee ever participate in any professional capacity in any case that was pending in this Court during the employee's tenure.

Rule 8. Disbarment and Disciplinary Action

1. Whenever a member of the Bar of this Court has been disbarred or suspended from practice in any court of record, or has engaged in conduct unbecoming a member of the Bar of this Court, the Court will enter an order suspending that member from practice before this Court and affording the member an opportunity to show cause, within 40 days, why a disbarment order should not be entered. Upon response, or if no response is timely filed, the Court will enter an appropriate order.

2. After reasonable notice and an opportunity to show cause why disciplinary action should not be taken, and after a hearing if material facts are in dispute, the Court may take any appropriate disciplinary action against any attorney who is admitted to practice before it for conduct unbecoming a member of the Bar or for failure to comply with these Rules or any Rule or order of the Court.

Rule 9. Appearance of Counsel

1. An attorney seeking to file a document in this Court in a representative capacity must first be admitted to practice before this Court as provided in Rule 5, except that admission to the Bar of this Court is not required for an attorney appointed under the Criminal Justice Act of 1964, see 18 U.S.C. § 3006A(d)(6), or under any other applicable federal statute. The attorney whose name, address, and telephone number appear on the cover of a document presented for filing is considered counsel of record, and a separate notice of appearance need not be filed. If the name of more than one attorney is shown on the cover of the document, the attorney who is counsel of record shall be clearly identified.

2. An attorney representing a party who will not be filing a document shall enter a separate notice of appearance as counsel of record indicating the name of the party represented. A separate notice of

appearance shall also be entered whenever an attorney is substituted as counsel of record in a particular case.

PART III. JURISDICTION ON WRIT OF CERTIORARI

Rule 10. Considerations Governing Review on Certiorari

Review on a writ of certiorari is not a matter of right, but of judicial discretion. A petition for a writ of certiorari will be granted only for compelling reasons. The following, although neither controlling nor fully measuring the Court's discretion, indicate the character of the reasons the Court considers:

(a) a United States court of appeals has entered a decision in conflict with the decision of another United States court of appeals on the same important matter; has decided an important federal question in a way that conflicts with a decision by a state court of last resort; or has so far departed from the accepted and usual course of judicial proceedings, or sanctioned such a departure by a lower court, as to call for an exercise of this Court's supervisory power;

(b) a state court of last resort has decided an important federal question in a way that conflicts with the decision of another state court of last resort or of a United States court of appeals;

(c) a state court or a United States court of appeals has decided an important question of federal law that has not been, but should be, settled by this Court, or has decided an important federal question in a way that conflicts with relevant decisions of this Court.

A petition for a writ of certiorari is rarely granted when the asserted error consists of erroneous factual findings or the misapplication of a properly stated rule of law.

Rule 11. Certiorari to a United States Court of Appeals Before Judgment

A petition for a writ of certiorari to review a case pending in a United States court of appeals, before judgment is entered in that court, will be granted only upon a showing that the case is of such imperative public importance as to justify deviation from normal appellate practice and to require immediate determination in this Court. See 28 U.S.C. § 2101(e).

Rule 12. Review on Certiorari: How Sought; Parties

1. Except as provided in paragraph 2 of this Rule, the petitioner shall file 40 copies of a petition for a writ of certiorari, prepared as required by Rule 33.1, and shall pay the Rule 38(a) docket fee.

2. A petitioner proceeding in forma pauperis under Rule 39 shall file an original and 10 copies of a petition for a writ of certiorari prepared as required by Rule 33.2, together with an original and 10 copies of the motion for leave to proceed in forma pauperis. A copy of the

motion shall precede and be attached to each copy of the petition. An inmate confined in an institution, if proceeding in forma pauperis and not represented by counsel, need file only an original petition and motion.

3. Whether prepared under Rule 33.1 or Rule 33.2, the petition shall comply in all respects with Rule 14 and shall be submitted with proof of service as required by Rule 29. The case then will be placed on the docket. It is the petitioner's duty to notify all respondents promptly, on a form supplied by the Clerk, of the date of filing, the date the case was placed on the docket, and the docket number of the case. The notice shall be served as required by Rule 29.

4. Parties interested jointly, severally, or otherwise in a judgment may petition separately for a writ of certiorari; or any two or more may join in a petition. A party not shown on the petition as joined therein at the time the petition is filed may not later join in that petition. When two or more judgments are sought to be reviewed on a writ of certiorari to the same court and involve identical or closely related questions, a single petition for a writ of certiorari covering all the judgments suffices. A petition for a writ of certiorari may not be joined with any other pleading, except that any motion for leave to proceed in forma pauperis shall be attached.

5. No more than 30 days after a case has been placed on the docket, a respondent seeking to file a conditional cross-petition (i.e., a cross-petition that otherwise would be untimely) shall file, with proof of service as required by Rule 29, 40 copies of the cross-petition prepared as required by Rule 33.1, except that a cross-petitioner proceeding in forma pauperis under Rule 39 shall comply with Rule 12.2. The cross-petition shall comply in all respects with this Rule and Rule 14, except that material already reproduced in the appendix to the opening petition need not be reproduced again. A cross-petitioning respondent shall pay the Rule 38(a) docket fee or submit a motion for leave to proceed in forma pauperis. The cover of the cross-petition shall indicate clearly that it is a conditional cross-petition. The cross-petition then will be placed on the docket, subject to the provisions of Rule 13.4. It is the cross-petitioner's duty to notify all cross-respondents promptly, on a form supplied by the Clerk, of the date of filing, the date the cross-petition was placed on the docket, and the docket number of the cross-petition. The notice shall be served as required by Rule 29. A cross-petition for a writ of certiorari may not be joined with any other pleading, except that any motion for leave to proceed in forma pauperis shall be attached. The time to file a conditional cross-petition will not be extended.

6. All parties to the proceeding in the court whose judgment is sought to be reviewed are deemed parties entitled to file documents in this Court, unless the petitioner notifies the Clerk of this Court in writing of the petitioner's belief that one or more of the parties below have no interest in the outcome of the petition. A copy of such notice shall be served as required by Rule 29 on all parties to the proceeding

below. A party noted as no longer interested may remain a party by notifying the Clerk promptly, with service on the other parties, of an intention to remain a party. All parties other than the petitioner are considered respondents, but any respondent who supports the position of a petitioner shall meet the petitioner's time schedule for filing documents, except that a response supporting the petition shall be filed within 20 days after the case is placed on the docket, and that time will not be extended. Parties who file no document will not qualify for any relief from this Court.

7.   The clerk of the court having possession of the record shall keep it until notified by the Clerk of this Court to certify and transmit it. In any document filed with this Court, a party may cite or quote from the record, even if it has not been transmitted to this Court. When requested by the Clerk of this Court to certify and transmit the record, or any part of it, the clerk of the court having possession of the record shall number the documents to be certified and shall transmit therewith a numbered list specifically identifying each document transmitted. If the record, or stipulated portions, have been printed for the use of the court below, that printed record, plus the proceedings in the court below, may be certified as the record unless one of the parties or the Clerk of this Court requests otherwise. The record may consist of certified copies, but if the lower court is of the view that original documents of any kind should be seen by this Court, that court may provide by order for the transport, safekeeping, and return of such originals.

Rule 13.   Review on Certiorari: Time for Petitioning

1.   Unless otherwise provided by law, a petition for a writ of certiorari to review a judgment in any case, civil or criminal, entered by a state court of last resort or a United States court of appeals (including the United States Court of Appeals for the Armed Forces) is timely when it is filed with the Clerk of this Court within 90 days after entry of the judgment. A petition for a writ of certiorari seeking review of a judgment of a lower state court that is subject to discretionary review by the state court of last resort is timely when it is filed with the Clerk within 90 days after entry of the order denying discretionary review.

2.   The Clerk will not file any petition for a writ of certiorari that is jurisdictionally out of time. See, e.g., 28 U.S.C. § 2101(c).

3.   The time to file a petition for a writ of certiorari runs from the date of entry of the judgment or order sought to be reviewed, and not from the issuance date of the mandate (or its equivalent under local practice). But if a petition for rehearing is timely filed in the lower court by any party, the time to file the petition for a writ of certiorari for all parties (whether or not they requested rehearing or joined in the petition for rehearing) runs from the date of the denial of the petition for rehearing or, if the petition for rehearing is granted, the subsequent entry of judgment.

4.   A cross-petition for a writ of certiorari is timely when it is filed with the Clerk as provided in paragraphs 1, 3, and 5 of this Rule, or in Rule 12.5. However, a conditional cross-petition (which except for Rule 12.5 would be untimely) will not be granted unless another party's timely petition for a writ of certiorari is granted.

5.   For good cause, a Justice may extend the time to file a petition for a writ of certiorari for a period not exceeding 60 days. An application to extend the time to file shall set out the basis for jurisdiction in this Court, identify the judgment sought to be reviewed, include a copy of the opinion and any order respecting rehearing, and set out specific reasons why an extension of time is justified. The application must be received by the Clerk at least 10 days before the date the petition is due, except in extraordinary circumstances. For the time and manner of presenting the application, see Rules 21, 22, 30, and 33.2. An application to extend the time to file a petition for a writ of certiorari is not favored.

Rule 14.   Content of a Petition for a Writ of Certiorari

1.   A petition for a writ of certiorari shall contain, in the order indicated:

(a) The questions presented for review, expressed concisely in relation to the circumstances of the case, without unnecessary detail. The questions should be short and should not be argumentative or repetitive. If the petitioner or respondent is under a death sentence that may be affected by the disposition of the petition, the notation "capital case" shall precede the questions presented. The questions shall be set out on the first page following the cover, and no other information may appear on that page. The statement of any question presented is deemed to comprise every subsidiary question fairly included therein. Only the questions set out in the petition, or fairly included therein, will be considered by the Court.

(b) A list of all parties to the proceeding in the court whose judgment is sought to be reviewed (unless the caption of the case contains the names of all the parties), and a list of parent companies and nonwholly owned subsidiaries as required by Rule 29.6.

(c) If the petition exceeds five pages, a table of contents and a table of cited authorities.

(d) Citations of the official and unofficial reports of the opinions and orders entered in the case by courts or administrative agencies.

(e) A concise statement of the basis for jurisdiction in this Court, showing:

(i) the date the judgment or order sought to be reviewed was entered (and, if applicable, a statement that the petition is filed under this Court's Rule 11);

(ii) the date of any order respecting rehearing, and the date and terms of any order granting an extension of time to file the petition for a writ of certiorari;

(iii) express reliance on Rule 12.5, when a cross-petition for a writ of certiorari is filed under that Rule, and the date of docketing of the petition for a writ of certiorari in connection with which the cross-petition is filed;

(iv) the statutory provision believed to confer on this Court jurisdiction to review on a writ of certiorari the judgment or order in question; and

(v) if applicable, a statement that the notifications required by Rule 29.4(b) or (c) have been made.

(f) The constitutional provisions, treaties, statutes, ordinances, and regulations involved in the case, set out verbatim with appropriate citation. If the provisions involved are lengthy, their citation alone suffices at this point, and their pertinent text shall be set out in the appendix referred to in subparagraph 1(i).

(g) A concise statement of the case setting out the facts material to consideration of the questions presented, and also containing the following:

(i) If review of a state-court judgment is sought, specification of the stage in the proceedings, both in the court of first instance and in the appellate courts, when the federal questions sought to be reviewed were raised; the method or manner of raising them and the way in which they were passed on by those courts; and pertinent quotations of specific portions of the record or summary thereof, with specific reference to the places in the record where the matter appears (e.g., court opinion, ruling on exception, portion of court's charge and exception thereto, assignment of error), so as to show that the federal question was timely and properly raised and that this Court has jurisdiction to review the judgment on a writ of certiorari. When the portions of the record relied on under this subparagraph are voluminous, they shall be included in the appendix referred to in subparagraph 1(i).

(ii) If review of a judgment of a United States court of appeals is sought, the basis for federal jurisdiction in the court of first instance.

(h) A direct and concise argument amplifying the reasons relied on for allowance of the writ. See Rule 10.

(i) An appendix containing, in the order indicated:

(i) the opinions, orders, findings of fact, and conclusions of law, whether written or orally given and transcribed, entered in conjunction with the judgment sought to be reviewed;

(ii) any other relevant opinions, orders, findings of fact, and conclusions of law entered in the case by courts or administrative agencies, and, if reference thereto is necessary to ascertain the grounds of the judgment, of those in companion cases (each document shall include the caption showing the name of the issuing court or agency, the title and number of the case, and the date of entry);

(iii) any order on rehearing, including the caption showing the name of the issuing court, the title and number of the case, and the date of entry;

(iv) the judgment sought to be reviewed if the date of its entry is different from the date of the opinion or order required in sub-subparagraph (i) of this subparagraph;

(v) material required by subparagraphs 1(f) or 1(g)(i); and

(vi) any other material the petitioner believes essential to understand the petition.

If the material required by this subparagraph is voluminous, it may be presented in a separate volume or volumes with appropriate covers.

2. All contentions in support of a petition for a writ of certiorari shall be set out in the body of the petition, as provided in subparagraph 1(h) of this Rule. No separate brief in support of a petition for a writ of certiorari may be filed, and the Clerk will not file any petition for a writ of certiorari to which any supporting brief is annexed or appended.

3. A petition for a writ of certiorari should be stated briefly and in plain terms and may not exceed the page limitations specified in Rule 33.

4. The failure of a petitioner to present with accuracy, brevity, and clarity whatever is essential to ready and adequate understanding of the points requiring consideration is sufficient reason for the Court to deny a petition.

5. If the Clerk determines that a petition submitted timely and in good faith is in a form that does not comply with this Rule or with Rule 33 or Rule 34, the Clerk will return it with a letter indicating the deficiency. A corrected petition received no more than 60 days after the date of the Clerk's letter will be deemed timely.

Rule 15. Briefs in Opposition; Reply Briefs; Supplemental Briefs

1. A brief in opposition to a petition for a writ of certiorari may be filed by the respondent in any case, but is not mandatory except in a capital case, see Rule 14.1(a), or when ordered by the Court.

2. A brief in opposition should be stated briefly and in plain terms and may not exceed the page limitations specified in Rule 33. In addition to presenting other arguments for denying the petition, the brief in opposition should address any perceived misstatement of fact or law in the petition that bears on what issues properly would be before the Court if certiorari were granted. Counsel are admonished that they have an obligation to the Court to point out in the brief in opposition, and not later, any perceived misstatement made in the petition. Any objection to consideration of a question presented based on what occurred in the

proceedings below, if the objection does not go to jurisdiction, may be deemed waived unless called to the Court's attention in the brief in opposition.

3.   Any brief in opposition shall be filed within 30 days after the case is placed on the docket, unless the time is extended by the Court or a Justice, or by the Clerk under Rule 30.4. Forty copies shall be filed, except that a respondent proceeding in forma pauperis under Rule 39, including an inmate of an institution, shall file the number of copies required for a petition by such a person under Rule 12.2, together with a motion for leave to proceed in forma pauperis, a copy of which shall precede and be attached to each copy of the brief in opposition. If the petitioner is proceeding in forma pauperis, the respondent may file an original and 10 copies of a brief in opposition prepared as required by Rule 33.2. Whether prepared under Rule 33.1 or Rule 33.2, the brief in opposition shall comply with the requirements of Rule 24 governing a respondent's brief, except that no summary of the argument is required. A brief in opposition may not be joined with any other pleading, except that any motion for leave to proceed in forma pauperis shall be attached. The brief in opposition shall be served as required by Rule 29.

4.   No motion by a respondent to dismiss a petition for a writ of certiorari may be filed. Any objections to the jurisdiction of the Court to grant a petition for a writ of certiorari shall be included in the brief in opposition.

5.   The Clerk will distribute the petition to the Court for its consideration upon receiving an express waiver of the right to file a brief in opposition, or, if no waiver or brief in opposition is filed, upon the expiration of the time allowed for filing. If a brief in opposition is timely filed, the Clerk will distribute the petition, brief in opposition, and any reply brief to the Court for its consideration no less than 10 days after the brief in opposition is filed.

6.   Any petitioner may file a reply brief addressed to new points raised in the brief in opposition, but distribution and consideration by the Court under paragraph 5 of this Rule will not be deferred pending its receipt. Forty copies shall be filed, except that petitioner proceeding in forma pauperis under Rule 39, including an inmate of an institution, shall file the number of copies required for a petition by such a person under Rule 12.2. The reply brief shall be served as required by Rule 29.

7.   If a cross-petition for a writ of certiorari has been docketed, distribution of both petitions will be deferred until the cross-petition is due for distribution under this Rule.

8.   Any party may file a supplemental brief at any time while a petition for a writ of certiorari is pending, calling attention to new cases, new legislation, or other intervening matter not available at the time of the party's last filing. A supplemental brief shall be restricted to new matter and shall follow, insofar as applicable, the form for a brief in opposition prescribed by this Rule. Forty copies shall be filed, except that a party proceeding in forma pauperis under Rule 39, including an inmate

of an institution, shall file the number of copies required for a petition by such a person under Rule 12.2. The supplemental brief shall be served as required by Rule 29.

Rule 16.   Disposition of a Petition for a Writ of Certiorari

1.   After considering the documents distributed under Rule 15, the Court will enter an appropriate order. The order may be a summary disposition on the merits.

2.   Whenever the Court grants a petition for a writ of certiorari, the Clerk will prepare, sign, and enter an order to that effect and will notify forthwith counsel of record and the court whose judgment is to be reviewed. The case then will be scheduled for briefing and oral argument. If the record has not previously been filed in this Court, the Clerk will request the clerk of the court having possession of the record to certify and transmit it. A formal writ will not issue unless specially directed.

3.   Whenever the Court denies a petition for a writ of certiorari, the Clerk will prepare, sign, and enter an order to that effect and will notify forthwith counsel of record and the court whose judgment was sought to be reviewed. The order of denial will not be suspended pending disposition of a petition for rehearing except by order of the Court or a Justice.

PART IV.   OTHER JURISDICTION

Rule 17.   Procedure in an Original Action

1.   This Rule applies only to an action invoking the Court's original jurisdiction under Article III of the Constitution of the United States. See also 28 U.S.C. § 1251 and U.S. Const., Amdt. 11. A petition for an extraordinary writ in aid of the Court's appellate jurisdiction shall be filed as provided in Rule 20.

2.   The form of pleadings and motions prescribed by the Federal Rules of Civil Procedure is followed. In other respects, those Rules and the Federal Rules of Evidence may be taken as guides.

3.   The initial pleading shall be preceded by a motion for leave to file, and may be accompanied by a brief in support of the motion. Forty copies of each document shall be filed, with proof of service. Service shall be as required by Rule 29, except that when an adverse party is a State, service shall be made on both the Governor and the Attorney General of that State.

4.   The case will be placed on the docket when the motion for leave to file and the initial pleading are filed with the Clerk. The Rule 38(a) docket fee shall be paid at that time.

5.   No more than 60 days after receiving the motion for leave to file and the initial pleading, an adverse party shall file 40 copies of any brief in opposition to the motion, with proof of service as required by Rule 29. The Clerk will distribute the filed documents to the Court for its

consideration upon receiving an express waiver of the right to file a brief in opposition, or, if no waiver or brief is filed, upon the expiration of the time allowed for filing. If a brief in opposition is timely filed, the Clerk will distribute the filed documents to the Court for its consideration no less than 10 days after the brief in opposition is filed. A reply brief may be filed, but consideration of the case will not be deferred pending its receipt. The Court thereafter may grant or deny the motion, set it for oral argument, direct that additional documents be filed, or require that other proceedings be conducted.

6. A summons issued out of this Court shall be served on the defendant 60 days before the return day specified therein. If the defendant does not respond by the return day, the plaintiff may proceed ex parte.

7. Process against a State issued out of this Court shall be served on both the Governor and the Attorney General of that State.

Rule 18. Appeal from a United States District Court

1. When a direct appeal from a decision of a United States district court is authorized by law, the appeal is commenced by filing a notice of appeal with the clerk of the district court within the time provided by law after entry of the judgment sought to be reviewed. The time to file may not be extended. The notice of appeal shall specify the parties taking the appeal, designate the judgment, or part thereof, appealed from and the date of its entry, and specify the statute or statutes under which the appeal is taken. A copy of the notice of appeal shall be served on all parties to the proceeding as required by Rule 29, and proof of service shall be filed in the district court together with the notice of appeal.

2. All parties to the proceeding in the district court are deemed parties entitled to file documents in this Court, but a party having no interest in the outcome of the appeal may so notify the Clerk of this Court and shall serve a copy of the notice on all other parties. Parties interested jointly, severally, or otherwise in the judgment may appeal separately, or any two or more may join in an appeal. When two or more judgments involving identical or closely related questions are sought to be reviewed on appeal from the same court, a notice of appeal for each judgment shall be filed with the clerk of the district court, but a single jurisdictional statement covering all the judgments suffices. Parties who file no document will not qualify for any relief from this Court.

3. No more than 60 days after filing the notice of appeal in the district court, the appellant shall file 40 copies of a jurisdictional statement and shall pay the Rule 38 docket fee, except that an appellant proceeding in forma pauperis under Rule 39, including an inmate of an institution, shall file the number of copies required for a petition by such a person under Rule 12.2, together with a motion for leave to proceed in forma pauperis, a copy of which shall precede and be attached to each copy of the jurisdictional statement. The jurisdictional statement shall

follow, insofar as applicable, the form for a petition for a writ of certiorari prescribed by Rule 14, and shall be served as required by Rule 29. The case will then be placed on the docket. It is the appellant's duty to notify all appellees promptly, on a form supplied by the Clerk, of the date of filing, the date the case was placed on the docket, and the docket number of the case. The notice shall be served as required by Rule 29. The appendix shall include a copy of the notice of appeal showing the date it was filed in the district court. For good cause, a Justice may extend the time to file a jurisdictional statement for a period not exceeding 60 days. An application to extend the time to file a jurisdictional statement shall set out the basis for jurisdiction in this Court; identify the judgment sought to be reviewed; include a copy of the opinion, any order respecting rehearing, and the notice of appeal; and set out specific reasons why an extension of time is justified. For the time and manner of presenting the application, see Rules 21, 22, and 30. An application to extend the time to file a jurisdictional statement is not favored.

4. No more than 30 days after a case has been placed on the docket, an appellee seeking to file a conditional cross-appeal (i.e., a cross-appeal that otherwise would be untimely) shall file, with proof of service as required by Rule 29, a jurisdictional statement that complies in all respects (including number of copies filed) with paragraph 3 of this Rule, except that material already reproduced in the appendix to the opening jurisdictional statement need not be reproduced again. A cross-appealing appellee shall pay the Rule 38 docket fee or submit a motion for leave to proceed in forma pauperis. The cover of the cross-appeal shall indicate clearly that it is a conditional cross-appeal. The cross-appeal then will be placed on the docket. It is the cross-appellant's duty to notify all cross-appellees promptly, on a form supplied by the Clerk, of the date of filing, the date the cross-appeal was placed on the docket, and the docket number of the cross-appeal. The notice shall be served as required by Rule 29. A cross-appeal may not be joined with any other pleading, except that any motion for leave to proceed in forma pauperis shall be attached. The time to file a cross-appeal will not be extended.

5. After a notice of appeal has been filed in the district court, but before the case is placed on this Court's docket, the parties may dismiss the appeal by stipulation filed in the district court, or the district court may dismiss the appeal on the appellant's motion, with notice to all parties. If a notice of appeal has been filed, but the case has not been placed on this Court's docket within the time prescribed for docketing, the district court may dismiss the appeal on the appellee's motion, with notice to all parties, and may make any just order with respect to costs. If the district court has denied the appellee's motion to dismiss the appeal, the appellee may move this Court to docket and dismiss the appeal by filing an original and 10 copies of a motion presented in conformity with Rules 21 and 33.2. The motion shall be accompanied by proof of service as required by Rule 29, and by a certificate from the clerk of the district court, certifying that a notice of appeal was filed and

that the appellee's motion to dismiss was denied. The appellant may not thereafter file a jurisdictional statement without special leave of the Court, and the Court may allow costs against the appellant.

6. Within 30 days after the case is placed on this Court's docket, the appellee may file a motion to dismiss, to affirm, or in the alternative to affirm or dismiss. Forty copies of the motion shall be filed, except that an appellee proceeding in forma pauperis under Rule 39, including an inmate of an institution, shall file the number of copies required for a petition by such a person under Rule 12.2, together with a motion for leave to proceed in forma pauperis, a copy of which shall precede and be attached to each copy of the motion to dismiss, to affirm, or in the alternative to affirm or dismiss. The motion shall follow, insofar as applicable, the form for a brief in opposition prescribed by Rule 15, and shall comply in all respects with Rule 21.

7. The Clerk will distribute the jurisdictional statement to the Court for its consideration upon receiving an express waiver of the right to file a motion to dismiss or to affirm or, if no waiver or motion is filed, upon the expiration of the time allowed for filing. If a motion to dismiss or to affirm is timely filed, the Clerk will distribute the jurisdictional statement, motion, and any brief opposing the motion to the Court for its consideration no less than 10 days after the motion is filed.

8. Any appellant may file a brief opposing a motion to dismiss or to affirm, but distribution and consideration by the Court under paragraph 7 of this Rule will not be deferred pending its receipt. Forty copies shall be filed, except that an appellant proceeding in forma pauperis under Rule 39, including an inmate of an institution, shall file the number of copies required for a petition by such a person under Rule 12.2. The brief shall be served as required by Rule 29.

9. If a cross-appeal has been docketed, distribution of both jurisdictional statements will be deferred until the cross-appeal is due for distribution under this Rule.

10. Any party may file a supplemental brief at any time while a jurisdictional statement is pending, calling attention to new cases, new legislation, or other intervening matter not available at the time of the party's last filing. A supplemental brief shall be restricted to new matter and shall follow, insofar as applicable, the form for a brief in opposition prescribed by Rule 15. Forty copies shall be filed, except that a party proceeding in forma pauperis under Rule 39, including an inmate of an institution, shall file the number of copies required for a petition by such a person under Rule 12.2. The supplemental brief shall be served as required by Rule 29.

11. The clerk of the district court shall retain possession of the record until notified by the Clerk of this Court to certify and transmit it. See Rule 12.7.

12. After considering the documents distributed under this Rule, the Court may dispose summarily of the appeal on the merits, note

probable jurisdiction, or postpone consideration of jurisdiction until a hearing of the case on the merits. If not disposed of summarily, the case stands for briefing and oral argument on the merits. If consideration of jurisdiction is postponed, counsel, at the outset of their briefs and at oral argument, shall address the question of jurisdiction. If the record has not previously been filed in this Court, the Clerk of this Court will request the clerk of the court in possession of the record to certify and transmit it.

13.   If the Clerk determines that a jurisdictional statement submitted timely and in good faith is in a form that does not comply with this Rule or with Rule 33 or Rule 34, the Clerk will return it with a letter indicating the deficiency. If a corrected jurisdictional statement is received no more than 60 days after the date of the Clerk's letter, its filing will be deemed timely.

Rule 19.   Procedure on a Certified Question

1.   A United States court of appeals may certify to this Court a question or proposition of law on which it seeks instruction for the proper decision of a case. The certificate shall contain a statement of the nature of the case and the facts on which the question or proposition of law arises. Only questions or propositions of law may be certified, and they shall be stated separately and with precision. The certificate shall be prepared as required by Rule 33.2 and shall be signed by the clerk of the court of appeals.

2.   When a question is certified by a United States court of appeals, this Court, on its own motion or that of a party, may consider and decide the entire matter in controversy. See 28 U.S.C. § 1254(2).

3.   When a question is certified, the Clerk will notify the parties and docket the case. Counsel shall then enter their appearances. After docketing, the Clerk will submit the certificate to the Court for a preliminary examination to determine whether the case should be briefed, set for argument, or dismissed. No brief may be filed until the preliminary examination of the certificate is completed.

4.   If the Court orders the case briefed or set for argument, the parties will be notified and permitted to file briefs. The Clerk of this Court then will request the clerk of the court in possession of the record to certify and transmit it. Any portion of the record to which the parties wish to direct the Court's particular attention should be printed in a joint appendix, prepared in conformity with Rule 26 by the appellant or petitioner in the court of appeals, but the fact that any part of the record has not been printed does not prevent the parties or the Court from relying on it.

5.   A brief on the merits in a case involving a certified question shall comply with Rules 24, 25, and 33.1, except that the brief for the party who is the appellant or petitioner below shall be filed within 45 days of the order requiring briefs or setting the case for argument.

Rule 20.   Procedure on a Petition for an Extraordinary Writ

1.   Issuance by the Court of an extraordinary writ authorized by 28 U.S.C. § 1651(a) is not a matter of right, but of discretion sparingly exercised. To justify the granting of any such writ, the petition must show that the writ will be in aid of the Court's appellate jurisdiction, that exceptional circumstances warrant the exercise of the Court's discretionary powers, and that adequate relief cannot be obtained in any other form or from any other court.

2.   A petition seeking a writ authorized by 28 U.S.C. § 1651(a), § 2241, or § 2254(a) shall be prepared in all respects as required by Rules 33 and 34. The petition shall be captioned "In re [name of petitioner]" and shall follow, insofar as applicable, the form of a petition for a writ of certiorari prescribed by Rule 14. All contentions in support of the petition shall be included in the petition. The case will be placed on the docket when 40 copies of the petition are filed with the Clerk and the docket fee is paid, except that a petitioner proceeding in forma pauperis under Rule 39, including an inmate of an institution, shall file the number of copies required for a petition by such a person under Rule 12.2, together with a motion for leave to proceed in forma pauperis, a copy of which shall precede and be attached to each copy of the petition. The petition shall be served as required by Rule 29 (subject to subparagraph 4(b) of this Rule).

3.   (a) A petition seeking a writ of prohibition, a writ of mandamus, or both in the alternative shall state the name and office or function of every person against whom relief is sought and shall set out with particularity why the relief sought is not available in any other court. A copy of the judgment with respect to which the writ is sought, including any related opinion, shall be appended to the petition together with any other document essential to understanding the petition.

(b) The petition shall be served on every party to the proceeding with respect to which relief is sought. Within 30 days after the petition is placed on the docket, a party shall file 40 copies of any brief or briefs in opposition thereto, which shall comply fully with Rule 15. If a party named as a respondent does not wish to respond to the petition, that party may so advise the Clerk and all other parties by letter. All persons served are deemed respondents for all purposes in the proceedings in this Court.

4.   (a) A petition seeking a writ of habeas corpus shall comply with the requirements of 28 U.S.C. §§ 2241 and 2242, and in particular with the provision in the last paragraph of § 2242, which requires a statement of the "reasons for not making application to the district court of the district in which the applicant is held." If the relief sought is from the judgment of a state court, the petition shall set out specifically how and where the petitioner has exhausted available remedies in the state courts or otherwise comes within the provisions of 28 U.S.C. § 2254(b). To justify the granting of a writ of habeas corpus, the petitioner must show that exceptional circumstances warrant the exercise of the Court's

discretionary powers, and that adequate relief cannot be obtained in any other form or from any other court. This writ is rarely granted.

(b) Habeas corpus proceedings, except in capital cases, are ex parte, unless the Court requires the respondent to show cause why the petition for a writ of habeas corpus should not be granted. A response, if ordered, or in a capital case, shall comply fully with Rule 15. Neither the denial of the petition, without more, nor an order of transfer to a district court under the authority of 28 U.S.C. § 2241(b), is an adjudication on the merits, and therefore does not preclude further application to another court for the relief sought.

5.   The Clerk will distribute the documents to the Court for its consideration when a brief in opposition under subparagraph 3(b) of this Rule has been filed, when a response under subparagraph 4(b) has been ordered and filed, when the time to file has expired, or when the right to file has been expressly waived.

6.   If the Court orders the case set for argument, the Clerk will notify the parties whether additional briefs are required, when they shall be filed, and, if the case involves a petition for a common-law writ of certiorari, that the parties shall prepare a joint appendix in accordance with Rule 26.

PART V. MOTIONS AND APPLICATIONS

Rule 21.   Motions to the Court

1.   Every motion to the Court shall clearly state its purpose and the facts on which it is based and may present legal argument in support thereof. No separate brief may be filed. A motion should be concise and shall comply with any applicable page limits. Rule 22 governs an application addressed to a single Justice.

2.   (a) A motion in any action within the Court's original jurisdiction shall comply with Rule 17.3.

(b) A motion to dismiss as moot (or a suggestion of mootness), a motion for leave to file a brief as amicus curiae, and any motion the granting of which would dispose of the entire case or would affect the final judgment to be entered (other than a motion to docket and dismiss under Rule 18.5 or a motion for voluntary dismissal under Rule 46) shall be prepared as required by Rule 33.1, and 40 copies shall be filed, except that a movant proceeding in forma pauperis under Rule 39, including an inmate of an institution, shall file a motion prepared as required by Rule 33.2, and shall file the number of copies required for a petition by such a person under Rule 12.2. The motion shall be served as required by Rule 29.

(c) Any other motion to the Court shall be prepared as required by Rule 33.2; the moving party shall file an original and 10 copies. The Court subsequently may order the moving party to prepare the motion as required by Rule 33.1; in that event, the party shall file 40 copies.

3.   A motion to the Court shall be filed with the Clerk and shall be accompanied by proof of service as required by Rule 29. No motion may be presented in open Court, other than a motion for admission to the Bar, except when the proceeding to which it refers is being argued. Oral argument on a motion will not be permitted unless the Court so directs.

4.   Any response to a motion shall be filed as promptly as possible considering the nature of the relief sought and any asserted need for emergency action, and, in any event, within 10 days of receipt, unless the Court or a Justice, or the Clerk under Rule 30.4, orders otherwise. A response to a motion prepared as required by Rule 33.1, except a response to a motion for leave to file an amicus curiae brief (see Rule 37.5), shall be prepared in the same manner if time permits. In an appropriate case, the Court may act on a motion without waiting for a response.

Rule 22. Applications to Individual Justices

1.   An application addressed to an individual Justice shall be filed with the Clerk, who will transmit it promptly to the Justice concerned if an individual Justice has authority to grant the sought relief.

2.   The original and two copies of any application addressed to an individual Justice shall be prepared as required by Rule 33.2, and shall be accompanied by proof of service as required by Rule 29.

3.   An application shall be addressed to the Justice allotted to the Circuit from which the case arises. When the Circuit Justice is unavailable for any reason, the application addressed to that Justice will be distributed to the Justice then available who is next junior to the Circuit Justice; the turn of the Chief Justice follows that of the most junior Justice.

4.   A Justice denying an application will note the denial thereon. Thereafter, unless action thereon is restricted by law to the Circuit Justice or is untimely under Rule 30.2, the party making an application, except in the case of an application for an extension of time, may renew it to any other Justice, subject to the provisions of this Rule. Except when the denial is without prejudice, a renewed application is not favored. Renewed application is made by a letter to the Clerk, designating the Justice to whom the application is to be directed, and accompanied by 10 copies of the original application and proof of service as required by Rule 29.

5.   A Justice to whom an application for a stay or for bail is submitted may refer it to the Court for determination.

6.   The Clerk will advise all parties concerned, by appropriately speedy means, of the disposition made of an application.

Rule 23. Stays

1.   A stay may be granted by a Justice as permitted by law.

2.   A party to a judgment sought to be reviewed may present to a Justice an application to stay the enforcement of that judgement See 28 U.S.C. § 2101(f).

3.   An application for a stay shall set out with particularity why the relief sought is not available from any other court or judge. Except in the most extraordinary circumstances, an application for a stay will not be entertained unless the relief requested was first sought in the appropriate court or courts below or from a judge or judges thereof. An application for a stay shall identify the judgment sought to be reviewed and have appended thereto a copy of the order and opinion, if any, and a copy of the order, if any, of the court or judge below denying the relief sought, and shall set out specific reasons why a stay is justified. The form and content of an application for a stay are governed by Rules 22 and 33.2.

4.   A judge, court, or Justice granting an application for a stay pending review by this Court may condition the stay on the filing of a supersedeas bond having an approved surety or sureties. The bond will be conditioned on the satisfaction of the judgment in full, together with any costs, interest, and damages for delay that may awarded. If a part of the judgment sought to be reviewed has already been satisfied, or is otherwise secured, the bond may be conditioned on the satisfaction of the part of the judgment not otherwise secured or satisfied, together with costs, interest, and damages.

PART VI.   BRIEFS ON THE MERITS AND ORAL ARGUMENT

Rule 24.   Briefs on the Merits: In General

1.   A brief on the merits for a petitioner or an appellant shall comply in all respects with Rule 33.1 and 34 and shall contain in the order here indicated:

(a) The questions presented for review under Rule 14.1(a). The questions shall be set out on the first page following the cover, and no other information may appear on that page. The phrasing of the questions presented need not be identical with that in the petition for a writ of certiorari or the jurisdictional statement, but the brief may not raise additional questions or change the substance of the questions already presented in those documents. At its option, however, the Court may consider a plain error not among the questions presented but evident from the record and otherwise within its jurisdiction to decide.

(b) A list of all parties to the proceeding in the court whose judgment is under review (unless the caption of the case in this Court contains the names of all parties). Any amended list of parent companies and nonwholly owned subsidiaries as required by Rule 29.6 shall be placed here.

(c) If the brief exceeds five pages, a table of contents and a table of cited authorities.

(d) Citations of the official and unofficial reports of the opinions and orders entered in the case by courts and administrative agencies.

(e) A concise statement of the basis for jurisdiction in this Court, including the statutory provisions and time factors on which jurisdiction rests.

(f) The constitutional provisions, treaties, statutes, ordinances, and regulations involved in the case, set out verbatim with appropriate citation. If the provisions involved are lengthy, their citation alone suffices at this point, and their pertinent text, if not already set out in the petition for a writ of certiorari, jurisdictional statement, or an appendix to either document, shall be set out in an appendix to the brief.

(g) A concise statement of the case, setting out the facts material to the consideration of the questions presented, with appropriate references to the joint appendix, e.g., App. 12, or to the record, e.g., Record 12.

(h) A summary of the argument, suitably paragraphed. The summary should be a clear and concise condensation of the argument made in the body of the brief; mere repetition of the headings under which the argument is arranged is not sufficient.

(i) The argument, exhibiting clearly the points of fact and of law presented and citing the authorities and statutes relied on.

(j) A conclusion specifying with particularity the relief the party seeks.

2. A brief on the merits for a respondent or an appellee shall conform to the foregoing requirements, except that items required by subparagraphs 1(a), (b), (d), (e), (f), and (g) of this Rule need not be included unless the respondent or appellee is dissatisfied with their presentation by the opposing party.

3. A brief on the merits may not exceed the page limitations specified in Rule 33.1(g). An appendix to a brief may include only relevant material, and counsel are cautioned not to include in an appendix arguments or citations that properly belong in the body of the brief.

4. A reply brief shall conform to those portions of this Rule applicable to the brief for a respondent or an appellee, but, if appropriately divided by topical headings, need not contain a summary of the argument.

5. A reference to the joint appendix or to the record set out in any brief shall indicate the appropriate page number. If the reference is to an exhibit, the page numbers at which the exhibit appears, at which it was offered in evidence, and at which it was ruled on by the judge shall be indicated, e.g., Pl.Exh. 14, Record 199, 2134.

6. A brief shall be concise, logically arranged with proper headings, and free of irrelevant, immaterial, or scandalous matter. The Court may disregard or strike a brief that does not comply with this paragraph.

Rule 25. Briefs on the Merits: Number of Copies and Time to File

1. The petitioner or appellant shall file 40 copies of the brief on the merits within 45 days of the order granting the writ of certiorari, noting probable jurisdiction, or postponing consideration of jurisdiction. Any respondent or appellee who supports the petitioner or appellant shall meet the petitioner's or appellant's time schedule for filing documents.

2. The respondent or appellee shall file 40 copies of the brief on the merits within 30 days after receiving the brief for the petitioner or appellant.

3. The petitioner or appellant shall file 40 copies of the reply brief, if any, within 30 days after receiving the brief for the respondent or appellee, but any reply brief must actually be received by the Clerk not later than one week before the date of oral argument. Any respondent or appellee supporting the petitioner or appellant may file a reply brief.

4. The time periods stated in paragraphs 1 and 2 of this Rule may be extended as provided in Rule 30. An application to extend the time to file a brief on the merits is not favored. If a case is advanced for hearing, the time to file briefs on the merits may be abridged as circumstances require pursuant to an order of the Court on its own motion or that of a party.

5. A party wishing to present late authorities, newly enacted legislation, or other intervening matter that was not available in time to be included in a brief may file 40 copies of a supplemental brief, restricted to such new matter and otherwise presented in conformity with these Rules, up to the time the case is called for oral argument or by leave of the Court thereafter.

6. After a case has been argued or submitted, the Clerk will not file any brief, except that of a party filed by leave of the Court.

7. The Clerk will not file any brief that is not accompanied by proof of service as required by Rule 29.

Rule 26. Joint Appendix

1. Unless the Clerk has allowed the parties to use the deferred method described in paragraph 4 of this Rule, the petitioner or appellant, within 45 days after entry of the order granting the writ of certiorari, noting probable jurisdiction, or postponing consideration of jurisdiction, shall file 40 copies of a joint appendix, prepared as required by Rule 33.1. The joint appendix shall contain: (1) the relevant docket entries in all the courts below; (2) any relevant pleadings, jury instructions, findings, conclusions, or opinions; (3) the judgment, order, or decision under review; and (4) any other parts of the record that the

parties particularly wish to bring to the Court's attention. Any of the foregoing items already reproduced in a petition for a writ of certiorari, jurisdictional statement, brief in opposition to a petition for a writ of certiorari, motion to dismiss or affirm, or any appendix to the foregoing, that was prepared as required by Rule 33.1, need not be reproduced again in the joint appendix. The petitioner or appellant shall serve three copies of the joint appendix on each of the other parties to the proceeding as required by Rule 29.

2.   The parties are encouraged to agree on the contents of the joint appendix. In the absence of agreement, the petitioner or appellant, within 10 days after entry of the order granting the writ of certiorari, noting probable jurisdiction, or postponing consideration of jurisdiction, shall serve on the respondent or appellee a designation of parts of the record to be included in the joint appendix. Within 10 days after receiving the designation, a respondent or appellee who considers the parts of the record so designated insufficient shall serve on the petitioner or appellant a designation of additional parts to be included in the joint appendix, and the petitioner or appellant shall include the parts so designated. If the Court has permitted the respondent or appellee to proceed in forma pauperis, the petitioner or appellant may seek by motion to be excused from printing portions of the record the petitioner or appellant considers unnecessary. In making these designations, counsel should include only those materials the Court should examine; unnecessary designations should be avoided. The record is on file with the Clerk and available to the Justices, and counsel may refer in briefs and in oral argument to relevant portions of the record not included in the joint appendix.

3.   When the joint appendix is filed, the petitioner or appellant immediately shall file with the Clerk a statement of the cost of printing 50 copies and shall serve a copy of the statement on each of the other parties as required by Rule 29. Unless the parties agree otherwise, the cost of producing the joint appendix shall be paid initially by the petitioner or appellant; but a petitioner or appellant who considers that parts of the record designated by the respondent or appellee are unnecessary for the determination of the issues presented may so advise the respondent or appellee, who then shall advance the cost of printing the additional parts, unless the Court or a Justice otherwise fixes the initial allocation of the costs. The cost of printing the joint appendix is taxed as a cost in the case, but if a party unnecessarily causes matter to be included in the joint appendix or prints excessive copies, the Court may impose these costs on that party.

4.   (a) On the parties' request, the Clerk may allow preparation of the joint appendix to be deferred until after the briefs have been filed. In that event, the petitioner or appellant shall file the joint appendix no more than 14 days after receiving the brief for the respondent or appellee. The provisions of paragraphs 1, 2, and 3 of this Rule shall be followed, except that the designations referred to therein shall be made

by each party when that party's brief is served. Deferral of the joint appendix is not favored.

(b) If the deferred method is used, the briefs on the merits may refer to the pages of the record. In that event, the joint appendix shall include in brackets on each page thereof the page number of the record where that material may be found. A party wishing to refer directly to the pages of the joint appendix may serve and file copies of its brief prepared as required by Rule 33.2 within the time provided by Rule 25, with appropriate references to the pages of the record. In that event, within 10 days after the joint appendix is filed, copies of the brief prepared as required by Rule 33.1 containing references to the pages of the joint appendix in place of, or in addition to, the initial references to the pages of the record, shall be served and filed. No other change may be made in the brief as initially served and filed, except that typographical errors may be corrected.

5.   The joint appendix shall be prefaced by a table of contents showing the parts of the record that it contains, in the order in which the parts are set out, with references to the pages of the joint appendix at which each part begins. The relevant docket entries shall be set out after the table of contents, followed by the other parts of the record in chronological order. When testimony contained in the reporter's transcript of proceedings is set out in the joint appendix, the page of the transcript at which the testimony appears shall be indicated in brackets immediately before the statement that is set out. Omissions in the transcript or in any other document printed in the joint appendix shall be indicated by asterisks. Immaterial formal matters (e.g., captions, subscriptions, acknowledgments) shall be omitted. A question and its answer may be contained in a single paragraph.

6.   Exhibits designated for inclusion in the joint appendix may be contained in a separate volume or volumes suitably indexed. The transcript of a proceeding before an administrative agency, board, commission, or officer used in an action in a district court or court of appeals is regarded as an exhibit for the purposes of this paragraph.

7.   The Court, on its own motion or that of a party, may dispense with the requirement of a joint appendix and may permit a case to be heard on the original record (with such copies of the record, or relevant parts thereof, as the Court may require) or on the appendix used in the court below, if it conforms to the requirements of this Rule.

8.   For good cause, the time limits specified in this Rule may be shortened or extended by the Court or a Justice, or by the Clerk under Rule 30.4.

Rule 27.   Calendar

1.   From time to time, the Clerk will prepare a calendar of cases ready for argument. A case ordinarily will not be called for argument less

than two weeks after the brief on the merits for the respondent or appellee is due.

2.   The Clerk will advise counsel when they are required to appear for oral argument and will publish a hearing list in advance of each argument session for the convenience of counsel and the information of the public.

3.   The Court, on its own motion or that of a party, may order that two or more cases involving the same or related questions be argued together as one case or on such other terms as the Court may prescribe.

Rule 28.   Oral Argument

1.   Oral argument should emphasize and clarify the written arguments in the briefs on the merits. Counsel should assume that all Justices have read the briefs before oral argument. Oral argument read from a prepared text is not favored.

2.   The petitioner or appellant shall open and may conclude the argument. A cross-writ of certiorari or cross-appeal will be argued with the initial writ of certiorari or appeal as one case in the time allowed for that one case, and the Court will advise the parties who shall open and close.

3.   Unless the Court directs otherwise, each side is allowed one-half hour for argument. Counsel is not required to use all the allotted time. Any request for additional time to argue shall be presented by motion under Rule 21 no more than 15 days after the petitioner's or appellant's brief on the merits is filed, and shall set out specifically and concisely why the case cannot be presented within the half-hour limitation. Additional time is rarely accorded.

4.   Only one attorney will be heard for each side, except by leave of the Court on motion filed no more than 15 days after the respondent's or appellee's brief on the merits is filed. Any request for divided argument shall be presented by motion under Rule 21 and shall set out specifically and concisely why more than one attorney should be allowed to argue. Divided argument is not favored.

5.   Regardless of the number of counsel participating in oral argument, counsel making the opening argument shall present the case fairly and completely and not reserve points of substance for rebuttal.

6.   Oral argument will not be allowed on behalf of any party for whom a brief has not been filed.

7.   By leave of the Court, and subject to paragraph 4 of this Rule, counsel for an amicus curiae whose brief has been filed as provided in Rule 37 may argue orally on the side of a party, with the consent of that party. In the absence of consent, counsel for an amicus curiae may seek leave of the Court to argue orally by a motion setting out specifically and concisely why oral argument would provide assistance to the Court not otherwise available. Such a motion will be granted only in the most extraordinary circumstances.

PART VII.   PRACTICE AND PROCEDURE

Rule 29.   Filing and Service of Documents; Special Notifications; Corporate Disclosure Statement

1.   Any document required or permitted to be presented to the Court or to a Justice shall be filed with the Clerk.

2.   A document is timely filed if it is received by the Clerk within the time specified for filing; or if it is sent to the Clerk through the United States Postal Service by first-class mail (including express or priority mail), postage prepaid, and bears a postmark showing that the document was mailed on or before the last day for filing. Commercial postage meter labels alone are not acceptable. If submitted by an inmate confined in an institution, a document is timely filed if it is deposited in the institution's internal mail system on or before the last day for filing and is accompanied by a notarized statement or declaration in compliance with 28 U.S.C. § 1746 setting out the date of deposit and stating that first-class postage has been prepaid. If the postmark is missing or not legible, the Clerk will require the person who mailed the document to submit a notarized statement or declaration in compliance with 28 U.S.C. § 1746 setting out the details of the mailing and stating that the mailing took place on a particular date within the permitted time. A document also is timely filed if it is forwarded through a private delivery or courier service and is actually received by the Clerk within the time permitted for filing.

3.   Any document required by these Rules to be served may be served personally or by mail on each party to the proceeding at or before the time of filing. If the document has been prepared as required by Rule 33.1, three copies shall be served on each other party separately represented in the proceeding. If the document has been prepared as required by Rule 33.2, service of a single copy on each other separately represented party suffices. If personal service is made, it shall consist of delivery at the office of the counsel of record, either to counsel or to an employee therein. If service is by mail, it shall consist of depositing the document with the United States Postal Service, with no less than first-class postage prepaid, addressed to counsel of record at the proper post office address. When a party is not represented by counsel, service shall be made on the party, personally or by mail.

4.   (a) If the United States or any federal department, office, agency, officer, or employee is a party to be served, service shall be made on the Solicitor General of the United States, Room 5614, Department of Justice, 10th St. and Constitution Ave., N.W., Washington, DC 20530. When an agency of the United States that is a party is authorized by law to appear before this Court on its own behalf, or when an officer or employee of the United States is a party, the agency, officer, or employee shall be served in addition to the Solicitor General.

(b) In any proceeding in this Court in which the constitutionality of an Act of Congress is drawn into question, and neither the

United States nor any federal department, office, agency, officer, or employee is a party, the initial document filed in this Court shall recite that 28 U.S.C. § 2403(a) may apply and shall be served on the Solicitor General of the United States, Room 5614, Department of Justice, 10th St. and Constitution Ave., N.W., Washington, DC 20530. In such a proceeding from any court of the United States, as defined by 28 U.S.C. § 451, the initial document also shall state whether that court, pursuant to 28 U.S.C. § 2403(a), certified to the Attorney General the fact that the constitutionality of an Act of Congress was drawn into question. See Rule 14.1(e)(v).

(c) In any proceeding in this Court in which the constitutionality of any statute of a State is drawn into question, and neither the State nor any agency, officer, or employee thereof is a party, the initial document filed in this Court shall recite that 28 U.S.C. § 2403(b) may apply and shall be served on the Attorney General of that State. In such a proceeding from any court of the United States, as defined by 28 U.S.C. § 451, the initial document also shall state whether that court, pursuant to 28 U.S.C. § 2403(b), certified to the State Attorney General the fact that the constitutionality of a statute of that State was drawn into question. See Rule 14.1(e)(v).

5. Proof of service, when required by these Rules, shall accompany the document when it is presented to the Clerk for filing and shall be separate from it. Proof of service shall contain, or be accompanied by, a statement that all parties required to be served have been served, together with a list of the names, addresses, and telephone numbers of counsel indicating the name of the party or parties each counsel represents. It is not necessary that service on each party required to be served be made in the same manner or evidenced by the same proof. Proof of service may consist of any one of the following:

(a) an acknowledgment of service, signed by counsel of record for the party served, and bearing the address and telephone number of such counsel;

(b) a certificate of service, reciting the facts and circumstances of service in compliance with the appropriate paragraph or paragraphs of this Rule, and signed by a member of the Bar of this Court representing the party on whose behalf service is made or by an attorney appointed to represent that party under the Criminal Justice Act of 1964, see 18 U.S.C. § 3006A(d)(6), or under any other applicable federal statute; or

(c) a notarized affidavit or declaration in compliance with 28 U.S.C. § 1746, reciting the facts and circumstances of service in accordance with the appropriate paragraph or paragraphs of this Rule, whenever service is made by any person not a member of the Bar of this Court and not an attorney appointed to represent a party under the Criminal Justice Act of 1964, see 18 U.S.C. § 3006A(d)(6), or under any other applicable federal statute.

6.   Every document, except a joint appendix or amicus curiae brief, filed by or on behalf of a nongovernmental corporation shall contain a corporate disclosure statement identifying the parent corporations and listing any publicly held company that owns 10% or more of the corporation's stock. If there is no parent or publicly held company owning 10% or more of the corporation's stock, a notation to this effect shall be included in the document. If a statement has been included in a document filed earlier in the case, reference may be made to the earlier document (except when the earlier statement appeared in a document prepared under Rule 33.2) and only amendments to the statement to make it current need be included in the document being filed.

Rule 30.   Computation and Extension of Time

1.   In the computation of any period of time prescribed or allowed by these Rules, by order of the Court, or by an applicable statute, the day of the act, event, or default from which the designated period begins to run is not included. The last day of the period shall be included, unless it is a Saturday, Sunday, federal legal holiday listed in 5 U.S.C. § 6103, or day on which the Court building is closed by order of the Court or the Chief Justice, in which event the period shall extend until the end of the next day that is not a Saturday, Sunday, federal legal holiday, or day on which the Court building is closed.

2.   Whenever a Justice or the Clerk is empowered by law or these Rules to extend the time to file any document, an application seeking an extension shall be filed within the period sought to be extended. An application to extend the time to file a petition for a writ of certiorari or to file a jurisdictional statement must be received by the Clerk at least 10 days before the specified final filing date as computed under these Rules; if received less than 10 days before the final filing date, such application will not be granted except in the most extraordinary circumstances.

3.   An application to extend the time to file a petition for a writ of certiorari, to file a jurisdictional statement, to file a reply brief on the merits, or to file a petition for rehearing shall be made to an individual Justice and presented and served on all other parties as provided by Rule 22. Once denied, such an application may not be renewed.

4.   An application to extend the time to file any document or paper other than those specified in paragraph 3 of this Rule may be presented in the form of a letter to the Clerk setting out specific reasons why an extension of time is justified. The letter shall be served on all other parties as required by Rule 29. The application may be acted on by the Clerk in the first instance, and any party aggrieved by the Clerk's action may request that the application be submitted to a Justice or to the Court. The Clerk will report action under this paragraph to the Court as instructed.

Rule 31.   Translations

Whenever any record to be transmitted to this Court contains material written in a foreign language without a translation made under the authority of the lower court, or admitted to be correct, the clerk of the court transmitting the record shall advise the Clerk of this Court immediately so that this Court may order that a translation be supplied and, if necessary, printed as part of the joint appendix.

Rule 32.   Models, Diagrams, and Exhibits

1.   Models, diagrams, and exhibits of material forming part of the evidence taken in a case and brought to this Court for its inspection shall be placed in the custody of the Clerk at least two weeks before the case is to be heard or submitted.

2.   All models, diagrams, exhibits, and other items placed in the custody of the Clerk shall be removed by the parties no more than 40 days after the case is decided. If this is not done, the Clerk will notify counsel to remove the articles forthwith. If they are not removed within a reasonable time thereafter, the Clerk will destroy them or dispose of them in any other appropriate way.

Rule 33.   Document Preparation: Booklet Format; 8 1/2—by 11– inch Paper Format

1.   *Booklet Format*:

(a) Except for a document expressly permitted by these Rules to be submitted on 8 1/2–by 11–inch paper, see, e.g., Rules 21, 22, and 39, every document filed with the Court shall be prepared in a 6 1/8—9 1/4–inch booklet format using a standard typesetting process (e.g., hot metal, photocomposition, or computer typesetting) to produce text printed in typographic (as opposed to typewriter) characters. The process used must produce a clear black image on white paper. The text must be reproduced with a clarity that equals or exceeds the output of a laser printer.

(b) The text of every booklet-format document, including any appendix thereto, shall be typeset in roman 11–point or larger type with 2–point or more leading between lines. The typeface should be similar to that used in current volumes of the United States Reports. Increasing the amount of text by using condensed or thinner typefaces, or by reducing the space between letters, is strictly prohibited. Type size and face shall be consistent throughout. Quotations in excess of 50 words shall be indented. The typeface of footnotes shall be 9–point or larger with 2–point or more leading between lines. The text of the document must appear on both sides of the page.

(c) Every booklet-format document, shall be produced on paper that is opaque, unglazed, and not less than 60 pounds in weight, and shall have margins of at least three-fourths of an inch on all sides. The text field, including footnotes may not exceed 4 1/8 by 7 1/8 inches. The document shall be bound firmly in at least two places along the left margin (saddle stitch or perfect binding preferred) so as to permit easy opening, and no part of the text should be obscured by the binding. Spiral, plastic, metal, and string bindings may not be used. Copies of patent documents, except opinions, may be duplicated in such size as is necessary in a separate appendix.

(d) Every booklet-format document, shall comply with the page limits shown on the chart in subparagraph 1(g) of this Rule. The page limits do not include the questions presented, the list of parties and corporate disclosure statement, the table of contents, the table of cited authorities, or any appendix. Verbatim quotations required under Rule 14.1(f), if set out in the text of a brief rather than in the appendix, are also excluded. For good cause, the Court or a Justice may grant leave to file a document in excess of the page limits, but application for such leave is not favored. An application to exceed page limits shall comply with Rule 22 and must be received by the Clerk at least 15 days before the filing date of the document in question, except in the most extraordinary circumstances.

(e) Every booklet-format document, shall have a suitable cover consisting of 65—pound weight paper in the color indicated on the chart in subparagraph 1(g) of this Rule. If a separate appendix to any document is filed, the color of its cover shall be the same as that of the cover of the document it supports. The Clerk will furnish a color chart upon request. Counsel shall ensure that there is adequate contrast between the printing and the color of the cover. A document filed by the United States, or by any other federal party represented by the Solicitor General, shall have a gray cover. A joint appendix, answer to a bill of complaint, motion for leave to intervene, and any other document not listed in subparagraph 1(g) of this Rule shall have a tan cover.

(f) Forty copies of a booklet-format document shall be filed.

(g) Page limits and cover colors for booklet-format documents are as follows:

Type of Document	Page Limits	Color of Cover
(i) Petition for a Writ of Certiorari (Rule 14); Motion for Leave to File a Bill of Complaint and Brief in Support (Rule 17.3); Jurisdictional Statement (Rule 18.3); Petition for an Extraordinary Writ (Rule 20.2)	30	white
(ii) Brief in Opposition (Rule 15.3); Brief in Opposition to Motion for Leave to File an Original Action (Rule 17.5); Motion to Dismiss or Affirm (Rule 18.6); Brief in Opposition to Mandamus or Prohibition (Rule 20.3(b)); Response to a Petition for Habeas Corpus (Rule 20.4)	30	orange

Type of Document	Page Limits	Color of Cover
(iii) Reply to Brief in Opposition (Rules 15.6 and 17.5); Brief Opposing a Motion to Dismiss or Affirm (Rule 18.8)	10	tan
(iv) Supplemental Brief (Rules 15.8, 17, 18.10, and 25.5)	10	tan
(v) Brief on the Merits for Petitioner or Appellant (Rule 24); Exceptions by Plaintiff to Report of Special Master (Rule 17)	50	light blue
(vi) Brief on the Merits for Respondent or Appellee (Rule 24.2); Brief on the Merits for Respondent or Appellee Supporting Petitioner or Appellant (Rule 12.6); Exceptions by Party Other Than Plaintiff to Report of Special Master (Rule 17)	50	light red
(vii) Reply Brief on the Merits (Rule 24.4)	20	yellow
(viii) Reply to Plaintiff's Exceptions to Report of Special Master (Rule 17)	50	orange
(ix) Reply to Exceptions by Party Other Than Plaintiff to Report of Special Master (Rule 17)	50	yellow
(x) Brief for an Amicus Curiae at the Petition Stage (Rule 37.2)	20	cream
(xi) Brief for an Amicus Curiae in Support of the Plaintiff, Petitioner, or Appellant, or in Support of Neither Party, on the Merits or in an Original Action at the Exceptions Stage (Rule 37.3)	30	light green
(xii) Brief for an Amicus Curiae in Support of the Defendant, Respondent, or Appellee, on the Merits or in an Original Action at the Exceptions Stage (Rule 37.3)	30	dark green
(xiii) Petition for Rehearing (Rule 44)	10	tan

2. *8 1/2–by 11–Inch Paper Format:*

   (a) The text of every document, including any appendix thereto, expressly permitted by these Rules to be presented to the Court on 8 1/2–by 11–inch paper shall appear double spaced, except for indented quotations, which shall be single spaced, on opaque, unglazed, white paper. The document shall be stapled or bound at the upper left-hand corner. Copies, if required, shall be produced on the same type of paper and shall be legible. The original of any such document (except a motion to dismiss or affirm under Rule 18.6) shall be signed by the party proceeding pro se or by counsel of record who must be a member of the Bar of this Court or an attorney appointed under the Criminal Justice Act of 1964, see 18 U.S.C. § 3006A(d)(6), or under any other applicable federal statute. Subparagraph 1(g) of this Rule does not apply to documents prepared under this paragraph.

(b) Page limits for documents presented on 8 1/2–by 11–inch paper are: 40 pages for a petition for a writ of certiorari, jurisdictional statement, petition for an extraordinary writ, brief in opposition, or motion to dismiss or affirm; and 15 pages for a reply to a brief in opposition, brief opposing a motion to dismiss or affirm, supplemental brief, or petition for rehearing. The page exclusions specified in subparagraph 1(d) of this Rule apply.

Rule 34. Document Preparation: General Requirements

Every document, whether prepared under Rule 33.1 or Rule 33.2, shall comply with the following provisions:

1. Each document shall bear on its cover, in the order indicated, from the top of the page:

(a) the docket number of the case or, if there is none, a space for one;

(b) the name of this Court;

(c) the caption of the case as appropriate in this Court;

(d) the nature of the proceeding and the name of the court from which the action is brought (e.g., "On Petition for Writ of Certiorari to the United States Court of Appeals for the Fifth Circuit"; or, for a merits brief, "On Writ of Certiorari to the United States Court of Appeals for the Fifth Circuit");

(e) the title of the document (e.g., "Petition for Writ of Certiorari," "Brief for Respondent," "Joint Appendix");

(f) the name of the attorney who is counsel of record for the party concerned (who must be a member of the Bar of this Court except as provided in Rule 33.2), and on whom service is to be made, with a notation directly thereunder identifying the attorney as counsel of record and setting out counsel's office address and telephone number. Only one counsel of record may be noted on a single document. The names of other members of the Bar of this Court or of the bar of the highest court of a State acting as counsel, and, if desired, their addresses, may be added, but counsel of record shall be clearly identified. Names of persons other than attorneys admitted to a state bar may not be listed, unless the party is appearing pro se, in which case the party's name, address, and telephone number shall appear. The foregoing shall be displayed in an appropriate typographic manner and, except for the identification of counsel, may not be set in type smaller than standard 11–point, if the document is prepared as required by Rule 33.1.

2. Every document exceeding five pages (other than a joint appendix), whether prepared under Rule 33.1 or Rule 33.2, shall contain a table of contents and a table of cited authorities (i.e., cases alphabetically arranged, constitutional provisions, statutes, treatises, and other materials) with references to the pages in the document where such authorities are cited.

3. The body of every document shall bear at its close the name of counsel of record and such other counsel, identified on the cover of the document in conformity with subparagraph 1(g) of this Rule, as may be desired.

Rule 35.   Death, Substitution, and Revivor; Public Officers

1. If a party dies after the filing of a petition for a writ of certiorari to this Court, or after the filing of a notice of appeal, the authorized representative of the deceased party may appear and, on motion, be substituted as a party. If the representative does not voluntarily become a party, any other party may suggest the death on the record and, on motion, seek an order requiring the representative to become a party within a designated time. If the representative then fails to become a party, the party so moving, if a respondent or appellee, is entitled to have the petition for a writ of certiorari or the appeal dismissed, and if a petitioner or appellant, is entitled to proceed as in any other case of nonappearance by a respondent or appellee. If the substitution of a representative of the deceased is not made within six months after the death of the party, the case shall abate.

2. Whenever a case cannot be revived in the court whose judgment is sought to be reviewed, because the deceased party's authorized representative is not subject to that court's jurisdiction, proceedings will be conducted as this Court may direct.

3. When a public officer who is a party to a proceeding in this Court in an official capacity dies, resigns, or otherwise ceases to hold office, the action does not abate and any successor in office is automatically substituted as a party. The parties shall notify the Clerk in writing of any such successions. Proceedings following the substitution shall be in the name of the substituted party, but any misnomer not affecting substantial rights of the parties will be disregarded.

4. A public officer who is a party to a proceeding in this Court in an official capacity may be described as a party by the officer's official title rather than by name, but the Court may require the name to be added.

Rule 36.   Custody of Prisoners in Habeas Corpus Proceedings

1. Pending review in this Court of a decision in a habeas corpus proceeding commenced before a court, Justice, or judge of the United States, the person having custody of the prisoner may not transfer

custody to another person unless the transfer is authorized under this Rule.

2. Upon application by a custodian, the court, Justice, or judge who entered the decision under review may authorize transfer and the substitution of a successor custodian as a party.

3. (a) Pending review of a decision failing or refusing to release a prisoner, the prisoner may be detained in the custody from which release is sought or in other appropriate custody or may be enlarged on personal recognizance or bail, as may appear appropriate to the court, Justice, or judge who entered the decision, or to the court of appeals, this Court, or a judge or Justice of either court.

(b) Pending review of a decision ordering release, the prisoner shall be enlarged on personal recognizance or bail, unless the court, Justice, or judge who entered the decision, or the court of appeals, this Court, or a judge or Justice of either court, orders otherwise.

4. An initial order respecting the custody or enlargement of the prisoner, and any recognizance or surety taken, shall continue in effect pending review in the court of appeals and in this Court unless for reasons shown to the court of appeals, this Court, or a judge or Justice of either court, the order is modified or an independent order respecting custody, enlargement, or surety is entered.

Rule 37. Brief for an Amicus Curiae

1. An amicus curiae brief that brings to the attention of the Court relevant matter not already brought to its attention by the parties may be of considerable help to the Court. An amicus curiae brief that does not serve this purpose burdens the Court, and its filing is not favored.

2. (a) An amicus curiae brief submitted before the Court's consideration of a petition for a writ of certiorari, motion for leave to file a bill of complaint, jurisdictional statement, or petition for an extraordinary writ, may be filed if accompanied by the written consent of all parties, or if the Court grants leave to file under subparagraph 2(b) of this Rule. The brief shall be submitted within the time allowed for filing a brief in opposition or for filing a motion to dismiss or affirm. The amicus curiae brief shall specify whether consent was granted, and its cover shall identify the party supported.

(b) When a party to the case has withheld consent, a motion for leave to file an amicus curiae brief before the Court's consideration of a petition for a writ of certiorari, motion for leave to file a bill of complaint, jurisdictional statement, or petition for an extraordinary writ may be presented to the Court. The motion, prepared as required by Rule 33.1 and as one document with the brief sought to be filed, shall be submitted within the time allowed for filing an amicus curiae brief, and shall indicate the party or parties who have withheld consent and state the nature of the movant's interest. Such a motion is not favored.

3. (a) An amicus curiae brief in a case before the Court for oral argument may be filed if accompanied by the written consent of all parties, or if the Court grants leave to file under subparagraph 3(b) of this Rule. The brief shall be submitted within the time allowed for filing the brief for the party supported, or if in support of neither party, within the time allowed for filing the petitioner's or appellant's brief. The amicus curiae brief shall specify whether consent was granted, and its cover shall identify the party supported or indicate whether it suggests affirmance or reversal. The Clerk will not file a reply brief for an amicus curiae, or a brief for an amicus curiae in support of, or in opposition to, a petition for rehearing.

(b) When a party to a case before the Court for oral argument has withheld consent, a motion for leave to file an amicus curiae brief may be presented to the Court. The motion, prepared as required by Rule 33.1 and as one document with the brief sought to be filed, shall be submitted within the time allowed for filing an amicus curiae brief, and shall indicate the party or parties who have withheld consent and state the nature of the movant's interest.

4. No motion for leave to file an amicus curiae brief is necessary if the brief is presented on behalf of the United States by the Solicitor General; on behalf of any agency of the United States allowed by law to appear before this Court when submitted by the agency's authorized legal representative; on behalf of a State, Commonwealth, Territory, or Possession when submitted by its Attorney General; or on behalf of a city, county, town, or similar entity when submitted by its authorized law officer.

5. A brief or motion filed under this Rule shall be accompanied by proof of service as required by Rule 29, and shall comply with the applicable provisions of Rules 21, 24, and 33.1 (except that it suffices to set out in the brief the interest of the amicus curiae, the summary of the argument, the argument, and the conclusion). A motion for leave to file may not exceed five pages. A party served with the motion may file an objection thereto, stating concisely the reasons for withholding consent; the objection shall be prepared as required by Rule 33.2.

6. Except for briefs presented on behalf of amicus curiae listed in Rule 37.4, a brief filed under this Rule shall indicate whether counsel for a party authored the brief in whole or in part and shall identify every person or entity, other than the amicus curiae, its members, or its counsel, who made a monetary contribution to the preparation or submission of the brief. The disclosure shall be made in the first footnote on the first page of text.

Rule 38.   Fees

Under 28 U.S.C. § 1911, the fees charged by the Clerk are:

(a) for docketing a case on a petition for a writ of certiorari or on appeal or for docketing any other proceeding, except a certified question or a motion to docket and dismiss an appeal under Rule 18.5, $300;

(b) for filing a petition for rehearing or a motion for leave to file a petition for rehearing, $200;

(c) for reproducing and certifying any record or paper, $1 per page; and for comparing with the original thereof any photographic reproduction of any record or paper, when furnished by the person requesting its certification, $.50 per page;

(d) for a certificate bearing the seal of the Court, $10; and

(e) for a check paid to the Court, Clerk, or Marshal that is returned for lack of funds, $35.

Rule 39. Proceedings in Forma Pauperis

1. A party seeking to proceed in forma pauperis shall file a motion for leave to do so, together with the party's notarized affidavit or declaration (in compliance with 28 U.S.C. § 1746) in the form prescribed by the Federal Rules of Appellate Procedure, Form 4. The motion shall state whether leave to proceed in forma pauperis was sought in any other court and, if so, whether leave was granted. If the United States district court or the United States court of appeals has appointed counsel under the Criminal Justice Act of 1964, 18 U.S.C. § 3006A, or under any other applicable federal statute, no affidavit or declaration is required, but the motion shall cite the statute under which counsel was appointed.

2. If leave to proceed in forma pauperis is sought for the purpose of filing a document, the motion, and an affidavit or declaration if required, shall be filed together with that document and shall comply in every respect with Rule 21. As provided in that Rule, it suffices to file an original and 10 copies, unless the party is an inmate confined in an institution and is not represented by counsel, in which case the original, alone, suffices. A copy of the motion shall precede and be attached to each copy of the accompanying document.

3. Except when these Rules expressly provide that a document shall be prepared as required by Rule 33.1, every document presented by a party proceeding under this Rule shall be prepared as required by Rule 33.2 (unless such preparation is impossible). Every document shall be legible. While making due allowance for any case presented under this Rule by a person appearing pro se, the Clerk will not file any document if it does not comply with the substance of these Rules or is jurisdictionally out of time.

4. When the documents required by paragraphs 1 and 2 of this Rule are presented to the Clerk, accompanied by proof of service as required by Rule 29, they will be placed on the docket without the payment of a docket fee or any other fee.

5. The respondent or appellee in a case filed in forma pauperis shall respond in the same manner and within the same time as in any other case of the same nature, except that the filing of an original and 10

copies of a response prepared as required by Rule 33.2, with proof of service as required by Rule 29, suffices. The respondent or appellee may challenge the grounds for the motion for leave to proceed in forma pauperis in a separate document or in the response itself.

6.   Whenever the Court appoints counsel for an indigent party in a case set for oral argument, the briefs on the merits submitted by that counsel, unless otherwise requested, shall be prepared under the Clerk's supervision. The Clerk also will reimburse appointed counsel for any necessary travel expenses to Washington, D.C., and return in connection with the argument.

7.   In a case in which certiorari has been granted, probable jurisdiction noted, or consideration of jurisdiction postponed, this Court may appoint counsel to represent a party financially unable to afford an attorney to the extent authorized by the Criminal Justice Act of 1964, 18 U.S.C. § 3006A, or by any other applicable federal statute.

8.   If satisfied that a petition for a writ of certiorari, jurisdictional statement, or petition for an extraordinary writ is frivolous or malicious, the Court may deny leave to proceed in forma pauperis.

Rule 40.   Veterans, Seamen, and Military Cases

1.   A veteran suing to establish reemployment rights under any provision of law exempting veterans from the payment of fees or court costs, may file a motion for leave to proceed on papers prepared as required by Rule 33.2. The motion shall ask leave to proceed as a veteran and be accompanied by an affidavit or declaration setting out the moving party's veteran status. A copy of the motion shall precede and be attached to each copy of the petition for a writ of certiorari or other substantive document filed by the veteran.

2.   A seaman suing under 28 U.S.C. § 1916 may proceed without prepayment of fees or costs or furnishing security therefor, but is not entitled to proceed under Rule 33.2, except as authorized by the Court on separate motion under Rule 39.

3.   An accused person petitioning for a writ of certiorari to review a decision of the United States Court of Appeals for the Armed Forces under 28 U.S.C. § 1259 may proceed without prepayment of fees or costs or furnishing security therefor and without filing an affidavit of indigency, but is not entitled to proceed on papers prepared as required by Rule 33.2, except as authorized by the Court on separate motion under Rule 39.

PART VIII.   DISPOSITION OF CASES

Rule 41.   Opinions of the Court

Opinions of the Court will be released by the Clerk immediately upon their announcement from the bench, or as the Court otherwise directs. Thereafter, the Clerk will cause the opinions to be issued in slip form, and the Reporter of Decisions will prepare them for publication in the preliminary prints and bound volumes of the United States Reports.

Rule 42.   Interest and Damages

1.   If a judgment for money in a civil case is affirmed, any interest allowed by law is payable from the date the judgment under review was entered. If a judgment is modified or reversed with a direction that a judgment for money be entered below, the mandate will contain instructions with respect to the allowance of interest. Interest in cases arising in a state court is allowed at the same rate that similar judgments bear interest in the courts of the State in which judgment is directed to be entered. Interest in cases arising in a court of the United States is allowed at the interest rate authorized by law.

2.   When a petition for a writ of certiorari, an appeal, or an application for other relief is frivolous, the Court may award the respondent or appellee just damages, and single or double costs under Rule 43. Damages or costs may be awarded against the petitioner, appellant, or applicant, against the party's counsel, or against both party and counsel.

Rule 43.   Costs

1.   If the Court affirms a judgment, the petitioner or appellant shall pay costs unless the Court otherwise orders.

2.   If the Court reverses or vacates a judgment, the respondent or appellee shall pay costs unless the Court otherwise orders.

3.   The Clerk's fees and the cost of printing the joint appendix are the only taxable items in this Court. The cost of the transcript of the record from the court below is also a taxable item, but shall be taxable in that court as costs in the case. The expenses of printing briefs, motions, petitions, or jurisdictional statements are not taxable.

4.   In a case involving a certified question, costs are equally divided unless the Court otherwise orders, except that if the Court decides the whole matter in controversy, as permitted by Rule 19.2, costs are allowed as provided in paragraphs 1 and 2 of this Rule.

5.   To the extent permitted by 28 U.S.C. § 2412, costs under this Rule are allowed for or against the United States or an officer or agent thereof, unless expressly waived or unless the Court otherwise orders.

6.   When costs are allowed in this Court, the Clerk will insert an itemization of the costs in the body of the mandate or judgment sent to the court below. The prevailing side may not submit a bill of costs.

7.   In extraordinary circumstances the Court may adjudge double costs.

Rule 44.   Rehearing

1.   Any petition for the rehearing of any judgment or decision of the Court on the merits shall be filed within 25 days after entry of the judgment or decision, unless the Court or a Justice shortens or extends

the time. The petitioner shall file 40 copies of the rehearing petition and shall pay the filing fee prescribed by Rule 38(b), except that a petitioner proceeding in forma pauperis under Rule 39, including an inmate of an institution, shall file the number of copies required for a petition by such a person under Rule 12.2. The petition shall state its grounds briefly and distinctly and shall be served as required by Rule 29. The petition shall be presented together with certification of counsel (or of a party unrepresented by counsel) that it is presented in good faith and not for delay; one copy of the certificate shall bear the signature of counsel (or of a party unrepresented by counsel). A copy of the certificate shall follow and be attached to each copy of the petition. A petition for rehearing is not subject to oral argument and will not be granted except by a majority of the Court, at the instance of a Justice who concurred in the judgment or decision.

2.   Any petition for the rehearing of an order denying a petition for a writ of certiorari or extraordinary writ shall be filed within 25 days after the date of the order of denial and shall comply with all the form and filing requirements of paragraph 1 of this Rule, including the payment of the filing fee if required, but its grounds shall be limited to intervening circumstances of a substantial or controlling effect or to other substantial grounds not previously presented. The petition shall be presented together with certification of counsel (or of a party unrepresented by counsel) that it is restricted to the grounds specified in this paragraph and that it is presented in good faith and not for delay; one copy of the certificate shall bear the signature of counsel (or of a party unrepresented by counsel). The certificate shall be bound with each copy of the petition. The Clerk will not file a petition without a certificate. The petition is not subject to oral argument.

3.   The Clerk will not file any response to a petition for rehearing unless the Court requests a response. In the absence of extraordinary circumstances, the Court will not grant a petition for rehearing without first requesting a response.

4.   The Clerk will not file consecutive petitions and petitions that are out of time under this Rule.

5.   The Clerk will not file any brief for an amicus curiae in support of, or in opposition to, a petition for rehearing.

Rule 45.   Process; Mandates

1.   All process of this Court issues in the name of the President of the United States.

2.   In a case on review from a state court, the mandate issues 25 days after entry of the judgment, unless the Court or a Justice shortens or extends the time, or unless the parties stipulate that it issue sooner. The filing of a petition for rehearing stays the mandate until disposition of the petition, unless the Court orders otherwise. If the petition is denied, the mandate issues forthwith.

3. In a case on review from any court of the United States, as defined by 28 U.S.C. § 451, a formal mandate does not issue unless specially directed; instead, the Clerk of this Court will send the clerk of the lower court a copy of the opinion or order of this Court and a certified copy of the judgment. The certified copy of the judgment, prepared and signed by this Court's Clerk, will provide for costs if any are awarded. In all other respects, the provisions of paragraph 2 of this Rule apply.

Rule 46. Dismissing Cases

1. At any stage of the proceedings, whenever all parties file with the Clerk an agreement in writing that a case be dismissed, specifying the terms for payment of costs, and pay to the Clerk any fees then due, the Clerk, without further reference to the Court, will enter an order of dismissal.

2. (a) A petitioner or appellant may file a motion to dismiss the case, with proof of service as required by Rule 29, tendering to the Clerk any fees due and costs payable. No more than 15 days after service thereof, an adverse party may file an objection, limited to the amount of damages and costs in this Court alleged to be payable or to showing that the moving party does not represent all petitioners or appellants. The Clerk will not file any objection not so limited.

(b) When the objection asserts that the moving party does not represent all the petitioners or appellants, the party moving for dismissal may file a reply within 10 days, after which time the matter will be submitted to the Court for its determination.

(c) If no objection is filed—or if upon objection going only to the amount of damages and costs in this Court, the party moving for dismissal tenders the additional damages and costs in full within 10 days of the demand therefor—the Clerk, without further reference to the Court, will enter an order of dismissal. If, after objection as to the amount of damages and costs in this Court, the moving party does not respond by a tender within 10 days, the Clerk will report the matter to the Court for its determination.

3. No mandate or other process will issue on a dismissal under this Rule without an order of the Court.

PART IX. DEFINITIONS AND EFFECTIVE DATE

Rule 47. Reference to "State Court" and "State Law"

The term "state court," when used in these Rules, includes the District of Columbia Court of Appeals and the Supreme Court of the Commonwealth of Puerto Rico. See 28 U.S.C. §§ 1257 and 1258. References in these Rule to the common law and statutes of a State include the common law and statutes of the District of Columbia and of the Commonwealth of Puerto Rico.

Rule 48.   Effective Date of Rules

1.   These Rules, adopted July 26, 1995, will be effective October 2, 1995.

2.   The Rules govern all proceedings after their effective date except to the extent that, in the opinion of the Court, their application to a pending matter would not be feasible or would work an injustice, in which event the former procedure applies.

Appendix B

FEDERAL RULES OF APPELLATE PROCEDURE

As revised effective December 1, 1998

TITLE I. APPLICABILITY OF RULES

TITLE II. APPEAL FROM A JUDGMENT OR ORDER OF A DISTRICT COURT

APPENDIX OF FORMS

FORM

4. Affidavit Accompanying Motion for Permission to Appeal In Forma Pauperis.
5. Notice of Appeal to a Court of Appeals from a Judgment or Order of a District Court or a Bankruptcy Appellate Panel.

TITLE I. APPLICABILITY OF RULES

Rule 1. Scope of Rules; Title

(a) Scope of Rules.

(1) These rules govern procedure in the United States courts of appeals.

(2) When these rules provide for filing a motion or other document in the district court, the procedure must comply with the practice of the district court.

(b) Rules Do Not Affect Jurisdiction. These rules do not extend or limit the jurisdiction of the courts of appeals.

(c) Title. These rules are to be known as the Federal Rules of Appellate Procedure.

Rule 2. Suspension of Rules

On its own or a party's motion, a court of appeals may—to expedite its decision or for other good cause—suspend any provision of these rules in a particular case and order proceedings as it directs, except as otherwise provided in Rule 26(b).

TITLE II. APPEAL FROM A JUDGMENT OR ORDER OF A DISTRICT COURT

Rule 3. Appeal as of Right—How Taken

(a) Filing the Notice of Appeal.

(1) An appeal permitted by law as of right from a district court to a court of appeals may be taken only by filing a notice of appeal with the district clerk within the time allowed by Rule 4. At the time of filing, the appellant must furnish the clerk with enough copies of the notice to enable the clerk to comply with Rule 3(d).

(2) An appellant's failure to take any step other than the timely filing of a notice of appeal does not affect the validity of the appeal, but is ground only for the court of appeals to act as it considers appropriate, including dismissing the appeal.

(3) An appeal from a judgment by a magistrate judge in a civil case is taken in the same way as an appeal from any other district court judgment.

(4) An appeal by permission under 28 U.S.C. § 1292(b) or an appeal in a bankruptcy case may be taken only in the manner prescribed by Rules 5 and 6, respectively.

(b) Joint or Consolidated Appeals.

(1) When two or more parties are entitled to appeal from a district-court judgment or order, and their interests make joinder practicable, they may file a joint notice of appeal. They may then proceed on appeal as a single appellant.

(2) When the parties have filed separate timely notices of appeal, the appeals may be joined or consolidated by the court of appeals.

(c) Contents of the Notice of Appeal.

(1) The notice of appeal must:

(A) specify the party or parties taking the appeal by naming each one in the caption or body of the notice, but an attorney representing more than one party may describe those parties with such terms as "all plaintiffs," "the defendants," "the plaintiffs A, B, et al.," or "all defendants except X";

(B) designate the judgment, order, or part thereof being appealed; and

(C) name the court to which the appeal is taken.

(2) A pro se notice of appeal is considered filed on behalf of the signer and the signer's spouse and minor children (if they are parties), unless the notice clearly indicates otherwise.

(3) In a class action, whether or not the class has been certified, the notice of appeal is sufficient if it names one person qualified to bring the appeal as representative of the class.

(4) An appeal must not be dismissed for informality of form or title of the notice of appeal, or for failure to name a party whose intent to appeal is otherwise clear from the notice.

(5) Form 1 in the Appendix of Forms is a suggested form of a notice of appeal.

(d) Serving the Notice of Appeal.

(1) The district clerk must serve notice of the filing of a notice of appeal by mailing a copy to each party's counsel of record— excluding the appellant's—or, if a party is proceeding pro se, to the party's last known address. When a defendant in a criminal case appeals, the clerk must also serve a copy of the notice of appeal on the defendant, either by personal service or by mail addressed to the defendant. The clerk must promptly send a copy of the notice of appeal and of the docket entries—and any later docket entries—to the clerk of the court of appeals named in the notice. The district clerk must note, on each copy, the date when the notice of appeal was filed.

(2) If an inmate confined in an institution files a notice of appeal in the manner provided by Rule 4(c), the district clerk must also note the date when the clerk docketed the notice.

(3) The district clerk's failure to serve notice does not affect the validity of the appeal. The clerk must note on the docket the names of the parties to whom the clerk mails copies, with the date of mailing. Service is sufficient despite the death of a party or the party's counsel.

(e) Payment of Fees. Upon filing a notice of appeal, the appellant must pay the district clerk all required fees. The district clerk receives the appellate docket fee on behalf of the court of appeals.

Rule 3.1 Appeal from a Judgment of a Magistrate Judge in a Civil Case [Abrogated]

Rule 4. Appeal as of Right—When Taken

(a) Appeal in a Civil Case.

(1) Time for Filing a Notice of Appeal.

(A) In a civil case, except as provided in Rules 4(a)(1)(B), 4(a)(4), and 4(c), the notice of appeal required by Rule 3 must be filed with the district clerk within 30 days after the judgment or order appealed from is entered.

(B) When the United States or its officer or agency is a party, the notice of appeal may be filed by any party within 60 days after the judgment or order appealed from is entered.

(2) Filing Before Entry of Judgment. A notice of appeal filed after the court announces a decision or order—but before the entry of the judgment or order—is treated as filed on the date of and after the entry.

(3) Multiple Appeals. If one party timely files a notice of appeal, any other party may file a notice of appeal within 14 days after the date when the first notice was filed, or within the time otherwise prescribed by this Rule 4(a), whichever period ends later.

(4) Effect of a Motion on a Notice of Appeal.

(A) If a party timely files in the district court any of the following motions under the Federal Rules of Civil Procedure, the time to file an appeal runs for all parties from the entry of the order disposing of the last such remaining motion:

(i) for judgment under Rule 50(b);

(ii) to amend or make additional factual findings under Rule 52(b), whether or not granting the motion would alter the judgment;

(iii) for attorney's fees under Rule 54 if the district court extends the time to appeal under Rule 58;

(iv) to alter or amend the judgment under Rule 59;

(v) for a new trial under Rule 59; or

(vi) for relief under Rule 60 if the motion is filed no later than 10 days (computed using Federal Rule of Civil Procedure 6(a)) after the judgment is entered.

(B) (i) If a party files a notice of appeal after the court announces or enters a judgment—but before it disposes of any motion listed in Rule 4(a)(4)(A)—the notice becomes effective to appeal a judgment or order, in whole or in part, when the order disposing of the last such remaining motion is entered.

(ii) A party intending to challenge an order disposing of any motion listed in Rule 4(a)(4)(A), or a judgment altered or amended upon such a motion, must file a notice of appeal, or an amended notice of appeal—in compliance with Rule 3(c)—within the time prescribed by this Rule measured from the entry of the order disposing of the last such remaining motion.

(iii) No additional fee is required to file an amended notice.

(5) Motion for Extension of Time.

(A) The district court may extend the time to file a notice of appeal if:

(i) a party so moves no later than 30 days after the time prescribed by this Rule 4(a) expires; and

(ii) that party shows excusable neglect or good cause.

(B) A motion filed before the expiration of the time prescribed in Rule 4(a)(1) or (3) may be ex parte unless the court requires otherwise. If the motion is filed after the expiration of the prescribed time, notice must be given to the other parties in accordance with local rules.

(C) No extension under this Rule 4(a)(5) may exceed 30 days after the prescribed time or 10 days after the date when the order granting the motion is entered, whichever is later.

(6) Reopening the Time to File an Appeal. The district court may reopen the time to file an appeal for a period of 14 days after the date when its order to reopen is entered, but only if all the following conditions are satisfied:

(A) the motion is filed within 180 days after the judgment or order is entered or within 7 days after the moving party receives notice of the entry, whichever is earlier;

(B) the court finds that the moving party was entitled to notice of the entry of the judgment or order sought to be appealed but did not receive the notice from the district court or any party within 21 days after entry; and

(C) the court finds that no party would be prejudiced.

(7) Entry Defined. A judgment or order is entered for purposes of this Rule 4(a) when it is entered in compliance with Rules 58 and 79(a) of the Federal Rules of Civil Procedure.

(b) Appeal in a Criminal Case.

(1) Time for Filing a Notice of Appeal.

(A) In a criminal case, a defendant's notice of appeal must be filed in the district court within 10 days after the later of:

(i) the entry of either the judgment or the order being appealed; or

(ii) the filing of the government's notice of appeal.

(B) When the government is entitled to appeal, its notice of appeal must be filed in the district court within 30 days after the later of:

(i) the entry of the judgment or order being appealed; or

(ii) the filing of a notice of appeal by any defendant.

(2) Filing Before Entry of Judgment. A notice of appeal filed after the court announces a decision, sentence, or order—but before the entry of the judgment or order—is treated as filed on the date of and after the entry.

(3) Effect of a Motion on a Notice of Appeal.

(A) If a defendant timely makes any of the following motions under the Federal Rules of Criminal Procedure, the notice of appeal from a judgment of conviction must be filed within 10 days after the entry of the order disposing of the last such remaining motion, or within 10 days after the entry of the judgment of conviction, whichever period ends later. This provision applies to a timely motion:

(i) for judgment of acquittal under Rule 29;

(ii) for a new trial under Rule 33, but if based on newly discovered evidence, only if the motion is made no later than 10 days after the entry of the judgment; or

(iii) for arrest of judgment under Rule 34.

(B) A notice of appeal filed after the court announces a decision, sentence, or order—but before it disposes of any of the motions referred to in Rule 4(b)(3)(A)—becomes effective upon the later of the following:

(i) the entry of the order disposing of the last such remaining motion; or

(ii) the entry of the judgment of conviction.

(C) A valid notice of appeal is effective—without amendment— to appeal from an order disposing of any of the motions referred to in Rule 4(b)(3)(A).

(4) Motion for Extension of Time. Upon a finding of excusable neglect or good cause, the district court may—before or after the time has expired, with or without motion and notice—extend the time to file a notice of appeal for a period not to exceed 30 days from the expiration of the time otherwise prescribed by this Rule 4(b).

(5) Jurisdiction. The filing of a notice of appeal under this Rule 4(b) does not divest a district court of jurisdiction to correct a sentence under Federal Rule of Criminal Procedure 35(c), nor does the filing of a motion under 35(c) affect the validity of a notice of appeal filed before entry of the order disposing of the motion.

(6) Entry Defined. A judgment or order is entered for purposes of this Rule 4(b) when it is entered on the criminal docket.

(c) Appeal by an Inmate Confined in an Institution.

(1) If an inmate confined in an institution files a notice of appeal in either a civil or a criminal case, the notice is timely if it is deposited in the institution's internal mail system on or before the last day for filing. If an institution has a system designed for legal mail, the inmate must use that system to receive the benefit of this rule. Timely filing may be shown by a declaration in compliance with 28 U.S.C. § 1746 or by a notarized statement, either of which must set forth the date of deposit and state that first-class postage has been prepaid.

(2) If an inmate files the first notice of appeal in a civil case under this Rule 4(c), the 14–day period provided in Rule 4(a)(3) for another party to file a notice of appeal runs from the date when the district court dockets the first notice.

(3) When a defendant in a criminal case files a notice of appeal under this Rule 4(c), the 30–day period for the government to file its notice of appeal runs from the entry of the judgment or order appealed from or from the district court's docketing of the defendant's notice of appeal, whichever is later.

(d) Mistaken Filing in the Court of Appeals. If a notice of appeal in either a civil or a criminal case is mistakenly filed in the court of appeals, the clerk of that court must note on the notice the date when it was received and send it to the district clerk. The notice is then considered filed in the district court on the date so noted.

Rule 5. Appeal by Permission

(a) Petition for Permission to Appeal.

(1) To request permission to appeal when an appeal is within the court of appeals' discretion, a party must file a petition for permission to appeal. The petition must be filed with the circuit clerk with proof of service on all other parties to the district-court action.

(2) The petition must be filed within the time specified by the statute or rule authorizing the appeal or, if no such time is specified, within the time provided by Rule 4(a) for filing a notice of appeal.

(3) If a party cannot petition for appeal unless the district court first enters an order granting permission to do so or stating that the

necessary conditions are met, the district court may amend its order, either on its own or in response to a party's motion, to include the required permission or statement. In that event, the time to petition runs from entry of the amended order.

(b) Contents of the Petition; Answer or Cross–Petition; Oral Argument.

(1) The petition must include the following:

(A) the facts necessary to understand the question presented;

(B) the question itself;

(C) the relief sought;

(D) the reasons why the appeal should be allowed and is authorized by a statute or rule; and

(E) an attached copy of:

(i) the order, decree, or judgment complained of and any related opinion or memorandum, and

(ii) any order stating the district court's permission to appeal or finding that the necessary conditions are met.

(2) A party may file an answer in opposition or a cross-petition within 7 days after the petition is served.

(3) The petition and answer will be submitted without oral argument unless the court of appeals orders otherwise.

(c) Form of Papers; Number of Copies. All papers must conform to Rule 32(a)(1). An original and 3 copies must be filed unless the court requires a different number by local rule or by order in a particular case.

(d) Grant of Permission; Fees; Cost Bond; Filing the Record.

(1) Within 10 days after the entry of the order granting permission to appeal, the appellant must:

(A) pay the district clerk all required fees; and

(B) file a cost bond if required under Rule 7.

(2) A notice of appeal need not be filed. The date when the order granting permission to appeal is entered serves as the date of the notice of appeal for calculating time under these rules.

(3) The district clerk must notify the circuit clerk once the petitioner has paid the fees. Upon receiving this notice, the circuit clerk must enter the appeal on the docket. The record must be forwarded and filed in accordance with Rules 11 and 12(c).

Rule 5.1   Appeal by Leave under 28 U.S.C. § 636(c)(5) [Abrogated]

Rule 6.   Appeal in a Bankruptcy Case from a Final Judgment, Order, or Decree of a District Court or Bankruptcy Appellate Panel

(a) Appeal From a Judgment, Order, or Decree of a District Court Exercising Original Jurisdiction in a Bankruptcy Case. An appeal to a court of appeals from a final judgment, order, or decree of a district court exercising jurisdiction under 28 U.S.C. § 1334 is taken as any other civil appeal under these rules.

(b) Appeal From a Judgment, Order, or Decree of a District Court or Bankruptcy Appellate Panel Exercising Appellate Jurisdiction in a Bankruptcy Case.

(1) Applicability of Other Rules. These rules apply to an appeal to a court of appeals under 28 U.S.C. § 158(d) from a final judgment, order, or decree of a district court or bankruptcy appellate panel exercising appellate jurisdiction under 28 U.S.C. § 158(a) or (b). But there are 3 exceptions:

(A) Rules 4(a)(4), 4(b), 9, 10, 11, 12(b), 13–F20, 22–23, and 24(b) do not apply;

(B) the reference in Rule 3(c) to "Form 1 in the Appendix of Forms" must be read as a reference to Form 5; and

(C) when the appeal is from a bankruptcy appellate panel, the term "district court," as used in any applicable rule, means "appellate panel."

(2) Additional Rules. In addition to the rules made applicable by Rule 6(b)(1), the following rules apply:

(A) Motion for rehearing.

(i) If a timely motion for rehearing under Bankruptcy Rule 8015 is filed, the time to appeal for all parties runs from the entry of the order disposing of the motion. A notice of appeal filed after the district court or bankruptcy appellate panel announces or enters a judgment, order, or decree—but before disposition of the motion for rehearing—becomes effective when the order disposing of the motion for rehearing is entered.

(ii) Appellate review of the order disposing of the motion requires the party, in compliance with Rules 3(c) and 6(b)(1)(B), to amend a previously filed notice of appeal. A party intending to challenge an altered or amended judgment, order, or decree must file a notice of appeal or amended notice of appeal within the time prescribed by Rule 4—excluding Rules 4(a)(4) and 4(b)—measured from the entry of the order disposing of the motion.

(iii) No additional fee is required to file an amended notice.

(B) The record on appeal.

(i) Within 10 days after filing the notice of appeal, the appellant must file with the clerk possessing the record assembled in accordance with Bankruptcy Rule 8006—and serve on the appellee—a statement of the issues to be presented on appeal and a designation of the record to be certified and sent to the circuit clerk.

(ii) An appellee who believes that other parts of the record are necessary must, within 10 days after being served with the appellant's designation, file with the clerk and serve on the appellant a designation of additional parts to be included.

(iii) The record on appeal consists of:

• the redesignated record as provided above;

• the proceedings in the district court or bankruptcy appellate panel; and

• a certified copy of the docket entries prepared by the clerk under Rule 3(d).

(C) Forwarding the record.

(i) When the record is complete, the district clerk or bankruptcy appellate panel clerk must number the documents constituting the record and send them promptly to the circuit clerk together with a list of the documents correspondingly numbered and reasonably identified. Unless directed to do so by a party or the circuit clerk, the clerk will not send to the court of appeals documents of unusual bulk or weight, physical exhibits other than documents, or other parts of the record designated for omission by local rule of the court of appeals. If the exhibits are unusually bulky or heavy, a party must arrange with the clerks in advance for their transportation and receipt.

(ii) All parties must do whatever else is necessary to enable the clerk to assemble and forward the record. The court of appeals may provide by rule or order that a certified copy of the docket entries be sent in place of the redesignated record, but any party may request at any time during the pendency of the appeal that the redesignated record be sent.

(D) Filing the record. Upon receiving the record—or a certified copy of the docket entries sent in place of the redesignated record—the circuit clerk must file it and immediately notify all parties of the filing date.

Rule 7. Bond for Costs on Appeal in a Civil Case

In a civil case, the district court may require an appellant to file a bond or provide other security in any form and amount necessary to ensure payment of costs on appeal. Rule 8(b) applies to a surety on a bond given under this rule.

Rule 8. Stay or Injunction Pending Appeal

(a) Motion for Stay.

(1) Initial Motion in the District Court. A party must ordinarily move first in the district court for the following relief:

(A) a stay of the judgment or order of a district court pending appeal;

(B) approval of a supersedeas bond; or

(C) an order suspending, modifying, restoring, or granting an injunction while an appeal is pending.

(2) Motion in the Court of Appeals; Conditions on Relief. A motion for the relief mentioned in Rule 8(a)(1) may be made to the court of appeals or to one of its judges.

(A) The motion must:

(i) show that moving first in the district court would be impracticable; or

(ii) state that, a motion having been made, the district court denied the motion or failed to afford the relief requested and state any reasons given by the district court for its action.

(B) The motion must also include:

(i) the reasons for granting the relief requested and the facts relied on;

(ii) originals or copies of affidavits or other sworn statements supporting facts subject to dispute; and

(iii) relevant parts of the record.

(C) The moving party must give reasonable notice of the motion to all parties.

(D) A motion under this Rule 8(a)(2) must be filed with the circuit clerk and normally will be considered by a panel of the court. But in an exceptional case in which time requirements make that procedure impracticable, the motion may be made to and considered by a single judge.

(E) The court may condition relief on a party's filing a bond or other appropriate security in the district court.

(b) Proceeding Against a Surety. If a party gives security in the form of a bond or stipulation or other undertaking with one or more sureties, each surety submits to the jurisdiction of the district court and irrevocably appoints the district clerk as the surety's agent on whom any papers affecting the surety's liability on the bond or undertaking may be served. On motion, a surety's liability may be enforced in the district court without the necessity of an independent action. The motion and any notice that the district court prescribes may be served on the district clerk, who must promptly mail a copy to each surety whose address is known.

(c) Stay in a Criminal Case. Rule 38 of the Federal Rules of Criminal Procedure governs a stay in a criminal case.

Rule 9.   Release in a Criminal Case

(a) Release Before Judgment of Conviction.

(1) The district court must state in writing, or orally on the record, the reasons for an order regarding the release or detention of a defendant in a criminal case. A party appealing from the order must file with the court of appeals a copy of the district court's order and the court's statement of reasons as soon as practicable after filing the notice of appeal. An appellant who questions the factual basis for the district court's order must file a transcript of the release proceedings or an explanation of why a transcript was not obtained.

(2) After reasonable notice to the appellee, the court of appeals must promptly determine the appeal on the basis of the papers, affidavits, and parts of the record that the parties present or the court requires. Unless the court so orders, briefs need not be filed.

(3) The court of appeals or one of its judges may order the defendant's release pending the disposition of the appeal.

(b) Release After Judgment of Conviction. A party entitled to do so may obtain review of a district-court order regarding release after a judgment of conviction by filing a notice of appeal from that order in the district court, or by filing a motion in the court of appeals if the party has already filed a notice of appeal from the judgment of conviction. Both the order and the review are subject to Rule 9(a). The papers filed by the party seeking review must include a copy of the judgment of conviction.

(c) Criteria for Release. The court must make its decision regarding release in accordance with the applicable provisions of 18 U.S.C. §§ 3142, 3143, and 3145(c).

Rule 10. The Record on Appeal

(a) Composition of the Record on Appeal. The following items constitute the record on appeal:

(1) the original papers and exhibits filed in the district court;

(2) the transcript of proceedings, if any; and

(3) a certified copy of the docket entries prepared by the district clerk.

(b) The Transcript of Proceedings.

(1) Appellant's Duty to Order. Within 10 days after filing the notice of appeal or entry of an order disposing of the last timely remaining motion of a type specified in Rule 4(a)(4)(A), whichever is later, the appellant must do either of the following:

(A) order from the reporter a transcript of such parts of the proceedings not already on file as the appellant considers necessary, subject to a local rule of the court of appeals and with the following qualifications:

(i) the order must be in writing;

(ii) if the cost of the transcript is to be paid by the United States under the Criminal Justice Act, the order must so state; and

(iii) the appellant must, within the same period, file a copy of the order with the district clerk; or

(B) file a certificate stating that no transcript will be ordered.

(2) Unsupported Finding or Conclusion. If the appellant intends to urge on appeal that a finding or conclusion is unsupported by the evidence or is contrary to the evidence, the appellant must include in the record a transcript of all evidence relevant to that finding or conclusion.

(3) Partial Transcript. Unless the entire transcript is ordered:

(A) the appellant must—within the 10 days provided in Rule 10(b)(1)—file a statement of the issues that the appellant intends to present on the appeal and must serve on the appellee a copy of both the order or certificate and the statement;

(B) if the appellee considers it necessary to have a transcript of other parts of the proceedings, the appellee must, within 10 days after the service of the order or certificate and the statement of the issues, file and serve on the appellant a designation of additional parts to be ordered; and

(C) unless within 10 days after service of that designation the appellant has ordered all such parts, and has so notified the appellee, the appellee may within the following 10 days either order the parts or move in the district court for an order requiring the appellant to do so.

(4) Payment. At the time of ordering, a party must make satisfactory arrangements with the reporter for paying the cost of the transcript.

(c) Statement of the Evidence When the Proceedings Were Not Recorded or When a Transcript Is Unavailable. If the transcript of a hearing or trial is unavailable, the appellant may prepare a statement of the evidence or proceedings from the best available means, including the appellant's recollection. The statement must be served on the appellee, who may serve objections or proposed amendments within 10 days after being served. The statement and any objections or proposed amendments must then be submitted to the district court for settlement and approval. As settled and approved, the statement must be included by the district clerk in the record on appeal.

(d) Agreed Statement as the Record on Appeal. In place of the record on appeal as defined in Rule 10(a), the parties may prepare, sign, and submit to the district court a statement of the case showing how the issues presented by the appeal arose and were decided in the district court. The statement must set forth only those facts averred and proved or sought to be proved that are essential to the court's resolution of the issues. If the statement is truthful, it—together with any additions that the district court may consider necessary to a full presentation of the issues on appeal—must be approved by the district court and must then be certified to the court of appeals as the record on appeal. The district clerk must then send it to the circuit clerk within the time provided by Rule 11. A copy of the agreed statement may be filed in place of the appendix required by Rule 30.

(e) Correction or Modification of the Record.

(1) If any difference arises about whether the record truly discloses what occurred in the district court, the difference must be submitted to and settled by that court and the record conformed accordingly.

(2) If anything material to either party is omitted from or misstated in the record by error or accident, the omission or misstatement may be corrected and a supplemental record may be certified and forwarded:

(A) on stipulation of the parties;

(B) by the district court before or after the record has been forwarded; or

(C) by the court of appeals.

(3) All other questions as to the form and content of the record must be presented to the court of appeals.

Rule 11. Forwarding the Record

(a) Appellant's Duty. An appellant filing a notice of appeal must comply with Rule 10(b) and must do whatever else is necessary to enable the clerk to assemble and forward the record. If there are multiple appeals from a judgment or order, the clerk must forward a single record.

(b) Duties of Reporter and District Clerk.

(1) Reporter's Duty to Prepare and File a Transcript. The reporter must prepare and file a transcript as follows:

(A) Upon receiving an order for a transcript, the reporter must enter at the foot of the order the date of its receipt and the expected completion date and send a copy, so endorsed, to the circuit clerk.

(B) If the transcript cannot be completed within 30 days of the reporter's receipt of the order, the reporter may request the circuit clerk to grant additional time to complete it. The clerk must note on the docket the action taken and notify the parties.

(C) When a transcript is complete, the reporter must file it with the district clerk and notify the circuit clerk of the filing.

(D) If the reporter fails to file the transcript on time, the circuit clerk must notify the district judge and do whatever else the court of appeals directs.

(2) District Clerk's Duty to Forward. When the record is complete, the district clerk must number the documents constituting the record and send them promptly to the circuit clerk together with a list of the documents correspondingly numbered and reasonably identified. Unless directed to do so by a party or the circuit clerk, the district clerk will not send to the court of appeals documents of unusual bulk or weight, physical exhibits other than documents, or other parts of the record designated for omission by local rule of the court of appeals. If the exhibits are unusually bulky or heavy, a party must arrange with the clerks in advance for their transportation and receipt.

(c) Retaining the Record Temporarily in the District Court for Use in Preparing the Appeal. The parties may stipulate, or the district court on motion may order, that the district clerk retain the record temporarily for the parties to use in preparing the papers on appeal. In that event the district clerk must certify to the circuit clerk that the record on appeal is complete. Upon receipt of the appellee's brief, or earlier if the court orders or the parties agree, the appellant must request the district clerk to forward the record.

(d) [Abrogated.]

(e) Retaining the Record by Court Order.

(1) The court of appeals may, by order or local rule, provide that a certified copy of the docket entries be forwarded instead of the entire record. But a party may at any time during the appeal request that designated parts of the record be forwarded.

(2) The district court may order the record or some part of it retained if the court needs it while the appeal is pending, subject, however, to call by the court of appeals.

(3) If part or all of the record is ordered retained, the district clerk must send to the court of appeals a copy of the order and the docket entries together with the parts of the original record allowed by the district court and copies of any parts of the record designated by the parties.

(f) Retaining Parts of the Record in the District Court by Stipulation of the Parties. The parties may agree by written stipulation filed in the district court that designated parts of the record be retained in the district court subject to call by the court of appeals or request by a party. The parts of the record so designated remain a part of the record on appeal.

(g) Record for a Preliminary Motion in the Court of Appeals. If, before the record is forwarded, a party makes any of the following motions in the court of appeals:

• for dismissal;

• for release;

• for a stay pending appeal;

• for additional security on the bond on appeal or on a supersedeas bond; or

• for any other intermediate order—

the district clerk must send the court of appeals any parts of the record designated by any party.

Rule 12. Docketing the Appeal; Filing a Representation Statement; Filing the Record

(a) Docketing the Appeal. Upon receiving the copy of the notice of appeal and the docket entries from the district clerk under Rule 3(d), the circuit clerk must docket the appeal under the title of the district-court action and must identify the appellant, adding the appellant's name if necessary.

(b) Filing a Representation Statement. Unless the court of appeals designates another time, the attorney who filed the notice of appeal must, within 10 days after filing the notice, file a statement with the circuit clerk naming the parties that the attorney represents on appeal.

(c) Filing the Record, Partial Record, or Certificate. Upon receiving the record, partial record, or district clerk's certificate as provided in Rule 11, the circuit clerk must file it and immediately notify all parties of the filing date.

TITLE III.   REVIEW OF A DECISION OF THE UNITED STATES TAX COURT

Rule 13.   Review of a Decision of the Tax Court

(a) How Obtained; Time for Filing Notice of Appeal.

(1) Review of a decision of the United States Tax Court is commenced by filing a notice of appeal with the Tax Court clerk within 90 days after the entry of the Tax Court's decision. At the time of filing, the appellant must furnish the clerk with enough copies of the notice to enable the clerk to comply with Rule 3(d). If one party files a timely notice of appeal, any other party may file a notice of appeal within 120 days after the Tax Court's decision is entered.

(2) If, under Tax Court rules, a party makes a timely motion to vacate or revise the Tax Court's decision, the time to file a notice of appeal runs from the entry of the order disposing of the motion or from the entry of a new decision, whichever is later.

(b) Notice of Appeal; How Filed. The notice of appeal may be filed either at the Tax Court clerk's office in the District of Columbia or by mail addressed to the clerk. If sent by mail the notice is considered filed on the postmark date, subject to § 7502 of the Internal Revenue Code, as amended, and the applicable regulations.

(c) Contents of the Notice of Appeal; Service; Effect of Filing and Service. Rule 3 prescribes the contents of a notice of appeal, the manner of service, and the effect of its filing and service. Form 2 in the Appendix of Forms is a suggested form of a notice of appeal.

(d) The Record on Appeal; Forwarding; Filing.

(1) An appeal from the Tax Court is governed by the parts of Rules 10, 11, and 12 regarding the record on appeal from a district court, the time and manner of forwarding and filing, and the docketing in the court of appeals. References in those rules and in Rule 3 to the district court and district clerk are to be read as referring to the Tax Court and its clerk.

(2) If an appeal from a Tax Court decision is taken to more than one court of appeals, the original record must be sent to the court named in the first notice of appeal filed. In an appeal to any other court of appeals, the appellant must apply to that other court to make provision for the record.

Rule 14. Applicability of Other Rules to the Review of a Tax Court Decision

All provisions of these rules, except Rules 4–9, 15–20, and 22–23, apply to the review of a Tax Court decision.

TITLE IV.   REVIEW OR ENFORCEMENT OF AN ORDER OF AN ADMINISTRATIVE AGENCY, BOARD, COMMISSION, OR OFFICER

Rule 15. Review or Enforcement of an Agency Order—How Obtained; Intervention

(a) Petition for Review; Joint Petition.

(1) Review of an agency order is commenced by filing, within the time prescribed by law, a petition for review with the clerk of a court of appeals authorized to review the agency order. If their interests make joinder practicable, two or more persons may join in a petition to the same court to review the same order.

(2) The petition must:

(A) name each party seeking review either in the caption or the body of the petition—using such terms as "et al.," "petitioners," or "respondents" does not effectively name the parties;

(B) name the agency as a respondent (even though not named in the petition, the United States is a respondent if required by statute); and

(C) specify the order or part thereof to be reviewed.

(3) Form 3 in the Appendix of Forms is a suggested form of a petition for review.

(4) In this rule "agency" includes an agency, board, commission, or officer; "petition for review" includes a petition to enjoin, suspend, modify, or otherwise review, or a notice of appeal, whichever form is indicated by the applicable statute.

(b) Application or Cross–Application to Enforce an Order; Answer; Default.

(1) An application to enforce an agency order must be filed with the clerk of a court of appeals authorized to enforce the order. If a petition is filed to review an agency order that the court may enforce, a party opposing the petition may file a cross-application for enforcement.

(2) Within 20 days after the application for enforcement is filed, the respondent must serve on the applicant an answer to the application and file it with the clerk. If the respondent fails to answer in time, the court will enter judgment for the relief requested.

(3) The application must contain a concise statement of the proceedings in which the order was entered, the facts upon which venue is based, and the relief requested.

(c) Service of the Petition or Application. The circuit clerk must serve a copy of the petition for review, or an application or cross-application to enforce an agency order, on each respondent as prescribed by Rule 3(d), unless a different manner of service is prescribed by statute. At the time of filing, the petitioner must:

(1) serve, or have served, a copy on each party admitted to participate in the agency proceedings, except for the respondents;

(2) file with the clerk a list of those so served; and

(3) give the clerk enough copies of the petition or application to serve each respondent.

(d) Intervention. Unless a statute provides another method, a person who wants to intervene in a proceeding under this rule must file a motion for leave to intervene with the circuit clerk and serve a copy on all parties. The motion—or other notice of intervention authorized by statute—must be filed within 30 days after the petition for review is filed and must contain a concise statement of the interest of the moving party and the grounds for intervention.

(e) Payment of Fees. When filing any separate or joint petition for review in a court of appeals, the petitioner must pay the circuit clerk all required fees.

Rule 15.1 Briefs and Oral Argument in a National Labor Relations Board Proceeding

In either an enforcement or a review proceeding, a party adverse to the National Labor Relations Board proceeds first on briefing and at oral argument, unless the court orders otherwise.

Rule 16.   The Record on Review or Enforcement

(a) Composition of the Record. The record on review or enforcement of an agency order consists of:

(1) the order involved;

(2) any findings or report on which it is based; and

(3) the pleadings, evidence, and other parts of the proceedings before the agency.

(b) Omissions From or Misstatements in the Record. The parties may at any time, by stipulation, supply any omission from the record or correct a misstatement, or the court may so direct. If necessary, the court may direct that a supplemental record be prepared and filed.

Rule 17.   Filing the Record

(a) Agency to File; Time for Filing; Notice of Filing. The agency must file the record with the circuit clerk within 40 days after being served with a petition for review, unless the statute authorizing review provides otherwise, or within 40 days after it files an application for enforcement unless the respondent fails to answer or the court orders otherwise. The court may shorten or extend the time to file the record. The clerk must notify all parties of the date when the record is filed.

(b) Filing—What Constitutes.

(1) The agency must file:

(A) the original or a certified copy of the entire record or parts designated by the parties; or

(B) a certified list adequately describing all documents, transcripts of testimony, exhibits, and other material constituting the record, or describing those parts designated by the parties.

(2) The parties may stipulate in writing that no record or certified list be filed. The date when the stipulation is filed with the circuit clerk is treated as the date when the record is filed.

(3) The agency must retain any portion of the record not filed with the clerk. All parts of the record retained by the agency are a part of the record on review for all purposes and, if the court or a party so requests, must be sent to the court regardless of any prior stipulation.

Rule 18.   Stay Pending Review

(a) Motion for a Stay.

(1) Initial Motion Before the Agency. A petitioner must ordinarily move first before the agency for a stay pending review of its decision or order.

(2) Motion in the Court of Appeals. A motion for a stay may be made to the court of appeals or one of its judges.

(A) The motion must:

(i) show that moving first before the agency would be impracticable; or

(ii) state that, a motion having been made, the agency denied the motion or failed to afford the relief requested and state any reasons given by the agency for its action.

(B) The motion must also include:

(i) the reasons for granting the relief requested and the facts relied on;

(ii) originals or copies of affidavits or other sworn statements supporting facts subject to dispute; and

(iii) relevant parts of the record.

(C) The moving party must give reasonable notice of the motion to all parties.

(D) The motion must be filed with the circuit clerk and normally will be considered by a panel of the court. But in an exceptional case in which time requirements make that procedure impracticable, the motion may be made to and considered by a single judge.

(b) Bond. The court may condition relief on the filing of a bond or other appropriate security.

Rule 19. Settlement of a Judgment Enforcing an Agency Order in Part

When the court files an opinion directing entry of judgment enforcing the agency's order in part, the agency must within 14 days file with the clerk and serve on each other party a proposed judgment conforming to the opinion. A party who disagrees with the agency's proposed judgment must within 7 days file with the clerk and serve the agency with a proposed judgment that the party believes conforms to the opinion. The court will settle the judgment and direct entry without further hearing or argument.

Rule 20. Applicability of Rules to the Review or Enforcement of an Agency Order

All provisions of these rules, except Rules 3–14 and 22–23, apply to the review or enforcement of an agency order. In these rules, "appellant" includes a petitioner or applicant, and "appellee" includes a respondent.

TITLE V.   EXTRAORDINARY WRITS

Rule 21. Writs of Mandamus and Prohibition, and Other Extraordinary Writs

(a) Mandamus or Prohibition to a Court: Petition, Filing, Service, and Docketing.

(1) A party petitioning for a writ of mandamus or prohibition directed to a court must file a petition with the circuit clerk with proof of service on all parties to the proceeding in the trial court. The party must also provide a copy to the trial-court judge. All parties to the proceeding in the trial court other than the petitioner are respondents for all purposes.

(2) (A) The petition must be titled "In re [name of petitioner]."

(B) The petition must state:

(i) the relief sought;

(ii) the issues presented;

(iii) the facts necessary to understand the issue presented by the petition; and

(iv) the reasons why the writ should issue.

(C) The petition must include a copy of any order or opinion or parts of the record that may be essential to understand the matters set forth in the petition.

(3) Upon receiving the prescribed docket fee, the clerk must docket the petition and submit it to the court.

(b) Denial; Order Directing Answer; Briefs; Precedence.

(1) The court may deny the petition without an answer. Otherwise, it must order the respondent, if any, to answer within a fixed time.

(2) The clerk must serve the order to respond on all persons directed to respond.

(3) Two or more respondents may answer jointly.

(4) The court of appeals may invite or order the trial-court judge to address the petition or may invite an amicus curiae to do so. The trial-court judge may request permission to address the petition but may not do so unless invited or ordered to do so by the court of appeals.

(5) If briefing or oral argument is required, the clerk must advise the parties, and when appropriate, the trial-court judge or amicus curiae.

(6) The proceeding must be given preference over ordinary civil cases.

(7) The circuit clerk must send a copy of the final disposition to the trial-court judge.

(c) Other Extraordinary Writs. An application for an extraordinary writ other than one provided for in Rule 21(a) must be made by filing a petition with the circuit clerk with proof of service on the respondents. Proceedings on the application must conform, so far as is practicable, to the procedures prescribed in Rule 21(a) and (b).

(d) Form of Papers; Number of Copies. All papers must conform to Rule 32(a)(1). An original and 3 copies must be filed unless the court requires the filing of a different number by local rule or by order in a particular case.

TITLE VI.   HABEAS CORPUS; PROCEEDINGS IN FORMA PAUPERIS

Rule 22.   Habeas Corpus and Section 2255 Proceedings

(a) Application for the Original Writ. An application for a writ of habeas corpus must be made to the appropriate district court. If made to a circuit judge, the application must be transferred to the appropriate district court. If a district court denies an application made or transferred to it, renewal of the application before a circuit judge is not permitted. The applicant may, under 28 U.S.C. § 2253, appeal to the court of appeals from the district court's order denying the application.

(b) Certificate of Appealability.

(1) In a habeas corpus proceeding in which the detention complained of arises from process issued by a state court, or in a 28 U.S.C. § 2255 proceeding, the applicant cannot take an appeal unless a circuit justice or a circuit or district judge issues a certificate of appealability under 28 U.S.C. § 2253(c). If an applicant files a notice of appeal, the district judge who rendered the judgment must either issue a certificate of appealability or state why a certificate should not issue. The district clerk must send the certificate or statement to the court of appeals with the notice of appeal and the file of the district-court proceedings. If the district judge has denied the certificate, the applicant may request a circuit judge to issue the certificate.

(2) A request addressed to the court of appeals may be considered by a circuit judge or judges, as the court prescribes. If no express request for a certificate is filed, the notice of appeal constitutes a request addressed to the judges of the court of appeals.

(3) A certificate of appealability is not required when a state or its representative or the United States or its representative appeals.

Rule 23.   Custody or Release of a Prisoner in a Habeas Corpus Proceeding

(a) Transfer of Custody Pending Review. Pending review of a decision in a habeas corpus proceeding commenced before a court, justice, or judge of the United States for the release of a prisoner, the person having custody of the prisoner must not transfer custody to another unless a transfer is directed in accordance with this rule. When, upon application, a custodian shows the need for a transfer, the court, justice, or judge rendering the decision under review may authorize the transfer and substitute the successor custodian as a party.

(b) Detention or Release Pending Review of Decision Not to Release. While a decision not to release a prisoner is under review, the court or judge rendering the decision, or the court of appeals, or the Supreme Court, or a judge or justice of either court, may order that the prisoner be:

(1) detained in the custody from which release is sought;

(2) detained in other appropriate custody; or

(3) released on personal recognizance, with or without surety.

(c) Release Pending Review of Decision Ordering Release. While a decision ordering the release of a prisoner is under review, the prisoner must—unless the court or judge rendering the decision, or the court of appeals, or the Supreme Court, or a judge or justice of either court orders otherwise—be released on personal recognizance, with or without surety.

(d) Modification of the Initial Order on Custody. An initial order governing the prisoner's custody or release, including any recognizance or surety, continues in effect pending review unless for special reasons shown to the court of appeals or the Supreme Court, or to a judge or justice of either court, the order is modified or an independent order regarding custody, release, or surety is issued.

Rule 24. Proceeding in Forma Pauperis

(a) Leave to Proceed in Forma Pauperis.

(1) Motion in the District Court. Except as stated in Rule 24(a)(3), a party to a district-court action who desires to appeal in forma pauperis must file a motion in the district court. The party must attach an affidavit that:

(A) shows in the detail prescribed by Form 4 of the Appendix of Forms, the party's inability to pay or to give security for fees and costs;

(B) claims an entitlement to redress; and

(C) states the issues that the party intends to present on appeal.

(2) Action on the Motion. If the district court grants the motion, the party may proceed on appeal without prepaying or giving security for fees and costs. If the district court denies the motion, it must state its reasons in writing.

(3) Prior Approval. A party who was permitted to proceed in forma pauperis in the district-court action, or who was determined to be financially unable to obtain an adequate defense in a criminal case, may proceed on appeal in forma pauperis without further authorization, unless the district court—before or after the notice of appeal is filed—certifies that the appeal is not taken in good faith or finds that the party is not otherwise entitled to proceed in forma pauperis. In that event, the district court must state in writing its reasons for the certification or finding.

(4) Notice of District Court's Denial. The district clerk must immediately notify the parties and the court of appeals when the district court does any of the following:

(A) denies a motion to proceed on appeal in forma pauperis;

(B) certifies that the appeal is not taken in good faith; or

(C) finds that the party is not otherwise entitled to proceed in forma pauperis.

(5) Motion in the Court of Appeals. A party may file a motion to proceed on appeal in forma pauperis in the court of appeals within 30 days after service of the notice prescribed in Rule 24(a)(4). The motion must include a copy of the affidavit filed in the district court and the district court's statement of reasons for its action. If no affidavit was filed in the district court, the party must include the affidavit prescribed by Rule 24(a)(1).

(b) Leave to Proceed in Forma Pauperis on Appeal or Review of an Administrative–Agency Proceeding. When an appeal or review of a proceeding before an administrative agency, board, commission, or officer (including for the purpose of this rule the United States Tax Court) proceeds directly in a court of appeals, a party may file in the court of appeals a motion for leave to proceed on appeal in forma pauperis with an affidavit prescribed by Rule 24(a)(1).

(c) Leave to Use Original Record. A party allowed to proceed on appeal in forma pauperis may request that the appeal be heard on the original record without reproducing any part.

TITLE VII.   GENERAL PROVISIONS

Rule 25.   Filing and Service

(a) Filing.

(1) Filing with the Clerk. A paper required or permitted to be filed in a court of appeals must be filed with the clerk.

(2) Filing: Method and Timeliness.

(A) In general. Filing may be accomplished by mail addressed to the clerk, but filing is not timely unless the clerk receives the papers within the time fixed for filing.

(B) A brief or appendix. A brief or appendix is timely filed, however, if on or before the last day for filing, it is:

(i) mailed to the clerk by First–Class Mail, or other class of mail that is at least as expeditious, postage prepaid; or

(ii) dispatched to a third-party commercial carrier for delivery to the clerk within 3 calendar days.

(C) Inmate filing. A paper filed by an inmate confined in an institution is timely if deposited in the institution's internal mailing system on or before the last day for filing. If an institution has a system designed for legal mail, the inmate must use that system to receive the benefit of this rule. Timely filing may be shown by a declaration in compliance with 28 U.S.C. § 1746 or by a notarized statement, either of which must set forth the date of deposit and state that first-class postage has been prepaid.

(D) Electronic filing. A court of appeals may by local rule permit papers to be filed, signed, or verified by electronic means that are consistent with technical standards, if any, that the Judicial Conference of the United States establishes. A paper filed by electronic means in compliance with a local rule constitutes a written paper for the purpose of applying these rules.

(3) Filing a Motion with a Judge. If a motion requests relief that may be granted by a single judge, the judge may permit the motion to be filed with the judge; the judge must note the filing date on the motion and give it to the clerk.

(4) Clerk's Refusal of Documents. The clerk must not refuse to accept for filing any paper presented for that purpose solely because it is not presented in proper form as required by these rules or by any local rule or practice.

(b) Service of All Papers Required. Unless a rule requires service by the clerk, a party must, at or before the time of filing a paper, serve a copy on the other parties to the appeal or review. Service on a party represented by counsel must be made on the party's counsel.

(c) Manner of Service. Service may be personal, by mail, or by third-party commercial carrier for delivery within 3 calendar days. When reasonable considering such factors as the immediacy of the relief sought, distance, and cost, service on a party must be by a manner at least as expeditious as the manner used to file the paper with the court. Personal service includes delivery of the copy to a responsible person at the office of counsel. Service by mail or by commercial carrier is complete on mailing or delivery to the carrier.

(d) Proof of Service.

(1) A paper presented for filing must contain either of the following:

(A) an acknowledgment of service by the person served; or

(B) proof of service consisting of a statement by the person who made service certifying:

(i) the date and manner of service;

(ii) the names of the persons served; and

(iii) their mailing addresses or the addresses of the places of delivery.

(2) When a brief or appendix is filed by mailing or dispatch in accordance with Rule 25(a)(2)(B), the proof of service must also state the date and manner by which the document was mailed or dispatched to the clerk.

(3) Proof of service may appear on or be affixed to the papers filed.

(e) Number of Copies. When these rules require the filing or furnishing of a number of copies, a court may require a different number by local rule or by order in a particular case.

Rule 26.   Computing and Extending Time

(a) Computing Time. The following rules apply in computing any period of time specified in these rules or in any local rule, court order, or applicable statute:

(1) Exclude the day of the act, event, or default that begins the period.

(2) Exclude intermediate Saturdays, Sundays, and legal holidays when the period is less than 7 days, unless stated in calendar days.

(3) Include the last day of the period unless it is a Saturday, Sunday, legal holiday, or—if the act to be done is filing a paper in court—a day on which the weather or other conditions make the clerk's office inaccessible.

(4) As used in this rule, "legal holiday" means New Year's Day, Martin Luther King, Jr.'s Birthday, Presidents' Day, Memorial Day, Independence Day, Labor Day, Columbus Day, Veterans' Day, Thanksgiving Day, Christmas Day, and any other day declared a holiday by the President, Congress, or the state in which is located either the district court that rendered the challenged judgment or order, or the circuit clerk's principal office.

(b) Extending Time. For good cause, the court may extend the time prescribed by these rules or by its order to perform any act, or may permit an act to be done after that time expires. But the court may not extend the time to file:

(1) a notice of appeal (except as authorized in Rule 4) or a petition for permission to appeal; or

(2) a notice of appeal from or a petition to enjoin, set aside, suspend, modify, enforce, or otherwise review an order of an administrative agency, board, commission, or officer of the United States, unless specifically authorized by law.

(c) Additional Time after Service. When a party is required or permitted to act within a prescribed period after a paper is served on that party, 3 calendar days are added to the prescribed period unless the paper is delivered on the date of service stated in the proof of service.

Rule 26.1   Corporate Disclosure Statement

(a) Who Must File. Any nongovernmental corporate party to a proceeding in a court of appeals must file a statement identifying all its parent corporations and listing any publicly held company that owns 10% or more of the party's stock.

(b) Time for Filing. A party must file the statement with the principal brief or upon filing a motion, response, petition, or answer in the court of appeals, whichever occurs first, unless a local rule requires earlier filing. Even if the statement has already been filed, the party's principal brief must include the statement before the table of contents.

(c) Number of Copies. If the statement is filed before the principal brief, the party must file an original and 3 copies unless the court requires a different number by local rule or by order in a particular case.

Rule 27.   Motions

(a) In General.

(1) Application for Relief. An application for an order or other relief is made by motion unless these rules prescribe another form. A motion must be in writing unless the court permits otherwise.

(2) Contents of a Motion.

(A) Grounds and relief sought. A motion must state with particularity the grounds for the motion, the relief sought, and the legal argument necessary to support it.

(B) Accompanying documents.

(i) Any affidavit or other paper necessary to support a motion must be served and filed with the motion.

(ii) An affidavit must contain only factual information, not legal argument.

(iii) A motion seeking substantive relief must include a copy of the trial court's opinion or agency's decision as a separate exhibit.

(C) Documents barred or not required.

(i) A separate brief supporting or responding to a motion must not be filed.

(ii) A notice of motion is not required.

(iii) A proposed order is not required.

(3) Response.

(A) Time to file. Any party may file a response to a motion; Rule 27(a)(2) governs its contents. The response must be filed within 10 days after service of the motion unless the court shortens or extends the time. A motion authorized by Rules 8, 9, 18, or 41 may be granted before the 10–day period runs only if the court gives reasonable notice to the parties that it intends to act sooner.

(B) Request for affirmative relief. A response may include a motion for affirmative relief. The time to respond to the new motion, and to reply to that response, are governed by Rule 27(a)(3)(A) and (a)(4). The title of the response must alert the court to the request for relief.

(4) Reply to Response. Any reply to a response must be filed within 7 days after service of the response. A reply must not present matters that do not relate to the response.

(b) Disposition of a Motion for a Procedural Order. The court may act on a motion for a procedural order—including a motion under Rule 26(b)—at any time without awaiting a response, and may, by rule or by order in a particular case, authorize its clerk to act on specified types of procedural motions. A party adversely affected by the court's, or the clerk's, action may file a motion to reconsider, vacate, or modify that action. Timely opposition filed after the motion is granted in whole or in part does not constitute a request to reconsider, vacate, or modify the disposition; a motion requesting that relief must be filed.

(c) Power of a Single Judge to Entertain a Motion. A circuit judge may act alone on any motion, but may not dismiss or otherwise determine an appeal or other proceeding. A court of appeals may provide by rule or by order in a particular case that only the court may act on any motion or class of motions. The court may review the action of a single judge.

(d) Form of Papers; Page Limits; and Number of Copies.

(1) Format.

(A) Reproduction. A motion, response, or reply may be reproduced by any process that yields a clear black image on light paper. The paper must be opaque and unglazed. Only one side of the paper may be used.

(B) Cover. A cover is not required but there must be a caption that includes the case number, the name of the court, the title of the case, and a brief descriptive title indicating the purpose of the motion and identifying the party or parties for whom it is filed.

(C) Binding. The document must be bound in any manner that is secure, does not obscure the text, and permits the document to lie reasonably flat when open.

(D) Paper size, line spacing, and margins. The document must be on 8½ by 11 inch paper. The text must be double-spaced, but quotations more than two lines long may be indented and single-spaced. Headings and footnotes may be single-spaced. Margins must be at least one inch on all four sides. Page numbers may be placed in the margins, but no text may appear there.

(2) Page Limits. A motion or a response to a motion must not exceed 20 pages, exclusive of the corporate disclosure statement and accompanying documents authorized by Rule 27(a)(2)(B), unless the court permits or directs otherwise. A reply to a response must not exceed 10 pages.

(3) Number of Copies. An original and 3 copies must be filed unless the court requires a different number by local rule or by order in a particular case.

(e) Oral Argument. A motion will be decided without oral argument unless the court orders otherwise.

Rule 28. Briefs

(a) Appellant's Brief. The appellant's brief must contain, under appropriate headings and in the order indicated:

(1) a corporate disclosure statement if required by Rule 26.1;

(2) a table of contents, with page references;

(3) a table of authorities—cases (alphabetically arranged), statutes, and other authorities—with references to the pages of the brief where they are cited;

(4) a jurisdictional statement, including:

(A) the basis for the district court's or agency's subject-matter jurisdiction, with citations to applicable statutory provisions and stating relevant facts establishing jurisdiction;

(B) the basis for the court of appeals' jurisdiction, with citations to applicable statutory provisions and stating relevant facts establishing jurisdiction;

(C) the filing dates establishing the timeliness of the appeal or petition for review; and

(D) an assertion that the appeal is from a final order or judgment that disposes of all parties' claims, or information establishing the court of appeals' jurisdiction on some other basis;

(5) a statement of the issues presented for review;

(6) a statement of the case briefly indicating the nature of the case, the course of proceedings, and the disposition below;

(7) a statement of facts relevant to the issues submitted for review with appropriate references to the record (see Rule 28(e));

(8) a summary of the argument, which must contain a succinct, clear, and accurate statement of the arguments made in the body of the brief, and which must not merely repeat the argument headings;

(9) the argument, which must contain:

(A) appellant's contentions and the reasons for them, with citations to the authorities and parts of the record on which the appellant relies; and

(B) for each issue, a concise statement of the applicable standard of review (which may appear in the discussion of the issue or under a separate heading placed before the discussion of the issues);

(10) a short conclusion stating the precise relief sought; and

(11) the certificate of compliance, if required by Rule 32(a)(7).

(b) Appellee's Brief. The appellee's brief must conform to the requirements of Rule 28(a)(1)–(9) and (11), except that none of the following need appear unless the appellee is dissatisfied with the appellant's statement:

(1) the jurisdictional statement;

(2) the statement of the issues;

(3) the statement of the case;

(4) the statement of the facts; and

(5) the statement of the standard of review.

(c) Reply Brief. The appellant may file a brief in reply to the appellee's brief. An appellee who has cross-appealed may file a brief in reply to the appellant's response to the issues presented by the cross-appeal. Unless the court permits, no further briefs may be filed. A reply brief must contain a table of contents, with page references, and a table of authorities—cases (alphabetically arranged), statutes, and other authorities—with references to the pages of the reply brief where they are cited.

(d) References to Parties. In briefs and at oral argument, counsel should minimize use of the terms "appellant" and "appellee." To make briefs clear, counsel should use the parties' actual names or the designations used in the lower court or agency proceeding, or such descriptive terms as "the employee," "the injured person," "the taxpayer," "the ship," "the stevedore."

(e) References to the Record. References to the parts of the record contained in the appendix filed with the appellant's brief must be to the pages of the appendix. If the appendix is prepared after the briefs are filed, a party referring to the record must follow one of the methods detailed in Rule 30(c). If the original record is used under Rule 30(f) and is not consecutively paginated, or if the brief refers to an unreproduced part of the record, any reference must be to the page of the original document. For example:

• Answer p. 7;

• Motion for Judgment p. 2;

• Transcript p. 231.

Only clear abbreviations may be used. A party referring to evidence whose admissibility is in controversy must cite the pages of the appendix or of the transcript at which the evidence was identified, offered, and received or rejected.

(f) Reproduction of Statutes, Rules, Regulations, etc. If the court's determination of the issues presented requires the study of statutes, rules, regulations, etc., the relevant parts must be set out in the brief or in an addendum at the end, or may be supplied to the court in pamphlet form.

(g) [Reserved]

(h) Briefs in a Case Involving a Cross–Appeal. If a cross-appeal is filed, the party who files a notice of appeal first is the appellant for the purposes of this rule and Rules 30, 31, and 34. If notices are filed on the same day, the plaintiff in the proceeding below is the appellant. These designations may be modified by agreement of the parties or by court order. With respect to appellee's cross-appeal and response to appellant's brief, appellee's brief must conform to the requirements of Rule 28(a)(1)–(11). But an appellee who is satisfied with appellant's statement need not include a statement of the case or of the facts.

(i) Briefs in a Case Involving Multiple Appellants or Appellees. In a case involving more than one appellant or appellee, including consolidated cases, any number of appellants or appellees may join in a brief, and any party may adopt by reference a part of another's brief. Parties may also join in reply briefs.

(j) Citation of Supplemental Authorities. If pertinent and significant authorities come to a party's attention after the party's brief has been filed—or after oral argument but before decision—a party may promptly advise the circuit clerk by letter, with a copy to all other parties, setting forth the citations. The letter must state without argument the reasons for the supplemental citations, referring either to the page of the brief or to a point argued orally. Any response must be made promptly and must be similarly limited.

Rule 29.   Brief of an Amicus Curiae

(a) When Permitted. The United States or its officer or agency, or a State, Territory, Commonwealth, or the District of Columbia may file an amicus-curiae brief without the consent of the parties or leave of court. Any other amicus curiae may file a brief only by leave of court or if the brief states that all parties have consented to its filing.

(b) Motion for Leave to File. The motion must be accompanied by the proposed brief and state:

(1) the movant's interest; and

(2) the reason why an amicus brief is desirable and why the matters asserted are relevant to the disposition of the case.

(c) Contents and Form. An amicus brief must comply with Rule 32. In addition to the requirements of Rule 32, the cover must identify the party or parties supported and indicate whether the brief supports affirmance or reversal. If an amicus curiae is a corporation, the brief must include a disclosure statement like that required of parties by Rule

26.1. An amicus brief need not comply with Rule 28, but must include the following:

(1) a table of contents, with page references;

(2) a table of authorities—cases (alphabetically arranged), statutes and other authorities—with references to the pages of the brief where they are cited;

(3) a concise statement of the identity of the amicus curiae, its interest in the case, and the source of its authority to file;

(4) an argument, which may be preceded by a summary and which need not include a statement of the applicable standard of review; and

(5) a certificate of compliance, if required by Rule 32(a)(7).

(d) Length. Except by the court's permission, an amicus brief may be no more than one-half the maximum length authorized by these rules for a party's principal brief. If the court grants a party permission to file a longer brief, that extension does not affect the length of an amicus brief.

(e) Time for Filing. An amicus curiae must file its brief, accompanied by a motion for filing when necessary, no later than 7 days after the principal brief of the party being supported is filed. An amicus curiae that does not support either party must file its brief no later than 7 days after the appellant's or petitioner's principal brief is filed. A court may grant leave for later filing, specifying the time within which an opposing party may answer.

(f) Reply Brief. Except by the court's permission, an amicus curiae may not file a reply brief.

(g) Oral Argument. An amicus curiae may participate in oral argument only with the court's permission.

Rule 30. Appendix to the Briefs

(a) Appellant's Responsibility.

(1) Contents of the Appendix. The appellant must prepare and file an appendix to the briefs containing:

(A) the relevant docket entries in the proceeding below;

(B) the relevant portions of the pleadings, charge, findings, or opinion;

(C) the judgment, order, or decision in question; and

(D) other parts of the record to which the parties wish to direct the court's attention.

(2) Excluded Material. Memoranda of law in the district court should not be included in the appendix unless they have independent relevance. Parts of the record may be relied on by the court or the parties even though not included in the appendix.

(3) Time to File; Number of Copies. Unless filing is deferred under Rule 30(c), the appellant must file 10 copies of the appendix with the brief and must serve one copy on counsel for each party separately represented. An unrepresented party proceeding in forma pauperis must file 4 legible copies with the clerk, and one copy must be served on counsel for each separately represented party. The court may by local rule or by order in a particular case require the filing or service of a different number.

(b) All Parties' Responsibilities.

(1) Determining the Contents of the Appendix. The parties are encouraged to agree on the contents of the appendix. In the absence of an agreement, the appellant must, within 10 days after the record is filed, serve on the appellee a designation of the parts of the record the appellant intends to include in the appendix and a statement of the issues the appellant intends to present for review. The appellee may, within 10 days after receiving the designation, serve on the appellant a designation of additional parts to which it wishes to direct the court's attention. The appellant must include the designated parts in the appendix. The parties must not engage in unnecessary designation of parts of the record, because the entire record is available to the court. This paragraph applies also to a cross-appellant and a cross-appellee.

(2) Costs of Appendix. Unless the parties agree otherwise, the appellant must pay the cost of the appendix. If the appellant considers parts of the record designated by the appellee to be unnecessary, the appellant may advise the appellee, who must then advance the cost of including those parts. The cost of the appendix is a taxable cost. But if any party causes unnecessary parts of the record to be included in the appendix, the court may impose the cost of those parts on that party. Each circuit must, by local rule, provide for sanctions against attorneys who unreasonably and vexatiously increase litigation costs by including unnecessary material in the appendix.

(c) Deferred Appendix.

(1) Deferral Until After Briefs Are Filed. The court may provide by rule for classes of cases or by order in a particular case that preparation of the appendix may be deferred until after the briefs have been filed and that the appendix may be filed 21 days after the appellee's brief is served. Even though the filing of the appendix may be deferred, Rule 30(b) applies; except that a party must designate the parts of the record it wants included in the appendix when it serves its brief, and need not include a statement of the issues presented.

(2) References to the Record.

(A) If the deferred appendix is used, the parties may cite in their briefs the pertinent pages of the record. When the appendix is prepared, the record pages cited in the briefs must be indicated by inserting record page numbers, in brackets, at places in the appendix where those pages of the record appear.

(B) A party who wants to refer directly to pages of the appendix may serve and file copies of the brief within the time required by Rule 31(a), containing appropriate references to pertinent pages of the record. In that event, within 14 days after the appendix is filed, the party must serve and file copies of the brief, containing references to the pages of the appendix in place of or in addition to the references to the pertinent pages of the record. Except for the correction of typographical errors, no other changes may be made to the brief.

(d) Format of the Appendix. The appendix must begin with a table of contents identifying the page at which each part begins. The relevant docket entries must follow the table of contents. Other parts of the record must follow chronologically. When pages from the transcript of proceedings are placed in the appendix, the transcript page numbers must be shown in brackets immediately before the included pages. Omissions in the text of papers or of the transcript must be indicated by asterisks. Immaterial formal matters (captions, subscriptions, acknowledgments, etc.) should be omitted.

(e) Reproduction of Exhibits. Exhibits designated for inclusion in the appendix may be reproduced in a separate volume, or volumes, suitably indexed. Four copies must be filed with the appendix, and one copy must be served on counsel for each separately represented party. If a transcript of a proceeding before an administrative agency, board, commission, or officer was used in a district-court action and has been designated for inclusion in the appendix, the transcript must be placed in the appendix as an exhibit.

(f) Appeal on the Original Record Without an Appendix. The court may, either by rule for all cases or classes of cases or by order in a particular case, dispense with the appendix and permit an appeal to proceed on the original record with any copies of the record, or relevant parts, that the court may order the parties to file.

Rule 31. Serving and Filing Briefs

(a) Time to Serve and File a Brief.

(1) The appellant must serve and file a brief within 40 days after the record is filed. The appellee must serve and file a brief within 30 days after the appellant's brief is served. The appellant may serve and file a reply brief within 14 days after service of the appellee's brief but a reply brief must be filed at least 3 days before argument, unless the court, for good cause, allows a later filing.

(2) A court of appeals that routinely considers cases on the merits promptly after the briefs are filed may shorten the time to

serve and file briefs, either by local rule or by order in a particular case.

(b) Number of Copies. Twenty-five copies of each brief must be filed with the clerk and 2 copies must be served on counsel for each separately represented party. An unrepresented party proceeding in forma pauperis must file 4 legible copies with the clerk, and one copy must be served on counsel for each separately represented party. The court may by local rule or by order in a particular case require the filing or service of a different number.

(c) Consequence of Failure to File. If an appellant fails to file a brief within the time provided by this rule, or within an extended time, an appellee may move to dismiss the appeal. An appellee who fails to file a brief will not be heard at oral argument unless the court grants permission.

Rule 32.   Form of Briefs, Appendices, and Other Papers

(a) Form of a Brief.

(1) Reproduction.

(A) A brief may be reproduced by any process that yields a clear black image on light paper. The paper must be opaque and unglazed. Only one side of the paper may be used.

(B) Text must be reproduced with a clarity that equals or exceeds the output of a laser printer.

(C) Photographs, illustrations, and tables may be reproduced by any method that results in a good copy of the original; a glossy finish is acceptable if the original is glossy.

(2) Cover. Except for filings by unrepresented parties, the cover of the appellant's brief must be blue; the appellee's, red; an intervenor's or amicus curiae's, green; and any reply brief, gray. The front cover of a brief must contain:

(A) the number of the case centered at the top;

(B) the name of the court;

(C) the title of the case (see Rule 12(a));

(D) the nature of the proceeding (e.g., Appeal, Petition for Review) and the name of the court, agency, or board below;

(E) the title of the brief, identifying the party or parties for whom the brief is filed; and

(F) the name, office address, and telephone number of counsel representing the party for whom the brief is filed.

(3) Binding. The brief must be bound in any manner that is secure, does not obscure the text, and permits the brief to lie reasonably flat when open.

(4) Paper Size, Line Spacing, and Margins. The brief must be on 8½ by 11 inch paper. The text must be double-spaced, but quotations more than two lines long may be indented and single-spaced. Headings and footnotes may be single-spaced. Margins must be at least one inch on all four sides. Page numbers may be placed in the margins, but no text may appear there.

(5) Typeface. Either a proportionally spaced or a monospaced face may be used.

(A) A proportionally spaced face must include serifs, but sans-serif type may be used in headings and captions. A proportionally spaced face must be 14–point or larger.

(B) A monospaced face may not contain more than 10½ characters per inch.

(6) Type Styles. A brief must be set in a plain, roman style, although italics or boldface may be used for emphasis. Case names must be italicized or underlined.

(7) Length.

(A) Page limitation. A principal brief may not exceed 30 pages, or a reply brief 15 pages, unless it complies with Rule 32(a)(7)(B) and (C).

(B) Type-volume limitation.

(i) A principal brief is acceptable if:

• it contains no more than 14,000 words; or

• it uses a monospaced face and contains no more than 1,300 lines of text.

(ii) A reply brief is acceptable if it contains no more than half of the type volume specified in Rule 32(a)(7)(B)(i).

(iii) Headings, footnotes, and quotations count toward the word and line limitations. The corporate disclosure statement, table of contents, table of citations, statement with respect to oral argument, any addendum containing statutes, rules or regulations, and any certificates of counsel do not count toward the limitation.

(C) Certificate of compliance. A brief submitted under Rule 32(a)(7)(B) must include a certificate by the attorney, or an unrepresented party, that the brief complies with the type-volume limitation. The person preparing the certificate may rely on the word or line count of the word-processing system used to prepare the brief. The certificate must state either:

(i) the number of words in the brief; or

(ii) the number of lines of monospaced type in the brief.

(b) Form of an Appendix. An appendix must comply with Rule 32(a)(1), (2), (3), and (4), with the following exceptions:

(1) The cover of a separately bound appendix must be white.

(2) An appendix may include a legible photocopy of any document found in the record or of a printed judicial or agency decision.

(3) When necessary to facilitate inclusion of odd-sized documents such as technical drawings, an appendix may be a size other than 8½ by 11 inches, and need not lie reasonably flat when opened.

(c) Form of Other Papers.

(1) **Motion.** The form of a motion is governed by Rule 27(d).

(2) **Other Papers.** Any other paper, including a petition for rehearing and a petition for rehearing en banc, and any response to such a petition, must be reproduced in the manner prescribed by Rule 32(a), with the following exceptions:

(A) a cover is not necessary if the caption and signature page of the paper together contain the information required by Rule 32(a)(2); and

(B) Rule 32(a)(7) does not apply.

(d) Local Variation. Every court of appeals must accept documents that comply with the form requirements of this rule. By local rule or order in a particular case a court of appeals may accept documents that do not meet all of the form requirements of this rule.

Rule 33.   Appeal Conferences

The court may direct the attorneys—and, when appropriate, the parties—to participate in one or more conferences to address any matter that may aid in disposing of the proceedings, including simplifying the issues and discussing settlement. A judge or other person designated by the court may preside over the conference, which may be conducted in person or by telephone. Before a settlement conference, the attorneys must consult with their clients and obtain as much authority as feasible to settle the case. The court may, as a result of the conference, enter an order controlling the course of the proceedings or implementing any settlement agreement.

Rule 34.   Oral Argument

(a) In General.

(1) **Party's Statement.** Any party may file, or a court may require by local rule, a statement explaining why oral argument should, or need not, be permitted.

(2) **Standards.** Oral argument must be allowed in every case unless a panel of three judges who have examined the briefs and record unanimously agrees that oral argument is unnecessary for any of the following reasons:

(A) the appeal is frivolous;

(B) the dispositive issue or issues have been authoritatively decided; or

(C) the facts and legal arguments are adequately presented in the briefs and record, and the decisional process would not be significantly aided by oral argument.

(b) Notice of Argument; Postponement. The clerk must advise all parties whether oral argument will be scheduled, and, if so, the date, time, and place for it, and the time allowed for each side. A motion to postpone the argument or to allow longer argument must be filed reasonably in advance of the hearing date.

(c) Order and Contents of Argument. The appellant opens and concludes the argument. Counsel must not read at length from briefs, records, or authorities.

(d) Cross–Appeals and Separate Appeals. If there is a cross-appeal, Rule 28(h) determines which party is the appellant and which is the appellee for purposes of oral argument. Unless the court directs otherwise, a cross-appeal or separate appeal must be argued when the initial appeal is argued. Separate parties should avoid duplicative argument.

(e) Nonappearance of a Party. If the appellee fails to appear for argument, the court must hear appellant's argument. If the appellant fails to appear for argument, the court may hear the appellee's argument. If neither party appears, the case will be decided on the briefs, unless the court orders otherwise.

(f) Submission on Briefs. The parties may agree to submit a case for decision on the briefs, but the court may direct that the case be argued.

(g) Use of Physical Exhibits at Argument; Removal. Counsel intending to use physical exhibits other than documents at the argument must arrange to place them in the courtroom on the day of the argument before the court convenes. After the argument, counsel must remove the exhibits from the courtroom, unless the court directs otherwise. The clerk may destroy or dispose of the exhibits if counsel does not reclaim them within a reasonable time after the clerk gives notice to remove them.

Rule 35.   En Banc Determination

(a) When Hearing or Rehearing En Banc May Be Ordered. A majority of the circuit judges who are in regular active service may order that an appeal or other proceeding be heard or reheard by the court of appeals en banc. An en banc hearing or rehearing is not favored and ordinarily will not be ordered unless:

(1) en banc consideration is necessary to secure or maintain uniformity of the court's decisions; or

(2) the proceeding involves a question of exceptional importance.

(b) Petition for Hearing or Rehearing En Banc. A party may petition for a hearing or rehearing en banc.

(1) The petition must begin with a statement that either:

(A) the panel decision conflicts with a decision of the United States Supreme Court or of the court to which the petition is addressed (with citation to the conflicting case or cases) and consideration by the full court is therefore necessary to secure and maintain uniformity of the court's decisions; or

(B) the proceeding involves one or more questions of exceptional importance, each of which must be concisely stated; for example, a petition may assert that a proceeding presents a question of exceptional importance if it involves an issue on which the panel decision conflicts with the authoritative decisions of every other United States Court of Appeals that has addressed the issue.

(2) Except by the court's permission, a petition for an en banc hearing or rehearing must not exceed 15 pages, excluding material not counted under Rule 32.

(3) For purposes of the page limit in Rule 35(b)(2), if a party files both a petition for panel rehearing and a petition for rehearing en banc, they are considered a single document even if they are filed separately, unless separate filing is required by local rule.

(c) Time for Petition for Hearing or Rehearing En Banc. A petition that an appeal be heard initially en banc must be filed by the date when the appellee's brief is due. A petition for a rehearing en banc must be filed within the time prescribed by Rule 40 for filing a petition for rehearing.

(d) Number of Copies. The number of copies to be filed must be prescribed by local rule and may be altered by order in a particular case.

(e) Response. No response may be filed to a petition for an en banc consideration unless the court orders a response.

(f) Call for a Vote. A vote need not be taken to determine whether the case will be heard or reheard en banc unless a judge calls for a vote.

Rule 36. Entry of Judgment; Notice

(a) Entry. A judgment is entered when it is noted on the docket. The clerk must prepare, sign, and enter the judgment:

(1) after receiving the court's opinion—but if settlement of the judgment's form is required, after final settlement; or

(2) if a judgment is rendered without an opinion, as the court instructs.

(b) Notice. On the date when judgment is entered, the clerk must mail to all parties a copy of the opinion—or the judgment, if no opinion was written—and a notice of the date when the judgment was entered.

Rule 37. Interest on Judgment

(a) When the Court Affirms. Unless the law provides otherwise, if a money judgment in a civil case is affirmed, whatever interest is allowed by law is payable from the date when the district court's judgment was entered.

(b) When the Court Reverses. If the court modifies or reverses a judgment with a direction that a money judgment be entered in the district court, the mandate must contain instructions about the allowance of interest.

Rule 38. Frivolous Appeal—Damages and Costs

If a court of appeals determines that an appeal is frivolous, it may, after a separately filed motion or notice from the court and reasonable opportunity to respond, award just damages and single or double costs to the appellee.

Rule 39. Costs

(a) Against Whom Assessed. The following rules apply unless the law provides or the court orders otherwise:

(1) if an appeal is dismissed, costs are taxed against the appellant, unless the parties agree otherwise;

(2) if a judgment is affirmed, costs are taxed against the appellant;

(3) if a judgment is reversed, costs are taxed against the appellee;

(4) if a judgment is affirmed in part, reversed in part, modified, or vacated, costs are taxed only as the court orders.

(b) Costs For and Against the United States. Costs for or against the United States, its agency, or officer will be assessed under Rule 39(a) only if authorized by law.

(c) Costs of Copies. Each court of appeals must, by local rule, fix the maximum rate for taxing the cost of producing necessary copies of a brief or appendix, or copies of records authorized by Rule 30(f). The rate must not exceed that generally charged for such work in the area where the clerk's office is located and should encourage economical methods of copying.

(d) Bill of Costs: Objections; Insertion in Mandate.

(1) A party who wants costs taxed must—within 14 days after entry of judgment—file with the circuit clerk, with proof of service, an itemized and verified bill of costs.

(2) Objections must be filed within 10 days after service of the bill of costs, unless the court extends the time.

(3) The clerk must prepare and certify an itemized statement of costs for insertion in the mandate, but issuance of the mandate must not be delayed for taxing costs. If the mandate issues before costs are finally determined, the district clerk must—upon the circuit clerk's request—add the statement of costs, or any amendment of it, to the mandate.

(e) Costs on Appeal Taxable in the District Court. The following costs on appeal are taxable in the district court for the benefit of the party entitled to costs under this rule:

(1) the preparation and transmission of the record;

(2) the reporter's transcript, if needed to determine the appeal;

(3) premiums paid for a supersedeas bond or other bond to preserve rights pending appeal; and

(4) the fee for filing the notice of appeal.

Rule 40.   Petition for Panel Rehearing

(a) Time to File; Contents; Answer; Action by the Court if Granted.

(1) Time. Unless the time is shortened or extended by order or local rule, a petition for panel rehearing may be filed within 14 days after entry of judgment. But in a civil case, if the United States or its officer or agency is a party, the time within which any party may seek rehearing is 45 days after entry of judgment, unless an order shortens or extends the time.

(2) Contents. The petition must state with particularity each point of law or fact that the petitioner believes the court has overlooked or misapprehended and must argue in support of the petition. Oral argument is not permitted.

(3) Answer. Unless the court requests, no answer to a petition for panel rehearing is permitted. But ordinarily rehearing will not be granted in the absence of such a request.

(4) Action by the Court. If a petition for panel rehearing is granted, the court may do any of the following:

(A) make a final disposition of the case without reargument;

(B) restore the case to the calendar for reargument or resubmission; or

(C) issue any other appropriate order.

(b) Form of Petition; Length. The petition must comply in form with Rule 32. Copies must be served and filed as Rule 31 prescribes. Unless the court permits or a local rule provides otherwise, a petition for panel rehearing must not exceed 15 pages.

Rule 41. Mandate: Contents; Issuance and Effective Date; Stay

(a) Contents. Unless the court directs that a formal mandate issue, the mandate consists of a certified copy of the judgment, a copy of the court's opinion, if any, and any direction about costs.

(b) When Issued. The court's mandate must issue 7 days after the time to file a petition for rehearing expires, or 7 days after entry of an order denying a timely petition for panel rehearing, rehearing en banc, or motion for stay of mandate, whichever is later. The court may shorten or extend the time.

(c) Effective Date. The mandate is effective when issued.

(d) Staying the Mandate.

(1) On Petition for Rehearing or Motion. The timely filing of a petition for panel rehearing, petition for rehearing en banc, or motion for stay of mandate, stays the mandate until disposition of the petition or motion, unless the court orders otherwise.

(2) Pending Petition for Certiorari.

(A) A party may move to stay the mandate pending the filing of a petition for a writ of certiorari in the Supreme Court. The motion must be served on all parties and must show that the certiorari petition would present a substantial question and that there is good cause for a stay.

(B) The stay must not exceed 90 days, unless the period is extended for good cause or unless the party who obtained the stay files a petition for the writ and so notifies the circuit clerk in writing within the period of the stay. In that case, the stay continues until the Supreme Court's final disposition.

(C) The court may require a bond or other security as a condition to granting or continuing a stay of the mandate.

(D) The court of appeals must issue the mandate immediately when a copy of a Supreme Court order denying the petition for writ of certiorari is filed.

Rule 42. Voluntary Dismissal

(a) Dismissal in the District Court. Before an appeal has been docketed by the circuit clerk, the district court may dismiss the appeal on the filing of a stipulation signed by all parties or on the appellant's motion with notice to all parties.

(b) Dismissal in the Court of Appeals. The circuit clerk may dismiss a docketed appeal if the parties file a signed dismissal agreement specifying how costs are to be paid and pay any fees that are due. But no mandate or other process may issue without a court order. An appeal may be dismissed on the appellant's motion on terms agreed to by the parties or fixed by the court.

Rule 43. Substitution of Parties

(a) Death of a Party.

(1) After Notice of Appeal Is Filed. If a party dies after a notice of appeal has been filed or while a proceeding is pending in the court of appeals, the decedent's personal representative may be substituted as a party on motion filed with the circuit clerk by the representative or by any party. A party's motion must be served on the representative in accordance with Rule 25. If the decedent has no representative, any party may suggest the death on the record, and the court of appeals may then direct appropriate proceedings.

(2) Before Notice of Appeal Is Filed—Potential Appellant. If a party entitled to appeal dies before filing a notice of appeal, the decedent's personal representative—or, if there is no personal representative, the decedent's attorney of record—may file a notice of appeal within the time prescribed by these rules. After the notice of appeal is filed, substitution must be in accordance with Rule 43(a)(1).

(3) Before Notice of Appeal Is Filed—Potential Appellee. If a party against whom an appeal may be taken dies after entry of a judgment or order in the district court, but before a notice of appeal is filed, an appellant may proceed as if the death had not occurred. After the notice of appeal is filed, substitution must be in accordance with Rule 43(a)(1).

(b) Substitution for a Reason Other Than Death. If a party needs to be substituted for any reason other than death, the procedure prescribed in Rule 43(a) applies.

(c) Public Officer: Identification; Substitution.

(1) Identification of Party. A public officer who is a party to an appeal or other proceeding in an official capacity may be described as a party by the public officer's official title rather than by name. But the court may require the public officer's name to be added.

(2) Automatic Substitution of Officeholder. When a public officer who is a party to an appeal or other proceeding in an official capacity dies, resigns, or otherwise ceases to hold office, the action does not abate. The public officer's successor is automatically substituted as a party. Proceedings following the substitution are to be in the name of the substituted party, but any misnomer that does not affect the substantial rights of the parties may be disregarded. An order of substitution may be entered at any time, but failure to enter an order does not affect the substitution.

Rule 44. Case Involving a Constitutional Question When the United States Is Not a Party

If a party questions the constitutionality of an Act of Congress in a proceeding in which the United States or its agency, officer, or employee is not a party in an official capacity, the questioning party must give written notice to the circuit clerk immediately upon the filing of the record or as soon as the question is raised in the court of appeals. The clerk must then certify that fact to the Attorney General.

Rule 45. Clerk's Duties

(a) General Provisions.

(1) Qualifications. The circuit clerk must take the oath and post any bond required by law. Neither the clerk nor any deputy clerk may practice as an attorney or counselor in any court while in office.

(2) When Court Is Open. The court of appeals is always open for filing any paper, issuing and returning process, making a motion, and entering an order. The clerk's office with the clerk or a deputy in attendance must be open during business hours on all days except Saturdays, Sundays, and legal holidays. A court may provide by local rule or by order that the clerk's office be open for specified hours on Saturdays or on legal holidays other than New Year's Day, Martin Luther King, Jr.'s Birthday, Presidents' Day, Memorial Day, Independence Day, Labor Day, Columbus Day, Veterans' Day, Thanksgiving Day, and Christmas Day.

(b) Records.

(1) The Docket. The circuit clerk must maintain a docket and an index of all docketed cases in the manner prescribed by the Director of the Administrative Office of the United States Courts. The clerk must record all papers filed with the clerk and all process, orders, and judgments.

(2) Calendar. Under the court's direction, the clerk must prepare a calendar of cases awaiting argument. In placing cases on the calendar for argument, the clerk must give preference to appeals in criminal cases and to other proceedings and appeals entitled to preference by law.

(3) Other Records. The clerk must keep other books and records required by the Director of the Administrative Office of the United States Courts, with the approval of the Judicial Conference of the United States, or by the court.

(c) Notice of an Order or Judgment. Upon the entry of an order or judgment, the circuit clerk must immediately serve by mail a notice of entry on each party to the proceeding, with a copy of any opinion, and must note the mailing on the docket. Service on a party represented by counsel must be made on counsel.

(d) Custody of Records and Papers. The circuit clerk has custody of the court's records and papers. Unless the court orders or instructs otherwise, the clerk must not permit an original record or paper to be taken from the clerk's office. Upon disposition of the case, original papers constituting the record on appeal or review must be returned to the court or agency from which they were received. The clerk must preserve a copy of any brief, appendix, or other paper that has been filed.

Rule 46. Attorneys

(a) Admission to the Bar.

(1) Eligibility. An attorney is eligible for admission to the bar of a court of appeals if that attorney is of good moral and professional character and is admitted to practice before the Supreme Court of the United States, the highest court of a state, another United States court of appeals, or a United States district court (including the district courts for Guam, the Northern Mariana Islands, and the Virgin Islands).

(2) Application. An applicant must file an application for admission, on a form approved by the court that contains the applicant's personal statement showing eligibility for membership. The applicant must subscribe to the following oath or affirmation:

> "I, _____, do solemnly swear [or affirm] that I will conduct myself as an attorney and counselor of this court, uprightly and according to law; and that I will support the Constitution of the United States."

(3) Admission Procedures. On written or oral motion of a member of the court's bar, the court will act on the application. An applicant may be admitted by oral motion in open court. But, unless the court orders otherwise, an applicant need not appear before the court to be admitted. Upon admission, an applicant must pay the clerk the fee prescribed by local rule or court order.

(b) Suspension or Disbarment.

(1) Standard. A member of the court's bar is subject to suspension or disbarment by the court if the member:

(A) has been suspended or disbarred from practice in any other court; or

(B) is guilty of conduct unbecoming a member of the court's bar.

(2) Procedure. The member must be given an opportunity to show good cause, within the time prescribed by the court, why the member should not be suspended or disbarred.

(3) Order. The court must enter an appropriate order after the member responds and a hearing is held, if requested, or after the time prescribed for a response expires, if no response is made.

(c) Discipline. A court of appeals may discipline an attorney who practices before it for conduct unbecoming a member of the bar or for failure to comply with any court rule. First, however, the court must

afford the attorney reasonable notice, an opportunity to show cause to the contrary, and, if requested, a hearing.

Rule 47. Local Rules by Courts of Appeals

(a) Local Rules.

(1) Each court of appeals acting by a majority of its judges in regular active service may, after giving appropriate public notice and opportunity for comment, make and amend rules governing its practice. A generally applicable direction to parties or lawyers regarding practice before a court must be in a local rule rather than an internal operating procedure or standing order. A local rule must be consistent with—but not duplicative of—Acts of Congress and rules adopted under 28 U.S.C. § 2072 and must conform to any uniform numbering system prescribed by the Judicial Conference of the United States. Each circuit clerk must send the Administrative Office of the United States Courts a copy of each local rule and internal operating procedure when it is promulgated or amended.

(2) A local rule imposing a requirement of form must not be enforced in a manner that causes a party to lose rights because of a nonwillful failure to comply with the requirement.

(b) Procedure When There Is No Controlling Law. A court of appeals may regulate practice in a particular case in any manner consistent with federal law, these rules, and local rules of the circuit. No sanction or other disadvantage may be imposed for noncompliance with any requirement not in federal law, federal rules, or the local circuit rules unless the alleged violator has been furnished in the particular case with actual notice of the requirement.

Rule 48. Masters

(a) Appointment; Powers. A court of appeals may appoint a special master to hold hearings, if necessary, and to recommend factual findings and disposition in matters ancillary to proceedings in the court. Unless the order referring a matter to a master specifies or limits the master's powers, those powers include, but are not limited to, the following:

(1) regulating all aspects of a hearing;

(2) taking all appropriate action for the efficient performance of the master's duties under the order;

(3) requiring the production of evidence on all matters embraced in the reference; and

(4) administering oaths and examining witnesses and parties.

(b) Compensation. If the master is not a judge or court employee, the court must determine the master's compensation and whether the cost is to be charged to any party.

APPENDIX OF FORMS

Form 1. Notice of Appeal to a Court of Appeals From a Judgment or Order of a District Court

United States District Court for the _____ District of _____
File Number _____

A.B., Plaintiff	)	
	)	
v.	)	Notice of Appeal
	)	
C.D., Defendant	)	

Notice is hereby given that [*(here name all parties taking the appeal)*, (plaintiffs) (defendants) in the above named case,[1]] hereby appeal to the United States Court of Appeals for the _____ Circuit (from the final judgment) (from an order (describing it)) entered in this action on the _____ day of _____, 19__.

(s) _____
Attorney for [_____]
[Address: _____]

(As amended Apr. 22, 1993, eff. Dec. 1, 1993.)

[1] See Rule 3(c) for permissible ways of identifying appellants.

Form 2. Notice of Appeal to a Court of Appeals From a Decision of the United States Tax Court

UNITED STATES TAX COURT
Washington, D.C.

A.B., Petitioner	)	
	)	
v.	)	Docket No. _____
	)	
Commissioner of Internal Revenue,	)	
Respondent	)	

Notice of Appeal

Notice is hereby given that *(here name all parties taking the appeal* [1] *)*, hereby appeals to the United States Court of Appeals for the _____ Circuit from (that part of) the decision of this court entered in the above captioned proceeding on the _____ day of _____, 19__ (relating to _____).

(s) _____
Counsel for [_____]
[Address: _____]

(As amended Apr. 22, 1993, eff. Dec. 1, 1993.)

[1] See Rule 3(c) for permissible ways of identifying appellants.

Form 3. Petition for Review of Order of an Agency, Board, Commission or Officer

United States Court of Appeals for the _____ Circuit

A.B., Petitioner   )
)
                v.   )   Petition for Review
)
XYZ Commission, Respondent   )

[(here name all parties bringing the petition [1])] hereby petitions the court for review of the Order of the XYZ Commission (describe the order) entered on _____, 19___.

[(s)] _____
Attorney for Petitioners
Address: _____

(As amended Apr. 22, 1993, eff. Dec. 1, 1993.)

[1] See Rule 15.

Form 4. Affidavit Accompanying Motion for Permission to Appeal In Forma Pauperis

United States District Court for the _____ District of _____

A.B., Plaintiff

v.   **Case No. _____**

C.D., Defendant

Affidavit in Support of Motion

I swear or affirm under penalty of perjury that, because of my poverty, I cannot prepay the docket fees of my appeal or post a bond for them. I believe I am entitled to redress. I swear or affirm under penalty of perjury under United States laws that my answers on this form are true and correct. (28 U.S.C. § 1746; 18 U.S.C. § 1621.)

Instructions

Complete all questions in this application and then sign it. Do not leave any blanks: if the answer to a question is "0," "none," or "not applicable (N/A)," write in that response. If you need more space to answer a question or to explain your answer, attach a separate sheet of paper identified with your name, your case's docket number, and the question number.

Signed: _____   Date: _____

My issues on appeal are:

1. For both you and your spouse estimate the average amount of money received from each of the following sources during the past 12 months. Adjust any amount that was received weekly, biweekly, quarterly, semiannually, or annually to show the monthly rate. Use gross amounts, that is, amounts before any deductions for taxes or otherwise.

Income source	**Average monthly amount during the past 12 months**	**Amount expected next month**
	You	**You**
Employment	$_____	$_____
Self-employment	$_____	$_____
Income from real property (such as rental income)	$_____	$_____
Interest and dividends	$_____	$_____
Gifts	$_____	$_____
Alimony	$_____	$_____
Child support	$_____	$_____
Retirement (such as social security, pensions, annuities, insurance)	$_____	$_____
Disability (such as social security, insurance payments)	$_____	$_____
Unemployment payments	$_____	$_____
Public-assistance (such as welfare)	$_____	$_____
Other (specify):_____	$_____	$_____
Total monthly income:	$_____	$_____

2. List your employment history, most recent employer first. (Gross monthly pay is before taxes or other deductions.)

Employer	Address	Dates of employment	Gross monthly pay
_____	_____	_____	_____
_____	_____	_____	_____
_____	_____	_____	_____

3. List your spouse's employment history, most recent employer first. (Gross monthly pay is before taxes or other deductions.)

Employer	Address	Dates of employment	Gross monthly pay
_____	_____	_____	_____
_____	_____	_____	_____
_____	_____	_____	_____

4. How much cash do you and your spouse have? $_____
Below, state any money you or your spouse have in bank accounts or in any other financial institution.

Financial institution	Type of account	Amount you have	Amount your spouse has
_____	_____	$_____	$_____
_____	_____	$_____	$_____
_____	_____	$_____	$_____

If you are a prisoner, you must attach a statement certified by the appropriate institutional officer showing all receipts, expenditures, and balances during the last six months in your institutional accounts. If you have multiple accounts, perhaps because you have been in multiple institutions, attach one certified statement of each account.

5. List the assets, and their values, which you own or your spouse owns. Do not list clothing and ordinary household furnishings.

Home	(Value)	Other real estate	(Value)	Motor vehicle # 1	(Value)
_____		_____		Make & year: _____	
_____		_____		Model: _____	
_____		_____		Registration #: _____	

Motor vehicle # 2	(Value)	Other assets	(Value)	Other assets	(Value)
Make & year: _____		_____		_____	
Model: _____		_____		_____	
Registration #: _____		_____		_____	

6. State every person, business, or organization owing you or your spouse money, and the amount owed.

Person owing you or your spouse money	Amount owed to you	Amount owed to your spouse
_____	_____	_____
_____	_____	_____
_____	_____	_____

7.   State the persons who rely on you or your spouse for support.

Name	Relationship	Age
_____	_____	_____
_____	_____	_____
_____	_____	_____

8.   Estimate the average monthly expenses of you and your family. Show separately the amounts paid by your spouse.   Adjust any payments that are made weekly, biweekly, quarterly, semiannually, or annually to show the monthly rate.

	You	**Your Spouse**
Rent or home-mortgage payment (include lot rented for mobile home) Are real-estate taxes included? ☐ Yes ☐ No Is property insurance included? ☐ Yes ☐ No	$_____	$_____
Utilities (electricity, heating fuel, water, sewer, and Telephone)	$_____	$_____
Home maintenance (repairs and upkeep)	$_____	$_____
Food	$_____	$_____
Clothing	$_____	$_____
Laundry and dry-cleaning	$_____	$_____
Medical and dental expenses	$_____	$_____
Transportation (not including motor vehicle payments)	$_____	$_____
Recreation, entertainment, newspapers, magazines, etc.	$_____	$_____
Insurance (not deducted from wages or included in Mortgage payments)	$_____	$_____
Homeowner's or renter's	$_____	$_____
Life	$_____	$_____
Health	$_____	$_____
Motor Vehicle	$_____	$_____
Other: _____	$_____	$_____
Taxes (not deducted from wages or included in Mortgage payments) (specify):_____	$_____	$_____
Installment payments	$_____	$_____
Motor Vehicle	$_____	$_____
Credit card (name): _____	$_____	$_____
Department store (name): _____	$_____	$_____
Other: _____	$_____	$_____
Alimony, maintenance, and support paid to others	$_____	$_____
Regular expenses for operation of business, profession, or farm (attach detailed statement)	$_____	$_____

Other (specify): _____ $_____ $_____
          Total monthly expenses: $_____ $_____

9. Do you expect any major changes to your monthly income or expenses or in your assets or liabilities during the next 12 months?

☐ Yes ☐ No   If yes, describe on an attached sheet.

10. Have you paid—or will you be paying—an attorney any money for services in connection with this case, including the completion of this form? ☐ Yes ☐ No

If yes, how much? $_____

If yes, state the attorney's name, address, and telephone number:

_____

_____

_____

11. Have you paid—or will you be paying—anyone other than an attorney (such as a paralegal or a typist) any money for services in connection with this case, including the completion of this form?

☐ Yes ☐ No

If yes, how much? $_____

If yes, state the person's name, address, and telephone number:

_____

_____

_____

12. Provide any other information that will help explain why you cannot pay the docket fees for your appeal.

13. State the address of your legal residence.

_____

_____

Your daytime phone number: (___) _____

Your age: _____ Your years of schooling: _____

Your social-security number: _____

(As amended Apr. 24, 1998, eff. Dec. 1, 1998).

Form 5.   Notice of Appeal to a Court of Appeals from a Judgment or Order of a District Court or a Bankruptcy Appellate Panel

United States District Court for the ....
District of ....

In re   )
)
......................,   )
          Debtor   )
)   File No. ....
......................,   )
          Plaintiff   )
)

     v.   )
)
. . . . ,   )
   Defendant   )

Notice of Appeal to United States Court of
Appeals for the . . . . Circuit

 . . . . , the plaintiff [or defendant or other party] appeals
to the United States Court of Appeals for the . . . . Circuit
from the final judgment [or order or decree] of the district court for the
district of . . . . [or bankruptcy appellate panel of the
. . . . circuit], entered in this case on . . . . , 19. . .
[here describe the judgment, order, or decree] . . . .

 The parties to the judgment [or order or decree] appealed from and
the names and addresses of their respective attorneys are as follows:

           Dated . . . .
           Signed . . . .
           Attorney for Appellant
           Address: . . . .
           . . . .

(Added Apr. 25, 1989, eff. Dec. 1, 1989.)

Appendix C

BRIEF FOR THE PETITIONER

I have selected the Petitioner's brief, the Respondent's brief and the Petitioner's reply brief of the recently-decided case on executive immunity involving the President of the United States, i.e. *Clinton v. Jones*. While ultimately the central issues presented in the complaint will be resolved, this case will stand as a milestone on the issue of whether executive immunity will be recognized in a situation in which the alleged actions of the President occurred prior to his election and subsequent term in the office.

For purposes of studying and evaluating written appellate advocacy, briefs in the following three appendices illustrate contrasting styles and approaches. It is not suggested any one approach is preferable, but the briefs should be studied carefully to assess their strengths and weaknesses.

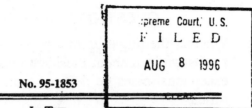

No. 95-1853

IN THE

𝕾𝖚𝖕𝖗𝖊𝖒𝖊 𝕮𝖔𝖚𝖗𝖙 𝕺𝖋 𝕿𝖍𝖊 𝖀𝖓𝖎𝖙𝖊𝖉 𝕾𝖙𝖆𝖙𝖊𝖘

October Term, 1995

WILLIAM JEFFERSON CLINTON,

Petitioner,

vs.

PAULA CORBIN JONES,

Respondent.

**On Writ Of Certiorari To The
United States Court Of Appeals
For The Eighth Circuit**

BRIEF FOR THE PETITIONER

Robert S. Bennett
   Counsel of Record
Carl S. Rauh
Alan Kriegel
Amy R. Sabrin
Of Counsel: Stephen P. Vaughn
David A. Strauss   SKADDEN, ARPS, SLATE,
Geoffrey R. Stone   MEAGHER & FLOM
1111 East 60th Street   1440 New York Avenue, N.W.
Chicago, Illinois 60637   Washington, D.C. 20005
(312) 702-9601   (202) 371-7000

Attorneys for the Petitioner
President William Jefferson Clinton

Balmar Legal Publishing Department, Washington, D.C.

QUESTIONS PRESENTED

1. Whether the litigation of a private civil damages action against an incumbent President must in all but the most exceptional cases be deferred until the President leaves office.

2. Whether a district court, as a proper exercise of judicial discretion, may stay such litigation until the President leaves office.

PARTIES TO THE PROCEEDING

Petitioner, President William Jefferson Clinton, was a defendant in the district court and appellant in the court of appeals. Respondent Paula Corbin Jones was the plaintiff in the district court and cross-appellant in the court of appeals. Danny Ferguson was a defendant in the district court.

TABLE OF CONTENTS

PAGE

PAGE

TABLE OF AUTHORITIES

Cases   **Page(s)**

Other Authorities   **Page(s)**

No. 95-1853

IN THE

𝔖upreme ℭourt 𝔒f 𝔗he 𝔘nited 𝔖tates

October Term, 1995

WILLIAM JEFFERSON CLINTON,

Petitioner,

vs.

PAULA CORBIN JONES,

Respondent.

**On Writ Of Certiorari To The
United States Court Of Appeals
For The Eighth Circuit**

BRIEF FOR THE PETITIONER

OPINIONS BELOW

The opinion of the court of appeals (Pet. App. 1) is reported at 72 F.3d 1354. The court of appeals' order denying the petition for rehearing (Pet. App. 32) is reported at 81 F.3d 78. The principal opinion of the district court (Pet. App. 54) is reported at 869 F. Supp. 690. Other published opinions of the district court (Pet. App. at 40 and 74) appear at 858 F. Supp. 902 and 879 F. Supp. 86.

JURISDICTION

The judgment of the United States Court of Appeals for the Eighth Circuit was entered on January 9, 1996. A petition for rehearing was filed on January 23, 1996, and denied on March 28, 1996. A petition for certiorari was filed on May 15, 1996, and granted on June 24, 1996. This Court's jurisdiction is based on 28 U.S.C. § 1254(1) (1994).

LEGAL PROVISIONS INVOLVED IN THIS CASE

U.S. CONST. art. II, § 1, cl. 1

U.S. CONST. art. II, §§ 2-4

U.S. CONST. amend. XXV

42 U.S.C. § 1983 (1994)

42 U.S.C. § 1985 (1994)

FED. R. CIV. P. 40

These provisions are set forth at Pet. App. 79-85.

STATEMENT

Petitioner William Jefferson Clinton is President of the United States. On May 6, 1994, respondent Paula Corbin Jones filed this civil damages action against the President in the United States District Court for the Eastern District of Arkansas. The complaint was based principally on conduct alleged to have occurred three years earlier, before the President took office. The complaint included two claims arising under federal civil rights statutes and two arising under state tort law, and sought $175,000 in actual and punitive damages for each of the four counts.[1] Jurisdiction was asserted under 28 U.S.C. §§ 1331, 1332 and 1343 (1994).

---

[1] The first two counts allege that in 1991, when the President was Governor of Arkansas and respondent a state employee, he subjected respondent to sexual harassment and thereby deprived her of her civil rights in violation of 42 U.S.C. §§ 1983, 1985 (1994). A third claim alleges that the President thereby inflicted emotional distress upon respondent. Finally, the complaint alleges that in 1994, while he was President, petitioner defamed respondent through statements attributed to the White House Press Secretary and the President's lawyer, denying her much-publicized allegations against the President.

Arkansas State Trooper Danny Ferguson was named as co-defendant in two counts. Respondent alleges that Trooper Ferguson approached her on the President's behalf, thereby conspiring with the President to deprive

(continued . . .)

The President moved to stay the litigation or to dismiss it without prejudice to its reinstatement when he left office. He asserted that such a course was warranted by the singular nature of the President's Article II duties and by principles of separation of powers. The district court stayed the trial until the President left office, but held that discovery could proceed immediately "as to all persons including the President himself." Pet. App. 71.

The district court reasoned that "the case most applicable to this one is *Nixon v. Fitzgerald*, [457 U.S. 731 (1982)]" (Pet. App. 67), which held that a President is absolutely immune from any civil liability for his official acts as President. The district court noted that the holding of *Fitzgerald* did not directly apply to this case because President Clinton was sued primarily for actions taken before he became President, but concluded that a significant part of the rationale in *Fitzgerald* did apply here:

> [T]he majority opinion by Justice Powell [in *Fitzgerald*] is sweeping and quite firm in the view that to disturb the President with defending civil litigation that does not demand immediate attention . . . would be to interfere with the conduct of the duties of the office.

Pet. App. 68-69. The district court stated that these concerns "are not lessened by the fact that [the conduct alleged] preceded his Presidency." Pet. App. 69. In this connection, the district

---

[1](. . . continued)
respondent of her civil rights in violation of 42 U.S.C. § 1985. Respondent also alleges that Mr. Ferguson defamed her in statements about a woman identified only as "Paula," which were attributed to an anonymous trooper in an article about President Clinton's personal conduct published in *The American Spectator* magazine. Neither the publication nor the author was named as a defendant in the suit.

court stated that "this [is not] a case that would likely be tried with few demands on Presidential time." Pet. App. 70.

The district court also stated that "[t]his is not a case in which any necessity exists to rush to trial." Pet. App. 70. Noting that respondent "filed this action two days before the three-year statute of limitations expired" and that she "[o]bviously . . . was in no rush to get her case to court," the district court found that "a delay in trial . . . will not harm [respondent's] right to recover or cause her undue inconvenience." *Id.* Invoking Federal Rule of Civil Procedure 40 and the court's equitable power to manage its own docket, the district judge concluded that the trial should be stayed, "[t]o protect the Office of President . . . from unfettered civil litigation, and to give effect to the policy of separation of powers." Pet. App. 72.[2] The trial court ruled, however, that there was "no reason why the discovery and deposition process could not proceed," and said that this would avoid the possible loss of evidence with the passage of time. Pet. App. 71.

The President and respondent both appealed.[3] A divided panel of the court of appeals reversed the district court's order staying trial, and affirmed its decision allowing discovery to proceed. The majority opinion, by Judge Bowman, determined that the Constitution does not confer on the President any protection from civil actions that arise from his unofficial

---

[2] The stay of trial encompassed the claims against Trooper Ferguson as well, because the court found that there was "too much interdependency of events and testimony to proceed piecemeal," and that "it would not be possible to try the Trooper adequately without testimony from the President." Pet. App. 71.

[3] The court of appeals' jurisdiction over the President's appeal was based on 28 U.S.C. § 1291 (1994). *See Mitchell v. Forsyth*, 472 U.S. 511, 526 (1985); *Nixon v. Fitzgerald*, 457 U.S. 731, 743 (1982). In our view, however, the court of appeals lacked jurisdiction to entertain respondent Jones's cross-appeal. *See infra* pp. 43-45.

acts. Pet. App. 16. Judge Bowman acknowledged that "the fundamental authority" on the question before the Court was *Nixon v. Fitzgerald*, but stated that the reasoning of *Fitzgerald* is "inapposite where only personal, private conduct by a President is at issue." Pet. App. 8, 11. After asserting that the court of appeals had "pendent appellate jurisdiction" to entertain respondent's challenge to the stay of trial issued by the district court (Pet. App. 5 n.4), Judge Bowman overturned even that limited stay as an abuse of discretion. Pet. App. 13 n.9.

Judge Bowman also put aside concerns that a trial court's exercise of control over the President's time and priorities through the supervision of discovery and trial would do violence to the separation of powers. Pet. App. 12-14. He stated that any separation of powers problems could be avoided by "judicial case management sensitive to the burdens of the presidency and the demands of the President's schedule." Pet. App. 13.

Judge Beam "concur[red] in the conclusions reached by Judge Bowman." Pet. App. 17. He acknowledged that the issues in this case "raise matters of substantial concern given the constitutional obligations of the office" of the Presidency. *Id.* He also recognized that "judicial branch interference with the functioning of the presidency should this suit be allowed to go forward" is a matter of "major concern." Pet. App. 21. He asserted, however, that this litigation could be managed with a "minimum of impact on the President's schedule." Pet. App. 23. This could be accomplished, he suggested, by the President's not attending his own trial and not participating in discovery, and by limiting the number of pretrial encounters between the President and respondent's counsel. Pet. App. 23-24.

Judge Ross dissented. Pet. App. 25-31. Noting that "[n]o other branch of government is entrusted to a single person," he stated: "It is this singularity of the President's constitutional position that calls for protection from civil litigation." Pet. App. 26.

> The burdens and demands of civil litigation can be expected to impinge on the President's discharge of his constitutional office by forcing him to divert his energy and attention from the rigorous demands of his office to the task of protecting himself against personal liability. That result would disserve the substantial public interest in the President's unhindered execution of his duties and would impair the integrity of the role assigned to the President by Article II of the Constitution.

Id. Judge Ross concluded that "unless exigent circumstances can be shown, private actions for damages against a sitting President of the United States, even though based on unofficial acts, must be stayed until the completion of the President's term." Pet. App. 25. He stated that this conclusion was compelled by the "language, logic and intent" of *Fitzgerald.* Pet. App. 25.

Judge Ross further explained that a lawsuit against a sitting President would "create opportunities for the judiciary to intrude upon the Executive[]" and "set the stage for potential constitutional confrontations between courts and a President." Pet. App. 28. In addition, he noted, such litigation "permit[s] the civil justice system to be used for partisan political purposes." *Id.* At the same time, he stated, postponing litigation "will rarely defeat a plaintiff's ability to ultimately obtain meaningful relief." Pet. App. 30. Judge Ross concluded that litigation should proceed against a sitting President only if a plaintiff can "demonstrate convincingly both that delay will seriously prejudice the plaintiff's interests and that . . . [it] will not significantly impair the President's ability to attend to the duties of his office." Pet. App. 31.

The court of appeals denied the President's request for rehearing *en banc.* Three judges did not participate, and

Judge McMillian dissented. Judge McMillian stated that the panel majority's holding "demean[ed] the Office of the President." Pet. App. 32. He further stated that the holding "would put all the problems of our nation on pilot control and treat as more urgent a private lawsuit that even the [respondent] delayed filing for at least *three* years," and would "allow judicial interference with, and control of, the President's time." Pet. App. 33.

SUMMARY OF ARGUMENT

I.A. The President, unlike any other federal official, has the sole responsibility for an entire branch of the federal government. For that reason, litigation against the individual who is serving as President unavoidably impinges on the constitutional responsibilities of the Executive Branch. The Framers explicitly recognized this point, as has this Court, on several occasions.

A personal damages action is bound to be burdensome and disruptive. This is especially so in a lawsuit that seeks to impugn a defendant's reputation and threatens him with enormous financial liability. It is inconceivable that anyone, including the President, could remain disengaged from such proceedings. Even if a President ultimately prevails, protracted personal damages litigation would make it impossible for him to devote his undivided energies to one of the most demanding jobs in the world. Judge Learned Hand once commented that, as a potential litigant, he would "dread a lawsuit beyond anything else short of sickness and death." [4] In this respect the President is like any other litigant. The President's litigation, however, like the President's illness, becomes the nation's problem.

---

[4] 3 *Lectures on Legal Topics*, Assn. of the Bar of the City of New York 105 (1926), *quoted in Fitzgerald*, 457 U.S. at 763 n.6 (Burger, C.J., concurring).

There is also no reason to believe that, if it is established that private damages actions against sitting Presidents may go forward, such suits would be rare. To the contrary, parties seeking publicity, partisan advantage or a quick settlement will not forbear from using such litigation to advance their objectives. The usual means of discouraging or disposing of unfounded civil complaints would be especially ineffective in these cases.

B. Even the panel majority did not dispute the basic point that personal damages litigation against an incumbent President threatens the functioning of the Executive Branch. Deferral of litigation against an incumbent President would wholly eliminate this problem, while still enabling courts to provide effective relief for wrongdoing. The panel, however, rejected deferral of the litigation as a remedy, and instead concluded that "case management" by the trial court could adequately protect the interests at stake. But "case management" only exacerbates separation of powers problems, by entangling the Executive and Judicial Branches in an ongoing and mutually damaging relationship.

In concrete terms, trial court "case management" means that whenever a President believes that his responsibilities require a change in the schedule of litigation against him, he will have to seek the approval of the trial judge, state or federal. That judge will be authorized to insist on an explanation of the President's reasons for seeking a schedule change, a problematic state of affairs in itself. The trial judge will then review the President's explanation and decide whether to accept it, or whether the President should instead rearrange his official priorities to devote more time and attention to the litigation.

The President's priorities, however, are inseparable from the priorities of the Executive Branch of the federal government. Judges should not be in the position of reviewing those priorities. If they are, the effect will be to enmesh the President and the judiciary, to the great detriment of both branches, in a series of controversies over highly sensitive and, in an important sense, deeply political issues about the President's official priorities.

Moreover, state courts are likely to become the natural venue for private civil damages actions against an incumbent President, because such suits often will not involve federal claims. The Framers were well aware of the potential for conflict between the states and the federal government, particularly the Executive Branch of the federal government. They could not possibly have contemplated that state trial judges would have the power to control a President that is inherent in "case management" -- much less that they would have the power to compel an incumbent President to stand trial in a state court. This further demonstrates that deferral, not "case management," is more consistent with our constitutional scheme.

C. The temporary deferral that the President seeks here is not, contrary to the court of appeals, an extraordinary remedy, and it does not place the President "above the law." In a variety of circumstances -- ranging from the automatic stay in bankruptcy to the doctrine of primary jurisdiction to the suspension of civil actions while criminal proceedings are pending -- litigation is delayed in our system in order to protect significant public or institutional interests. The public interest in protecting the Presidency from disruption is at least as strong as, if not stronger than, the interests underlying these well-established doctrines.

Deferral also does not place unreasonable burdens on respondent. In many cases -- for example, where absolute, qualified, or diplomatic immunities apply -- settled doctrines deny recovery outright to innocent individuals who may have been grievously injured. Deferral of this litigation, by contrast, will not preclude respondent from ultimately seeking a remedy and, if warranted, recovering damages. Deferral leaves the President no less accountable for his conduct. Only the timing of the litigation is affected.

II. Respondent's suit, in particular, should be deferred under separation of powers principles. The suit is based on conduct that occurred before the President took office, and therefore presents no risk of abuse of Presidential power. Respondent seeks only damages, and can be made whole even if the proceedings are delayed. The suit involves the President personally and directly, not peripherally, so it is especially likely to impinge on his ability to perform his official duties. And respondent could have sought relief long before the President assumed office, or sought other avenues of relief, but chose not to do so.

For these and all the reasons set forth more fully below, the decision of the court of appeals should be reversed, and this litigation should be deferred in its entirety until the President leaves office.

ARGUMENT

I. **PRIVATE CIVIL DAMAGES LITIGATION AGAINST AN INCUMBENT PRESIDENT MUST, IN ALL BUT THE MOST EXCEPTIONAL CASES, BE DEFERRED UNTIL THE PRESIDENT LEAVES OFFICE.**

  A. **A Personal Damages Action Against An Incumbent President Would Interfere With The Discharge Of A President's Article II Responsibilities And Jeopardize The Separation Of Powers.**

   1. **The President, Unlike Any Other Official, Bears Sole Responsibility For An Entire Branch Of Government.**

Under our system of government, the Executive Branch is the sole responsibility of the individual who has been elected President. Anything that significantly affects that individual will affect the functioning of the Executive Branch as well. For this reason, even a private lawsuit against the President impinges on the Presidency and the operations of the Executive.

That the President "occupies a unique position in the constitutional scheme" (*Nixon v. Fitzgerald*, 457 U.S. 731, 749 (1982)) has been a central and all but undisputed axiom of our constitutional system since the Founding. It is borne out by the statements of the Framers, the decisions of this Court, and of course the text and structure of the Constitution itself.

Article II, § 1, vests the entire "executive Power" in "a President," who is indispensable to the execution of that power. The President alone is director of all the executive departments and Commander-In-Chief of the armed forces. The Constitution places on him the responsibility to take care that the laws are faithfully executed. U.S. CONST. art. II, §§ 2-3. The Framers recognized that their decision to vest the executive power in a single individual, instead of in a group or council, was a crucial aspect of the constitutional plan, and in the Federalist papers they devoted as much attention to that decision as they did to any single provision of the Constitution. *See* THE FEDERALIST Nos. 70-77 (Alexander Hamilton).[5]

The extraordinary character of the Presidency in this respect is woven into the very fabric of the Constitution. The Constitution envisions that Congress will be in session for a period of time and then adjourn. U.S. CONST. art. I, §§ 4, 5, 7. The Presidency, however, is always "in session;" the Presidency never adjourns.[6] The Constitution further provides specific steps to replace the President in the event of his disability. U.S. CONST. amend. XXV, §§ 3-4. These provisions, made for no other federal officer, further confirm that the Presidency is inseparable from the individual who is President.

The unadorned words of the Constitution do not fully convey the momentous and unrelenting burdens on every President. "[T]he President, for all practical purposes . . . affords the only means through which we can act as a nation."[7]

The range of the President's functions is enormous.
He is ceremonial head of the state. He is a vital

---

[5]   *See* PHILIP B. KURLAND, WATERGATE AND THE CONSTITUTION 135 (1978): "The President is . . . the only officer of the United States whose duties under the Constitution are entirely his responsibility and his responsibility alone. He is the sole indispensable man in government, and his duties are of such a nature that he should not be called from them at the instance of any . . . branch of government."

[6]   Akhil R. Amar & Neal K. Katyal, *Executive Privileges and Immunities: The Nixon And Clinton Cases*, 108 HARV. L. REV. 701, 713 (1995) ("Unlike federal lawmakers and judges, the President is at 'Session' twenty-four hours a day, every day. Constitutionally speaking, the President never sleeps.").

[7]   George E. Reedy, *Discovering the Presidency*, N.Y. TIMES, Jan. 20, 1985, at G1, *quoted in* LOU CANNON, PRESIDENT REAGAN -- THE ROLE OF A LIFETIME 147 (1991).

source of legislative suggestion. He is the final
source of all executive decision. He is the authoritative exponent of the nation's foreign policy.[8]

Although he has many advisers, the President alone is ultimately accountable for a myriad of decisions affecting pro-
foundly important questions of national and international
policy -- such as dispatching military forces as exigencies require; helping to negotiate peace in regions vital to our national interest; deciding whether to sign or veto legislation;
and negotiating with Congress on budgetary, tax and many
other crucial issues. The President's obligations to the office,
moreover, never cease; serious crises can, and often do, erupt
unexpectedly, commanding the President's immediate attention.[9]

To combine all [this] with the continuous need to be
at once the representative man of the nation and the
leader of his political party is clearly a call upon the

---

[8] HAROLD J. LASKI, THE AMERICAN PRESIDENCY, AN INTERPRE-
TATION 26 (1940), *quoted in* CANNON, *supra* note 7, at 147.

[9] This has been true of every modern Presidency. To give just a few
examples, President Reagan was aroused from sleep to deal with the Lib-
yan downing of two American Navy fighter planes; approved U.S. participation in a multinational peacekeeping force in Lebanon while at his
ranch in Santa Barbara; and attended to the crisis occasioned by the Soviet
downing of KAL Flight 007 while on vacation. CANNON, *supra* note 7, at
191, 399, 420. President Carter spent one vacation reading psychological
profiles of Anwar el-Sadat and Menachem Begin in preparation for the
Camp David Summit. JIMMY CARTER, KEEPING FAITH -- MEMOIRS OF A
PRESIDENT 57 (1982).   President Clinton was notified of the terrorist
bombing of U.S. military personnel on the eve of the G-7 economic summit, causing him both to change his priorities for the summit and to return
to the U.S. before it was over to attend memorial services. Associated
Press, *Clinton Calls For Unity Against Terrorism*, CHI. TRIB., June 27,
1996, at A1.

energies of a single man unsurpassed by the exigencies of any other political office in the world.[10]

2. **To Subject An Incumbent President To Civil Litigation In His Personal Capacity Would Be Inconsistent With The Historic Understanding Of Relations Between The Executive And Judicial Branches.**

The nation's courts "traditionally have recognized the President's constitutional responsibilities and status as factors counseling judicial deference and restraint." *Fitzgerald*, 457 U.S. at 753 & n.34. Accordingly, courts historically have refrained from exercising jurisdiction over the President personally, except in cases of imperative need, and then only to the most limited extent possible. *See id.* at 753-54.

This Court repeatedly has recognized that the President's unique status and range of responsibilities under the Constitution distinguish him from all other federal officers. *Id.* at 749-50. A President is absolutely immune from personal liability for any action taken in connection with his official duties. *Id.* at 749. A President's communications are presumptively privileged, and that privilege can be overridden only in cases of exceptionally strong public need. *United States v. Nixon*, 418 U.S. 683, 705 (1974). Similarly, there is an "apparently unbroken historical tradition . . . implicit in the separation of powers" that a President may not be ordered by the Judiciary to perform particular executive acts. *Franklin v. Massachusetts*, 505 U.S. 788, 827 (1992) (Scalia, J., concurring); *see id.* at 802-03 (plurality opinion of O'Connor, J.). And the Department of Justice, speaking through then-Solicitor General Robert H. Bork, has taken the position -- based on explicit language in *The Federalist* -- that while an incumbent Vice-President is subject to criminal prosecution, the President

---

[10] LASKI, *supra* note 8, at 26.

must be impeached and removed from office before he can be prosecuted.[11] All of these protections are "functionally mandated incident[s] of the President's unique office, rooted in the constitutional tradition of the separation of powers and supported by our history." *Fitzgerald*, 457 U.S. at 749.[12]

This tradition of judicial deference and restraint toward the Presidency -- a tradition that "can be traced far back into our constitutional history" (*Fitzgerald*, 457 U.S. at 753 n.34) -- bars personal damages litigation against an incumbent President. Over 150 years ago, Justice Story explained why such litigation cannot go forward while the President is in office:

> There are . . . incidental powers, belonging to the executive department, which are necessarily implied from the nature of the functions, which are confided to it. Among these, must necessarily be included

---

[11] *See* THE FEDERALIST No. 69, at 416 (Alexander Hamilton) (Clinton Rossiter ed., 1961); *id.* No. 77, at 464 (Alexander Hamilton); *id.* No. 65, at 398-99 (Alexander Hamilton); 2 MAX FARRAND, THE RECORDS OF THE FEDERAL CONVENTION OF 1787 500 (rev. ed. 1966) (noting the comment of Gouvenour Morris); *id.* at 626 (comment of James Wilson). Solicitor General Bork explained that the unique burdens of the President's duties distinguished him in this regard from all other federal officers:

> [The Framers] assumed that the nation's Chief Executive, responsible as no other single officer is for the affairs of the United States, would not be taken from duties that only he can perform unless and until it is determined that he is to be shorn of those duties by the Senate.

Memorandum for the United States Concerning the Vice President's Claim of Constitutional Immunity at 17, *In re Proceedings of The Grand Jury Impaneled Dec. 5, 1972*, (No. 73-965) (D. Md. filed Oct. 5, 1973) (C.A. App. 92).

[12] This Court repeatedly has stated that a specific textual basis is not necessary to support such incidents of the President's office. *Fitzgerald*, 457 U.S. at 750 n.31; *Nixon*, 418 U.S. at 705 n.16.

the power to perform them .... The president cannot, therefore, be liable to arrest, imprisonment, or detention, while he is in the discharge of the duties of his office; and for this purpose his person must be deemed, in civil cases at least, to possess an official inviolability.

3 JOSEPH STORY, COMMENTARIES ON THE CONSTITUTION OF THE UNITED STATES § 1563, pp. 418-19 (1st ed. 1833), *quoted in Fitzgerald*, 457 U.S. at 749.

The second and third Presidents of the United States held the same view. John Adams explained that the President personally is not subject to any process whatever, for to permit otherwise would "put it in the power of a common Justice to exercise any Authority over him and Stop the Whole Machine of Government."[13] President Jefferson was even more emphatic:

> [W]ould the executive be independent of the judiciary, if he were subject to the *commands* of the latter, & to imprisonment for disobedience; if the several courts could bandy him from pillar to post, keep him constantly trudging from north to south & east to west, and withdraw him entirely from his constitutional duties?[14]

As this court stated in *Fitzgerald*, "nothing in [the Framers'] debates suggests an expectation that the President would be

---

[13] THE DIARY OF WILLIAM MACLAY AND OTHER NOTES ON SENATE DEBATES 168 (recording a discussion between then-Vice President Adams and Senator Oliver Ellsworth during the first Congress) (Kenneth R. Bowling and Helen E. Veit eds., 1988).

[14] 10 THE WORKS OF THOMAS JEFFERSON 404 n. (Paul L. Ford ed., 1905) (emphasis in original), *quoted in Fitzgerald*, 457 U.S. at 751 n.31.

subjected to the distraction of suits by disappointed private citizens." 457 U.S. at 751 n.31.[15]

The traditional practice has been fully consistent with this historical doctrine. It is, of course, "settled law that the separation-of-powers doctrine does not bar every exercise of jurisdiction over the President," *Fitzgerald*, 457 U.S. at 753-54, and Presidents, including this one, have sought to accommodate the interests of the courts, particularly their interest in the fair administration of criminal justice, where accommodation can be accomplished consistent with Presidential functions. *See infra* pp. 26-28. These interests have not heretofore been thought to require an incumbent President's participation as a defendant in a private civil damages suit, however.

To the contrary, it "has been taken for granted for nearly two centuries," *Fitzgerald*, 457 U.S. at 758 (Burger, C.J., concurring), that one could not hale an incumbent President into court and seek damages from him personally. So far as can be determined, no President has ever been required even to give evidence in a civil proceeding, let alone appear as a defendant. No President has ever been compelled to appear personally and testify at trial in any case, civil or criminal. President Jefferson was sued for official actions he took while he was President, but notably, not until after he left office.[16] Three other Presidents had civil damages litigation pending against

---

[15] While there are some statements by contemporaries of the Framers that questioned the notion of Presidential immunity to civil suit, the majority in *Fitzgerald* observed in response that "historical evidence must be weighed as well as cited. When the weight of evidence is considered, we think we must place our reliance on the contemporary understanding of John Adams, Thomas Jefferson, and Oliver Ellsworth." 457 U.S. at 752 n.31.

[16] *Livingston v. Jefferson*, 15 F. Cas. 660, 663 (C.C.D. Va. 1811) (No. 8.411) (suit for trespass, based on federal seizure of land, dismissed for want of venue).

them during their tenure in office, but in each case, suit was filed before they took office; two were effectively disposed of before the President was sworn in; and none was actively litigated while the defendant served as President.[17] This "prolonged reticence" about suing an incumbent President is powerful evidence of a nearly universal understanding that such litigation is inconsistent with our constitutional scheme. *See Plaut v. Spendthrift Farm, Inc.*, 115 S. Ct. 1447, 1458 (1995).

In *Fitzgerald*, the Court explained that historically the President has been subjected to a court's jurisdiction only when necessary to serve a compelling, broad-based constitu-

---

[17] In *New York ex rel. Hurley v. Roosevelt*, 179 N.Y. 544 (1904), Theodore Roosevelt was sued in his capacity as Chairman of the New York City Police Board, a position he held in 1895. An intermediate court of appeals affirmed dismissal of the complaint on January 25, 1901, *id.*, nine months before he assumed the Presidency. The New York Court of Appeals affirmed the dismissal without opinion in 1904 while President Roosevelt was in office. *Id.*

In *DeVault v. Truman*, 194 S.W.2d 29 (Mo. 1946), the plaintiff alleged that in 1931 Harry Truman and other judges in Jackson County, Missouri, improperly committed him to a mental institution. The action was initiated in November 1944, *id.* at 31, and the trial court granted the defendants' motion to dismiss. Mr. Truman became President in April 1945. One year later, the Supreme Court of Missouri affirmed the order dismissing the complaint. *Id.* at 32.

A suit was filed against Senator John F. Kennedy during his 1960 campaign and settled after he took office. Certain delegates to the 1960 Democratic convention sought to hold him liable for injuries incurred while riding in a car leased to his campaign. Complaint, *Bailey v. Kennedy*, No. 757200, and *Hills v. Kennedy*, No. 757201 (Los Angeles County Superior Court, both filed Oct. 27, 1960 and subsequently consolidated) (C.A. App. 128, 135) (hereinafter "*Bailey*"). The court did not permit the plaintiffs to take the President's deposition, permitting the President to respond by way of written interrogatories. *Bailey*, Order Denying Motion for Deposition (Aug. 27, 1962) (C.A. App. 155). The case was settled before further discovery against the President. *See infra* note 22.

tional or public interest, and only when the exercise of jurisdiction would not unduly intrude on the functions of the office. 457 U.S. at 753-54. The Court gave two examples of such exceptional cases: those seeking to curb abuses of Presidential authority and maintain separation of powers, *id.* (citing *Youngstown Sheet & Tube Co. v. Sawyer*, 343 U.S. 579 (1952)); and those seeking to vindicate the public interest in criminal prosecutions. *Id.* (citing *United States v. Nixon*, 418 U.S. at 703-13). Noting that there is a lesser public interest in actions for civil damages than in criminal proceedings, *id.* at 754 n.37, the Court in *Fitzgerald* concluded that a "merely private suit for damages based on a President's official acts" does not warrant the exercise of jurisdiction over a President. *Id.* at 754.[18]

Until the unprecedented decision by the court of appeals in this case, private civil damages litigation has not been thought to warrant an exception to the teaching of the Framers. To the contrary, such litigation does not serve the broad-based, compelling public or constitutional interests enumerated in *Fitzgerald*. To allow it to proceed would be an abrupt break with well-established principles of American jurisprudence.

---

[18] In the few cases where plaintiffs have sought to compel or restrain official action by a President, courts consistently have resorted to procedural or jurisdictional devices to dismiss the claims or to avoid issuing relief directed at the President personally. *See, e.g., Mississippi v. Johnson*, 71 U.S. (4 Wall.) 475, 500-01 (1866) (discretionary Presidential decision-making held unreviewable); *Dellums v. Bush*, 752 F. Supp. 1141 (D.D.C. 1990) (dismissed for lack of ripeness). *See also Franklin v. Massachusetts*, 505 U.S. 788, 802-03 (1992) (plurality opinion of O'Connor, J.) (relief may be directed to defendants other than President); *Youngstown Sheet & Tube Co. v. Sawyer*, 343 U.S. 579 (1952) (same).

3.   **Civil Damages Litigation Against A Sitting President Would Seriously Impair The President's Ability To Discharge His Constitutional Responsibilities.**

In *Nixon v. Fitzgerald*, this Court held that the President enjoys absolute immunity from damages liability for acts within the "outer perimeter" of his official duties. 457 U.S. at 756. The logic of *Fitzgerald* compels the conclusion that incumbent Presidents are entitled to the much more modest relief sought here -- the temporary deferral of private civil litigation.

Fitzgerald relied upon three significant grounds. First, the Court was concerned that to subject a President to liability for official conduct would inhibit him in carrying out his duties fearlessly and impartially, and would inject courts improperly into Presidential decision-making. *Id.* at 752 & n.32. Second, the Court stated, "[b]ecause of the singular importance of the President's duties," the "diversion of his energies by concern with private lawsuits would raise unique risks to the effective functioning of government." *Id.* at 751. And third, the Court was concerned that the "sheer prominence of the President's office" would make him "an easily identifiable target for suits for civil damages." *Id.* at 752-53.

This case is different from *Fitzgerald*, of course, in that it largely does not touch upon official actions. Accordingly, it does not warrant, and the President does not seek, any immunity from liability. But because this case involves a sitting President, it directly implicates the two other critical concerns that prompted the decision in *Fitzgerald*: the President's vulnerability to civil damages actions and the diversion of the President's time and attention to attend to such litigation. These concerns are equally present whether the lawsuit is based on private conduct or official conduct. Defending a suit based on private conduct is not any less of an imposition on the President's ability to attend to his constitutional responsibilities, or any less of a "risk[] to the effective functioning of government." *Id.* at 751. Protection for the Presidency therefore is still required, albeit the much more limited protection of holding litigation in abeyance until the President leaves office.

A protracted lawsuit not only "ties up the defendant's time [but] prolongs the uncertainty and anxiety that are often the principal costs of being sued." *Ball v. City of Chicago*, 2 F.3d 752, 759 (7th Cir. 1993). The discovery phase alone of civil damages litigation would be an enormous imposition on a President's time and attention. "No one disputes any longer that today the process requires lawyers to try their cases twice: once during discovery and, if they manage to survive that ordeal, once again at trial."[19] Discovery, "used as a weapon to burden, discourage or exhaust the opponent," makes even a relatively minor case a costly and lengthy ordeal.[20] As this Court has recognized, "pretrial discovery . . . has a significant potential for abuse. This abuse is not limited to matters of delay and expense; discovery also may seriously implicate privacy interests of litigants and third parties." *Seattle Times Co. v. Rhinehart*, 467 U.S. 20, 34-35 (1984) (footnote omitted).

The instant case clearly illustrates these points. Respondent's counsel have revealed their intention to pursue discovery aggressively, stating that, "all is on the table in . . . discovery . . . including evidence that can lead to admissible evidence." They announced that they will "fully pursue, and exhaustively pursue" allegations of purportedly related

---

[19] Griffin B. Bell, Chilton D. Varner, & Hugh Q. Gottschalk, *Automatic Disclosure in Discovery -- The Rush to Reform*, 27 GA. L. REV. 1, 11 (1992).

[20] Hon. William W. Schwarzer, *Slaying The Monsters Of Cost And Delay: Would Disclosure Be More Effective Than Discovery?*, 74 JUDICATURE 178, 179 (1991).

wrongdoing that go far beyond the limited contacts between the President and the respondent alleged in the complaint, ostensibly for the purpose of showing an alleged "pattern" of harassment and the purported misuse of government resources. They also have suggested they will ask the trial court to compel an unprecedented physical examination of the President.[21]

No President could ignore, or leave to others to handle, a lawsuit such as this, which focuses on his personal conduct, aims to impugn his integrity, and seeks to impose hundreds of thousands of dollars in damages on him personally. Indeed, one of the most significant misconceptions in the panel majority's reasoning is the notion that the President can remain disengaged from a personal damages action brought against him. The panel majority seemed to envision that, perhaps apart from giving a deposition and consulting briefly on a few occasions with his trial counsel, the President can essentially ignore the litigation. It was even suggested that the President could forego attending his own trial. Pet. App. 23-24 (Beam, J., concurring). In fact, if the President is a defendant, he will be entitled to -- and, as a practical matter, will simply have to -- devote considerable time and attention to his defense.

This would be true whether the litigation involved allegations regarding personal misconduct, as here, or a disputed commercial transaction. Any case relating to events in which the President personally was involved would require the President's participation at almost every stage. In order to protect his interests adequately, the President, like any responsible litigant, would be required to review the complaint and answer; prepare and assure the veracity of discovery re-

---

[21] Transcript, *Daybreak* (CNN television broadcast, Dec. 29, 1994) at 3-4 (comments of Joseph Cammarata) (C.A. App. 117-18); Transcript, *Nightline* (ABC television broadcast, Dec. 28, 1994) at 3-4 (comments of Gilbert Davis) (C.A. App. 122-23).

sponses; retrieve and review documents; assist counsel to prepare for other witnesses' depositions; review those depositions and other evidence in the case; review the opposition's pleadings and motions; and consult with counsel throughout the case. He also would have the right and the obligation to review and approve all pleadings and motions filed on his behalf. Beyond that, the President would have to prepare for and participate in his own deposition, and finally, attend trial -- perhaps for weeks -- in a courtroom far from Washington.

The panel majority's antiseptic notion that the President can remain aloof from a personal damages action against him simply does not conform to reality. The litigation would command a significant part of the President's time, while the urgent business of the nation competed for his attention. The President would be put to an impossible choice between attending to his official duties or protecting his personal interests in the litigation -- a choice that is unfair not just to the President, but more importantly, to the nation he serves.

Even one lawsuit would have the potential seriously to disrupt the President's conduct of his official duties, just as one lawsuit could disrupt the professional and personal life of any individual. But if the Court allows private civil damages litigation to proceed against a sitting President, there is no reason to think that such lawsuits will be isolated events. As this Court has envisioned, Presidents likely would become "easily identifiable target[s]" for private civil damages actions in the future. *Fitzgerald*, 457 U.S. at 753. Those seeking publicity, financial gain or partisan political advantage would be altogether too willing to use the judicial system as an instrument to advance their private agendas at the expense of the public's interest in unimpeded constitutional governance.

In particular, any President is especially vulnerable to politically motivated "strike suits" financed or stimulated by partisan opponents of whatever stripe, hoping to undermine a President's pursuit of his policy objectives or to attack his integrity, and thereby diminish his effectiveness as a leader. Partisan opponents would also be tempted to file suit in order to take advantage of modern discovery techniques, unknown throughout most of our history, to uncover personal and financial information about the President, his family and close associates.[22] Use of the judicial system in this manner would corrode the political process.

Even if a claimant has a legitimate grievance, litigation against an incumbent President can deflect the exercise of the popular will by appropriating the President's time and energy, which properly belong not to the individual who sued the President, but to the nation as a whole. Therefore, "[w]e should hesitate before arming each citizen with a kind of legal assault weapon enabling him or her to commandeer the President's time, drag him from the White House, and haul him before any judge in America."[23]

Respondent and the panel majority suggest that there are procedural devices available to protect incumbent Presidents

---

[22] The suit against John F. Kennedy, *supra* note 17, illustrates how plaintiffs can use litigation for purposes of political mischief and potential extortion. The plaintiffs believed President Kennedy's policies were inimical to their state. *Bailey*, Reply to Objections to Cross-Interrogatories at 4-5 (Sept. 28, 1962) (C.A. App. 156). They attempted to propound politically embarrassing interrogatories to Attorney General Robert F. Kennedy, who had been the President's campaign manager. They also sought to obtain information about Kennedy family finances, and used pleadings to allege that the President was using his office to harass them and their state. *See Bailey*, Cross-Interrogatories to Robert F. Kennedy (Sept. 20, 1962) (C.A. App. 162); *Bailey*, Reply To Objections To Cross-Interrogatories at 3-4 (Sept. 28, 1962) (C.A. App. 156). As fatuous as the allegations were, President Kennedy settled the suit for $17,750, a significant sum in 1963. *Two Suits Against Kennedy Settled*, L.A. HERALD-EXAMINER, Apr. 2, 1963 (C.A. App. 181). Not all Presidents will have access to personal wealth to dispose of vexatious litigation in the interest of an unimpeded Presidency.

[23] Amar & Katyal, *supra* note 6, at 713.

against meritless lawsuits filed for purposes of harassment, publicity or partisanship. *See* Pet. App. 15; Resp. C.A. Br. 30, 32-33. But those devices are far from foolproof, and for a variety of reasons, are likely to be ineffective in protecting the President.

The strongest deterrent of unfounded lawsuits is typically financial: usually an individual will not incur the expense of suit if there is no prospect of prevailing, and will not risk sanctions under Rule 11 of the Federal Rules of Civil Procedure if the suit is found to be frivolous. But financial restraints are overcome by other incentives when -- as many prominent business, entertainment and public figures have learned to their dismay -- plaintiffs can attain instant celebrity status or political impact simply by including allegations against such figures in a complaint filed in court. The notoriety that accompanies such a lawsuit is lucrative in and of itself, in the form of book or movie contracts, for both client and lawyer. Likewise, a frivolous but embarrassing claim may be filed because the target is perceived, as a President surely would be, as vulnerable to quick settlement. As Chief Justice Burger observed, suits against Presidents can be "used as mechanisms of extortion." *Fitzgerald*, 457 U.S. at 763 (Burger, C.J., concurring). And a party whose objective is to divert the President's energy and resources, or to uncover information through discovery, or to embarrass the President by making sensational allegations, might willingly incur the costs of litigation even if there is no hope of success on the merits.

Nor does a motion to dismiss or for summary judgment promise swift or painless relief for the target of meritless litigation. A potential private action easily could be drafted to entangle a President in embarrassing or protracted litigation simply by alleging claims based on unwitnessed one-on-one encounters, or by otherwise raising credibility issues. These kinds of claims are exceedingly difficult to dispose of under the standards that govern pre-trial motions. And, as Chief Justice Burger recognized in *Fitzgerald*, "even a lawsuit ultimately found to be frivolous . . . often requires significant expenditures of time and money" to defend. "Ultimate vindication on the merits does not repair the damage." 457 U.S. at 763 (Burger, C.J., concurring).

4. Criminal Cases Where A President Has Been A Third-Party Witness Provide No Precedent For Requiring A Sitting President To Participate As A Defendant In Civil Damages Litigation.

The respondent and the panel majority below minimized the disruptive effect of civil litigation on the Presidency by comparing the full-scale defense of a personal damages action to the few occasions when a President has testified as a nonparty witness in a criminal or legislative proceeding. *See* Pet. App. 22-23 (Beam, J., concurring). This comparison is not plausible. The isolated event of giving testimony in a proceeding to which one is not a party bears no resemblance to the burdens borne by a defendant in a civil action for damages. In fact, the lesson of cases involving Presidential testimony is more nearly the opposite of what respondent and the panel majority say: those cases show that requiring an incumbent President to submit as a defendant in a private damages action would go beyond anything a court has done before, with less justification.

As this Court has emphasized, the interests at stake in criminal cases are of an altogether different magnitude from the interests affected by private damages actions. *See, e.g., Fitzgerald*, 457 U.S. at 754; *United States v. Gillock*, 445 U.S. 360, 371-72 (1980). Not only is the public interest in the accurate outcome of a criminal prosecution far greater, *see, e.g., Berger v. United States*, 295 U.S. 78, 88 (1935), but the defendant has a constitutional right under the Compulsory Process Clause of the Sixth Amendment to obtain evidence in a criminal proceeding. *United States v. Burr*, 25 F. Cas. 30, 33

(C.C.D. Va. 1807) (No. 14,692d). This right, of course, has no constitutional counterpart in civil cases.

Only once in our history, in *United States v. Nixon*, 418 U.S. 683 (1974), has the Supreme Court required a sitting President to give evidence. That case, of course, involved physical evidence, not the President's own testimony. Even so, the Court could not have been clearer that the limitation on Presidential autonomy was warranted only because of the "primary constitutional duty of the Judicial Branch to do justice in criminal prosecutions." *Id.* at 707. The Court expressly declined to extend its holding to civil proceedings. *See Nixon*, 418 U.S. at 709-10, 711-12 & n.19. In addition, the Court quoted, not once but twice, Justice Marshall's statement that "[i]n no case of this kind would a court be required to proceed against the president as against an ordinary individual." *Id.* at 708 and 715 (quoting *United States v. Burr*, 25 F. Cas. 187, 192 (C.C.D. Va. 1807) (No. 14,694)).

Consistent with *Nixon* and *Burr*, lower courts have required a strong showing of need for the President's testimony.[24] Even then, courts have allowed it to be obtained only in a manner that limits the disruption of the President's offi-

---

[24] *See Nixon*, 418 U.S. at 713 (subpoena enforced against the President because there was a "demonstrated, specific need for evidence in a pending criminal trial"); *see also United States v. Branscum*, No. LR-CR-96-49 (E.D. Ark. June 7, 1996) (President would be compelled to provide testimony for criminal trial only if court is "satisfied that his testimony would be material as tested by a meticulous standard, as well as being necessary in the sense of being a more logical and more persuasive source of evidence than alternatives that might be suggested") (quoting *United States v. Poindexter*, 732 F. Supp. 142, 147 (D.D.C. 1990)); *United States v. North*, 713 F. Supp. 1448, 1449 (D.D.C. 1989) (quashing subpoena to President when defendant failed to show "that the ... President's testimony is essential to assure the defendant a fair trial"), *aff'd*, 910 F.2d 843 (D.C. Cir. 1990), *cert. denied*, 500 U.S. 941 (1991).

cial functions, such as by videotaped deposition.[25] Thus, obtaining even third-party evidence from a President is a complex and delicate matter, to be done only in cases of great public need or where the constitutional right to compulsory process is at stake.

Neither of these factors is present, however, in ordinary civil litigation. Criminal prosecutions additionally carry certain important safeguards that are absent in civil litigation: they must be approved by a public official, premised on a finding of probable cause, and often require approval by a grand jury. Civil litigation, by contrast, can be filed by any individual out of any motive. Accordingly, this Court has been careful never to suggest that a sitting President could be compelled even to give evidence as a third party in a civil proceeding. *See United States v. Nixon*, 418 U.S. at 712 n.19.

The issue here, of course, is not whether the President can be compelled to testify as a mere witness. It is, rather, whether he can be sued as a defendant. Whatever difficulties may be involved in arranging for the President to testify as a third-party witness, those difficulties would be increased exponentially if the President were made a defendant in a civil action for damages, which has the potential to interfere much more severely, over a much more extended period, with his ability to fulfill the unique and extraordinarily demanding responsibilities of his office. It would be highly incongruous to subject the Presi-

---

[25] *See Nixon*, 418 U.S. at 711-15 (requiring in camera inspection of presumptively privileged Presidential tapes to ensure that only relevant, admissible material was provided to grand jury); *Branscum, supra* note 24 (videotaped deposition); *United States v. McDougal*, No. LR-CR-95-173 (E.D. Ark. Mar. 20, 1996) (videotaped deposition at the White House supervised by trial court via videoconferencing, after which only directly relevant parts would be shown at trial); *Poindexter*, 732 F. Supp. at 146-47 (videotaped deposition); *United States v. Fromme*, 405 F. Supp. 578, 583 (E.D. Cal. 1975) (videotaped deposition).

dent -- and the nation -- to these burdens solely on the basis of a civil complaint filed against him by a private party, when the alternative -- deferral -- avoids these problems entirely and provides reasonable protection for the interests of all parties.

B. "Case Management" By The Trial Court Does Not Mitigate, But Instead Exacerbates, The Separation Of Power Problems Created By Suits Against An Incumbent President.

1. "Case Management" By Federal District Courts Impermissibly Entangles The Branches Of Government By Permitting Courts To Examine, And Re-order, Executive Branch Priorities.

Even the panel majority did not deny that private damages actions against a sitting President threaten to interfere with the integrity of the Executive Branch and to undermine the separation of powers. Its solution to these problems, however, was not deferral, but was instead "judicial case management sensitive to the burdens of the presidency and the demands of the President's schedule." Pet. App. 13. This supposed cure is worse than the disease. "Case management" by the judiciary of a suit against the Chief Executive entangles the two branches in an ongoing and mutually harmful relationship, instead of maintaining the separation of the branches, as the Constitution envisions.

The panel majority suggested that throughout the litigation, a President could "pursue motions for rescheduling, additional time, or continuances" if he could show that the proceedings "interfer[ed] with specific, particularized, clearly articulated presidential duties." Pet. App. 16. Under this approach, the President would have to provide detailed information about the nature of pending Executive Branch matters requiring his attention, and the trial judge would have to pass judgment on the President's priorities. If the trial court -- state or federal -- decided that the President should devote more time to the private litigation than to official duties, the question would arise whether it could enforce that decision by threatening the President with contempt of court or sanctions. *See* FED. R. CIV. P. 16(f). If the President disagreed with a decision of the trial court, he could "petition [the court of appeals] for a writ of mandamus or prohibition." Pet. App. 16.

Such a state of affairs is an extraordinary affront to the separation of powers. A trial judge -- state or federal -- would be examining the official priorities of the individual in whom the whole of "the executive Power" is vested. And the judge would be not merely reviewing the President's priorities, but conceivably could order the President to rearrange them.

The nature of the President's responsibilities makes it especially inappropriate for the courts to insist on answers to the kinds of questions that inevitably would be posed under this regime. In situations involving matters of national security, sensitive diplomatic issues, or confidential intelligence or law enforcement operations -- to take just a few obvious examples -- the trial judge immediately would be enmeshed in disputes that could ripen into deeply troubling constitutional confrontations. Moreover, even seemingly minor changes in the President's schedule are imbued with significant portent by observers, both foreign and domestic. It is therefore not uncommon for a President to seek to maintain a pretense of "business as usual" to mask an impending crisis, while simultaneously having to attend to the urgent matter at hand.[26]

---

[26] The experiences of Presidents Carter and Reagan provide dramatic examples: when the invasion of Grenada was being planned, President Reagan was week-ending at a Georgia golf club. He wanted to hurry back to Washington, but his advisors told him "that a change in [his] schedule might draw attention to the possibility of U.S. intervention." He decided to remain in Georgia, but participated in meetings by way of telephone. CANNON, *supra* note 7, at 441-42. Similarly, during the 1980 mission to rescue the hostages in Iran, President Carter "wanted to spend every moment monitoring the progress of the rescue mission, but had to stick to

(continued . . .)

In such circumstances, simply having to ask a court for a change in the litigation schedule obviously could be highly damaging.

Even in areas not involving sensitive foreign or domestic concerns, a trial court would, under the panel's "case management" approach, be able to second-guess judgments that are properly made only by the President. A myriad of important Presidential activities might warrant a change in a litigation schedule: foreign or domestic travel; contacting members of Congress to persuade them to vote for legislation; meetings with groups of citizens to call public attention to an issue; intensive briefings from advisers on complex subjects. If the President moved for a change in the litigation schedule to accommodate these interests, the denial of such a motion would effectively preempt the priorities of the Executive Branch.[27]

The panel majority seemed to believe that untoward consequences can be averted so long as "case management" is "sensitive" enough to the demands of the President's office. Pet. App. 13. But this misunderstands both the nature of the problem and the nature of separated powers. Because the President embodies a branch of government, his priorities *are* the priorities of the Executive Branch. It follows that "case management," when the President is the defendant, necessar-

---

[26](... continued)
[his] regular schedule and act as though nothing of the kind was going on." CARTER, *supra* note 9, at 514.

[27] President Carter, for example, cut short a vacation to return to Washington to urge the passage of natural gas legislation that he deemed crucial to his national energy policy. CARTER, *supra* note 9, at 322. If the President had been involved in some aspect of litigation rather than on vacation, under the panel majority's scenario, he would have had to ask a court -- perhaps even a state court -- for permission to change his plans. The court then would be deciding if the President's interest in passage of the natural gas legislation was sufficiently important to warrant an interruption in judicial proceedings.

ily means management of the business of the Executive Branch -- both in setting priorities for the President's time and in controlling the disclosure of information about the President's schedule.

"Case management" by trial judges not only threatens the independence of the Executive from the Judicial Branch; it also unfairly places judges in a position they should not have to occupy -- the political arena. In suits against the President, the trial judge will be operating in an atmosphere that is almost certain to be highly charged politically. Any significant decision that a judge makes will be scrutinized for signs of partisan bias for or against the President. Decisions that are routine in any other case, such as a decision to postpone the defendant's deposition, will if the President is the deponent become the subject of partisan speculation and comment.

Moreover, judges attempting to assess the sufficiency of a President's explanation inevitably will be asked to distinguish between a President's "political" activities, on the one hand, and his "official" activities on the other. Political activity, of course, is one of the responsibilities of a democratically-elected official, and, as has often been recognized, these kinds of distinctions are inappropriate for judges to make.[28] These problems can, and should, be avoided altogether by holding the litigation in abeyance until the defendant is no longer President.

---

[28] *See United States ex rel. Joseph v. Cannon*, 642 F.2d 1373, 1379 (D.C. Cir. 1981) (courts lack "manageable standards" by which to distinguish between political and official functions), *cert. denied*, 455 U.S. 999 (1982); *Winpisinger v. Watson*, 628 F.2d 133, 140 (D.C. Cir.) (claim deemed not justiciable because it required judicial determination of whether executive actions were motivated by genuine concern for public interest or by "political expediency"), *cert. denied,* 446 U.S. 929 (1980).

2. "Case Management" By State Trial Courts Is Inconsistent With Principles Of Federalism Inherent In The Constitutional Scheme.

Perhaps the clearest evidence of the superiority of deferral to "case management," given the postulates of our constitutional system, emerges when one considers that if private civil actions can be brought against a sitting President, they are likely to be brought in state courts. Two of the claims in this case are state tort claims, and one would expect that civil suits in damages against a President for matters unrelated to his official duties will often, as here, involve causes of action under state law.[29] If suit is brought in state court, decisions about the activities and priorities of the Executive Branch of the federal government will be made in the first instance by state trial court judges, including those chosen by partisan election. The President, moreover, may not be able to obtain immediate review of these decisions in a federal forum. The availability of interlocutory review would turn on the judicial procedures of the state forum, and then, the only federal forum available to the President would likely be this Court.

The vast majority of state judges would, of course, be highly conscientious in carrying out their responsibilities in such a situation, but even the possibility that an incumbent President could be subject to the jurisdiction of a state court further demonstrates that suits against a sitting President are inconsistent with our constitutional scheme. The Framers were well aware that state governments might come into conflict with the federal government, and particularly with the Executive Branch. It would take little ingenuity to contrive a

---

[29] In the absence of diversity jurisdiction, suits based on a President's personal conduct ordinarily would not be removable. *See* 28 U.S.C. §§ 1441(b), 1442(a) (1994); *Mesa v. California*, 489 U.S. 121, 138-39 (1989).

state law damages action against a President unrelated to the conduct of his office. In an atmosphere of local partisan hostility to the President, the ability to bring such a suit in state court would be a powerful weapon in the hands of state interests -- one that the Framers could not possibly have intended to permit. This is further evidence that the approach most faithful to our constitutional scheme is not "case management," but the simple deferral of litigation until after the President leaves office, at which time any risk of disruption of the orderly functioning of the Executive is eliminated.

C. The Relief Sought Here Is Not Extraordinary, And Would Not Place the President "Above The Law."

A recurrent theme of both respondent and the panel majority is that the President's claim in this case is somehow extraordinary, both in the relief that it seeks and in the burden that it would place on respondent. This is wrong. The relief that the President seeks does not provide, in the panel majority's words, a "degree of protection from suit for his private wrongs enjoyed by no other public official (much less ordinary citizens)". Pet. App. 13. On the contrary, the relief that the President seeks is afforded in a variety of circumstances to public officials and private citizens alike. At the same time, the burdens that temporary deferral of the litigation would impose on plaintiffs are limited and reasonable.

1. Deferring Litigation Is Not Extraordinary.

The deferral that the President seeks is properly classified with an unexceptional group of doctrines that provide for litigation to be stayed to protect important institutional or public interests. There are numerous such instances where civil plaintiffs must accept the temporary postponement of litigation:

• The automatic stay provision of the Bankruptcy Code provides that litigation against a debtor must be stayed as soon as a party files a bankruptcy petition. The institutional interest in the orderly resolution of the bankruptcy estate justifies the imposition of delay on the plaintiff's claims. The stay ordinarily remains in effect until the bankruptcy proceeding is completed or the bankruptcy court lifts the stay. 11 U.S.C. § 362 (1994). That stay affects all litigation that "was or could have been commenced" prior to the filing of the petition. *Id.* Under this provision, civil actions can be stayed for extended periods.[30] Thus, if respondent had sued a party who entered bankruptcy, respondent would automatically find herself in a position similar to that she would be in if the President prevails before this Court -- except that the bankruptcy stay is indefinite, while the stay in this case has a definite term, circumscribed by the constitutional limit on a President's tenure in office.

- Courts defer civil litigation until the conclusion of a related criminal prosecution against the same defendant, if doing so is in the interests of justice or the public's interest in criminal law enforcement. That process may, of course, take several years. During that time, the civil plaintiff -- who may have been injured by a party who engaged in criminal conduct -- is afforded no relief.[31]

---

[30] *See, e.g., Moser v. Universal Eng'g Corp.,* 11 F.3d 720, 721-22 (7th Cir. 1993); *Panzella v. Hills Stores Co.,* 171 B.R. 22, 23 (E.D. Pa. 1994). A bankruptcy judge also has discretion to order a stay even of third-party litigation, to which the debtor is not a party, if that litigation conceivably could have an effect on the bankruptcy estate. *See* 11 U.S.C. § 105 (1994); 2 COLLIER ON BANKRUPTCY ¶ 105.02 (Lawrence P. King ed., 15th ed. 1994), and cases cited therein.

[31] *See, e.g., Koester v. American Republic Invs., Inc.,* 11 F.3d 818, 823 (8th Cir. 1993); *Wehling v. Columbia Broadcasting Sys.,* 608 F.2d 1084 (5th Cir. 1979); *United States v. Mellon Bank, N.A.,* 545 F.2d 869 (3d Cir. 1976); *Texaco, Inc. v. Borda,* 383 F.2d 607 (3d Cir. 1967).

- The Soldiers' and Sailors' Civil Relief Act of 1940, 50 U.S.C. app. §§ 501-25 (1988 & Supp. V 1993), permits civil claims by or against military personnel to be tolled and stayed while they are on active duty. It provides yet another analogous example of a stay, though the President does not claim, and has not claimed, relief under the Act.[32]

- The doctrine of primary jurisdiction, where it applies, compels plaintiffs to postpone the litigation of their civil claims while they pursue administrative proceedings, even though the administrative proceedings may not provide the relief they seek. *See, e.g., Ricci v. Chicago Mercantile Exch.*, 409 U.S. 289, 302-06 (1973). The process, which can take several years, is needed to ensure that a regulatory agency will be able to pursue its institutional agenda in an orderly fashion. *See, e.g., United States v. Western Pac. R.R. Co.*, 352 U.S. 59, 63-65 (1956) (quoting *Far East Conference v. United States*, 342 U.S. 570, 574-75 (1952)).

- Public officials who unsuccessfully raise a qualified immunity defense in a trial court are entitled, in the usual case, to a stay of discovery while they pursue an interlocutory appeal. *Harlow v. Fitzgerald*, 457 U.S. 800, 818 (1982). Such appeals routinely can delay litigation for a substantial period, even though the official ultimately may be found not to be entitled to immunity. In fact the stay attaches only in those cases where a trial court has initially rejected the claim of immunity.

---

[32] President Clinton does not claim to be on active military status. Nor does he claim protection under this or any other legislation. Rather, the relief sought here emanates from the nature of the President's constitutional duties and principles of separation of powers.

We do not suggest that all of these doctrines operate in exactly the same way as the relief that the President seeks here. But these examples dispel any suggestion that the President, in asking that this litigation be deferred, is somehow seeking extraordinary relief, or that holding this or any other litigation in abeyance violates a plaintiff's right to access to the courts.

2. Presidents Remain Accountable For Private Misconduct.

The panel majority, invoking the term "immunity," also suggested at various points that the President was seeking a rule that would bar liability for alleged wrongful conduct committed outside the scope of his official responsibilities. This is untrue. The President seeks only to defer the litigation until he leaves office. He remains accountable for his conduct and will be amenable to potential liability at that time. Accordingly, relieving a President temporarily of the requirement to defend private civil damages action does not, as the respondent suggests, place the President "above the law." Resp. C.A. Br. 9.

Deferring damages litigation manifestly does not give Presidents free license to engage in private misconduct. As this Court has observed, there are formal and informal checks quite apart from civil damages that deter unlawful, tortious or unconstitutional behavior by Presidents or those who may run for office in the future. These include the prospect of impeachment in egregious cases, as well as "constant scrutiny by the press." *Fitzgerald*, 457 U.S. at 757. Plaintiffs can take their charges to the newspapers and broadcast media, as has been done here. "Other incentives to avoid misconduct . . . include a desire to earn reelection," *id.*, or in the case of those who seek the Presidency, the desire to be elected in the first instance. Further deterrence may be found in the concern of a President "for his historical stature." *Id.* And of course, a President would still remain liable for damages after leaving office.

Indeed, deferral stands in sharp contrast to much more sweeping protection -- absolute or qualified immunity from damages -- that the law provides to literally tens of thousands of public employees. These immunity doctrines do not just delay litigation, but leave innocent victims wholly without compensation, sometimes even in cases where an official's conduct amounts to gross abuse of individual rights.[33] Similarly, diplomats, members of their families and foreign heads of state are wholly immune from liability in this country, even for personal misconduct and criminal acts.[34] In all these cases, protection from liability is needed to "advance compelling public ends." *Fitzgerald*, 457 U.S. at 758. Temporarily excusing the President from the burdens of private civil litiga-

---

[33] For example, in *Stump v. Sparkman*, 435 U.S. 349 (1978), a judge was held absolutely immune from damages notwithstanding undisputed allegations that he ordered a mildly retarded teenager sterilized in an *ex parte* proceeding, without a hearing, without notice to the young woman, and without appointment of a guardian *ad litem*. In *Imbler v. Pachtman*, 424 U.S. 409 (1976), a prosecutor was held absolutely immune from damages even though the plaintiff had obtained habeas corpus relief on the ground that the prosecutor knowingly used false testimony at a trial which led to plaintiff's murder conviction and death sentence.

[34] *See, e.g., Lafontant v. Aristide*, 844 F. Supp. 128 (E.D.N.Y. 1994); *Skeen v. Brazil*, 566 F. Supp. 1414 (D.D.C. 1983); *In re Terrence K.*, 524 N.Y.S.2d 996 (N.Y. Fam. Ct. 1988). Head-of-state immunity, founded on long-standing principles of international common law, permits heads of state, including our own, "to freely perform their duties at home and abroad without the threat of civil and criminal liability in a foreign legal system." *Lafontant*, 844 F. Supp. at 132. Diplomatic immunity, founded on the Vienna Convention, is a reciprocal immunity that exists "[t]o protect United States diplomats from criminal and civil prosecution in foreign lands with differing cultural and legal norms as well as fluctuating political climates." *Tabion v. Mufti*, 877 F. Supp. 285, 293 (E.D. Va. 1995), *aff'd*, 73 F.3d 535 (4th Cir. 1996).

tion, a far more modest accommodation, serves even more "compelling public ends."[35]

In sum, the President asserts a limited form of protection that is calibrated to accommodate a plaintiff's right to seek redress in the courts and the right of the people to have the person they elected President available to perform the unique and demanding responsibilities of that office. Because the plaintiff's right ultimately to seek redress is preserved, deferral also is in accordance with Chief Justice Marshall's declaration that "[t]he very essence of civil liberty certainly consists in the right of every individual to claim the protection of the laws, whenever he receives an injury." *Marbury v. Madison*, 5 U.S. (1 Cranch) 137, 163 (1803).

II. THE LITIGATION OF THIS PARTICULAR PRIVATE DAMAGES SUIT AGAINST THE PRESIDENT SHOULD, IN ANY EVENT, BE DEFERRED.

A. Several Factors Weigh Heavily In Favor Of Deferring This Litigation In Its Entirety.

Even if it were determined that temporary insulation from private civil damages litigation is not presumptively mandated in every case involving the President, there remains the question of whether, under principles enunciated in this Court's separation of powers cases, litigation of this particular nature should go forward while the President is in office. We respectfully submit that it should not.

---

[35] Indeed, while we seek here only to defer the plaintiff's opportunity to pursue redress, we note that courts have, with few qualms, denied damages remedies altogether in other cases. "It never has been denied that . . . immunity may impose a regrettable cost on individuals whose rights have been violated. But . . . it is not true that our jurisprudence ordinarily supplies a remedy in civil damages for every legal wrong." *Fitzgerald*, 457 U.S. at 754 n.37.

In *Fitzgerald*, the Court framed the analysis that must be undertaken as follows: "a court, before exercising jurisdiction [over a President], must balance the constitutional weight of the interest to be served against the dangers of intrusion on the authority and functions of the Executive Branch." 457 U.S. at 754. As the Court recently explained, "the separation-of-powers doctrine requires that a branch not impair another in the performance of its constitutional duties." *Loving v. United States*, 116 S. Ct. 1737, 1743 (1996). Accordingly, when action by another branch -- in this case the judiciary -- has "the potential for disruption" of Executive Branch functions, a court must "determine whether that impact is justified by an overriding need to promote objectives within the constitutional authority" of the Judicial Branch. *Nixon v. Administrator of Gen. Servs.*, 433 U.S. 425, 443 (1977) (hereinafter "*Nixon v. GSA*").

Providing a forum for the redress of civil rights and common law torts is, of course, an appropriate and important objective within the constitutional authority of the federal judiciary. The issue here, though, is whether there is an "overriding need" to promote this objective at this time, if doing so has the potential to disrupt the President's ability to perform his constitutional functions. The key is "to resolve those competing interests in a manner that preserves the essential functions of each branch." *United States v. Nixon*, 418 U.S. 683, 707 (1974). Temporarily deferring this litigation does just that.

Under the separation of powers principles elaborated in *Fitzgerald*, *United States v. Nixon*, and *Nixon v. GSA*, there is no justification for requiring this litigation to proceed while the President is in office. First, this suit involves the President both directly and personally. He is not a peripheral figure or one among many co-defendants. As the district court found, he is the "central figure in this action." Pet. App. 77. Moreover, given the nature of the allegations, this is the kind of litigation that he must attend to personally. It alleges events in which only he and the respondent purportedly were involved, and directly attacks his reputation and integrity. Such litigation cannot be handled by, for example, the President's accountants or business associates. As discussed above, litigation of this nature is especially disruptive, because it would require the President's personal time and attention.

Second, this suit concerns alleged pre-Presidential conduct, rather than unofficial conduct that the President engaged in while in office. In a case of this kind, the plaintiff's need to press a claim during the President's incumbency is less compelling, because the plaintiff generally will have had an opportunity to sue before the President was elected, as was the case here. The public interest in allowing the suit to go forward is also less, because there is no risk that the defendant was seeking to take advantage of the Presidency at the time of the alleged wrong.

Third, and related, this is a case in which the plaintiff's delay in bringing suit after the President was elected is not readily understandable. Respondent claims that deferring the suit will prejudice her interests, but respondent is the author of her own predicament. This case does not involve a latent harm that only became known long after the fact. The facts alleged in the complaint were known to respondent at once, and the claims accrued well before the President took office. Moreover, respondent chose not to pursue other available avenues of potential recovery, such as a timely claim under Title VII, or a suit against the publisher and the author of the article in which she was allegedly defamed. Respondent instead waited three years to act, filing barely within the limitations period for civil rights actions, 16 months after the defendant became President. Irrespective of whether the doctrine of laches should formally apply, these facts suggest that deferral is especially appropriate here. When the plaintiff has delayed extensively before suing, there is reason to think that further delay will not harm the plaintiff's interests. By the same token, when a plaintiff waits to bring suit based on pre-Presidential conduct until the President is elected, and chooses not to pursue other available remedies, the danger that the suit was prompted by illegitimate motives is obviously greater.

Finally, as the district court observed, "[t]his is not a case in which any necessity exists to rush to trial." Pet. App. 70. Respondent seeks only damages. If she ultimately prevails, she will be made whole regardless of the delay.[36] Respondent also does not identify any special need for the damages she seeks and, in fact, has stated that she intends to donate any award to charity.[37] Again, in a suit seeking only damages, where a plaintiff can be made whole by prejudgment interest and has disclaimed personal or expedient need for financial recovery, the danger that respondent will be prejudiced is diminished, and the justification for the potential interference with the functioning of the Executive Branch is even further diminished.

Respondent's interest in vindicating her asserted rights, and the judiciary's interest in providing a forum for vindicating such rights, are not significantly impaired by deferring this litigation. When the burden on the Presidency is compared with the very minimal impairment of these interests, it becomes clear that this litigation should be deferred in its entirety until the President leaves office.

---

[36] Prejudgment interest generally is available in appropriate circumstances under 42 U.S.C. § 1983 (1994). *See Winter v. Cerro Gordo County Conservation Bd.*, 925 F.2d 1069, 1073 (8th Cir. 1991); *Foley v. City of Lowell*, 948 F.2d 10 (1st Cir. 1991). Prejudgment interest also is available under Arkansas law in appropriate cases. *Wooten v. McClendon*, 612 S.W.2d 105 (Ark. 1981) (prejudgment interest available in contract and tort actions, provided that at time of injury, damages are immediately ascertainable with relative certainty).

[37] Transcript, *CNN: Paula Jones Interview* (CNN television broadcast, June 27, 1994) (C.A. App. 85).

B. At A Minimum, The District Court's Decision To Stay Trial Should Have Been Sustained.

1. The Court Of Appeals Lacked Jurisdiction Over Respondent's Cross Appeal.

Respondent cross-appealed below to challenge the district court's order to stay trial. A district court's decision to stay proceedings, however, is ordinarily not a final decision for purposes of appeal. *Moses H. Cone Memorial Hosp. v. Mercury Constr. Corp.*, 460 U.S. 1, 10 n.11 (1983). While such orders may in some circumstances be reviewed on an interlocutory basis by way of writ of mandamus (*see* 28 U.S.C. § 651 (1994)), respondent never sought such a writ.[38]

Respondent instead asserted that the court of appeals had "pendent appellate jurisdiction" over respondent's cross-appeal. The panel majority agreed, even though this Court recently ruled that "pendent appellate jurisdiction" should not be used "to parlay *Cohen*-type collateral orders into multi-issue interlocutory appeal tickets." *Swint v. Chambers County Comm'n*, 115 S. Ct. 1203, 1211 (1995).

Swint exhibits strong skepticism toward the type of pendent jurisdiction exercised in this case. There, the Court explained that under 28 U.S.C § 1292(b), Congress gave a district court "circumscribed authority to certify for immediate appeal interlocutory orders deemed pivotal and debatable," thus

---

[38] Some courts recognize that exceptions may exist in cases in which a stay is "tantamount to a dismissal" because it "effectively ends the litigation." *See, e.g., Boushel v. Toro Co.*, 985 F.2d 406, 408 (8th Cir. 1993); *Cheyney State College Faculty v. Hufstedler*, 703 F.2d 732, 735 (3d Cir. 1983). Even assuming that this exception should be allowed, respondent did not assert this ground as a basis for jurisdiction, perhaps in recognition that it clearly is not applicable here, where the district court's order contemplated further proceedings in federal court. *See Boushel*, 985 F.2d at 408-09.

confer[ring] on district courts first line discretion to allow interlocutory appeals. If courts of appeals had discretion to append to a *Cohen*-authorized appeal from a collateral order further rulings of a kind neither independently appealable nor certified by the district court, then the two-tiered arrangement § 1292(b) mandates would be severely undermined.

115 S. Ct. at 1210 (footnote omitted). Notwithstanding this language, and without any certification of the issue by the district court, the Eighth Circuit asserted pendent appellate jurisdiction over the respondent's interlocutory appeal of the stay of trial.[39]

The panel majority reasoned that *Swint* did not apply because respondent's cross-appeal was "inextricably intertwined" with the President's appeal. Pet. App. 5 n.4. *See Swint*, 115 S. Ct. at 1212. The issues in the two appeals were not, however, "inextricably intertwined." That these two appeals raise very distinct issues is evident from the distinct nature of the inquiries they generate. The issue of whether the President can defer litigation raises a question of law; the issue of whether a district court can stay litigation is a discretionary determination based on the facts of a particular case. While a district court's legal decisions are entitled to no special deference, its exercise of discretion to stay proceedings is a determination that can be overturned only for abuse of that discretion. *Landis v. North Am. Co.*, 299 U.S. 248, 255 (1936).

---

[39] Since *Swint*, numerous other circuit courts have eschewed asserting pendent jurisdiction in appeals such as this. *See Woods v. Smith*, 60 F.3d 1161, 1166 & n.29 (5th Cir. 1995), *cert denied*, 116 S. Ct. 880 (1996); *Pickens v. Hollowell*, 59 F.3d 1203, 1208 (11th Cir. 1995); *Garraghty v. Virginia*, 52 F.3d 1274, 1279 n.5 (4th Cir. 1995); *McKesson Corp. v. Islamic Republic of Iran*, 52 F.3d 346, 353 (D.C. Cir. 1995), *cert. denied*, 116 S. Ct. 704 (1996).

The district court here, in deciding to postpone trial, invoked its discretionary powers over scheduling. Pet. App. 71 (citing FED. R. CIV. P. 40). The court then expressly based its decision on the particular circumstances of this case:

> This is not a case in which any necessity exists to rush to trial. . . . Neither is this a case that would likely be tried with few demands on Presidential time, such as an *in rem* foreclosure by a lending institution.

> The situation here is that the Plaintiff filed this action two days before the three-year statute of limitations expired. Obviously, Plaintiff Jones was in no rush to get her case to court . . . . Consequently, the possibility that Ms. Jones may obtain a judgment and damages in this matter does not appear to be of urgent nature for her, and a delay in trial of the case will not harm her right to recover or cause her undue inconvenience.

Pet. App. 70.

As this passage makes clear, the district court's decision to stay trial rested upon the particular facts at hand, and review of that stay -- unlike review of its decision to reject the President's position that the entire case must be deferred as matter of law -- must address these particular facts. Accordingly, even if the concept of "pendent appellate jurisdiction" survived *Swint*, the two appeals here were not "inextricably intertwined," and the panel majority's exercise of such jurisdiction over the interlocutory appeal was erroneous.

2. The Court Of Appeals Erred In Reversing The District Court's Decision To Stay Trial In This Case.

The district court clearly had the authority to stay trial in this case. In *Landis*, Justice Cardozo wrote for this Court that

the power to stay proceedings is incidental to the
power inherent in every court to control the disposition of the causes on its docket . . . . How this can
best be done calls for the exercise of judgment,
which must weigh competing interests and maintain
an even balance.

299 U.S. at 254-55. Indeed, the Court in *Landis* specifically
stated that

*[e]specially in cases of extraordinary public mo-
ment*, the [plaintiff] may be required to submit to
delay not immoderate in extent and not oppressive
in its consequences if the public welfare or convenience will thereby be promoted.

Id. at 256 (emphasis added). Obviously, a trial here, which
would require the heavy involvement of a sitting President, is
a case of "extraordinary public moment."

The panel majority in this case showed none of the deference to the district court's determination required by *Landis*.
Instead, it rejected the trial court's order with a single sentence: "Such an order, delaying the trial until Mr. Clinton is
no longer President, is the functional equivalent of a grant of
temporary immunity to which, as we hold today, Mr. Clinton
is not constitutionally entitled." Pet. App. 13 n.9. This
sweeping and conclusory ruling hardly represents the careful
weighing of particular facts and circumstances necessary to
support a conclusion that the trial court abused its discretion.

The district court, by contrast, specifically assessed the
case and appropriately concluded that trial here should not
proceed. For all the reasons enumerated above, the trial court
found that it simply would not be possible to try the case
without enormous and extraordinary demands on the President's time, and that the respondent's interests would be substantially preserved notwithstanding the stay. Due to these
case-specific factors, the district court correctly stayed trial
until the President left office. That decision was not an abuse

of discretion and, if reviewed at all, should have been sustained.

CONCLUSION

For all the foregoing reasons, the decision of the court of appeals should be reversed, and this litigation should be held in abeyance, in its entirety, until the President leaves office.

Respectfully Submitted,

Robert S. Bennett
  Counsel of Record
Carl S. Rauh
Alan Kriegel
Amy R. Sabrin
Stephen P. Vaughn
SKADDEN, ARPS, SLATE,
  MEAGHER & FLOM
1440 New York Avenue, N.W.
Washington, D.C. 20005
(202) 371-7000

Of Counsel:
David A. Strauss
Geoffrey R. Stone
1111 East 60th Street
Chicago, Illinois 60637
(312) 702-9601

Attorneys for the Petitioner
President William Jefferson Clinton

August 8, 1996

Appendix D

BRIEF FOR RESPONDENT

No. 95-1853

IN THE

Supreme Court of the United States

OCTOBER TERM, 1995

◆

WILLIAM JEFFERSON CLINTON,

Petitioner.

—v.—

PAULA CORBIN JONES,

Respondent.

ON WRIT OF CERTIORARI TO THE UNITED STATES
COURT OF APPEALS FOR THE EIGHTH CIRCUIT

BRIEF FOR RESPONDENT

GILBERT K. DAVIS
   Counsel of Record
9516-C Lee Highway
Fairfax. Virginia 22031
(703) 352-3850

JOSEPH CAMMARATA
9516-C Lee Highway
Fairfax. Virginia 22031
(703) 352-3850

Counsel for Respondent Paula Corbin Jones

September 9, 1996

QUESTIONS PRESENTED

This uncomplicated civil action for damages against petitioner, who is President of the United States, for acts committed before he became President, bears no possible relation to his official responsibilities. No showing was made in the district court that the lawsuit, or any aspect of it, would impair the functioning of the presidency. The court of appeals ordered the district court to refrain from "creating scheduling conflicts" for petitioner on remand. The following questions are presented:

1. Whether the court of appeals erred in holding that petitioner was not entitled as a matter of law to a postponement or a stay of all proceedings for the duration of his presidency, when such a postponement or stay would effectively operate as a grant of official immunity for acts beyond "the outer perimeter of [the President's] official responsibility," the limit for presidential immunity set forth in *Nixon v. Fitzgerald*, 457 U.S. 731 (1982).

2. Whether the court of appeals erred in reversing the district court's grant to petitioner of what the district court termed a "limited or temporary immunity from trial," Pet. App. 68, for acts beyond the outer perimeter of his official responsibility.

TABLE OF CONTENTS

TABLE OF AUTHORITIES

PAGE

Statutes and Rules

IN THE

Supreme Court of the United States

OCTOBER TERM, 1995

No. 95-1853

———◆———

WILLIAM JEFFERSON CLINTON,

Petitioner,

—v.—

PAULA CORBIN JONES,

Respondent.

ON WRIT OF CERTIORARI TO THE UNITED STATES
COURT OF APPEALS FOR THE EIGHTH CIRCUIT

———◆———

BRIEF FOR RESPONDENT

STATEMENT OF THE CASE

In Arkansas on May 8, 1991, respondent Paula Corbin
Jones was a $6.35-an-hour state employee, and petitioner
William Jefferson Clinton was the Governor. The complaint
alleges that both were at the Excelsior Hotel in Little Rock
that day for the Governor's Quality Management Conference.
While working at the conference registration desk, Mrs. Jones
(Miss Corbin at that time) and a coworker were approached
by Danny Ferguson, a state trooper assigned to Governor
Clinton's security detail. Trooper Ferguson told Mrs. Jones
that "[t]he Governor would like to meet with you" in a suite
in the hotel, and gave her a piece of paper with the suite

number written on it. When Mrs. Jones wondered what the Governor wanted, Trooper Ferguson responded: "It's okay, we do this all the time for the Governor." Trooper Ferguson then escorted Mrs. Jones to the Governor's floor. Complaint ¶¶ 6-13.

Mrs. Jones, who had never met the Governor before, entered his suite at his invitation. Small talk followed. Mr. Clinton asked Mrs. Jones about her job. The Governor noted that David Harrington, his appointee who served as the director of Mrs. Jones's agency and her superior there, was his "good friend." The Governor then made a series of verbal and physical sexual advances toward Mrs. Jones, and undressed himself from the waist down. Horrified, Mrs. Jones moved away from Mr. Clinton and said, "Look, I've got to go." Pulling up his pants, Mr. Clinton said, "If you get in trouble for leaving work, have Dave [Harrington] call me immediately and I'll take care of it." As Mrs. Jones left, the Governor looked at her sternly and said: "You are smart. Let's keep this between ourselves." Visibly shaken and upset, Mrs. Jones resumed her post downstairs. In the following hours and days, she told her coworker, friends and relatives about what had happened. Mrs. Jones made no immediate official or public complaint because of fear for her job and for her relationship with her fiancé, and because she felt there was no one to whom she could complain since both her ultimate boss and the police were involved. She remained at her agency for the next twenty-one months, where she both feared and experienced job retaliation for her refusal to submit to Mr. Clinton's advances. In 1993, Mrs. Jones moved to California, and Mr. Clinton became President of the United States. Complaint ¶¶ 14-40, 48.

In January 1994, a widely publicized magazine article reported that, while he was Governor of Arkansas, Mr. Clinton regularly used his state police security detail to solicit women for sex with him. The article, apparently based upon the accounts of various Arkansas state troopers, reported that an unidentified trooper (clearly Mr. Ferguson) told the magazine that, at Mr. Clinton's request, he had approached a woman named "Paula" and escorted her to Mr. Clinton's room at the Excelsior Hotel. The article reported (again clearly based upon statements of Mr. Ferguson) that Paula had told the trooper that "she was available to be Clinton's regular girlfriend if he so desired," and thus implied that Mrs. Jones was one of the many women who, according to the article, had consensual sexual relationships with Mr. Clinton. Upset that individuals in Arkansas could (and did) identify her as the "Paula" in the article, and angry at the falsehoods that had damaged her reputation, Mrs. Jones publicly stated in February 1994 that she had rebuffed Mr. Clinton's advances and asked that Mr. Clinton acknowledge that fact. Instead, through press spokespersons, Mr. Clinton denied ever having met Mrs. Jones, publicly branded her a liar, and thus further damaged her reputation. Complaint ¶¶ 41-51.

On May 6, 1994, only four months after learning about the damaging magazine article, and after attempting unsuccessfully to obtain an acceptable statement by Mr. Clinton to settle the matter and to restore her reputation, Mrs. Jones filed suit against Mr. Clinton and Mr. Ferguson in the United States District Court for the Eastern District of Arkansas. Alleging the facts summarized above, her complaint asserts a claim under 42 U.S.C. § 1983 (1994) that Mr. Clinton, acting under color of state law, violated her constitutional rights to equal protection and due process by sexually harassing and assaulting her, as well as a claim under 42 U.S.C. § 1985 that Mr. Clinton and Mr. Ferguson had conspired to violate those rights. Her complaint also asserts two claims under Arkansas common law, one for intentional infliction of emotional distress against Mr. Clinton, and one for defamation against both Mr. Clinton and Mr. Ferguson. Complaint ¶¶ 58-79.

Mr. Ferguson's answer to complaint admitted, among other things, "traveling in an elevator with plaintiff Paula Jones and pointing out a particular room of the hotel." Ferguson Answer

¶ 11. He disclaimed any "personal knowledge of what took place in the hotel room." *Id.* ¶ 14.

Mr. Clinton did not answer the complaint, but instead requested and obtained an order allowing him to defer a response pending a motion to dismiss on grounds of "presidential immunity." Pet App. 40. On August 10, 1994, he filed what he called a "Motion to Dismiss on Grounds of Presidential Immunity." *See* Pet. App. ii. Citing the same principal authorities he cites here, Mr. Clinton argued that "immunity for the duration of the President's tenure is constitutionally mandated in the instant case." Memorandum in Support of President Clinton's Motion To Dismiss on Grounds of Presidential Immunity 6, *Jones* v. *Clinton*, Civil Action No. LR-C-94-290 (E.D. Ark. filed Aug. 10, 1994). As the district court noted, Mr. Clinton's claim "that he may not be sued in a civil action while sitting as President, even when the facts asserted by the Plaintiff occurred, if at all, before he was elected or assumed the office," is "a claim of absolute immunity." Pet. App. 55. Mr. Clinton argued that the complaint should be dismissed without prejudice to being refiled after he leaves the White House; in the alternative, he argued that the district court should stay the case until that time. Pet App. 55.

Mr. Clinton's motion was predicated simply upon his occupancy of the Office of President of the United States. He made no factual showing that any aspect of the pretrial or trial proceedings would hinder him from carrying out the duties of that Office.

The district court denied the substance of Mr. Clinton's motion on December 28, 1994. Pet. App. 54. Rejecting Mr. Clinton's immunity claim, the court denied the motion to dismiss, and observed that "[n]owhere in the Constitution, congressional acts, or the writings of any judge or scholar, may any credible support . . . be found" for Mr. Clinton's claim that he has "immunity from civil causes of action arising prior to [his] assuming the office" of the presidency. Pet.

App. 68. The court found Mr. Clinton's contention to be "contrary to our form of government, which asserts as did the English in the Magna Carta and the Petition of Right, that even the sovereign is subject to God and the law." Pet. App. 68. Nevertheless, in a self-contradictory holding that was apparently premised upon isolated language in *Nixon* v. *Fitzgerald*, 457 U.S. 731 (1982), the district court granted Mr. Clinton what it called a "limited or temporary immunity from trial," Pet. App. 68; *see also id.* at 70 (noting that its holding "amounts to the granting of temporary or limited immunity from trial as *Fitzgerald* seems to require"). Without offering any reason why a trial, however brief and properly managed, would interfere with Mr. Clinton's official duties, the court ordered an indefinite postponement of the trial against both Mr. Clinton *and* Mr. Ferguson pending the completion of Mr. Clinton's term in office, whether that be 1997 or 2001. Pet. App. 68-71. The court nonetheless held that discovery could proceed because "[t]here would seem to be no reason why the discovery and deposition process could not proceed as to all persons including the President himself." Pet App. 71.

Mr. Clinton appealed the rejection of his full immunity defense, Mrs. Jones cross-appealed the grant of "limited or temporary immunity from trial," and on February 24, 1995, the district court ordered a stay of all proceedings, including discovery, pending the appeal. Pet. App. 74. Mr. Clinton asserted that appellate jurisdiction existed under the rule that "denials of immunity are subject to appeal as of right under section 1291 [and] the collateral order doctrine." Opening Brief of Appellant President William Jefferson Clinton 10, 23, *Jones* v. *Clinton*, No. 95-1050 (8th Cir. filed Apr. 5, 1995).

On January 9, 1996, a divided panel of the Court of Appeals for the Eighth Circuit affirmed in part and reversed in part. Pet. App. 1. The Eighth Circuit held that nothing in the Constitution or in this Court's immunity case law lent support to Mr. Clinton's claim of immunity, as there had *never* been "any case in which any public official . . . has been granted any immunity from suit for his *unofficial* acts." Pet App. 7 (emphasis added). The court of appeals noted that this Court's decision in *Nixon* v. *Fitzgerald* recognized a presidential immunity that extended only to " 'acts within the 'outer perimeter' of [the President's] official responsibility,' " and that "unofficial acts" are "[b]y definition . . . not within the perimeter of the President's official responsibility at all, even the outer perimeter." Pet. App. 8-9 (quoting *Fitzgerald,* 457 U.S. at 756). The court concluded that *Fitzgerald*'s rationale—"that, without protection from civil liability for his *official* acts, the President would make (or refrain from making) official decisions, not in the best interests of the nation, but in an effort to avoid lawsuits and personal liability"—is "inapposite where only personal, private conduct by a President is at issue." Pet. App. 11 (emphasis added). The district court's denial of Mr. Clinton's motion to dismiss was accordingly affirmed.

The court of appeals reversed the district court's grant of a "limited or temporary immunity from trial" for the same reasons. While recognizing that "[t]he trial court has broad discretion to control the scheduling of events in matters on its docket," Pet. App. 13 (footnote omitted), the court of appeals held that, to the extent the district court's ruling could be characterized as an attempt to exercise that discretion, it was an "abuse of discretion" because it was "the functional equivalent of a grant of temporary immunity to which . . . Mr. Clinton is not constitutionally entitled," *id.* at. 13 & n.9. The court of appeals stressed that the district court had considerable power to ensure that the litigation would not interfere with Mr. Clinton's official duties, and that the district court was to engage in "judicial case management sensitive to the burdens of the presidency and the demands of the President's schedule," Pet. App. 13:

> We have every confidence that the District Court will exercise its [scheduling] discretion in such a way that

this lawsuit may move forward with the reasonable dispatch that is desirable in all cases, without creating scheduling conflicts that would thwart the President's performance of his official duties. . . .

If, contrary to history and all reasonable expectations, a President ever becomes so burdened by private-wrong lawsuits that his attention to them would hinder him in carrying out the duties of his office, then clearly the courts would be duty-bound to exercise their discretion to control scheduling and the like so as to protect the President's ability to fulfill his constitutional responsibilities. . . .

The discretion of the courts in suits such as this one comes into play, not in deciding on a case-by-case basis whether a civil complaint alleging private wrongs is sufficiently compelling so as to be permitted to proceed with an incumbent President as defendant, but in controlling the scheduling of the case as necessary to avoid interference with specific, particularized, clearly articulated presidential duties. If the trial preliminaries or the trial itself become barriers to the effective performance of his official duties, Mr. Clinton's remedy is to pursue motions for rescheduling, additional time, or continuances.

Pet. App. 13-16.

Judge Beam, concurring, emphasized that Mr. Clinton had failed to point out *any* "specific hardship or inequity" that would justify any stay of the litigation under this Court's decision in *Landis* v. *North American Co.*, 299 U.S. 248, 254-56 (1936). Pet. App. 20. Judge Beam observed that Mr. Clinton had "greatly overstated" the potential for "interbranch interference" that would result if the lawsuit were allowed to proceed. Pet. App. 21. Citing numerous occasions upon which past Presidents had given testimony, Judge Beam explained that the potential for such interference in this particular case was "not appreciably greater than those faced in many other instances in which a sitting President interfaces as a party, witness, or target with the judicial and legislative branches of the government." Pet. App. 22. He concluded:

> Mrs. Jones's complaint presents relatively uncomplicated civil litigation, the discovery for which can and should be carried out with a minimum of impact on the President's schedule. It is doubtful, for instance, that more than one, perhaps two, face-to-face pretrial encounters between the President and Mrs. Jones's representatives need to occur. Indeed, there is not even a requirement that parties be present at the trial of civil litigation and with some frequency they are not. At the bottom line, the availability of written interrogatories, written requests for admissions and written stipulations of undisputed facts, as allowed by the Federal Rules of Civil Procedure, would indicate that the actual impact of this litigation on the duties of the presidency, if that is Mr. Clinton's real concern, is being vastly magnified, especially assuming the trial judge's careful supervision of the litigation with maximum consideration of the President's constitutional duties. . . .

> As I have attempted to stress, *nothing [in our decision] prohibits the trial judge from halting or delaying or rescheduling any proposed action by any party at any time should she find that the duties of the presidency are even slightly imperiled.*

Pet. App. 23-25 (emphasis added).

SUMMARY OF ARGUMENT

Mr. Clinton asks for the recognition of an entirely unprecedented presidential immunity, a purely personal privilege against lawsuits that have nothing to do with official, presidential duties. Nothing in *Nixon* v. *Fitzgerald,* 457 U.S. 731

(1982), or in this Court's immunity case law, however, supports his theory. The essential rationale of official immunity is that the imposition of personal damages liability on public officials for official acts would cause them to "hesitate to exercise their discretion in a way 'injuriously affect[ing] the claims of particular individuals.' " *Id.* at 744-75 (citation omitted). As a consequence, presidential immunity was limited in *Fitzgerald* to "acts within the *'outer perimeter'* of [the President's] *official responsibility,"* *id.* at 756 (emphasis added), and Chief Justice Burger's concurring opinion in that case made clear that Presidents "are *not* immune for acts outside official duties," *id.* at 759 (Burger, C.J., concurring). The claim that *Fitzgerald* supports protection for unofficial acts is based upon language taken out of context.

Mr. Clinton's other authorities do not support his immunity claim. The Framers did not intend to place the President above the law, and thus did not confer upon Presidents any personal privileges akin to those of a monarch who is sovereign in both person and office. Nor do *United States* v. *Burr,* 25 F. Cas. 30, 187 (C.C.D. Va. 1807) (Nos. 14,692d and 14,694), and *United States* v. *Nixon,* 418 U.S. 683 (1974), support immunity. They simply stand for the proposition that confidential and official presidential communications are presumptively protected by executive privilege, which may nonetheless be overcome upon a sufficient showing of need. Here, no official acts or confidential communications are involved, and no balancing of interests between privilege and need is required. This Court's cases, indeed, have always limited Presidential privileges to official communications and acts, and there is no reason to abandon that course here.

Nor is Mr. Clinton's immunity claim supported by separation-of-powers principles. He made no showing below that this case will actually prevent him from carrying out his duties. Nor could he, given the manifest simplicity of the case. Mr. Clinton is thus reduced to the contention that in general, litigation (including a hypothetical torrent of future cases) will always interfere with Presidential duties. Mr. Clinton overstates the vulnerability of his Office's work to civil litigation involving unofficial actions. In addition, Mr. Clinton also overstates a supposed danger that a trial court, by engaging in "judicial case management sensitive to the burdens of the presidency and the demands of the President's schedule," as the court of appeals directed, Pet. App. 13, will somehow interfere with the functioning of the Executive Branch.

ARGUMENT

I. THE TEMPORARY PRESIDENTIAL IMMUNITY ASSERTED BY PETITIONER IS LEGALLY INSUPPORTABLE AND IS UNNECESSARY TO PROTECT THE INTERESTS OF THE PRESIDENCY.

A. The immunity case law does not support petitioner's immunity claim.

Mr. Clinton, the Government, and the academic *amici* supporting him ask this Court to create a heretofore unrecognized presidential immunity: a purely personal privilege against lawsuits that have nothing to do with official, presidential duties. They argue that, even in cases having nothing to do with official action of any kind, "private civil damages litigation against an incumbent president must, in all but the most exceptional cases, be deferred until the president leaves office." Pet. Br. 11. And while Mr. Clinton now shies away from using the word "immunity" to describe the relief he seeks, the academic *amici* supporting him candidly do not. As they explain, the gist of Mr. Clinton's claim is that "*Nixon* v. *Fitzgerald* supports a temporary Presidential immunity for civil litigation even for claims based on private conduct." Br. *Amicus Curiae* of Law Profs. In Supp. of Pet. 11. Mr. Clinton and his *amici* indeed rely principally upon the leading presidential immunity case, *Nixon* v. *Fitzgerald*, 457 U.S. 731 (1982), which, they say, recognizes that, regardless of the basis of the claim, "one [cannot] hale an incumbent President into court and seek damages from him personally," Pet. Br. 17, and "indicates that the instant suit should be deferred," Br. for United States as *Amicus Curiae* 4. Neither the *Fitzgerald* holding nor its rationale, however, supports the extraordinary and novel immunity claim advanced here.

In *Fitzgerald*, a five-Justice majority of this Court held that Presidents are entitled to an absolute immunity for suits for civil damages relating to any of their official acts. Four Justices dissented, arguing that presidential immunity should be limited only to particular functions performed by the President. Both the majority and concurring opinions made clear that the President's official immunity only forecloses "damages liability for acts within the *'outer perimeter'* of [the President's] *official responsibility*." *Fitzgerald*, 457 U.S. at 756 (emphasis added). Chief Justice Burger explained that presidential immunity covers only *official* actions and "*does not extend beyond such actions*"—that "a President, like Members of Congress, judges, prosecutors or congressional aides . . . [is] *not* immune for acts outside official duties." *Id.* at 761 n.4, 759 (Burger, C.J., concurring; emphasis added). That very limitation, Chief Justice Burger observed, was precisely why the Court's decision did not "place[ ] a President 'above the law,' " as the dissent had vigorously argued. *Id.* (Burger, C.J., concurring); *see id.* at 766-67 (White, J., dissenting); *id.* at 797 (Blackmun, J., dissenting).

The limitation of immunity to official acts is backed by a long and unbroken line of authority cited in *Fitzgerald*. As Judge Learned Hand once explained, "[t]he decisions have, indeed, *always* imposed as a limitation upon the immunity that the official's act must have been within the scope of his powers." *Gregoire* v. *Biddle*, 177 F.2d 579, 581 (2d Cir. 1949) (emphasis added), *cert. denied*, 339 U.S. 949 (1950). The essential rationale of immunity is that imposing personal liability for *official* acts would distort official judgment or make officials unwilling to act. Thus, *Fitzgerald* observed that, "[i]n the absence of immunity, . . . executive officials would hesitate to exercise their discretion in a way 'injuriously affect[ing] the claims of particular individuals,' even when the public interest required bold and unhesitating action." *Fitzgerald,* 457 U.S. at 744-45 (quoting *Spalding* v. *Vilas,* 161 U.S. 483, 499 (1896)). The Court cited "the prospect that damages liability may render an official unduly cautious in the discharge of his official duties" as being "[a]mong the most persuasive reasons supporting official immunity." *Id.* at 752 n.32. Immunity, the Court explained, was necessary to "provid[e] an official 'the maximum ability to deal fearlessly and impartially with' the duties of his office." *Id.* at 752 (quoting *Ferri* v. *Ackerman,* 444 U.S. 193, 203 (1979)).[1]

In following this central rationale undergirding this Court's immunity cases, *Fitzgerald* held that official immunity could only be invoked as a defense in litigation involving official acts:

> Applying the principles of our cases to claims of this kind, we hold that petitioner, as a former President of the United States, is entitled to absolute immunity from damages liability predicated on his *official* acts.
>
> *   *   *
>
> In view of the special nature of the President's constitutional office and functions, we think it appropriate to recognize absolute Presidential immunity from damages liability for acts *within the 'outer perimeter' of his official responsibility.*

---

[1]   *See also, e.g., Mireles* v. *Waco,* 502 U.S. 9, 10-11 (1991) (per curiam) (judges immune for judicial acts so that they may act in official capacity without apprehension of personal liability); *Forrester* v. *White,* 484 U.S. 219, 226-29 (1988) (same); *Butz* v. *Economou,* 438 U.S. 478, 504-17 (1978) (same for executive agency officials); *Imbler* v. *Pachtman,* 424 U.S. 409, 424-31 (1976) (state prosecutors); *Scheuer* v. *Rhodes,* 416 U.S. 232, 240-49 (1974) (state executive officials); *Tenney* v. *Brandhove,* 341 U.S. 368, 376-79 (1951) (state legislators); *Bradley* v. *Fisher,* 80 U.S. (13 Wall.) 335, 347-53 (1872) (judges).

Id. at 749, 756 (emphasis added). These words were not mere dicta. Sharply disputed in *Fitzgerald* was the issue of which acts were to be subject to immunity. The Court noted that, in the past, it had linked absolute immunity to particular official functions: "Frequently our decisions have held that an official's absolute immunity should extend only to acts in performance of particular functions of his office." *Id.* at 755. But because of the variety of functions performed by the President, the Court selected the broadest scope of absolute immunity recognized in the case law: immunity "for acts within the 'outer perimeter' of . . . official responsibility." *Id.* at 756; *see, e.g., Spalding* v. *Vilas, supra,* 161 U.S. at 498; *Barr* v. *Matteo,* 360 U.S. 564, 575 (1959). The Court then applied its holding to the facts of the case. Citing a specific provision of the United States Code, it held that the alleged conduct for which President Nixon had been sued indeed fell within the outer perimeter of presidential responsibility. *Id.* at 757.

Conceding, as he must, that "[t]his case is different from *Fitzgerald* . . . in that it largely does not touch upon official actions," Mr. Clinton nevertheless contends that "[t]he logic of *Fitzgerald* compels the conclusion that incumbent Presidents are entitled to the much more modest relief sought here—the temporary deferral of private civil litigation." Pet. Br. 20. In support of this argument, Mr. Clinton points to two sentences in a single paragraph of *Fitzgerald*: one sentence stating that "[b]ecause of the singular importance of the President's duties, diversion of his energies by concern with private lawsuits would raise unique risks to the effective functioning of government"; and another stating that "the sheer prominence of the President's office [cannot] be ignored." *Fitzgerald, supra,* 457 U.S. at 751-53, *quoted in* Pet. Br. 20. This language, the argument goes, applies as fully to lawsuits involving private conduct as to those involving official conduct, and so requires recognition of the temporary immunity sought here. *See* Pet. Br. 20-21; *see also* Br. *Amicus Curiae* of Law Profs. In Supp. of Pet. 10; Br. for United States 16.

Mr. Clinton misreads *Fitzgerald* because, as even the Government admits, "[w]hen the President is sued for actions wholly unrelated to his official responsibilities, *Fitzgerald*'s concern for ensuring 'fearless[ ] and impartial[ ]' Presidential decision making is not directly implicated." Br. for United States 15. The language upon which Mr. Clinton relies simply cannot be stripped from the context of that concern. Indeed, it comes from the Court's explanation of why the absolute immunity given to "prosecutors and judges," rather than the qualified immunity given to "governors and cabinet officers," was appropriate for the President's official actions, *Fitzgerald*, 457 U.S. at 750-51; and it makes clear that the "unique risks to the effective functioning of government" to which the Court referred stemmed from private lawsuits concerning *official* acts. The Court said that the overriding policy consideration underlying official immunity—that lawsuits over official acts might compromise an official's " 'ability to deal fearlessly and impartially with' the duties of his office," 457 U.S. at 752 (quoting *Ferri* v. *Ackerman*, 444 U.S. 193, 203 (1979))—applied with greater force to the President because (1) the President's official acts were more likely to be controversial ones affecting "countless people" than those of other officials, and (2) the President's "sheer prominence" made him the most likely target for suits about controversial official acts of the Executive Branch. Thus, the relevant portion of the Court's opinion reads as follows:

> In arguing that the President is entitled only to qualified immunity, the respondent relies on cases in which we have recognized immunity of this scope for governors and cabinet officers. *E.g.*, *Butz* v. *Economou*, 438 U.S. 478 (1978); *Scheuer* v. *Rhodes*, 416 U.S. 232 (1974). We find these cases to be inapposite. The President's unique status under the Constitution distinguishes him from other officials.

> Because of the singular importance of the President's duties, diversion of his energies by concern with private

lawsuits would raise unique risks to the effective functioning of government. *As is the case with prosecutors and judges—for whom absolute immunity now is established—a President must concern himself with matters likely to "arouse the most intense feelings." Pierson v. Ray, 386 U.S., at 554. Yet, as our decisions have recognized, it is in precisely such cases that there exists the greatest public interest in providing an official "the maximum ability to deal fearlessly and impartially with" the duties of his office. Ferri v. Ackerman, 444 U.S. 193, 203 (1979). This concern is compelling where the office-holder must make the most sensitive and far-reaching decisions entrusted to any official under our constitutional system. Nor can the sheer prominence of the President's office be ignored. In view of the visibility of his office and the effect of his actions on countless people, the President would be an easily identifiable target for suits for civil damages. Cognizance of this personal vulnerability frequently could distract a President from his public duties, to the detriment of not only the President and his office but also the Nation that the presidency was designed to serve.*

457 U.S. at 751-53 (footnotes omitted; emphasis added). In short, the Court reasoned that the President was potentially more vulnerable than other officials to lawsuits for *official* acts, and that absolute, not qualified, immunity should therefore apply to those acts.

The Court's reasoning in *Fitzgerald* thus has no application to the case at bar. As the court of appeals concluded, "[i]t is clear from a careful reading of *Fitzgerald*" that this Court was "concern[ed] that the President's awareness of his essentially infinite potential personal liability for virtually every official action he takes would have an adverse influence on the presidential decision-making process," and might cause the President to "make (or refrain from making) official decisions, not in the best interests of the nation, but in an effort to avoid lawsuits and personal liability." Pet. App. 11. No such dangers arise, of course, from suits relating to personal conduct. Imposing liability for pre-presidential or other unofficial conduct will simply not cause Presidents to "hesitate to exercise their discretion in a way 'injuriously affect[ing] the claims of particular individuals.' " *Fitzgerald*, 457 U.S. at 744-45 (quoting *Spalding* v. *Vilas*, 161 U.S. at 499). It will not diminish a President's " 'ability to deal fearlessly and impartially with' the duties of his office." *Id.* at 752 (quoting *Ferri* v. *Ackerman*, 444 U.S. 193, 203 (1979)). It will not place the President " 'under an apprehension that the motives that control his official conduct may, at any time, become the subject of inquiry in a civil suit for damages.' " *Id.* at 745 (quoting *Spalding*, 161 U.S. at 498). And it will not require any court "to probe into the elements of Presidential decisionmaking," or to engage in "judicial questioning of Presidential acts, including the reasons for the decision, how it was arrived at, the information on which it was based, and who supplied the information." *Id.* at 761-62 (Burger, C.J., concurring).

> **B. Petitioner's immunity claim would be contrary to the intention of the Framers, is not supported by any decisions of this Court, and would place petitioner above the law.**

Mr. Clinton also contends that allowing this litigation to proceed would run contrary to the "teaching of the Framers," Pet. Br. 15, and would contravene both "historical doctrine" and "traditional practice," *id.* at 17. To the contrary, the Framers did not intend to place the President above the law, and did not invest the President with any personal privileges akin to those of the English King. As the district court wrote, "[n]owhere in the Constitution, congressional acts, or the writings of any judge or scholar, may any support . . . be found" for giving the President special protection from "civil causes of action arising prior to assuming the office." Pet App. 68. Mr. Clinton's claim is simply "contrary to our form of government." *Id.* Indeed, to the extent that there is any "traditional practice" on the point at all, it is that lawsuits involving a President's unofficial acts must be allowed to proceed.

The Framers believed that every constitutional power and every constitutional actor must be constrained. "Federalists and antifederalists both agreed . . . that no one should ever be entrusted with unqualified authority." Bernard Bailyn, *The Ideological Origins of the American Revolution* 368 (1992). Having fought to escape the reign of a king whose power was unchecked, they were certain "that any release of the constraints on the executive—any executive—was an invitation to disaster." *Id.* at 379 (citing remarks of Edward Rutledge); *see also* 4 Jonathan Elliot, *The Debates of the Several State Conventions on the Adoption of the Federal Constitution as Recommended by the General Convention of Philadelphia in 1787* 276 (2d ed., reprinted 1987).

As a result, the Framers adhered to a notion reflected time and again in this Court's decisions: "No man in this country is so high that he is above the law." *United States* v. *Lee*, 106 U.S. 196, 220 (1882). It was understood that the President had no personal privileges beyond those of an ordinary citizen:

> *His person is not so much protected as that of a member of the house of representatives; for he may be proceeded against like any other man in the ordinary course of law.*

An American Citizen (Tench Coxe) I, Independent Gazetteer (Philadelphia) September 26, 1787, reprinted in I Bernard Bailyn, ed., *The Debate on the Constitution* 20, 24 (1993) (emphasis in original). As Charles Coatsworth Pinckney, an important Framer, explained on the Senate floor only a few years after the Constituion's adoption, the Framers

> well knew how oppressively the power of undefined privileges had been exercised in Great Britain, and were determined no such authority should ever be exercised here.

Annals of Congress, March 5, 1800, at 72. Pinckney continued:

> let us inquire, why the Constitution should have been so attentive to each branch of Congress, so jealous of their privileges, and have shewn so little to the President of the United States in this respect. Why should the individual members of either branch, or either branch itself, have more privileges than him? . . . The Convention which formed the Constitution well knew that this was an important point, and no subject had been more abused than privilege. They therefore determined to set the example, in merely limiting privilege to what was necessary, and no more.

Id. at 74; *cf. Nixon* v. *Fitzgerald, supra,* 457 U.S. at 755 (immunity must be "closely related to [its] justifying purpose," and "the sphere of protected action must be related closely to the immunity's justifying purpose"). Similarly, James Wilson explained that the President

> is placed high, and is possessed of power far from being contemptible; *yet not a single privilege is annexed to his character*; far from being above the laws, *he is amenable to them in his private character as a citizen,* and in his public character by impeachment.

2 Elliot, *Debates on the Federal Constitution, supra,* at 480 (emphasis added and omitted).

Mr. Clinton's own description of the historical record only serves to confirm the district court's conclusion that he has no credible support for his claim. As he did below, Mr. Clinton relies primarily upon Justice Story's isolated statement that a President's "person must be deemed, in civil cases at least, to possess an official inviolability." Pet. Br. 16 (quoting 3 Joseph Story, *Commentaries on the Constitution of the United States* § 1563, pp. 418-19 (1st ed. 1833)). By its terms, however, Justice Story's statement referred only to the President's "*official* inviolability," and described only the protections for actions taken by a President "*while he is in the discharge of the duties of his office*," *id.* (citation omitted), and thus goes no farther than *Nixon* v. *Fitzgerald*, which did not recognize any "immun[ity] for acts *outside* official duties," *Fitzgerald*, 457 U.S. at 759 (Burger, C.J., concurring). Beyond this, Justice Story was referring only to a presidential privilege from "arrest, imprisonment, or detention"—none of which, of course, is involved here—and the "official inviolability" he described was only for "*this* purpose." Pet Br. 16 (citation omitted; emphasis added).[2] And as for Mr. Clinton's citation of Presidents Adams and Jefferson to the effect that "the President personally is not subject to any process whatsoever," Pet. Br. 16, that view was refuted by Chief Justice Marshall early in our Nation's history in *United States* v. *Burr*, 25 F. Cas. 187, 191 (C.C.D. Va. 1807) (No. 14,694) ("That the president of the United States may be subpoenaed, and examined as a witness, and required to produce any paper in his possession, is not controverted"). *See also Nixon* v. *Sirica*, 487 F.2d 700, 709 (D.C. Cir. 1973) (en banc; per curiam) (noting that Chief Justice Marshall "squarely ruled that a subpoena may be directed to the President).[3] It is thus now

---

[2]   An ordinary modern civil case, of course, presents no danger of arrest, imprisonment or detention of the defendant. Accordingly, the debate over whether a "President must be impeached and removed from office before he can be prosecuted" for a crime, Pet. Br. 14-15 & n.11; *see also* Br. for United States 15 n.8, is irrelevant here.

[3]   In fact, the Jefferson letter that Mr. Clinton quotes was one in which President Jefferson was expressing his criticisms of the Chief Justice's decision in *Burr*. *See Fitzgerald*, 457 U.S. at 751 n.31; *see also* Bradford E. Biegon, Note, *Presidential Immunity in Civil Actions: An Analysis Based Upon Text, History and Blackstone's* Commentaries, 82 Va. L. Rev. 677, 698 & nn.127-28 (1996) ("Jefferson's close of the letter is illustrative of the distemper that Marshall's opinion must have caused him").

As for President Adams, he is almost universally regarded as an exponent of an excessively expansive view of executive power. He was regarded by most of his contemporaries as being almost a monarchist. *See* "settled law that the separation-of-powers doctrine does not bar every exercise of jurisdiction over the President." *Nixon* v. *Fitzgerald*, 457 U.S. at 753-54.

The law ever since Chief Justice Marshall's pronouncement in *Burr, supra,* supports not a distinction between testimony in criminal and testimony in civil cases, as Mr. Clinton contends (*see, e.g.,* Pet. Br. 17, 26-27), but a line between matters that pertain to the President's official duties and those that do not—in other words, precisely the line followed in *Fitzgerald.*. Thus, in *Burr,* Chief Justice Marshall observed that the President was "subject to the general rules which apply to others," and recognized *only* a privilege "to withhold private letters . . . written . . . in consequence of [the President's] public character, and may relate to public concerns." *Burr,* 25 F. Cas. at 191-92. Similarly today, the threshold issue of whether there is a presidential privilege turns not upon whether a proceeding is civil or criminal, but upon the nature of the materials subpoenaed. When faced with a subpoena, a President may "legitimately assert privilege, of course, *only* to those materials whose contents fall within the scope of the privilege recognized in *United States* v. *Nixon*"—which is "limited to communications 'in performance of [a President's] responsibilities,' 'of his office,' and made 'in the process of shaping and making decisions.'" *Nixon* v. *Administrator of General Services,* 433 U.S. 425, 449 (1977) (quoting *United States* v. *Nixon,* 418 U.S. 683, 711, 713, 708 (1974)). Only if that stringent test is met is there a "presumptive privilege." *United States* v. *Nixon,* 418 U.S. at 708. But even this presumptive privilege may be overcome, since the interests of the Executive Branch must be balanced against "our historic commitment to the rule of law," which "depend[s] on full disclosure of all the facts, within the framework of the rules evidence." *Id.* at 709. Only when that balancing is required— where *official* acts and communications are at issue—does it

---

W. Page Smith, *John Adams* 755 (1962); *see also* Biegon, *supra,* 82 Va. L. Rev. at 696.

become relevant whether a judicial proceeding is civil or criminal in nature. *See id.* at 707-13.

Thus, the executive privilege recognized by this Court in *United States* v. *Nixon* in no way supports Mr. Clinton's argument. Executive privilege is analogous to the protection recognized in *Nixon* v. *Fitzgerald*, and its limitations are similar. Both protections are designed to preserve the presidential decision-making process, and both are narrowly crafted to achieve that end. Executive privilege is necessary because "[a] President and those who assist him must be free to explore alternatives in the process of shaping policies and making decisions and to do so in a way many would be unwilling to express except privately." *United States* v. *Nixon*, 418 U.S. at 708. Because official conduct and communications are not involved here, there is no warrant to engage in the balancing of interests required in *United States* v. *Nixon*, and no basis to hold that there must be Sixth Amendment interests at stake for this litigation to proceed.[4] This case would no more threaten "the public interest in candid, objective, and even blunt or harsh opinions in Presidential decisionmaking," *id.*, than it would threaten to cause Presidents "to hesitate to exercise their discretion in a way 'injuriously affect[ing] the claims of particular individuals,' " *Nixon* v.

---

[4]   Mr. Clinton is accordingly wrong to suggest that *United States* v. *Nixon* can be read as implying that the testimony of someone serving as President cannot be compelled in "civil proceedings." Pet. Br. 27. The Court simply left open the question whether the presumptive *executive privilege* for executive communications could be overcome in civil proceedings. *See Nixon*, 418 U.S. at 711-12 & n. 19. Here, of course, there is no question of privilege, and therefore no need to look to whether the need to produce evidence in a civil case may be overcome by the need to protect the privacy of official presidential deliberations. Similarly, Mr. Clinton's observation that the Court in *Nixon* twice quoted Chief Justice Marshall's statement that "[i]n no case of this kind would a court be required to proceed against the president as against an ordinary individual," Pet. Br. 27 (quoting *Nixon*, 418 U.S. at 708, 715 (quoting *Burr*, 25 F. Cas. at 192)) is beside the point: both Chief Justice Marshall in *Burr* and the *Nixon* Court were addressing the question of how claims of executive privilege must be handled by the courts.

Fitzgerald, 457 U.S. at 744-75 (quoting *Spalding* v. *Vilas*, 161 U.S. at 498-99).

This Court has recognized the distinction between official and unofficial acts when determining the President's amenability to suit in contexts other than civil damages actions as well. The judiciary "has no jurisdiction of a bill to enjoin the President in the performance of his official duties," *Mississippi* v. *Johnson*, 71 U.S. (4 Wall.) 475, 500-01 (1866); the courts "cannot direct the President to take a specified executive act," *Franklin* v. *Massachusetts*, 505 U.S. 788, 829 (1992) (Scalia, J., concurring in part and in judgment). This rule serves the same functions as the immunity recognized in *Fitzgerald, see Franklin*, 505 U.S. at 827-28 (Scalia, J., concurring in part and in judgment), and is likewise expressly limited to official acts. Indeed, in *Mississippi* v. *Johnson*, 71 U.S. (4 Wall.) at 501, "the bill contain[ed] a prayer that, if the relief sought cannot be had against Andrew Johnson, as President, it may be granted against Andrew Johnson as a citizen of Tennessee." In responding to this contention, the Court did not dispute that injunctive proceedings could be had against a citizen serving as President. Rather, the Court held that what was prohibited was "relief *as against the execution of an Act of Congress* by Andrew Johnson"—an injunction relating to the President's *official* acts. *Johnson*, 71 U.S. (4 Wall.) at 501 (emphasis added).

Finally, there is no support for Mr. Clinton's claim that the paucity of cases against Presidents for unofficial acts is due to a "nearly universal understanding that such litigation is inconsistent with our constitutional scheme." Pet. Br. 18. There has been no such understanding. None of the prior Presidents who were sued for nonpresidential acts (Presidents Theodore Roosevelt, Harry· Truman, and John Kennedy) asserted any immunity claim. Pet. App. 14 n.10.[5] And Presi-

---

[5]   President Kennedy attempted to obtain a stay under the Soldiers' and Sailors' Civil Relief Act of 1940, 50 U.S.C. app. §§ 501-25 (1988 &

dent Nixon *twice* conceded to this Court that Presidents could indeed be sued for nonpresidential acts: first, at oral argument in *United States* v. *Nixon, supra,* and then later, in his briefs in *Nixon* v. *Fitzgerald, supra.*[6] In any event, the understanding reflected in Mr. Clinton's brief is that such litigation may indeed be brought, but must be stayed. If *that* were the universal historical understanding, then plaintiffs with claims against Presidents for unofficial acts would not have withheld their claims, but would have *asserted* them to preserve their timeliness, even if the claims were going to be stayed.

In short, to create a blanket rule protecting a President from litigation relating to his unofficial acts would cross a line that this Court has never crossed and that the Framers never contemplated would be crossed. It would create the first purely personal presidential privilege. It would provide, as the court of appeals noted, a "degree of protection from suit for

---

Supp. V 1993), Pet. App. 14 n. 10, but the state trial court denied his motion, which was plainly meritless in light of this Court's decision in *Boone* v. *Lightner,* 319 U.S. 561 (1943).

[6]   At oral argument in *United States* v. *Nixon,* White House Special Counsel James D. St. Clair expressly conceded that presidents could be sued for their unofficial conduct in personal matters:

> QUESTION: A president could be sued, couldn't he, for back taxes or penalties or what not?

> MR. ST. CLAIR: Well, in questions of immunity I think individually he could be . . . I think the President could be sued for back taxes in his individual capacity. But in terms of his power to effect the responsibilities of his office, to protect the presidency from unwarranted intrusions into the confidentiality of his communications, that's not a personal matter.

Transcript of Oral Argument at 80, *United States* v. *Nixon,* Nos. 73-1766 and 73-1834 (U.S. argued July 8, 1974).

President Nixon made the same concession in his reply brief in the *Fitzgerald* case. He stated that it was "clear that a President, in his capacity as a citizen, *always remains subject to suit for private wrongs,* but for improper actions as President, whether denominated 'political' or of a 'public character,' impeachment is the intended remedy." Reply Brief for Petitioner Richard Nixon at 8-9 n.6, *Nixon* v. *Fitzgerald,* No. 79-1738 (U.S. filed Nov. 20, 1981) (emphasis added).

his private wrongs enjoyed by no other public official (much less ordinary citizens)." Pet. App. 13. It would violate the precept that "[n]o man in this country is so high that he is above the law," *United States* v. *Lee, supra,* 106 U.S. at 220, or, as President Theodore Roosevelt said, that "[n]o man is above the law, and no man is below it; nor do we ask any man's permission when we require him to obey it."[7]

This is so even though the relief sought here is termed a "temporary deferral," Pet. App. 13, as opposed to dismissal. For far from being a brief delay, Mr. Clinton's requested "deferral" may be very long indeed. This action was commenced in 1994, and discovery is currently stayed by order of the District Court, Pet. App. 74. If Mr. Clinton is reelected, and if his temporary immunity claim is upheld, *discovery* would not even begin until early 2001—almost *seven years* after the claim was first brought. As for a claim more complex than Mrs. Jones's that is brought at the beginning of a two-term President's service in office, it is likely that more than a *decade* (and possibly more) would pass before the claim is tried, and perhaps more than *dozen* years would pass before any judgment became final on appeal.

Even in an age of heavy dockets, delays of such length are extraordinary, and by any standard exceed the "bounds of moderation," *Landis* v. *North American Co.,* 299 U.S. 248 (1936); indeed, as any unbiased litigator would attest, they are a defendant's dream. For under Mr. Clinton's proposed scheme of "deferral," a President may, in his capacity as an ordinary citizen, fail to meet a contractual covenant, or to pay a debt; he may commit a battery or a trespass or other tort, or commit any type of civil violation of law; and yet, unlike any other citizen, for a period of possibly eight years or even more, he is privileged not to pay any judgment, to submit to

___

[7]   John Bartlett, *Familiar Quotations* 687 (15th ed. 1980). With more spice as an apt egalitarian principle, is Montaigne's aphorism that "on the highest throne in the world, we still sit only on our own bottom." *Id.* at 166.

a trial, to give a deposition, to produce any document, or even to admit or to deny any of the allegations of a complaint. During this period of many years, evidence inevitably will be lost, as witnesses become unavailable, memories fade, and documents are mislaid or destroyed, all to the likely detriment of the plaintiff, who still must bear the burden of proof. If such delay were commanded by law, a plaintiff might be wise not to bother to assert even the strongest of claims. And in a case such as this, where the plaintiff seeks vindication for damage to her reputation, no amount of prejudgment interest will compensate for any delay. The presumptive "deferral" rule sought by Mr. Clinton is indeed a special privilege or "immunity"—which is why Mr. Clinton repeatedly described it as such throughout the proceedings below.

Mr. Clinton's description of stays in other litigation contexts only serves to confirm the extraordinary nature of the privilege he seeks here. With one execption—the stay provision in the Soldiers' and Sailors' Civil Relief Act of 1940, 50 U.S.C. app. §§ 501-25 (1988 & Supp. V 1993) (Pet. Br. 36)—each of the examples of stays he cites are ones required in order to allow *other* judicial or administrative cases to proceed. And none of these examples involves the creation of a special, personal privilege. Thus, the automatic bankruptcy stay (Pet Br. 34-35), which is the product of a statute, 11 U.S.C. § 362 (1994), serves to allow claims to be immediately addressed in the bankruptcy forum; and it affords protection not only to debtor-defendants but to claimant-plaintiffs, by preserving the value of the bankrupt estate. And as for the protection afforded debtors, it is available to any person who may file a bankrupcy petition—and not to a special privileged class of one. Similarly, the stay of civil litigation in favor of criminal litigation (Pet. Br. 35) serves the interests of justice, judicial economy, and constitutional rights such as the privilege against self-incrimination, and, through the doctrines of res judicata or collateral estoppel, may even benefit the civil plaintiff. And facilitating the conduct of criminal litigation against the defendant hardly amounts to a privilege for the defendant. The doctrine of primary jurisdiction (*id.* at 36) likewise serves the interests of economy, and does not place any citizen above any other in the eyes of the law. Finally, a stay of proceedings pending appeal (*id.*), like that entered here, is hardly unique to official-immunity litigation; it serves to preserve an issue for appellate review and creates no privilege for anyone.

As for the Soldiers and Sailors' Civil Relief Act, its stay procedure was expressly created by Congress, which could have just as easily granted relief to Presidents, but has not. In any event, as this Court has held, stays under that Act are not to be liberally granted; for example, "[t]he Act cannot be construed to require continuance on [a] mere showing that the defendant was in Washington in the military service," *Boone* v. *Lightner*, 319 U.S. 561, 565 (1943), and thus could not help Mr. Clinton even if the Act's military-service requirement could be ignored. Unlike the examples he cites, the relief Mr. Clinton seeks is indeed extraordinary, and would unquestionably provide a "degree of protection from suit for . . . private wrongs enjoyed by no other public official (much less ordinary citizens)." Pet. App. 13. Indeed, as the example of the Soldiers and Sailors' Civil Relief Act shows, any such protection should not be for the courts to create, but for Congress to enact.

C. Petitioner's claim of temporal immunity cannot be justified under Article II or the separation of powers.

Mr. Clinton and *amici* also contend that Article II and separation-of-powers principles establish the temporary immunity from suit that he seeks. To make out a separation-of-powers violation under this Court's cases, however, Mr. Clinton must demonstrate how proceeding with this litigation would cause the "encroachment or aggrandizement of one branch at the expense of the other,' " *Metropolitan*

Washington Airports Authority v. Citizens for the Abatement of Aircraft Noise, Inc., 501 U.S. 252, 273 (1991) (quoting *Morrison v. Olson*, 487 U.S. 654, 693 (1988)), or would otherwise "prevent[ ] the Executive Branch from accomplishing its constitutionally assigned functions,' " *Mistretta v. United States*, 488 U.S. 361, 383, 384 (1989) (quoting *Nixon v. Administrator of General Services*, 433 U.S. 425, 443 (1977)). Mr. Clinton's burden of showing a separation-of-powers violation, or showing that a stay of all proceedings is otherwise justified, is unmet. Nor is a blanket temporary-immunity protection required in *every* personal action against the President as a matter of law.

1. **This simple civil case will not prevent the Executive Branch from accomplishing its constitutionally assigned functions.**

As the court of appeals observed, Mr. Clinton has presented a "sweeping claim that this suit . . . will violate the constitutional separation of powers doctrine . . . without detailing any specific responsibilities so explaining how or the degree to which they are affected by the suit." Pet. App. 12. He made no attempt in the district court to show how this case could possibly keep him from carrying out his official duties. He did not do so for a very simple reason—he cannot.

It is not even necessary to look to Mr. Clinton's duties to establish the point. Given its simple factual predicate and the utterly barren record, this case could not be deemed to impose hardship upon the Executive Branch. It has nothing to do with Mr. Clinton's official duties. It is at bottom a very simple dispute about what happened in a very short encounter between two people in a room. There are only a handful of potentially important witnesses. One is Mr. Clinton himself, and presumably he has already spent with his counsel the short time required to obtain his recollection of events, for according to what he has publicly said, his recollection is nonexistent. By its nature, the case will not require the production of many documents. Discovery and trial in this case will not be burdensome, and can be controlled by the ample powers of the district court to prevent any interference with Mr. Clinton's official duties. On the other hand, the dimming of memories and the risk that other evidence may be lost could prove fatal to corroboration of Mrs. Jones's claims, and possibly to the case itself.

In his brief, Mr. Clinton cites television reports describing "[r]espondent's counsel's . . . intention to pursue discovery aggressively." Pet. Br. 21. Even aggressive discovery, however, would not make this case very complex—as *Mr. Clinton's* own counsel has publicly acknowledged. Mr. Clinton's counsel has admitted that "[t]he President's case is not a complicated case," and has explained that "[i]f the President were Joe Schmo [*sic*], we wouldn't be wasting time with motions. I'd go to trial next week . . . ."[8] He has also publicly acknowledged that the trial in this case would be very short.[9] In short, of the sorts of lawsuits that one could imagine being brought against any individual, this one is just about the simplest—even in the view of Mr. Clinton's own counsel. But the Court certainly need not rely upon the press clippings offered by the parties to decide whether the case is really that simple. The allegations of the complaint bespeak their own factual simplicity, and Mr. Clinton can point to nothing in the record suggesting that this case cannot be quickly and easily tried.

Mr. Clinton has thus offered no case-specific facts to show that *this case* would actually be so burdensome that it would impair his ability to carry out his official duties. Instead, he and his *amici* devote most of their efforts to establishing— generally, and not with reference to *this* simple case—that his duties are so vast and litigation over personal matters so

---

[8]   Ruth Shalit, *The President's Lawyer*, N.Y. Times, Oct. 2, 1994, § 6, at 42, 47 (quoting Robert S. Bennett, Esq.).

[9]   Frank Deford, *The Fabulous Bennett Boys*, Vanity Fair, August 1994, at 80, 85.

potentially burdensome that the two are bound to conflict, and
a blanket rule requiring a stay is called for.

These arguments fail. The Chief Executive's duties are difficult and important, but the fact remains that they are, as
Chief Justice John Marshall once observed, "not unremitting,"
and do not "demand his whole time for national objects."
United States v. *Burr*, 25 F. Cas. 30, 34 (C.C.D. Va. 1807)
(No. 14692d). That is no doubt because, as common sense
makes clear, a President does not and cannot exercise all
executive power himself; unlike legislative or judicial powers, executive powers can be, and for the most part, are, del-
egated. "Although the Constitution says that '[t]he executive
Power shall be vested in a President of the United States of
America,' Art. II, it was never thought that the President
would have to exercise that power *personally*. He may generally authorize others to exercise executive powers, with full
effect of law, in his place." *Mistretta* v. *United States*, 488
U.S. 361, 424 (1989) (Scalia, J., dissenting) (emphasis in
original). The President's powers are mostly exercised
through others. As a result, Presidents have always had time
to fulfill personal commitments that do not involve the exercise of their Article II powers. Mr. Clinton's activities in the
weeks after his brief was filed, which are a matter of public
record, provide an apt example: a book that Mr. Clinton had
authored was published; he spent a week vacationing in
Wyoming, where he hiked and played golf; he spent a day in
New York to attend a large birthday party in his honor; he
spent four days riding a train through the Midwest; attended
a political convention in Chicago; went on a two-day bus trip
through another route in the Midwest and South; and spent a
day in Little Rock, where he played golf.[10] There is, of

---

[10]   *E.g.*, *Clinton's Book Reinforces Administration's Themes*, Wash.
Post, Aug. 22, 1996, at A8, col. 1; *Clinton Puts Off Politics As Vacation
Winds Down*, Wash. Post, Aug. 17, 1996, at A15, col. 1; Alison Mitchell,
Clinton Has $10 Million Wish for Birthday Bash, N.Y. Times, Aug. 19,
1996, at A1, col. 4; John F. Harris, *President Finds 'Heaven' on the Cam-
paign Rails*, Wash. Post, Aug. 27, 1996, at A1, col. 3; Dan Balz, *Despite*

course, absolutely nothing inappropriate with any of these
activities, because the business of the Executive Branch indisputably went on unimpaired. But they refute the claim that the
demands of this "civil damages litigation against a sitting
President would seriously impair the President's ability to
discharge his constitutional responsibilities." Pet. Br. 20.

The past experience of Presidents with judicial and other
legal proceedings likewise refutes Mr. Clinton's argument.
Presidents have given evidence under judicial supervision
even as to matters relating to their office, without any ill
effect.[11] Mr. Clinton's own experience with the Whitewater
affair by itself proves the point: In addition to giving grand
jury testimony by videotape on more than one occasion,
Mr. Clinton has given testimony by videotape in two separate
criminal trials in the district court, which successfully and
uncontroversially balanced his schedule with the rights of the
litigants and the evidentiary needs of the case.[12] Indeed, given

---

Key Strategist's Fall, President Says 'Hope Is Back', Wash. Post, Aug.
30, 1996, at A1, col. 5; Todd S. Purdum, *Campaigns Over, the Candi-
dates Take To the Road*, N.Y. Times, Aug. 31, 1996, at A1, col. 6; Todd
S. Purdum, *Clinton Starts at the Beginning Once Again*, N.Y. Times,
Sept. 2, 1996, § 1, p. 10, col. 1.

[11]   *E.g., United States* v. *Fromme*, 405 F. Supp. 578, 582-83 (E.D.
Cal. 1975); *see also United States* v. *Poindexter*, 732 F. Supp. 142, 143-
146, 149-160 (D.D.C. 1990); 1 Ronald D. Rotunda & John E. Nowak,
Treatise on Constitutional Law: Substance and Procedure § 7.1 (2d ed.
1992); Laurence H. Tribe, *American Constitutional Law* 78 (2d ed. 1988)
(rejecting the view "that the President [is] beyond the pale of judicial
direction").

[12]   *United States* v. *McDougal*, No. LR-CR-95-173 (E.D. Ark.);
United States v. *Branscum*, No. LR-CR-96-49 (E.D. Ark.) (Wright, J.);
see, e.g., Stephen Labaton, *Clinton Denies Any Link to Whitewater Case
Loan*, N.Y. Times, May 10, 1996, § A, p. 1, col. 1; Alison Mitchell,
Clinton Is Ordered To Testify in Ex-Partners' Fraud Trial, N.Y. Times,
Feb. 6, 1996, § A, p. 16, col. 5; Ronald Smothers, *Judge Rules Clinton
Testimony Will Be Videotaped for Trial*, N.Y. Times, Mar. 21, 1996, § A,
p. 16, col. 1; Hugh Aynesworth, *Clinton Deposition Could Take 8 Hours,
Judge Tells Lawyers*, Wash. Times, Apr. 18, 1996, part A, p. 18; Tim

the fact that they were indeed criminal proceedings, that Mr. Clinton is expressly a principal subject of the Independent Counsel's criminal investigation into Whitewater,[13] and given that this investigation encompasses a number of complex and disparate financial transactions, Mr. Clinton has surely already spent more time dealing with Whitewater than he ever will with this case. At the least, it is clear that he has had to do in the criminal realm the burdensome things he now claims he cannot do in any civil litigation against him: "to review [pleadings]; prepare and assure the veracity of discovery responses; retrieve and review documents; . . . review . . . other evidence in the case; review the opposition's pleadings and motions; . . . consult with counsel throughout the case"—and testify. Pet. Br. 23; *see also* Br. for United States 9. If the Independent Counsel's investigation has not kept Mr. Clinton from his official duties, neither will most personal civil cases—and *certainly* not *this* one.

The very trial judge who will try this case, indeed, was very solicitous of Mr. Clinton in one of the Whitewater trials,[14] and even came to Washington to moderate his videotaped deposition in that case. She also granted his request that the tape not be shown to third parties. Far from intruding into presidential business, she has managed litigation to prevent judicial intrusion. She would no doubt be very accomodating of Mr. Clinton's scheduling concerns in this case through the use of her case-management experience (and through *in camera* and *ex parte* conferences when needed), and could ensure that no presidential business would be impaired. And she would no doubt be highly cognizant of the public mistrust of

---

Weiner, *Clinton Testifies on Tape in Trial of Bankers*, N.Y. Times, July 8, 1996, § A, p. 11, col. 1.

[13]   Order, *In re Madison Guaranty Savs. & Loan Ass'n*, Div. No. 94-1 (D.C. Cir., Sp. Div. Aug. 5, 1994) (appointing Independent Counsel).

[14]   *United States* v. *Branscum*, No. LR-CR-96-49 (E.D. Ark.) (Wright, J.).

the justice system that would result if the President were not treated fairly in the conduct of litigation while he is President.

Only by *ipse dixit* does Mr. Clinton assert that, "if the Court allows private civil damages litigation to proceed against a sitting President, there is no reason to think that such lawsuits will be isolated events." Pet. Br. 23. As the court of appeals correctly noted, however, Mr. Clinton's assertion about a flood of future cases is "not only specula-tive, but historically unsupported." In the 220-year history of the Republic, there apparently have been "only three prior instances in which sitting Presidents have been involved in litigation concerning their acts outside official presidential duties." Pet App. 14 n.10; *see also* Br. for United States 6-7 n.4. The historical record reveals no presidential hardship caused by these cases. *Id.*[15]

The reason why there have been so few cases is precisely that identified in the opinion of the court of appeals. Very few people actually "traffic with the President in his *personal* capacity," Pet. App. 15, leaving even fewer who could have any conceivably colorable claim. It is fanciful to suggest that Presidents, who have absolute immunity from damages for their official acts under *Nixon* v. *Fitzgerald*, are "especially vulnerable to politically motivated 'strike suits' " for their unofficial acts. Pet. Br. 23. Even apart from the fact that plaintiffs would be few and far between, it is highly unlikely that political partisans would make litigation their attack vehicle of choice. As the Nation's political history shows, lit-igation is hardly necessary to accuse, attack, or embarrass a public figure. Indeed, if accusations against a public figure

---

[15]   The lawsuit against President Truman, in particular, was filed just a few months before he became President, and was actively litigated during his term of office. Biegon, *Presidential Immunity*, *supra*, 82 Va. L. Rev. at 711-12. But "[d]espite the enormous demands of the Presi-dency during this tumultuous period in history, Mr. Truman did not find it necessary to seek the tolling of Mr. DeVault's suit." *Id.*; *see DeVault* v. *Truman*, 194 S.W.2d 29 (Mo. 1946).

are unjustified or purely partisan, one would think that litigation—which gives the public figure access to discovery and to a neutral forum in which to obtain vindication—is the *least* likely mode of attack. Mrs. Jones, for example, has filed a verified complaint, subjected herself to discovery, and has submitted herself to the authority of a neutral, nonpartisan forum empowered not only to dismiss her claims, but to impose severe sanctions under Fed. R. Civ. P. 11, the proper and effective tool for dealing with frivolous lawsuits, including purely private ones against Presidents.

Further, Mrs. Jones's life as a plaintiff is not attractive. She is subject to scurrilous comments in the media and minute examination of her past, is living in a controlled environment to prevent unwanted intrusion, and is exposed to intense interest and comments whenever she is recognized in public by all manner of people. It takes a person with great courage to sue someone with more influence, wealth, privilege, and power. If anything, Mrs. Jones's experiences would discourage others from ever suing a sitting President, especially since her case has now been delayed for more than two years.[16]

---

[16]   To compound matters, a supposed delay in filing her claim is claimed by Mr. Clinton to suggest that Mrs. Jones's motives were bad. Pet. Br. 41-42. If a political strike suit was her desire, the presidential campaign of 1992 would have been the time to attempt to politically harm Mr. Clinton. The possibility that Mrs. Jones had no such motive, as proven by her lack of desire to sue for almost three years until she was libeled, does not suggest itself to Mr. Clinton, who can see no harm in any post-filing delay to Mrs. Jones's cause in quickly restoring her reputation.

An improper motive is also implied by Mr. Clinton when he notes that Mrs. Jones did not sue the publication that published the libel. Pet. Br. 3 n.1. But the standard of proving libel in the face of the First Amendment rights of the press is difficult.

2. **Proper judicial case management is sufficient to protect the interests of the Executive Branch in this case and would not violate the separation of powers.**

None of this is to say that the courts do not owe great deference to the presidency in overseeing litigation. What is needed in *this* case to protect the public's interest in the presidency, however, is exactly what the court of appeals prescribed. Emphasizing that "[t]he trial court has broad discretion to control the scheduling of events in matters on its docket," the court of appeals directed the district court to engage in "judicial case management sensitive to the burdens of the presidency and the demands of the President's schedule." Pet. App. 13. The district court was directed to "exercise its discretion in such a way that this lawsuit may move forward with the reasonable dispatch that is desirable in all cases, without creating scheduling conflicts that would thwart the President's performance of his official duties." *Id.* at 13-14.

The decision below recognizes that a stay, not yet shown to be warranted in this case, may be required in some *other* case, or upon changed circumstances in this one. The court of appeals reversed the district court's stay of trial as an "abuse of discretion" because the district court failed to identify, and the record failed to present, any particularized reason to believe that a trial would hinder Mr. Clinton's execution of official duty. *Id.* at 13 n.9. The district court actually saw "no reason why the discovery and deposition process could not proceed as to all persons including the President himself," and pointed to no burden unique to a trial that could justify a different result. *Id.* at 71. Given this holding, and given that Mr. Clinton and the Government claim that discovery would be at least as burdensome (if not more so) than a trial, *see* Pet. Br. 21; Br. for United States 24, it should be clear that there was "no reason why [a trial] could not proceed" as well on this record and in the particular circumstances of this case.

The opinion under review emphasized that a different
record could indeed lead to a different result, and that the district court is *required* to do everything necessary to allow the
President to carry out his constitutional duties:

> If, contrary to history and all reasonable expectations, a
> President ever becomes so burdened by private-wrong
> lawsuits that his attention to them would hinder him in
> carrying out the duties of his office, then clearly the
> courts would be duty-bound to exercise their discretion
> to control scheduling and the like so as to protect the
> President's ability to fulfill his constitutional responsi-
> bilities. Frivolous claims, a category with which the
> courts are quite familiar, generally can be handled expe-
> ditiously and ordinarily can be terminated with little or
> no involvement by the person sued.

Pet. App. 15. Thus, the trial judge remains completely free
under the circuit court's decision to "halt[ ] or delay[ ] or
reschedul[e] *any* proposed action by *any* party at *any* time
should she find that the duties of the presidency are even
slightly imperiled." Pet. App. 25 (Beam, J., concurring;
emphasis added). And Mr. Clinton remains free "to pursue
motions for rescheduling, additional time, or continuances."
Pet. App. 16.

Contrary to Mr. Clinton's assertions, such motions would
not "entangle[ ]" the Judicial and Executive Branches "in an
ongoing and mutually harmful relationship," would not
require "the President . . . to provide detailed information
about the nature of pending Executive Branch matters," and
would not involve "the trial judge . . . passing judgment on
the President's priorities." Pet. Br. 29. The court of appeals'
decision directs *deference* to the presidency and mandates
"judicial case management *sensitive* to the burdens of the
presidency and the demands of the President's schedule." Pet.
App. 13 (emphasis added). The circuit court's reference to the
need to "control[ ] the scheduling of the case as necessary
to avoid interference with specific, particularized, clearly

articulated presidential duties," Pet. App. 16, when read in
context, clearly does not invite scrutiny of Executive Branch
affairs; it was meant to convey that the proper approach to
protection of the presidency lay not in a blanket granting of
immunity, for which Mr. Clinton argued, but in deferentially
scheduling around the President's duties. While Mr. Clinton
may not take the approach he took the below—to assert that
his duties do not permit litigation of this or any case until he
leaves office—he may properly assert, for example, that on
particular days or weeks, he is not available for deposition or
trial testimony because of presidential business, or that any
matter, including his deposition, must be interrupted for official business. The district court is "duty-bound . . . to protect
the President's ability to fulfill his . . . responsibilities," and
thus "duty-bound" to defer to him. Pet. App. 15. For again,
"nothing prohibits the trial judge from halting or delaying or
rescheduling any proposed action by any party at any time
should she find that the duties of the presidency are even
slightly imperiled." Pet. App. 25 (Beam, J., concurring).

Nothing in the court of appeals' decision requires or permits a trial judge to engage in judicial second-guessing of
presidential priorities. The district court would have little
opportunity to do so in any event. Busy and important people,
like corporate chief executives and Cabinet secretaries, are
frequently defendants in litigation—litigation far more complex than this—but their constant involvement in the cases is
not required, because, like Mr. Clinton, they have good
lawyers and assistants. But as the opinion below directs, Mr.
Clinton will have even greater solicitude than would other
defendants. While the only possible time other busy defendants would have to appear personally before the district
court would be to testify, Mr. Clinton's appearance could be
avoided by allowing him to testify by videotape. Cf. Pet. App.
23 (Beam, J., concurring); Pet. Br. 28 & n.25 (noting Mr.
Clinton's videotaped testimony in Whitewater trials). Worry
over money for defense costs and payment of a judgment is

even mitigated here, because Mr. Clinton is reportedly covered by insurance for an amount in excess of the *ad damnum* and by a legal defense fund.

Mr. Clinton attempts to assail the benefits of judicial deference by postulating remote hypotheticals that in any event do not advance his claim. His "national security" scenarios, for example, raise no realistic specter of danger to the functioning of the Executive Branch. The trial judge, under the court of appeals' decision, is to show deference to presidential interests in all circumstances, and surely there is no reason to believe that this deference will not be maintained when national-security issues are at stake. *Ex parte* and *in camera* procedures, moreover, may be used to protect the interests of the presidency. As for the hypothetical crisis offered by Mr. Clinton in which a President must "seek to maintain a pretense of 'business as usual' " and "simply having to ask a court for a change in the litigation schedule . . . . could be highly damaging," Pet. App. 31, any difficulty there would not be caused or exacerbated by the litigation; if the President were previously scheduled to give a speech, attend a conference, play golf, conduct a meeting, or go on a campaign tour, "simply having to [seek] a change in the . . . schedule" would be just as "damaging" in those circumstances as well.

Mr. Clinton's assertions about hypothetical litigation in state courts do not help his argument. This case is in federal court, and there is no need for this Court to address events in a state-court litigation that may never occur. And if a President is ever to be sued for personal acts in a state court, it would most likely be in a court of his own home state, a forum that would likely be convenient and familiar to him.[17]

_____

[17]   One scenario would be assertion of purely state-law claims by a plaintiff from his own state, in which case there would be no diversity jurisdiction, 28 U.S.C. § 1332(a)(1) (1994). Such claims, given the citizenship of the parties, would most likely be brought in the state courts of that state. Another scenario would be the situation in which a diverse plaintiff chose to sue the President in the state courts of his home state,

In any event, Mr. Clinton's claim that " 'case management' by state trial courts is inconsistent with principles of federalism," Pet. Br. 33, actually stands those principles on their head. Under the principles of federalism repeatedly articulated by this Court, it may not be presumed that "state trial judges" will display "local partisan hostility," *id.* at 33-34, or that they will refuse to respect the constitutional duties of the President. The opposite presumption is required. "Article VI of the United States Constitution declares that 'the Judges in every State shall be bound' by the Federal Constitution, laws, and treaties." *Pennzoil* v. *Texaco*, 481 U.S. 1, 15 (1987). Accordingly, "[m]inimal respect for the state processes . . . precludes any presumption that the state courts will not safeguard federal constitutional rights." *Middlesex County Ethics Comm.* v. *Garden State Bar Ass'n*, 457 U.S. 423, 431 (1982). Even if this case had been brought in state court, this Court could not decide it by assuming that a state court would act unlawfully.[18]

The scheme of deference established by the court of appeals will not "work any judicial usurpation of properly executive functions," *Morrison* v. *Olson*, 487 U.S. 654, 695 (1988), and will not " 'prevent[ ] the Executive Branch from accomplishing its constitutionally assigned functions,' " *Mistretta* v. *United States*, 488 U.S. 361, 383, 384 (1989)

---

in which event the President would not be able to remove the action to federal court on diversity grounds, *id.* § 1441(b). But in all other cases in which a diverse plaintiff sued a President in state court on state-law claims, the action would of course be removable.

[18]   Nor is there any merit to Mr. Clinton's suggestion that this case should be deferred because, given the President's position as a political official, it would supposedly thrust the courts into the "political arena." Pet. Br. 32. Needless to say, there is no "political person" doctrine, and in fact the federal courts find it frequently necessary to address cases that, unlike this one, actually do involve questions of law and fact having direct and controversial implications in the political arena. *E.g.*, *Shaw* v. *Reno*, 116 S. Ct. 1894 (1996) (redistricting); *Romer* v. *Evans*, 116 S. Ct. 1620 (1996) (homosexual rights).

(quoting *Nixon v. Administrator of General Services*, 433 U.S. 425, 443 (1977)). It will instead ensure that this case will not cause even the slightest impairment of presidential business.

II. THE COURT OF APPEALS CORRECTLY FOUND THAT, ON THIS BARREN FACTUAL RECORD, THERE IS NO BASIS FOR A STAY OF THE TRIAL OR THE LITIGATION GENERALLY.

Mr. Clinton also claims error in the Court of Appeals' reversal of what the District Court *itself* called a grant of a "limited or temporary *immunity* from trial," an "immunity from trial as [*Nixon* v.] *Fitzgerald* seems to require." Pet. App. 68 (emphasis added); *see* Pet. Br. 45-47. Citing this Court's decision in *Landis* v. *North American Co.*, 299 U.S. 248 (1936), which governs the issuance of discretionary litigation stays, Mr. Clinton argues that the district court did not abuse its discretion in ordering a postponement of trial. But he made no record below that would justify *any* stay whatsoever under *Landis*. Accordingly, the Court of Appeals correctly found that what the District Court ordered—a postponement of the trial until perhaps the year *2001*—not only was "the functional equivalent of a grant of temporary immunity," but was a manifest abuse of discretion even if reviewed under the settled law governing discretionary litigation stays. Pet App. 13 n.9.[19]

In *Landis* v. *North American Co.*, 299 U.S. 248 (1936), the Court did indeed hold that "the power to stay proceedings is incidental to the power inherent in every court to control the

---

[19]   The district judge cited her equity powers and Fed. R. Civ. P. 40, together with a finding of a "temporary or limited immunity from trial," to put the case on hold as far as a trial is concerned. Pet. App. 70-71. But her equity powers and Rule 40 were invoked because she incorrectly found an immunity from trial, as both she and the court of appeals made clear. *Id.*; *accord id.* at 13 & n.9. Thus, if her holding as to an immunity from trial fails, so should the alternative grounds for postponement fail as an abuse of discretion.

disposition of the causes on its docket with economy of time and effort for itself, for counsel, and for litigants." *Id.* at 254. But the Court made clear that a stay of litigation could be granted "[o]nly in rare circumstances." *Id.* at 255. In particular, "the *suppliant* for a stay must make out a *clear* case of hardship or inequity in being required to go forward, if there is even a fair possibility that the stay for which he prays will work damage to some one else." *Id.* (emphasis added). "[T]he burden of making out the justice and wisdom of a departure from the beaten track lay heavily on the . . . suppliant[ ] for relief, and discretion [is] abused if the stay [is] not kept within the bounds of moderation." *Id.* at 256.

Under *Landis*, it was Mr. Clinton's "heav[y]" burden to show why a stay was required. As stated above, however, he made no effort to show why the litigation of *this* simple case would *in fact* present him, or the presidency, any "clear . . . hardship or inequity." Rather than try to make such a showing—which, given the simplicity of this case, was impossible to make—Mr. Clinton resorted to reliance on hypothetical circumstances. He chose to argue in the abstract, as he does here, that litigation generally (including a hypothetical torrent of future cases) could someday pose an undue burden upon his Office. Apart from being incorrect, that argument fails to meet the *Landis* criteria. It fails to establish—indeed, it fails really to assert—that there will in fact be "hardship or inequity" in *this* case, or that *this* case was of such an "extraordinary public moment," *Landis*, 299 U.S. at 256, that any part of it should not be allowed to proceed.

The court of appeals was entirely faithful to *Landis* in reversing the district court's categorical and indefinite postponement of trial. In granting trial "immunity" to Mr. Clinton, far from considering "the particular facts at hand" (Pet. Br. 45), the district court made no finding that Mr. Clinton had made any showing of an actual "clear case of hardship," and cited *no* facts that would support such a finding (and could not, because, again, Mr. Clinton did not even try to present such facts). The closest the district court came to a finding was a conclusory statement that "[n]either is this a case that would likely be tried with few demands on Presidential time"—a statement that not only came without any indication of whether those demands would amount to clear inequity or hardship, but was manifestly insupportable in a case centering upon a short encounter between two people in a room.

On the other side of the balance, as Judge Beam explained, the danger of harm to Mrs. Jones is manifest. She "faces real dangers of loss of evidence through the unforeseeable calamities inevitable with the passage of time." Pet. App. 17. The district court not only incorrectly disregarded this harm, but ignored Mrs. Jones's well-pleaded reasons why the commencement of this action was delayed, and ignored the fact that public aspersions upon Mrs. Jones reputation had made it necessary for her to proceed. Complaint ¶¶ 41-51.[20] Beyond this, the passage of time contemplated by the District Court's order—possibly into the next century—was surely "immoderate" and impermissible under *Landis*. Even in "cases of extraordinary public moment"—which this one, given the lack of burden, is not—*Landis* requires that a delay cannot be "immoderate in extent." 299 U.S. at 256. In *Landis* itself, the Court found "the limits of a fair discretion" to have been "exceeded" by a stay that had suspended "the proceedings in the District Court . . . more than a year." 299 U.S. at 256.

---

[20]   Throughout the briefs of Mr. Clinton's Solicitor General and academic *amici*, the importance of Mrs. Jones' case is downplayed because of a supposed delay in filing her case. As noted above, public defamation in early 1994 caused her to proceed immediately to file a case that would not otherwise have been brought when few people knew about the harassment in 1991. Also to be noted is that the defamation action had recently accrued when she sued in May 1994. Of course, the speed of filing has never, so far as we can tell, governed the speed of litigation. Otherwise, a litigant Smith, whose cause of action arose after another plaintiff, Jones, had filed a similar action just before the limitations deadline, would have precedence on the court's docket even if Smith filed one day after his cause of action arose!

The district court was neither presented with, nor did it point to, a record of "clear hardship and inequity" as required by *Landis*. What the district court really did was what it candidly said it had done: to create a new rule of law establishing a "limited or temporary *immunity* from trial," a new kind of immunity that it believed, quite incorrectly, "[*Nixon* v.] *Fitzgerald* seems to require." Pet. App. 68, 70 (emphasis added). Apart from being based upon a clear error of law, the district court's ruling was an abuse of discretion because it was *not* an exercise of discretion. Reversal of the district court's "stay" order, if anything, was all but *required* under *Landis*.

Mr. Clinton makes a final effort to restore the district court's "trial immunity" order by contending that the court of appeals lacked jurisdiction to review it. Pet. Br. 43-45. This argument, which Mr. Clinton has not even mentioned in his list of questions presented, is meritless.

In appealing the denial of his claim of "immunity" (which was the word Mr. Clinton repeatedly used in both courts below to describe his claim), Mr. Clinton argued that the district judge's decision was "inherently inconsistent," that the "result that the District Court arrived at here—deferring trial but not discovery"—was "illogical" because principles of "immunity" under *Nixon* v. *Fitzgerald* required deferral of both. Opening Brief of Appellant President William Jefferson Clinton at 10, 23, *Jones* v. *Clinton*, No. 95-1050 (8th Cir. filed Apr. 5, 1995). His "statement of issues" and list of principal authorities in that court thus read:

> 1. Whether the Constitution and principles of separation of powers require the dismissal without prejudice of this civil damages suit against an incumbent President and his co-defendant, and the tolling of any statutes of limitation applicable to the claims asserted therein, until such time as the President is no longer in office.
>
> *Nixon* v. *Fitzgerald*, 457 U.S. 731 (1982); . . . .

2. Whether the District Court erred in holding that the Supreme Court's decision in *Nixon* v. *Fitzgerald*, 457 U.S. 731 (1982), requires that sitting Presidents be immune only from trial, but not from the demands of litigating pretrial motions and conducting discovery, which are equally burdensome and distracting to the Office of the President.

> *Nixon* v. *Fitzgerald*, 457 U.S. 731 (1982); . . . .

3. Whether the District Court, having found that it is not in the national interest to distract the President with the burdens of trial in private civil litigation, erred in refusing on the same basis to stay the proceedings in their entirety, until such time as the President leaves office.

> *Nixon* v. *Fitzgerald*, 457 U.S. 731 (1982); . . . .

Id. at vii-ix.

All of Mr. Clinton's questions presented in the Eighth Circuit were to the same effect: *Nixon* v. *Fitzgerald* and the principles of immunity expressed in that case required the postponement of *both* discovery and trial (regardless of whether the postponement takes the form of a stay or dismissal). Jurisdiction over Mr. Clinton's appeal was premised upon the principle that "denials of immunity are subject to appeal as of right under section 1291 [and] the collateral order doctrine." *Id.* at vii (citing *Nixon* v. *Fitzgerald, supra*); *accord* Pet. Br. 4 n.3 (citing *Mitchell* v. *Forsyth*, 472 U.S. 511 (1985)). Mrs. Jones cross-appealed, arguing (as she does here) precisely the converse of what Mr. Clinton was arguing— namely, that *Nixon* v. *Fitzgerald* justified *neither* the postponement of discovery nor the postponement of trial—and argued that jursidicton over her cross-appeal was proper under principles of pendent appellate jurisdiction.

The Eighth Circuit correctly held that the cross-appeal could properly be entertained as an exercise of pendent appellate jurisdiction. As this Court has recognized, pendent appellate jurisdiction is a concept that has been "endorsed" by all the federal courts of appeals, *Swint* v. *Chambers County Comm'n*, 115 S. Ct. 1203, 1209 n.2 (1995) (citing cases from each Circuit); it is typically held to apply when the pendent issue is "inextricably intertwined with" the primary issue on review, *id. at 1212.* And if ever there were a case where such jurisdiction was justified, this is it. For the question whether Mr. Clinton is entitled to a postponement of just a trial, far from being "very distinct" (Pet. Br. 44) from the question whether he is entitled to a postponement of the litigation entirely, is part and parcel of it. Indeed, as Mr. Clinton's own questions presented below show, the questions were in his view one and the same. In both the district court and the court of appeals, *he* argued that he was entitled, *as a matter of law*, to an immunity or stay as to *all* proceedings, *including* the trial, for *one* reason, and one reason *alone*—the fact that he is President of the United States. Mrs. Jones' cross-appeal argued a point that indisputably was inextricably intertwined with, indeed subsumed within, Mr. Clinton's claim—namely, to borrow the district court's words, whether he was entitled to "a temporary or limited immunity from trial [under] *Fitzgerald.*" Pet. App. 70. The court of appeals reached the obvious conclusion that both appeals

> are resolved by answering one question: is a sitting President entitled to immunity, for the duration of his presidency from civil suit for his unofficial acts? It is difficult to imagine issues more "intertwined" than these, where answering one question of law resolves them all.

Pet. App. 5 n.4.

Finally, nothing in this Court's decision in *Swint* v. *Chambers County Commission, supra*, casts doubt upon the exercise of pendent jurisdiction in this case. At issue in *Swint* was a purported exercise of " 'pendent party' " appellate jurisdiction, *Swint*, 115 S. Ct. at 1206; there were "parties who were not involved in the appealable order but were parties to the pendent order," *Gilda Marx, Inc.* v. *Wildwood Exercise, Inc.*, 85 F.3d 675, 678 (D.C. Cir. 1996) (per curiam). One group of defendants appealed the denial of their summary judgment motion, which was based upon a claim of qualified immunity; that appeal was plainly proper under *Mitchell* v. *Forsyth, supra. See* 115 S. Ct. at 1207. Another defendant, the Chambers County Commission, appealed the denial of its separate summary judgment motion, which did not involve the immunity issue and was not independently appealable. *Id.* at 1207-08. This Court, noting that "[w]e need not definitively or preemptively settle here whether or when it may be proper for a court of appeals with jurisdiction over one ruling to review, conjunctively, related rulings that are not themselves independently appealable," held that pendent appellate jurisdiction was not proper because the parties did not, and could not, "contend that the District Court's decision to deny the Chambers County Commission's summary judgment motion was inextricably intertwined with that court's decision to deny the individual defendants' qualified immunity motions, or that review of the former decision was necessary to ensure meaningful review of the latter." *Id.* at 1212.

As noted in *Swint*, this Court "ha[s] not universally required courts of appeals to confine review to the precise decision independently subject to appeal." *Id.* at 1211 (citing cases). And since *Swint*, the courts of appeals have continued to recognize the validity of pendent appellate jurisdiction, and have carefully confined the exercise of that jurisdiction to questions that are "inextricably intertwined" with those as to which independent bases of jurisdiction exist.[21] There is no

---

[21]   *See, e.g., Martin* v. *Memorial Hospital*, 86 F.3d 1391, 1401 (5th Cir. 1996) (noting that *Swint* implied that pendent appellate jurisdiction was proper where "inextricably intertwined" standard was met); *Eagle* v. *Morgan*, 88 F.3d 620, 628 (8th Cir. 1996) (applying "inextricably intertwined" standard, and exercising pendent appellate jurisdiction); *Gilda Marx, Inc.* v. *Wildwood Exercise, Inc.*, 85 F.3d 675, 678-79 (D.C. Cir. 1996) (per curiam) (recognizing continued validity of pendent appellate jurisdiction under "inextricably intertwined" standard); *Cooper* v. *Town*

reason to depart from that course here. No pendent party was involved. And the pendent appellate question, whether there existed a "temporary immunity from trial," was bound up in the question that Mr. Clinton presented, which was whether there was a "temporary immunity" from all proceedings; the pendent issue was an integral part of the decision that Mr. Clinton appealed. There was thus no danger here of turning a "collateral order[ ] into [a] multi-issue interlocutory appeal ticket." *Swint*, 115 S. Ct. at 1211. Indeed, it would have been wasteful and illogical for the Eighth Circuit to have held that Mr. Clinton was not entitled to the full immunity from litigation that he claimed, but to have held itself powerless to correct the district court's erroneous holding that there existed a "temporary immunity from trial." This Court's cases "indicate that [the courts of appeals] should give the jurisdictional statutes a 'practical contstruction,' " *Gilda Marx* v. *Wildwood Exercise, supra*, 85 F.3d at 678(quoting *Swint*, 115 S. Ct. at 1207-08 (citation omitted)), and such a construction surely requires, at a minimum, the exercise of pendent jurisdiction here.

---

of East Hampton, 83 F.3d 31, 36 (2d Cir. 1996) (same); *Brennan* v. *Township of Northville,* 78 F.3d 1152, 1157 (6th Cir. 1996) (same); *Dolihite* v. *Maughon,* 74 F.3d 1027, 1035 (11th Cir. 1996) (same), *petition for cert. filed* (June 19, 1996); *Sevier* v. *City of Lawrence,* 60 F.3d 695, 701 (10th Cir. 1995) (same).

CONCLUSION

The judgment of the court of appeals should be affirmed.

Respectfully submitted,

GILBERT K. DAVIS	JOSEPH CAMMARATA
Counsel of Record	9516-C Lee Highway
9516-C Lee Highway	Fairfax, Virginia 22031
Fairfax, Virginia 22031	(703) 352-3850
(703) 352-3850	

Counsel for Respondent Paula Corbin Jones

September 9, 1996

Appendix E

REPLY BRIEF FOR THE PETITIONER

No. 95-1853

IN THE

Supreme Court Of The United States

October Term, 1995

WILLIAM JEFFERSON CLINTON,

Petitioner,

vs.

PAULA CORBIN JONES,

Respondent.

**On Writ Of Certiorari To The
United States Court Of Appeals
For The Eighth Circuit**

REPLY BRIEF FOR THE PETITIONER

Robert S. Bennett
  Counsel of Record
Carl S. Rauh
Alan Kriegel
Amy R. Sabrin
Stephen P. Vaughn
SKADDEN, ARPS, SLATE,
  MEAGHER & FLOM
1440 New York Avenue, N.W.
Washington, D.C. 20005
(202) 371-7000

Of Counsel:
David A. Strauss
Geoffrey R. Stone
1111 East 60th Street
Chicago, Illinois 60637
(312) 702-9601

Attorneys for the Petitioner
President William Jefferson Clinton

Balmar Legal Publishing Department, Washington, D.C.

TABLE OF CONTENTS

Page

TABLE OF AUTHORITIES

No. 95-1853

In The

Supreme Court Of The United States

October Term, 1995

WILLIAM JEFFERSON CLINTON,

Petitioner,

vs.

PAULA CORBIN JONES,

Respondent.

**On Writ Of Certiorari To The
United States Court Of Appeals
For The Eighth Circuit**

REPLY BRIEF FOR THE PETITIONER

The active litigation of a personal damages action against an incumbent President is unknown in our constitutional tradition. Such litigation would divert a President's energy and attention from his official duties, and would spawn a series of constitutional confrontations between the courts and the President. The litigation of such actions should therefore be deferred, in all but the most exceptional cases, until the President leaves office.

Respondent and her amici offer a number of unfounded arguments in opposition to deferral. They assert that litigation of this kind should not be viewed as an extraordinary event, even though history clearly shows that it is. They insist, in the face of overwhelming evidence to the contrary, that the burdens of the Presidency are not so great that such litigation would impede a President's ability to discharge his responsibilities. And they contend that deferral of such actions would place a President "above the law" -- even though the President would remain amenable to liability when he leaves office.

Ultimately, however, respondent and her amici concede that such litigation would jeopardize a President's ability to discharge his constitutional responsibilities, and that some means must be found to protect the proper functioning of government. The question is how this is to be done. Respondent's proposed solution -- ad hoc "case management" by state and federal trial judges -- is no solution at all. It would multiply the litigation burdens on the Presidency and invite the use of civil litigation as a political weapon. Most troubling, it would require trial judges repeatedly to make complex, fiercely contested, discretionary rulings as to whether the President should attend to private litigation at the expense of his official duties -- rulings that inevitably would enmesh the trial court in Executive Branch management.

Deferral, by contrast, eliminates these problems. This limited form of protection accommodates both a plaintiff's right to seek legal redress, and the public interest in having a President available to perform the unique and demanding duties of his office. Deferral also preserves the separation of powers, and comports with the historic tradition that courts are to refrain from asserting jurisdiction over a President in all but the most compelling circumstances.

A. Respondent's "Scheme Of Deference" Does Not Adequately Safeguard The Presidency Or The Separation Of Powers.

Perhaps the most striking feature of the briefs of respondent and her amici is the contrast between their abstract complaint that deferral would place the President "above the law,"[1] and their energetic assertions that trial courts should

---

[1]   Brief for Respondent ("Resp. Br.") 16. *See also* Brief of *Amicus Curiae* of Law Professors in Support of Respondent ("Resp. Prof. Br.") 3; Brief for *Amicus Curiae* Coalition of American Veterans ("CAV Br.") 10-11.

conduct litigation against the President in a fashion that is highly deferential to that office. Respondent, for example, states that trial courts "owe great deference to the presidency in overseeing litigation" (Resp. Br. 34) and that the President is owed "greater solicitude than . . . other defendants." *Id.* at 36. Respondent endorses what she calls "[t]he scheme of deference established by the court of appeals" (*id.* at 38), and confidently insists that this "scheme" should prevent "even the slightest impairment of presidential business." *Id.* at 39. She twice quotes, with emphasis, the concurring opinion below to the effect that the trial judge should " 'halt[] or delay[] or reschedul[e] *any* proposed action by *any* party at *any* time should she find that the duties of the presidency are even *slightly* imperiled.' " *Id.* at 35, 36 (quoting Pet. App. 25 (Beam, J., concurring)) (emphases added by respondent).

Respondent's amici further advocate special procedural rules in cases where the President is a defendant, such as holding the plaintiff to heightened pleading requirements; requiring the plaintiff to offer corroboration for her allegations before discovery can be obtained from the President; requiring the plaintiff to demonstrate that information she seeks by way of discovery is not available from any source other than the President; excusing the President from attending trial; and permitting him to testify on videotape instead of in person. Resp. Prof. Br. 21-22; *see also* Pet. App. 23 (Beam, J., concurring). These unusual provisions would be difficult to square with the Federal Rules of Civil Procedure -- unless one recognizes, as even Respondent's amici eventually do, that the President "is not like any other litigant."[2]

As this chorus of accommodation and deference illustrates, this case is not about whether the President is "above the law." Rather, this case is about identifying the proper means of protecting the compelling interests that are impli-

---

[2]   Brief of *Amicus Curiae* American Civil Liberties Union ("ACLU Br.") 6.

cated when a private civil damages suit is filed against a sitting President. Respondent's "scheme of deference," however, actually endangers these interests; that is why deferral is the proper approach.

To begin with, there simply is no assurance that a trial court will be as deferential as respondent assumes. Respondent emphasizes language from the concurring opinion below, which called for a high level of deference. But she does not repudiate the more demanding standard of the majority opinion, which would require the President to prove that each aspect of the litigation would interfere with "specific, particularized, clearly articulated presidential duties." Pet. App. 16. The inescapable fact is that a "deference" standard, however formulated, cannot predictably be relied on to protect the Presidency, because it necessarily gives capacious discretion to trial judges.

Moreover, in the real world of litigation, it is inevitable that whenever the President seeks to postpone some scheduled aspect of the litigation, or asserts that he is not required to submit to a deposition or some other procedural requirement, the plaintiff will object. These objections in all likelihood will include, as they have here, claims that the President is abusing his office to obtain some undeserved litigation advantage, or that he seeks delay for political purposes. The trial judge will then have to decide, in a highly adversarial and politicized setting, whether the President's claim warrants the deference he requests. To fulfill this function, the trial judge will have to examine the President's priorities and determine whether to require the President to devote more time and attention to the litigation, and less to some competing matter of governance. Such inquiries -- likely to occur repeatedly throughout the litigation -- present a serious threat to separation of powers, as well as to the integrity of sensitive information about matters of national concern. *See* Brief for the Petitioner ("Pet. Br.") 29-34. And it should be evident that these problems are far more intractable when the President is a defendant than when he is asked merely to give third-party testimony. *See id.* 26-29.

Ad hoc case management also cannot protect a President who is faced with an ever increasing number of civil damages actions. *See* Resp. Br. 7 (quoting Pet. App. 15). If more and more such suits are filed for purposes of publicity or partisan gain -- and in today's "no holds barred" political arena, there is every reason to believe that they will be -- it will be impossible for individual judges issuing piecemeal rulings in individual cases to manage the threat. However well-intentioned and deferential they may be, they will simply be unable to provide a coordinated response to the burgeoning obligations such litigation would impose on the President. Only a generally applicable prophylactic will adequately prevent overburdening the Presidency.

In short, the disadvantages of respondent's scheme are great when compared to a simple rule of deferral. Respondent's scheme necessarily creates serious separation of powers problems; deferral averts those problems. Respondent's scheme augments the litigation burdens placed on the President; deferral eliminates the prospect that litigation will divert the President from his official duties. Respondent's scheme does not deter the filing of unfounded suits against the President for illegitimate purposes; deferral minimizes that danger. Thus, even assuming that there is some marginal gain to legitimate claimants from respondent's scheme, it would not justify the substantial costs that it would inflict on our system of government.

B. Respondent's Scheme Cannot Be Reconciled With *Fitzgerald* And This Court's Other Immunity Decisions.

Contrary to respondent's contention, the deferral the President seeks here is not an expansion of the absolute immunity recognized in *Nixon v. Fitzgerald*, 457 U.S. 731 (1982). It is a considerably narrower remedy, because it does not insulate a President from liability. Deferral is, moreover, strongly supported by both the language and the underlying logic of *Fitzgerald* and this Court's other immunity decisions.

Respondent spends a great deal of energy arguing that *Fitzgerald* does not mean what it says. For example, respondent asserts that the Court in *Fitzgerald* was concerned only with ensuring that the threat of liability does not inhibit official decision-making. Resp. Br. at 11-16. The Court, however, noted how the simple fact of on-going litigation could interfere with the performance of official duties. The Court was quite explicit in saying that "diversion of [the President's] energies by concern with private lawsuits would raise unique risks to the effective functioning of government." *Fitzgerald*, 457 U.S. at 751. And the Court explained that the President's exceptional immunity is necessary because "[t]he President occupies a unique position in the constitutional scheme" (*id.* at 749) and performs "singular[ly] importan[t] . . . duties." *Id.* at 751. The Court went out of its way to note that the President is "an easily identifiable target for suits for civil damages," and found that "[c]ognizance of this personal vulnerability frequently could distract a President from his public duties, to the detriment of not only the President and his office but also the Nation that the Presidency was designed to serve." *Id.* at 753. Each of these rationales for absolute immunity in *Fitzgerald* also dictates the more modest remedy of deferral in this case.[3]

---

[3] *See also id.* at 763 (Burger, C.J., concurring) ("The need to defend damages suits would have the serious effect of diverting the attention of a President from his executive duties since defending a lawsuit today -- even a lawsuit ultimately found to be frivolous -- often requires significant expenditures of time and money . . . ."). Respondent contends that Chief Justice Burger's concurrence forecloses the argument that private civil damages actions against an incumbent President should be deferred, because the Chief Justice stated that immunity "does not extend beyond" official actions. Resp. Br. 11 (quoting *Fitzgerald*, 457 U.S. at 761 n.4 (Burger, C.J., concurring)). We of course, do not disagree with this statement, which addresses *absolute* immunity, in a case involving a *for-*

The logic of *Fitzgerald* and the Court's other immunity decisions further negates two of respondent's other principal arguments. First, respondent asserts that personal damages litigation against a President will not divert him from his duties because Presidents "have good lawyers and assistants" and so can minimize their personal involvement. Resp. Br. 36. But the Court's immunity decisions emphasize repeatedly that immunity is needed because the litigation of even unfounded claims can cause "the diversion of official energy from pressing public issues." *Harlow v. Fitzgerald*, 457 U.S. 800, 814 (1982).[4] A denial of immunity, qualified or absolute, is also immediately appealable, precisely because immunity is an "entitlement not to stand trial or face the other burdens of litigation." *Digital Equip. Corp. v. Desktop Direct, Inc.*, 511 U.S. 863, 870 (1994) (quoting *Mitchell v. Forsyth*, 472 U.S. 511, 526 (1985)).

These doctrines would make no sense if, as respondent supposes, damages litigation against public officials can simply be turned over to "lawyers and assistants" while the officials proceed with their jobs. To the contrary, the Court recognized that litigation can work a "distraction . . . from . . . dut[y]" (*Harlow*, 457 U.S. at 816), however good a public official's "lawyers and assistants" may be. This is so even

---

mer President. The Chief Justice's language quoted at the beginning of this note, however, demonstrates that he also was concerned that civil litigation would divert the President from his official duties. As this passage suggests, he did not endorse the notion that damages litigation of any kind could go forward against a sitting President. In fact, Mr. Fitzgerald's counsel (including the ACLU appearing as amici for respondent here) asserted in their brief that a civil damages suit against an incumbent President could be stayed. Brief for Respondent A. Ernest Fitzgerald, Nos. 78-1738 and 80-945 (Sup. Ct. filed Oct. 29, 1981) at 28.

[4] In *Harlow*, indeed, the Court reformulated the qualified immunity doctrine to eliminate the component that referred to an official's state of mind, precisely so as to avoid "subject[ing] government officials either to the costs of trial or to the burdens of broad-reaching discovery." *Id*. at 817-18.

when, as is typical in immunity cases, the defendant official is represented by government lawyers. Here, the suit concerns not official actions -- which subordinates may to some degree be able to defend -- but alleged personal conduct by the President. The complaint unjustifiably attacks the President's integrity, alleges serious wrongdoing, and seeks to hold him personally liable for hundreds of thousands of dollars in damages. In this context, respondent's notion that a President can largely disregard the litigation -- or that he would choose to do so -- and rely instead on his lawyers, is simply implausible. *See* Pet. Br. 22-23.

Fitzgerald and the Court's other immunity decisions also reject the notion, urged by respondent and her amici, that the Court should require the President to make a showing, at each stage of any case brought against him, that a particular aspect of the litigation has become too burdensome. Instead of such a piecemeal approach, the Court's immunity decisions adopt a general rule of immunity -- a rule that is a much greater imposition on potential plaintiffs than mere deferral.

Thus, for example, respondent and her amici assert that whatever might be said of other cases against a President, this case should proceed because it is one of "manifest simplicity" (Resp. Br. 9), and that it "[s]urely" would not be too burdensome for the President to file an answer "to a short complaint like [respondent's]." Resp. Prof. Br. 6. They also insist that courts can dispose of unfounded claims easily,[5] and that the President should be required to make a specific showing whenever he seeks protection from some aspect of discovery.[6] Finally, they maintain that the trial schedule can be adjusted in a way that adequately protects the President, upon a specific showing of need. Resp. Br. 35.

---

[5]   Resp. Br. 35 (quoting Pet. App. 16); ACLU Br. 12-13.

[6]   Resp. Br. 27; Resp. Prof. Br. 6; ACLU Br. 4.

Every one of these arguments could be said to militate against absolute Presidential immunity as well. Yet the Court in *Fitzgerald* embraced none of them. *Fitzgerald* did not attempt to differentiate "simple" suits from others -- for the obvious reason, among others, that it is impossible to be sure at the outset that a case will in fact be simple.[7] The Court in *Fitzgerald* also well understood that the mechanisms for weeding out unfounded suits are far from foolproof, and that such suits can impose severe burdens on a President even if the President ultimately prevails. 457 U.S. at 752 n.32 (quoting *Gregoire v. Biddle*, 177 F.2d 579, 581 (2d Cir. 1949), *cert. denied*, 339 U.S. 949 (1950)). Nor did *Fitzgerald* rely on ad hoc trial court determinations, based on particularized showings by the President, to protect the President from unduly burdensome discovery or trial obligations. Instead, the Court recognized that once a President is enmeshed in civil damages litigation directed at him personally, the damage to his ability to govern, and to the separation of powers, is already done. There is no reason to believe that a piecemeal scheme would be any more successful here.

---

[7] The instant suit is surely unpredictable on that score. In repeatedly asserting that this is a simple case (Resp. Br. 9, 27, 28, 40), respondent's counsel fail to credit their own statements that they intend "to fully pursue, and exhaustively pursue" a wide-ranging "pattern of conduct" by the President (C.A. App. 117-18, 122-23); that they will pursue this line of inquiry with the President and with numerous other witnesses (C.A. App. 117-18); and that they may seek to compel an unprecedented physical examination of the President. *Id.* As respondent's counsel told the press, litigation of this suit "will take some time." Stephen LaBaton, *Sexual Harassment Suit Should Not Be Tried While Clinton Is President, Judge Rules*, N.Y. TIMES, Dec. 29, 1994, at B6.

C.   Private Civil Damages Litigation Would Impair The President's Ability To Perform The Duties Of His Office.

Quoting Chief Justice Marshall, respondent contends that the burdens of the Presidency are "not unremitting," and that the President should be able to defend against private civil damages actions in his spare time. Resp. Br. 29 (quoting *United States v. Burr*, 25 F. Cas. 30, 34 (C.C.D. Va. 1807) (No. 14,692d)). President Jefferson refuted this assertion at the time it was made.[8] Since then, of course, the burdens on the Presidency have increased exponentially.

There simply is no basis for respondent's bald assertion that "Presidents have always had time to fulfill personal commitments." Resp. Br. 29. To the contrary, as documented in the Solicitor General's brief, almost every President has remarked on the incessant demands of the office.[9] This is not surprising, in view of the fact that the Constitution vests the entire power of the Executive Branch in a single individual. U.S. CONST. art. II, § 1.   As David McCullough, a pre-

---

[8]   President Jefferson responded:

The Judge [Marshall] says, "*it is apparent* that the President's duties as chief magistrate do not demand his whole time . . . ." If he alludes to our annual retirement from the seat of government, during the sickly season, he should be told that such arrangements are made for carrying on the public business, at and between the several stations we take, that it goes on as unremittingly there, as if we were at the seat of government. I pass more hours in public business at Monticello than I do here, every day; and it is much more laborious, because all must be done in writing. . . . It would be very different were we always on the road, or placed in the noisy and crowded taverns where courts are held.

Letter from Thomas Jefferson to George Hay, (June 20, 1807), 11 The Writings of Thomas Jefferson 239, 242 (Andrew A. Lipscomb ed., 1904).

[9]   Brief of *Amicus Curiae* United States, 10-12.

eminent biographer of Presidents, recently observed, to be the Chief Executive is to experience "unrelenting responsibility."

> It is a 24-hour-a-day job that you cannot walk away from. You're president not just today, but tomorrow and next week and the week after and the month after and the year after, every single hour.[10]

The Presidency, he concluded, is "the hardest job in the world." *Id.*[11]

---

[10] Mr. McCullough further observed:

> [W]e're hiring [the President] to do more than one human being can possibly deliver. He is the chief of state, head of state; he is the commander-in-chief of the armed forces; he is the head of his political party; he is the preacher for the country, in a way, standing, as Theodore Roosevelt called it, in the Bully Pulpit . . . . [H]e is the only person, the only individual who represents all the people.
>
>   . . . .
>
>   . . . It's beyond anyone's previous experience or natural ability. . . . I don't think anybody -- no historian, no journalist, no politician in the Senate or House or anywhere in the country can ever possibly understand what it is to be President without becoming President. And every single president, once becoming president, has written about or talked about how different it is from what they expected.

Comments of David McCullough, *Riding The Tiger* (CNN television broadcast, Sept. 8, 1996) (Tr. # 934-2, available in LEXIS, Nexis Library, Script File). Mr. McCullough is the author of *Truman* (Simon & Schuster 1992), and *Mornings On Horseback*, a biography of Theodore Roosevelt (Simon & Schuster 1981), and is currently working on a history of the Presidencies of John Adams and Thomas Jefferson.

[11] Respondent also states incorrectly that the lawsuit against President Truman was "actively litigated during his term in office." Resp. Br. 32 n.15. That suit was dismissed by the trial court on April 11, 1945, the day before President Roosevelt died and Harry Truman became President. Notice of Appeal, *DeVault v. Truman*, No. 498465, (Jackson County Cir. Ct., Mo.) filed April 18, 1945. As stated in our opening brief, the only activity in the case after President Truman took office was the appeal of the dismissal, which was sustained on purely legal grounds. *DeVault v.*

Separation of powers concerns, moreover, distinguish litigation against a President from those situations where a President briefly and voluntarily absents himself from official duties to engage in recreational or political activities. In the latter circumstances, the President -- not a judge or a civil plaintiff -- determines the priorities for the Chief Executive's time, and the President remains available to perform the duties of office continuously, irrespective of such other activities. A President may have to (and often does) interrupt such activities to attend to pressing official duties, and is free to do so without seeking permission from anyone. *See* Pet. Br. 13 n.9. In the litigation setting, however, the President would be subject to the jurisdiction of a federal or state court, and would have to seek approval of the court to change or interrupt a litigation commitment to attend to unexpected official business.

D.   Deferral Is Not An Extraordinary Remedy.

In the opening brief, we showed that the temporary deferral of litigation is far from unusual in our system, and we offered a number of analogous contexts in which litigation is stayed -- often with undeniable prejudice to the plaintiff -- in order to protect important institutional interests. Respondent and her amici seek to distinguish these analogies on the ground that they do not involve "a special, personal privilege." Resp. Br. 25; *see also* Resp. Prof. Br. 2. It is unclear what is meant by this phrase. The doctrine of deferral is no more a "personal privilege" of the President than any other incident of his office, or than any immunity or similar protection is for any other public official. Deferral is necessary to preserve the functioning of the Presidency, and to protect the compelling institutional interests of the Executive Branch. It

---

Truman, 194 S.W.2d 29 (Mo. 1946). Accordingly, President Truman was not involved in active litigation while in office.

attaches to the office, not the person. It is no different in this respect from the "deference" for which respondent argues.

Deferral is directly analogous to the other stay doctrines we mentioned, all of which -- whether based on statute, judicial discretion or court-made doctrine -- delay a civil plaintiff's ability to obtain relief. Pet. Br. 34-37.[12] Respondent simply cannot explain why the compelling interests at stake here -- the unimpaired operation of the Executive Branch and the preservation of the separation of powers -- are not at least as strong as those present in the analogous contexts, and do not also justify a temporary stay of proceedings. Nor can she explain why deferring litigation against a President would impermissibly violate a plaintiff's entitlement to access to the courts, any more than those other types of stays do.[13]

---

[12] In this regard, respondent incorrectly asserts that pursuant to the automatic stay in bankruptcy, a plaintiff's tort claims are simply transferred to bankruptcy court and "immediately addressed" there. Resp. Br. 25. This is not so. The litigation cannot proceed in any forum without leave from the bankruptcy court, which typically is not granted until the court approves a plan for the debtor's estate, a complicated process that can take months or years. *See, e.g., Picco v. Global Marine Drilling Co.*, 900 F.2d 846, 847-48 (5th Cir. 1990); *In re Washington Mfg. Co.*, 118 B.R. 555, 559-60 (Bankr. M.D. Tenn. 1990). The reality is that most claimants must wait long periods before their claims are addressed, if ever. *See, e.g., Moser v. Universal Eng'g Corp.*, 11 F.3d 720, 721-22 (7th Cir. 1993); *Easley v. Pettibone Mich. Corp.*, 990 F.2d 905, 907 (6th Cir. 1993).

[13] On a related point, respondent and her amici contend that authority to stay this litigation must be found, if at all, in an act of Congress. Resp. Br. 26; Resp. Prof. Br. 19 n.14; CVA Br., *passim*. In *Fitzgerald*, however, the Court recognized that certain privileges and immunities are "functionally mandated incident[s] of the President's unique office, rooted in the constitutional tradition of the separation of powers and supported by our history" (457 U.S. at 749), and that there need not be a textual basis in the Constitution for such privileges and immunities. *Id.* at 750 n.31. The protection the President here asserts is another such incident of office. With regard to congressional action, moreover, the Court in *Fitzgerald* took an approach opposite that for which respondent contends: the Court

E. Deferral Will Not Lead To Abuse Of Office.

Respondent raises the specter that deferral would shelter a variety of Presidential wrongdoing, from defaulting on a debt to committing battery. Resp. Br. 24. The notion that the rule we advocate would increase the likelihood of misconduct by a President is, in a word, fanciful. As we showed in our opening brief, and as the Court underscored in *Fitzgerald*, there already are abundant forces to deter a President from private wrongdoing. *See* Pet. Br. 37; *Fitzgerald*, 457 U.S. at 757. These deterrents -- coupled with the knowledge that a plaintiff could vigorously pursue a civil claim and subject a President to damages following his tenure in office -- are sufficient to discourage misconduct in his private affairs. Realistically, with respect to deterrence and accountability, the differences between deferral and the respondent's proposed "scheme of deference" are non-existent.

---

declined to presume that Congress intended to subject the Chief Executive to litigation, absent an explicit, affirmative expression of legislative intent to do so. *Id.* at 749 n.27. Similarly, in Section 1983 cases such as this, the Court has repeatedly declined to infer congressional intent to override immunities "well grounded in history and reason." *Buckley v. Fitzsimmons*, 509 U.S. 259, 268 (1993) (quoting *Tenney v. Brandhove*, 341 U.S. 367, 376 (1951)).

CONCLUSION

For these reasons and the reasons stated in our opening brief, the judgment of the court of appeals should be reversed.

Respectfully submitted,

Robert S. Bennett
   Counsel of Record
Carl S. Rauh
Alan Kriegel
Amy R. Sabrin
Of Counsel: Stephen P. Vaughn
David A. Strauss   SKADDEN, ARPS, SLATE,
Geoffrey R. Stone   MEAGHER & FLOM
1111 East 60th Street   1440 New York Avenue, N.W.
Chicago, Illinois 60637 Washington, D.C. 20005
(312) 702-9601   (202) 371-7000

Attorneys for the Petitioner
President William Jefferson Clinton

October 9, 1996

Appendix F

ORAL ARGUMENTS

The following three arguments logically follow from the previous three briefs in Appendices C, D, and E. They are the oral arguments of the issues presented in those briefs. In addition, they indicate how fluid and unpredictable oral arguments can be when delivered to the Supreme Court of the United States.

William Jefferson CLINTON, Petitioner, v. Paula Corbin JONES.

No. 95–1853.

United States Supreme Court Official Transcript Jan. 13, 1997.

The above-entitled matter came on for oral argument before the Supreme Court of the United States at 10:03 a.m.

APPEARANCES:

ROBERT S. BENNETT, ESQ., Washington, D.C., on behalf of the Petitioner.

WALTER DELLINGER, ESQ., Acting Solicitor General, Department of Justice, Washington, D.C.; on behalf of the United States, as amicus curiae, supporting the Petitioner.

GILBERT K. DAVIS, ESQ., Fairfax, Virginia, on behalf of the Respondent.

CHIEF JUSTICE REHNQUIST: We'll hear argument now in No. 95–1853, William Jefferson Clinton v. Paula Corbin Jones.

ORAL ARGUMENT OF ROBERT S. BENNETT ON BEHALF OF THE PETITIONER

MR. BENNETT: Mr. Chief Justice and may it please the Court:

I am here this morning on behalf of the of the President of the United States, who has asked this Court to defer a private civil damage suit for money damages against him until he leaves office.

QUESTION: Is the request to totally dismiss the suit or to permit delay of the trial and any court appearance—in-court appearance or that position or that sort of thing?

MR. BENNETT: It is to delay the trial of the case and to—

QUESTION: How about discovery?

MR. BENNETT: And the discovery of the case. There is—

QUESTION: How about discovery of people who are not the President, other witnesses and things like that?

MR. BENNETT: That is correct, Your Honor. We—as—

QUESTION: You—you want to delay that as well?

MR. BENNETT: I want to delay that as well. However—

QUESTION: Should that be a general rule if preservation of evidence becomes crucial in a case?

MR. BENNETT: As we discussed in the District Court below, Justice O'Connor, we have agreed, and the District Court noted, that if there's a danger of the loss of any evidence, that we would cooperate to preserve it and make use of the Federal Rules of Civil Procedure.

QUESTION: Well, what if you wouldn't go up and what if the District Court—what if the court below disagreed with you?

MR. BENNETT: Well, that's—

QUESTION: I mean, what—I'm trying to figure out what the rule of law you're urging upon us here.

MR. BENNETT: The rule of law that we are urging upon you, Justice Scalia, is unless there are exceptional circumstances in a case, the President of the United States should not be subject to litigation, either at trial or in discovery. Unless there is some compelling necessity, he should not be taken away from his constitutional duties.

QUESTION: Is that issue a Federal—is it a Federal—suppose the suit were in State court, and the State court decided that the testimony of someone who was not the President is important to be preserved. Does that become a Federal question?

MR. BENNETT: Yes, it's a Federal question, because—

QUESTION: So if that State court's jurisdiction would be appealable here, or would the whole case be removable to Federal court, or—

MR. BENNETT: Well, I don't know how you would move a case from State court unless there is diversity. And that's why this Court must issue a constitutional ruling in this case. Because, otherwise, this—this complaint, and other complaints, could be brought into any State court in the country and command the President's time.

QUESTION: But the constitutional ruling you're asking of us is not that the suit cannot be brought.

MR. BENNETT: Well, we're asking—

QUESTION: So you're saying that the suit can be brought. And presumably it can be brought in State court?

MR. BENNETT: We are saying the suit against the President of the United States can be brought. It can be brought in a State court.

QUESTION: Right.

MR. BENNETT: It can be brought in a Federal court. But—

QUESTION: Right. Now, these—these questions of whether you have to preserve the witnesses' testimony—it's important to the case or not—do they render the case removable to Federal court?

MR. BENNETT: Yes, Your Honor, I believe that they do.

QUESTION: They do.

QUESTION: And I take it, just fading memories of witnesses, over a period of, say, 4 or 5 years, would not be sufficient to invoke the exception provision that you're talking about?

MR. BENNETT: I believe that's correct, Your Honor, particularly in this case, where the plaintiff had almost 20 months when Mr. Clinton was—was the governor.

QUESTION: Mr. Bennett—

QUESTION: And I take it that—I take it that since you say—and I think you're correct that this must be a privilege that's applicable in State courts, otherwise it would be a loser and it wouldn't give the protection you think the President needs—I take it that means you cannot rely on separation of powers as the constitutional theory, as the constitutional premise, for your argument; you have to rely on some other constitutional doctrine?

MR. BENNETT: I don't agree with that, with all due respect, Your Honor. I think this is a separation of powers case. Because if this—if this Court permits this litigation or other litigation like it to go forward, any State judge in the country or any county court judge in the country could command the President's time.

QUESTION: Right. But separation of powers isn't a doctrine that we impose on the State. Separation of powers is designed to confine each branch of the Federal Government to its appropriate constitutional scope.

MR. BENNETT: Well, but I—I would find it hard to believe that this Court would say that separation of powers would apply in a Federal court proceeding, but that any county or State judge could virtually destroy the power of the President under the Constitution in his Article II reading.

QUESTION: Well, I—I understand there's a Federal interest. But it seems to me what you're saying is that the inherent nature of the President's office requires that the States be constrained in this way. But that's not separation of powers.

QUESTION: Then it's Federal sovereignty. But I—I agree with the concerns expressed in the question by Justice Kennedy that it's if it were a suit in State court. It is very difficult to shoehorn it into some kind of separation of powers notion.

MR. BENNETT: I—I understand.

QUESTION: The supremacy clause—I don't know whether that bears on it—but certainly not separation of powers.

MR. BENNETT: I—I understand that, Your Honor, but—

QUESTION: Mr. Bennett, is there any experience in States with the temporal immunity with respect to a governor that you are asserting here with respect to the chief officer—

MR. BENNETT: We have found none, Your Honor.

QUESTION: And is it necessary—you said you must decide this as a constitutional matter because of the State court situation—this could be dealt with in the Federal courts as a matter of Federal common law. Isn't that where the immunities come from of executive offices? And who knows if it would come up in a State court. A State court might have such a similar—recognize such a similar immunity as a matter of their common law.

So why must we now assume that the State courts will not have such a—such an immunity and reach out for a constitutional question instead of saying here's a suit in Federal court and we can deal with it as a matter of Federal common law?

MR. BENNETT: I'm not quite sure I understand the question, Your Honor, but I think I do. I am certainly saying that this Court could decide this case without deciding the constitutional issue. I think that this Court could say that when the District Court judge stayed the trial, she had an inherent power, under the Landis case—the Supreme—this Court's decision in Landis—to stay the trial. And I don't think you would have to get to the constitutional considerations.

QUESTION: Well, I—I find it difficult to adopt such a Federal common law rule if it were—if it were so easily frustratable. I mean to say that there is a Federal common law rule that you can interfere with the President's duties by—by subjecting him to civil suit would be silly if any State could subject him to silly—to civil suit. I mean, don't you have to—have to tell me that this Federal common law rule you're asking me to adopt is one that will have some effect? And it will have no effect if the States can do the same thing?

MR. BENNETT: Yes, I agree it would be very silly for any county judge or any State judge to start deciding on the priorities of the President of—of the United States.

QUESTION: So I have to get to State courts somehow. Any general rule we adopt surely has to be one that we can enforce upon State courts as well as Federal.

MR. BENNETT: Oh, that's of most importance to this Court, particularly since the fact that you now have long-arm statutes which were not common in the days of our founders, and you could drag the President into any court. You know, what's unprecedented here—what is unprecedented here is the notion of taking the President of the United States of America, in whom the full executive power resides, and subjecting that President to any State court or any local court in the country.

Is this Court—

QUESTION: Or even worse, any Federal court. Because there you have, in addition, separation of powers.

MR. BENNETT: Or any—or in any Federal court. And I think, interestingly, Your Honors, if you—if you just transpose the facts of this case to the Federal system—let's say that Miss Jones were a Federal employee and let's say that Mr. Clinton were the President, and let's say that instead of State troopers, we're talking about Secret Service people—it would be my view that your very far-reaching decision in the Fitzgerald case, which—which gave the President absolute immunity for—for acts within the outer perimeters, would probably—would probably prevent this case from—from going forward.

QUESTION: Well, the record in Fitzgerald was based on a fear that unless you gave the President absolute immunity, as I understand the opinion, you—you—he would not vigorously exercise his official powers as President. I don't see how that element is involved here.

MR. BENNETT: I agree with you, Mr. Justice—Mr. Chief Justice, that—that element is not present here. But in the Fitzgerald opinion, in which you joined with Justice Powell, the rationale for that decision goes way beyond the chilling effect. You talked about intrusion on the President's time.

QUESTION: But, Mr. Bennett, that sentence that you feature was followed up by—by these words, "as in the case of prosecutors and judges." And prosecutors and judges also enjoy absolute immunity for their acts in the course of their office. But do they enjoy any kind of immunity for—for conduct unrelated to their office?

MR. BENNETT: No. No, Justice Ginsburg. But—but you went much further. I don't mean you personally. But you went much further in the Fitzgerald case. This was the core of the dissent of Mr. Justice White. He said that you are not giving absolute immunity simply to core functions. You are giving absolute immunity to the outer perimeters of the office.

QUESTION: But I think we're mixing up two things. We're mixing up, one, the total immunity, because you want the decisionmaking to be unfettered, and then the immunity that's, as you say, temporary, temporal, just not whether but when.

MR. BENNETT: Right. We're not asking for—

QUESTION: And there are different considerations involved in the two, are there not?

MR. BENNETT: Yes. Yes, Justice Ginsburg. That—that is correct. But you must remember, the fundamental difference between the Fitzgerald case—or one of the fundamental differences is this Court extinguished Mr. Fitzgerald's rights for all time, involving a case where you didn't even have a sitting President. Mr. Nixon hadn't been in office, to the best of my recollection, for 4 years. Here you have a sitting President. And all we're saying is we'll give Miss Jones her day in court, but let's not do it now.

QUESTION: But, in effect, I—I assume you're arguing that it is interference or the risk of interference with the actual presidential duties during the 4–year term that is the source of whatever privilege you request; isn't that right?

MR. BENNETT: That's correct.

QUESTION: Right. Now, how does that take you from interference with the President himself, as—as a deponent or as a witness or simply as a party attending a trial, and—and go to the further extent of—of giving you some kind of a privilege to preclude discovery, which does not personally involve the President? How—how is the interference there enough for you?

MR. BENNETT: Well, Mr. Justice Souter, it's the realities of real-world litigation. Mr.—my brother at the bar, Mr. Davis—

QUESTION: Well, it's going to keep you busy. But the President presumably—

(Laughter.)

QUESTION:—I mean, the President isn't going to attend these depositions; you are.

MR. BENNETT: But in the real world of litigation, Mr. Justice Souter, do you think when Mr. Davis, as he—as he claims, that he's going to be deposing all of the troopers; and any time the President of the United States has come into contact with a member of the opposite sex, he intends to inquire of that; this is a conspiracy complaint; they talk about pattern of conduct—

QUESTION: Yes, but, Mr. Bennett—

MR. BENNETT:—don't you think I'm going to have to talk to the President of United States about all those events?

QUESTION: Well, I assume—

QUESTION: Mr. Bennett, do you think all those events are relevant to this case?

MR. BENNETT: I think some trial courts would say they are not and some trial courts might—might say they are. We haven't gotten to that question yet.

QUESTION: How long do you think—how long—how long do you think it will take to try this case?

MR. BENNETT: It's impossible to say. I can tell you the President has spent—personally spent a substantial amount of time on this case already. I mean, this is a personal—the very nature of this case is so personal that it would require his heavy involvement.

QUESTION: But—but there are—there are two elements here really—a concern about some conflict with a judge deciding how to weigh the interests of the President in attending a NATO meeting or something versus a desire to avoid damage control politically. I mean, is there an element of that in here? And does that enter into the constitutional balance?

MR. BENNETT: I—I think the President is a political figure and—and deals in the political—political marketplace.

QUESTION: Yet could be the concern about damage control, at bottom, would motivate, not necessarily this President, but any President, in wanting to spend a little time with the lawyer as these allegations are made. But is that part of our constitutional balance?

MR. BENNETT: Well, Your Honor, I don't think we can—I think—there's no perfect answer to this. But I certainly don't think that you can permit the courts to start deciding what presidential priorities are or are not.

QUESTION: Why can't we wait until the President asserts such a conflict? It's never happened in a couple of hundred years. Why can't we wait until the court says, Mr. President, I want you here for this deposition and, if you don't come, you're going to lose the case; and the President says, I'm sorry, I have to go to a NATO meeting? Why don't we wait for that, what seems to me, very unlikely situation to arise?

MR. BENNETT: Well, I'm not so sure, in today's climate, that it is unlikely to arise. But I suppose you could wait, as you say. But I have a specific case I have to deal with now.

QUESTION: Thank you, Mr. Bennett. General Dellinger, we'll hear from you.

ORAL ARGUMENT OF WALTER DELLINGER ON BEHALF OF THE UNITED STATES, AS AMICUS CURIAE, SUPPORTING PETITIONER

MR. DELLINGER: Mr. Chief Justice and may it please the Court:

Let me begin by responding to Justice Scalia's question about the source of law. It is constitutionally based. In our view, Justice Scalia, it comes from this Court's—the same basis that this Court stated in its different opinion in Fitzgerald, where they considered the immunity there, quote, a functionally mandated incident of the President's unique office. That is, it allows this from Article II. That's—

QUESTION: Yeah, but to the extent that Nixon v. Fitzgerald involved some activity of the President that relates to his duties in office as President, that is an element that does not extend to this case.

MR. DELLINGER: That is correct, Justice O'Connor.

QUESTION: And there may have been Folsom language, as there often is, in Court opinions. But we have to get back to the basic source of what is it in the Constitution that we look to, to govern this—this issue?

MR. DELLINGER: You are correct, Justice O'Connor, that there is a different issue in Fitzgerald. But what Fitzgerald stands for is the proposition that this Court can announce rules of law which are binding on State and Federal court, as the Fitzgerald immunity surely is binding in State and Federal courts.

QUESTION: Well, what is it in the Constitution that makes the immunity, let's say, of a Federal judge or the immunity of any Federal employee for acts of official duty binding in a State court, where that activity might itself constitute a tort under State law? What is it in the Constitution that binds the State courts so that the State court can't proceed? Is this the supremacy clause? I mean, I—

MR. DELLINGER: Yes. Yes. The—to the extent that it's based upon Federal law, it is the supremacy clause. To the extent that it's—

QUESTION: So if there is a separation of powers doctrine that creates a—a—call it a Federal common law-type immunity, then that immunity for judges or anyone else is binding upon the State courts because of the supremacy?

MR. DELLINGER: That is absolutely correct, Justice Scalia, in—

QUESTION: No, but not if it's based on the separation of powers.

MR. DELLINGER: I believe that the Fitzgerald immunity clearly applies to actions brought in State court. Surely the Court in Fitzgerald did not announce that a doctrine of immunity for presidential actions, in the official capacity—

QUESTION: But isn't the reason for that that the immunity in a Federal court would be meaningless if it were subject to an end run, and that's how the supremacy clause translates a separation of powers doctrine into a State court immunity; isn't that the way it works?

MR. DELLINGER: That is exactly correct.

QUESTION: But a good—a good deal of your Federal official immunity for Federal comes by statute from Congress, not from the Constitution.

MR. DELLINGER: Yes, some of that comes by—

QUESTION: And that of course isn't—we're not faced with a situation where Congress has passed a law granting this immunity.

MR. DELLINGER: That is correct, Mr. Chief Justice—

QUESTION: Let me—I don't understand how Nixon v. Fitzgerald requires you to say that it is separation of powers that somehow gets to the State courts. A State—you could not bring suit in the State court to stay a Federal actor, whether it's the President or not. It's simply the supremacy clause that says State courts don't muck around with—with Federal activities.

MR. DELLINGER: Well, Justice—

QUESTION: You don't need separation of powers to get there.

MR. DELLINGER: No. You need—what you need is Article II, as informed by the separation of powers.

QUESTION: Right, right.

MR. DELLINGER: Nixon v.—

QUESTION: So that keeps the State courts out. And then you have the doctrine of separation of powers, which keeps the Federal courts out.

MR. DELLINGER: Yes, that is correct.

QUESTION: Okay. Well, that's quite different from saying we've extended—somehow we make a ruling on separation of powers for the Federal courts and that automatically slops over to the State courts.

MR. DELLINGER: No.

QUESTION: On the other hand, the case such as Toddles case, which says that a State—or a State court—cannot enjoin a Federal official, have to do with a Federal official in the course of his duties.

MR. DELLINGER: That is correct, Justice Kennedy. The—in both instances, however, the public interest in the President's unimpaired performance of his duties must take precedence over a private litigant's interest in redress.

QUESTION: Mr. Dellinger, can I ask you about that?

MR. DELLINGER: Yes.

QUESTION: Your brief and the brief of the Petitioner both make a lot about the fact that the President is—you know, it's a full-time job and he—he's very—and any intrusion upon his time is intruding. I must say, I don't find that terribly persuasive. The fact is that—that that's a better reason why the Chief Justice or any of the Justices of this Court should have the kind of immunity you're talking about, or the Speaker of the House, or a member of Congress, none of whom can delegate any of their responsibilities.

The President is the one Federal officer at the highest level who is able to delegate.

MR. DELLINGER: Justice Scalia, the singularity and unitariness of the executive are what makes it distinguishable from every other official, and it's not possible—

QUESTION: But we see Presidents riding horseback, chopping firewood, fishing for stick fish—

(Laughter.)

QUESTION:—playing golf and so forth and so on. Why can't we leave it to the point where, if and when a court tells a President to be there or he's going to lose his case, and if and when a President has the intestinal fortitude to say, I am absolutely too busy—so that he'll never be seen playing golf for the rest of his administration—

(Laughter.)

QUESTION:—if and when that happens, we can—we can resolve the problem.

MR. DELLINGER: Justice Scalia—

QUESTION: But, really, the notion that he doesn't have a minute to spare is—is just not—not credible.

MR. DELLINGER: Justice Scalia, President Reagan said quite aptly, Presidents don't have vacations; they have a change of scenery. Every party to this litigation and every judge below agrees that a President cannot be subjected to litigation in the same manner as someone who is not at that time serving as President. What—what is at issue is not whether an action against the President has to be treated differently, but how that difference should be.

And the approach suggested by the court below of—of sensitive judicial case management would wholly fail both to protect the President and would enmesh the State and Federal courts in a politically charged task, lacking manageable judicial standards.

QUESTION: Perhaps you can help me with this aspect of that argument. And it's been troubling to me. When we talk about privileges and immunities, we're talking about balances of interests, the rights of the litigant, the necessities of the President. Here, it seems to me, that the President, during the course of the stay that this proceeding produces, is free with his staff and his resources to really, to continue to argue his case, to ruin the reputation of the plaintiff, to poison the well any way he can, just as the—as the other parties might try to do against him. But he's in a very dominant position.

There's really nothing we have that could stay the President's activity in this regard. That certainly is beyond the control of the Court. So it seems to me that the imbalance here is very substantial. And I know of no compensating balance mechanism to protect the plaintiff.

MR. DELLINGER: Well, I think that certainly political pressures would cut against that. But we have—we have acknowledged that delay could well have adverse consequences for a plaintiff suing any President. But that has never been treated dispositive. There is nothing anomalous about the proposition that individual civil damage remedies are precluded by public policy considerations.

Chief Justice Burger noted in Fitzgerald that there are at least 75,000 public officials that have absolute immunity, a different kind of immunity, but one which nonetheless precludes plaintiffs from being able to—

QUESTION: Well, Mr. Dellinger, suppose it's a child custody matter. Sometime in the future, we have some President who doesn't get along with a spouse, and there's a child custody problem. There's no right to go into a State court and get temporary relief, so that the child knows where the child is going to be for the next 8 years or whatever it is?

MR. DELLINGER: Justice O'Connor, I believe that that would be—that's the most appealing case for an exception I've heard. Now, we're not suggesting—and I have to be concerned about—

QUESTION: Well, so there's no automatic rule that the Court has to dismiss the minute the thing is filed; you acknowledge that?

MR. DELLINGER: Well—

QUESTION: Or suppose a President in the future owns some part—great parcel of land somewhere and it's bubbling up with poisons. And all the neighbors are upset because of the environmental damage. No temporary injunction possibility?

MR. DELLINGER: I am not suggesting that there's a balancing test or a case-by-case determination. We're suggesting that there ought to be a rule—and we have to be concerned not just with civil damage actions like this one, but with actions against all future Presidents—a rule—an operative rule that courts should postpone civil litigation until the President's term. But the existence of that does not mean we can assume, arguendo, that an extraordinary case like child custody you could make an exception.

Now, as to the President's—

QUESTION: Well, once you assume that, arguendo, you don't have a firm rule, and you begin to lose me.

MR. DELLINGER: No—

QUESTION: Because I don't like cases—I do not like courts engaging in case-by-case balancing and saying, This intrudes on the presidency too much, this doesn't intrude.

MR. DELLINGER: This is not a matter—

QUESTION: You give me a clear line, and I might buy it.

MR. DELLINGER: The fact that you have a rule, and an operative rule, and it tells courts what to do does not mean that you can never make an exception. That's true of prior restraints.

QUESTION: Is that right?

MR. DELLINGER: That's true of prior restraints. The—

QUESTION: General Dellinger, there was a list in many of the briefs. And it went: nuisance abatement, mortgage foreclosure, divorce, child custody. And those were presented as categorical exceptions. Are you saying that it would be a case-by-case thing or that there are certain kinds of cases that would be excluded from this temporal immunity?

MR. DELLINGER: We believe that there should be a rule that any civil litigation against a President should be postponed. Now, the President's attorney need worry only about civil damage actions. And it is hard, I think, given the way our legal culture treats civil damage actions, to make the case for an exception in that instance. But when you consider the demands on the presidency, we think, given the—

QUESTION: What are those demands in respect to a deposition, say, kept under seal, of non-White House witnesses? How does proceeding with discovery for non-White House witnesses—even, let's say, kept it under seal so it wasn't in the press, et cetera—how would that interfere with the daily workings of the presidency?

MR. DELLINGER: I think it could interfere with the workings of the presidency, and therefore would urge that discovery be postponed, except for lost evidence that Mr. Bennett has acknowledged that he would accommodate. Because I think litigation can be all-consuming and all-absorbing. I think there is—one has to have a sense of the extent to which someone who is involved in personal litigation can be totally absorbed by it. Advising on what questions should be asked of witnesses—

QUESTION: But surely the range of matters—

QUESTION: Surely that may be true of an individual with an ordinary job, but with all the pressing concerns that the President has, one would think it would be less true of him.

MR. DELLINGER: Mr. Chief Justice, the—when this country adopted the 25th amendment, it was a recognition by Congress and the courts that the President's office was singular, as Chairman Emmanuel Cellars said when he proposed the amendment to Congress, the Nation cannot permit the office of the President to be vacant even for a moment.

QUESTION: But let's say it is singular. Now, it seems to me you're talking about intrusion of the judiciary upon the executive's time. You also have, sometimes, intrusion by the legislature upon the executive's time. Now, the way we've chosen to handle that with respect in particular to claims of presidential privilege—not to testify, not turn over documents, not to give information to Congress—is we haven't adopted an absolute rule that, because it would be so intrusive upon the President, you can't make any such demands. We wait for the case to arise.

And if and when the President has the intestinal fortitude to say, as, for instance, Dwight Eisenhower did with respect to the Army McCarthy hearings, I am not going to give any testimony; I am not going to allow any of my people to give testimony. If and when that comes up, I'm willing to allow a total executive privilege at that point. Why can't we adopt the same rule here? If and when the President says, I just don't have the time to come when you subpoena me, I'll give him an absolute immunity in that situation.

MR. DELLINGER: Justice Scalia—

QUESTION: Why isn't that enough to protect the President from all that we're worried about?

MR. DELLINGER: Because I think that risks both, clearly to protect the President and risks undercutting the role of the courts. To put the President to the task with regard to each phase of a lawsuit—

QUESTION: The beautiful thing about it is it takes the courts out of the scene. They don't have to decide, is it too important, is it unimportant, blah, blah, blah, blah, which gets the courts involved.

MR. DELLINGER: It totally undercuts—

QUESTION: This way it's absolute. All the President has to do is stand up and say, I'm too busy to come to this hearing, and I will not come, and you have no power to enter judgment against me simply because of my refusal.

MR. DELLINGER: Justice Scalia, that would—the approach that would have litigation go on—and perhaps no President could responsibly agree to attend, which is why putting the President to a task at every step and putting the courts at that task of making a decision about which of the President's duties. The President's work makes it impossible—

QUESTION: But under that rule, the court wouldn't have to make any decision. Under the rule proposed by the question you were answering, the minute that is asserted, the court says, Hands off, I'm out of here.

MR. DELLINGER: You would put the President to the burden of being concerned with litigation constantly and having to raise at each point a refusal to participate or to cut off his testimony. You would put—you would put a—

QUESTION: General Dellinger—General, but you're not just talking about when the President is called to testify; you are talking about all the other people in the litigation—

MR. DELLINGER: That is correct.

QUESTION:—that's what makes it unlike the legislative hearing?

MR. DELLINGER: The—the absorption of the President with the less of the trial and the hearing places the Article III judiciary in a very difficult position. The petitioners in this case give a list of activities—I'm sorry, the Respondents—in their brief that they think would not have justified delay, including vacation activities where important work may have been done, including a good example of what would happen to the courts is a 4-day train trip they not that a President—this particular President took en route to a political convention.

Now, if you debate that example, half the people will say that's clearly nonofficial and shouldn't give way. They're absolutely right; it's not even paid for by the government. Others will say it's an important governmental function for a President to communicate during his reelection campaign.

QUESTION: Thank you, General Dellinger.

Mr. Davis, we'll hear from you.

ORAL ARGUMENT OF GILBERT K. DAVIS
ON BEHALF OF THE RESPONDENT

MR. DAVIS: Mr. Chief Justice, and may it please the Court:

William Jefferson Clinton, the citizen, who holds the office of the presidency of the United States, advances the novel claim of immunity from the progress of litigation while he is President. This immunity he derives, he says, from the separation of powers doctrine of our Constitution, and he further contends that the judicial branch of Government must suspend the processing of Paula Corbin Jones' lawsuit until he is out of office, potentially for a period of 7 years after the date of her filing of the suit.

This novel proposition has three fundamental errors. The first error is to confuse the office of the presidency, which has privileges and immunities which protect its institutional duties, with the person who holds that office who, in his private capacity and personal capacity has no such privileges and immunities and instead has the same rights and responsibilities as all other citizens.

QUESTION: Mr. Davis—

MR. DAVIS: Yes, sir.

QUESTION:—what do you do when a State court tells the President, you're going to lose this lawsuit unless you appear for a hearing on June 2, and the President says, you know, Your Honor, I have a NATO meeting I'm supposed to go to, heads of State, and you know, you have a testy district judge or local State court judge—you've encountered some of them—and they say, this is my courtroom and, you know, I expect you here on June 2.

MR. DAVIS: Your Honor—

QUESTION: And you say there's no remedy for that.

MR. DAVIS: Justice Scalia—no, I say that there is a remedy for that. First, the bright line test that the Court should seek here, I think, is that you look first to an actual, imminent interference with official duty.

QUESTION: And who judges that, the judge does? The judge says, well, Mr. President, this NATO meeting, I've sort of looked up the—it's not a very important NATO meeting.

(Laughter.)

QUESTION: You could send your Secretary of State. In fact, I think he's smarter than you are anyway.

(Laughter.)

QUESTION: Or the President says, it's top secret. I can't tell you, judge, why I can't be there.

MR. DAVIS: Justice Ginsburg—I'm not sure who I should respond to first, but—

QUESTION: It's the same question.

(Laughter.)

MR. DAVIS: Justice Ginsburg, there are ample traditional powers. We don't have to shift burdens of proof or any other special mechanism here. There are traditional powers of the court which must be presumed to exercise those to protect the President from interference with his job, ex parte conferences, and the like.

Justice Scalia, your question as to what do you do if a judge does not and is not sensitive to the demands of the presidency and the time required by the occupant of that office to perform the functions, I think there are several potential remedies. I'm not certain that I could exhaust them all, but mandamus, prohibition. Certainly all roads lead to this Court.

QUESTION: But what law would govern that? Is it just State law, be nice to Presidents? I—

MR. DAVIS: No, I think first the President must make the claim, if he—

QUESTION: And what law would control, Federal or State, when a President says I can't be there because I have to do something that's connected with my office?

MR. DAVIS: I hope I'm not on unsettling ground here, but I would suggest, as Justice O'Connor I think first mentioned, that the Supremacy Clause, the structure—and here is a separation of powers issue perhaps, at least where the Constitution parceled out, structurally, power and gave to the President all executive power.

If a State or Federal court, and I'm not certain that it makes any difference whatsoever, were to interfere in such a way or permit an interference—

QUESTION: And who decides that? What we're asking is, who decides? Does this Court decide whether the President is being interfered with too much, or is the simple assertion—

MR. DAVIS: I think the simple assertion—

QUESTION: The simple assertion by the President, if he's willing to take the political heat and say, I don't have enough time to come to this hearing—

MR. DAVIS: I think—

QUESTION:—would you allow that absolutely to control?

MR. DAVIS: I would allow it to control with this possible caveat. If it happened 10 times in a row, and there was a question of good faith, I think the Court—I don't think the Court can exercise any jurisdiction over his person.

QUESTION: Can't you leave political pressures to take care of that? No President's going to do it 10 times. He's going to look very bad.

MR. DAVIS: Well, I would agree.

QUESTION: What in your view is an interference? That is, suppose, for example, that the lawyers are deposing non-White House witnesses and it turns out that every statement they made is in the newspaper and the President says, but I have to respond to each of these. They're saying I was in a certain place at a certain time, or I said something to somebody only a month ago.

And then somebody else says something about what he didn't say, and then somebody says something about where there's a paper that somebody wrote it down, and then it goes into—we all know how those things work, and suppose the President says, look, I don't have time to go into all of these things. I don't have time to remember every single thing I said to everybody and anything that's tangentially related. It's interfering, right now.

Now, what in your view—is that an interference, or is—

MR. DAVIS: I think that the rule here, Justice Breyer, is an actual, imminent interference with his job and a claim that he makes.

QUESTION: I've just given you the example. Is that an interference, or he's saying this deposition, all these depositions interfere because I don't have time.

MR. DAVIS: Yes, sir.

QUESTION: That is an interference?

MR. DAVIS: I think that may well be an interference. It's the same kind of interference that you would have that's posed, this torrent of litigation that might occur.

QUESTION: Now, he comes and says that, and how in your view should this be decided? I'm just repeating now the question, that I want to be clear about.

MR. DAVIS: On the torrent of litigation, or how—

QUESTION: No, how—when the—when your side, for example, takes dozens of depositions, and each one turns up what I call peripheral or satellite issues about who said what to whom where, and where the paper is and where it isn't and so forth, and he says, I don't have time to talk to my lawyers about all of these details because there are so many, and they require so much thought, and that's his claim of interference. Now, how in your view is it supposed to work?

MR. DAVIS: Justice Breyer, if he relates that to his official duties so that it is taking his time and his mental processes away from his official duties, then I think that is an interference that would justify him not—

QUESTION: Well, so you don't defend the judgment of the court of appeals below. Did you file a cross-petition for certiorari then on some ground? The court below permitted, as I understand it, some discovery—

MR. DAVIS: Oh, no. No, sir—

QUESTION:—to go forward, but you take the position that that discovery may not go forward if the President asserts, gee, this is taking my time. You're deposing witness X out there in the State of Arkansas but it's consuming my time to look at it. Therefore, you're off the hook. Is that your position?

MR. DAVIS: No. No, I am defending—

QUESTION: But that is precisely what you just told Justice Breyer is the rule.

MR. DAVIS: No, Your Honor.

QUESTION: What is the thing you're asserting? I just am totally confused now.

MR. DAVIS: All right. Well, let me see if I can clear the confusion. What I am suggesting, and it's in the context of the depositions that Justice Breyer raised this—

QUESTION: Depositions of third parties out of State?

MR. DAVIS: It's hard to conceive that they would be—

QUESTION: But if the President comes in and says, look, I want to keep track of this stuff, I need to meet with my lawyer, and I want to see what's going on here, it's interfering with my duties, what is the lower court to do?

MR. DAVIS: Well, I think the lower court has its function and its duty to decide whether that is a good faith claim.

QUESTION: That goes beyond my question, you understand.

QUESTION: Let him answer Justice O'Connor's question. Go ahead.

MR. DAVIS: And if it is not, then you may have a conflict between the person of the President and a judge. He would respond. He would just go to the—

QUESTION: So the trial court judge at the State court level is to determine whether the offer—the complaint made by the President's lawyer is made in good faith or not?

MR. DAVIS: I think he must make the claim of actual interference with his duties, that as another example, the torrent of litigation has come—is so much, that I am only responding now to civil complaints.

QUESTION: But don't we know that that's inevitable in a suit like this? This argument here today is taking an hour. All the counsel and all participants in the argument have thought about it for at least the weekend if not a week.

(Laughter.)

QUESTION: There's an anxiety component, there's an intellectual commitment—

MR. DAVIS: Yes, sir.

QUESTION:—there's an emotional commitment—

MR. DAVIS: Yes, sir.

QUESTION:—that's far more extensive than some time chart would indicate.

MR. DAVIS: I don't—

QUESTION: And I think that's part of what the President is saying, is—

MR. DAVIS: Well—

QUESTION:—if he's going to defend this lawsuit it will absorb substantial energies.

MR. DAVIS: I don't believe, Justice Kennedy, that the Constitution protects him in his personal capacity.

QUESTION: Well, what if the President's attorney came before the Court at the cert stage and asserted in the petition for certiorari this is causing the President to spend too much time on this. You, Supreme Court, lay off. It's bothering my duties. I'm very interested in this issue, and it's taking my time. What is the Supreme Court of the United States to do?

MR. DAVIS: I don't think the Supreme Court of the United States is a fact-finding body on that subject.

QUESTION: But the only fact is—

QUESTION: But we have an issue of law that is consuming a great deal of time, effort, and anxiety.

MR. DAVIS: Yes, but that issue again is a matter to be addressed to a trial judge, who is—

QUESTION: But I thought the only issue was good faith. I thought you said a moment ago that if in fact the particular objection to the particular deposition and what-not was made in good faith, that it would be appropriate for the court to honor it, period.

MR. DAVIS: Well, I think the court—I think—perhaps I should also suggest that a court suspicious of the good faith of that assertion—

QUESTION: No, let's—

MR. DAVIS:—is entitled to require a showing, just as in the—

QUESTION: But all of this showing, all of this inquiry goes to the good faith of the request.

MR. DAVIS: Goes to the interference, whether—

QUESTION: Goes to—I thought you were saying it goes to the good faith of the claim of interference, and that is a different thing, I think, that you are allowing thereby from an inquiry into the degree of interference and whether the interference is serious enough to warrant the stay or what-not.

I think those are two different inquiries, and I understood you to be saying back when you were responding to Justice Breyer that it was the good faith inquiry that would be dispositive.

MR. DAVIS: I think as a practical matter, and I'm not suggesting the good faith as a rule of law, as a practical matter in—

QUESTION: Probably try to take it out of the immunity context with respect to lesser officers—you know, the Fitzgerald case has been featured in the briefs and in this argument, but Harlow came down the same day, and in that case this Court said that discovery can be peculiarly disruptive of effective government. That was in the case of a lesser officer. And so for that reason the Court said, although immunity is only qualified, we're going to decide that question at the top of the list before any discovery is allowed.

MR. DAVIS: Justice Ginsburg, I believe that the immunity question, if it exists, if the concept that has been suggested to this Court of temporal immunity, if it exists, bars proceedings whether they're pretrial or trial. If that arises under the separation of powers, then it bars it all. If it does not, it does not bar either the pretrial or the trial subject to an actual interference.

QUESTION: And I asked—

QUESTION: I thought you were arguing that—or conceding that if there was in fact a good faith assertion of the privilege in a given instance, that it would be appropriate to honor it. Is that—I am wrong?

MR. DAVIS: I don't think it's a privilege. I think what he would be saying is, a procedure has happened here. I can't—

QUESTION: Whatever you call it.

MR. DAVIS: Well, I think the best way to call this is a trial. Let's talk about a trial. He's anticipating 7 days worth of trial, and I can't be in court for 7 days, and—

QUESTION: No, no. This is third party depositions we were talking about.

QUESTION: May I ask a question in that regard about third party depositions, and we're concerned about their impact on the office of the President and so forth.

Would it be permissible for the trial judge in trying to control the litigation and recognize the special problems of the President to narrow discovery to matters that relate to the particular incident involved in the trial and say, no, you can't ask about the history for the last 10 years, or 45 other police officers and so forth. Would that be a permissible use of the trial judge's discretion?

MR. DAVIS: I think the trial judge always has the opportunity and the duty to balance the interests—

QUESTION: So it would be permissible to him to narrow discovery and the scope of inquiry—

QUESTION: Mr. Davis, I don't think you're answering some of the questions quite as frankly as we might hope you would. To say that the trial judge could consider it isn't to say whether he's bound by it.

MR. DAVIS: I don't think he is bound—

QUESTION: And there is a difference between a President's claim simply saying, I can't come now. Is that conclusive on the court? It seems to me—or does the court have an obligation, or at least is it permissible to weigh the court's own evaluation of the President's claim?

I think I would like and I think my colleagues would like your answers to those questions.

MR. DAVIS: I do believe, Chief Justice, that a court has, if it is suspicious of a President's assertion of a claim, has a right to inquire into the bona fides of that claim, and if the court found in its belief that the President did not make that claim and that there—properly that there was not an interference with his duties, I think the court would go—could—can't take any exercise of jurisdiction over his person, but could go forward with the other kinds of remedies that it might have.

QUESTION: Is that the holding of the Eighth Circuit that we're reviewing?

MR. DAVIS: The Eighth Circuit never considered, I don't think, the minutiae—

QUESTION: It sounds different to me than what we read in the Sixth—

MR. DAVIS: The Eighth Circuit said—

QUESTION:—in the Eighth Circuit opinion.

MR. DAVIS: No, the Eighth Circuit said that, sensitive to proper judicial case management and sensitive to the interests of the parties, including the President, this case should proceed, and I—

QUESTION: Mr. Davis—

MR. DAVIS:—responding as a sensitivity to those questions.

QUESTION: Mr. Davis, I am unlikely to favor a disposition that allows any judge, Federal or State, to sit in judgment of the President's assertion of whether his executive duties are too important or not.

What about an alternative to your proposal that would draw a distinction between the person of the President being hauled before a court and depositions of other people, and say the latter, and the worry about the trial, and all of that, is just like worry about his personal health or his financial affairs, or marital problems at home, or whatever. It's just something you've got to live with, even when you're President.

However, to be hauled personally before a judge is something else, and so give the President absolute immunity. If he makes the claim, I'm too busy to come, you cannot enter judgment against him simply because he refuses to appear, but the rest of the trial can proceed. Would that be acceptable to you?

MR. DAVIS: I would not find it acceptable because I think the presumption is that this case, which does not have a risk to it in the likely event that it goes forward—if it were to go forward does not have a risk of interference with the functions of the presidency, and it's a case of a—

QUESTION: Well, what if the President says so? I'm not saying the rest of the trial. I'm just saying, when he's subpoenaed to testify he says, I am too busy. I am President of the United States.

MR. DAVIS: Well, Justice Scalia—

QUESTION: And he has to make that claim.

MR. DAVIS:—he has given depositions, and he has arranged his calendar, and the court would—under the new Federal rules, as I understand it, would have a conference with him, what protections do you need, and would—could enter an order to that, and he gives available dates.

As a matter of fact, in most of these circumstances my brother Mr. Bennett I'm sure would be accommodating to arrange with us, without the involvement of the court at all, the time and place and date, and the availability of the President, and if he said, hey, I've got something else to do, I'm sure counsel would do it. If they didn't do it, then of course you go to the court, but to say—

QUESTION: But you still insist that the court pass judgment on—if the President can't come to some compromise, you think the court will sit in judgment on whether, indeed, he's too busy?

MR. DAVIS: Well, his option is just not to obey, because I have a—

QUESTION: And suffer judgment.

MR. DAVIS:—constitutional and statutory function to perform.

QUESTION: And suffer judgment.

MR. DAVIS: He could suffer judgment. There's the appellate process for that.

QUESTION: When you say that the President can in good faith make an assertion of privilege that would be honored if it's in good faith, it seems to me that you give away most of your case.

You leave two things for court inquiry, number 1, the existence of good faith, and number 2 whether or not it's a risk to the presidency. It seems to me that both of those inquiries are so very, very intrusive that it argues strongly for the absolute privilege that petitioners are suggesting.

MR. DAVIS: Well, the question came to me initially and my bright line rule was not the good faith rule, it was the actual imminent risk to the President performing his duties, and an assertion of the claim, and we got to the point of the assertion of the claim, and I merely suggested that the—that if the President was not in good faith 10 times in a row, that the court might make an inquiry into that.

I did not suggest to the Court that the—necessarily that that was a—the rule of law that we would necessarily seek.

I think the President would act in good faith. If he did not act in it, the court may have the right to inquire.

I don't think that is before us. What is before us is a private action. The President has a private capacity. He should be—he should go forward with the case, and if—

QUESTION: Mr. Davis, what is at risk for you taking into account two things. Mr. Bennett said that it would be appropriate to take depositions to perpetuate testimony if there's a danger that the testimony won't be available later and, should you prevail, you get interest on any damage award, so what is at stake in a postponement?

MR. DAVIS: Well, what is at stake, and this is—these interests I think are substantial to the plaintiff. She can lose her cause of action if either she or the President dies. It is extinguished, as the Eighth Circuit concurring opinion points out.

She has her reputation. You talk about how important this case is. It's a civil rights case partially and State's claims, but reputation is what we take to our grave probably more than anything else, and while she's alive that reputation is sullied.

The implicit—well, the implication of the article was that she was a compliant female. If that is the case, we can imagine that she goes for a job and an employers says, I'm not so sure whether you made a valid claim here or not. I don't want to be the next employer that you charge.

QUESTION: She hasn't alleged anything like that, has she?

MR. DAVIS: No, no, but you asked me what interests are involved in the delay.

In addition to that, obviously, the course of human experience, we don't know when witnesses will die. We certainly can't say, well, there's an emergency because somebody's going to die tomorrow who's not ill. That is a common experience, and that's why justice delayed has often—

QUESTION: Well, witnesses' memories also fade, do they not?

MR. DAVIS: They fade, and they become incapacitated. The documents get lost or mislaid. So her case could be utterly destroyed, and she could—

QUESTION: I thought as far as witnesses' memories were concerned, I thought that Mr. Bennett had conceded that you could have something like Rule 27 of the Federal Rules of Civil Procedure, depositions to perpetuate testimony?

MR. DAVIS: But discovery depositions, Your Honor?

QUESTION: Yes.

MR. DAVIS: Where leads are developed? I'm not certain that Mr. Bennett would permit that.

QUESTION: No. No, responding to the dim memory problem, that dim memory is a problem. Then you can get the current memory.

MR. DAVIS: Mr. Bennett I found to be very accommodating, but this Court is going to be enunciating a constitutional doctrine.

QUESTION: Well, I'm not so sure about that, because even in the Fitzgerald case Justice Powell had a footnote where he suggested that Congress might pass a law authorizing such a claim against the President. Now, if Congress could pass a law, then it can't be a constitutional matter, can it?

MR. DAVIS: That is the remedy that the President—that the President could seek if he fears this interference. I think if there's—

QUESTION: No, no. In the Fitzgerald case Justice Powell said that he was leaving over the—leaving open the possibility that Congress could do away with the absolute immunity—

MR. DAVIS: Oh, I think—

QUESTION:—by law.

MR. DAVIS: Yes.

QUESTION: By a mere law.

MR. DAVIS: I—the justice—Chief Justice Burger was very skeptical of that. There was a suggestion in it, in dicta, in Justice Powell's opinion.

My own view is that if there is an immunity that arises under the Constitution and the separation of powers, that Congress by some affirmative act that says a President now doesn't have that protection, I would be very skeptical whether Congress could do it.

QUESTION: And of course Congress can apparently make constitutional by statute what is otherwise unconstitutional under the Commerce Clause, can't it?

(Laughter.)

MR. DAVIS: Yes, sir, but that—

QUESTION: So even if that were true, it wouldn't be unheard of in our strange jurisprudence.

MR. DAVIS: Justice Scalia, I'm not sure I want to be a part of that.

QUESTION: No, but it's true.

(Laughter.)

QUESTION: The fact is true though. Is it not true that Congress by statute can—

QUESTION: Well, Congress gives power—

QUESTION:—cause something which otherwise would be held by this Court to violate the Commerce Clause not to violate it.

QUESTION: The Constitution gives Congress the power to regulate commerce. It doesn't give Congress the power to regulate immunities. I suppose there's a distinction.

MR. DAVIS: That would be mine.

(Laughter.)

MR. DAVIS: May it please the Court, there are other—

QUESTION: Well, it would if there's a Federal—if the immunity's as a matter of Federal common law and not Federal constitutional law.

MR. DAVIS: Yes, but it is not here. We would—and the Fitzgerald opinion did talk about presidential immunities and the sources of them, and there were four sources. The presidency was a recent, much more recent development than the development of the common law, and so look for any immunity that the President has in the Constitution itself, which deals with official power, and that's purely our point here.

Unless there is an immunity that arises constitutionally, then there should be no bar to the progress of this litigation with the courts sensitive to the burdens of the presidency and should be trusted to do so.

That's another, I think fundamental problem with our opponents, is that they do not have a presumption of trust that the court will deal with these matters—

QUESTION: Well, it's often true, and litigants always don't trust one another completely.

May I ask you the same question I asked your opponent. How long do you think it will take to try this case?

MR. DAVIS: This is a very, relatively simple, as far as fact pattern case.

QUESTION: I'm not asking you to describe the case.

MR. DAVIS: I—

QUESTION: I'm asking you to tell me how long you think it will take to try it.

MR. DAVIS: Depending on stipulations, Justice Stevens, I would say 4 or 5 days perhaps, but that's just a guess, and it may—and we don't know if the case will be narrowed by—

QUESTION: Why would it take 4 or 5 days?

MR. DAVIS: Well, I'm thinking of what some jurisdictions do. In Virginia, in Federal or State court it would take probably—it would take a half-an-hour in the Eastern District, but—

(Laughter.)

MR. DAVIS: But I don't think it will take very long, and there's a point to be made about that also. With today's technology, with live feeds or transcripts and continuances from day-to-day, or whenever the President feels that he can—

QUESTION: One of the major concerns, of course, is the extent to which you plan to go into collateral matters.

MR. DAVIS: I can't, and I wouldn't bind, because I'm not certain whether they are admissible. I'm not certain what they—if they would tend to show a fact that we need to prove I think I would be duty bound as counsel to pursue that.

QUESTION: Suppose, because there are other parties involved, that it were 10 days of trial, 2 working weeks, and—pick a number—15 depositions. Do you think that would be a substantial investment of the President's time?

MR. DAVIS: It could very well be. It could very well be, and—

QUESTION: And if it then were in that degree, you think that he'd be entitled to an order deferring the litigation?

MR. DAVIS: If there was no way, at that time—this is ab initio, but at that time, if there was no other way to accommodate his needs, the presidency's needs for him to perform that job, then a continuance might very well be appropriate.

QUESTION: That's something of a perverse incentive, then, because then he has the incentive to ask for a long trial.

MR. DAVIS: He may indeed—

QUESTION: Mr. Davis—

MR. DAVIS:—if he wants to avoid a trial.

QUESTION: Mr. Davis, if we can trust the court to make that judgment, and if we can trust the court to make all the specific judgments on an instance-by-instance basis which you think is the appropriate way, why can't we also trust the court to make a judgment up front that there are going to be so many specific instances, and the so many specific instances are going to be so costly to the President that the only practical thing is to make a blanket judgment now based upon its good judgment?

If we can trust the court to make the first two kinds of good judgments, why can't we trust a court to make that third kind?

MR. DAVIS: In an appropriate circumstance, and you're getting to the question of a stay by the district judge as a discretionary matter rather than as a—

QUESTION: Well, they're all discretionary.

MR. DAVIS: Well, I think she did this—

QUESTION: I mean, it's an exercise of the court's discretion in each instance. If we can trust them in the first two examples, which you concede, why not in the third, assuming there's an evidentiary basis for it?

MR. DAVIS: Well, the court needs to have a factual basis on which to exercise discretion.

QUESTION: Okay, and let's assume that the President's lawyers come in and they provide one.

MR. DAVIS: If they do provide a factual basis that justifies a continuance—

QUESTION: Okay.

MR. DAVIS:—then certainly the court has authority to do it.

QUESTION: So the only thing—

MR. DAVIS: That's a matter of discretion.

QUESTION: The only thing we're really arguing about, then, is whether there ought to be a blanket rule that can be invoked simply by saying, I want this deferral for 4 years.

MR. DAVIS: Exactly.

QUESTION: As distinct from a rule in which the President's lawyers are going to come in and say, these are the practical stakes involved, and they therefore justify a 4–year continuance. That's all we're really arguing about.

MR. DAVIS: That's all we're arguing about, yes, sir.

Let me just conclude by saying this, that what the President is seeking would require a number of changes. They suggest burden of—changes as to compelling cases, that he doesn't need this, that the burden be on the plaintiff, and to delay it is a situation that would be highly unusual in the normal course, and we don't need it. The power of the court to deal with this is ample. If it proves not to be ample, as in Justice Souter's example—

CHIEF JUSTICE REHNQUIST: Thank you, Mr. Davis. The case is submitted.

(Whereupon, at 11:03 a.m., the case in the above-entitled matter was submitted.)

Index

References are to Pages

†